New England
WATERFALLS

New England
WATERFALLS

A GUIDE TO MORE
THAN 400 CASCADES
AND WATERFALLS

Greg Parsons
&
Kate B. Watson

THE COUNTRYMAN PRESS
WOODSTOCK, VERMONT

If you believe any information found in this guide to be incorrect, please let the
authors and publisher know so that corrections may be made in future editions.
The authors also welcome your comments and suggestions. Address all
correspondence to:

> Editor
> *New England Waterfalls*
> The Countryman Press
> PO Box 748
> Woodstock, VT 05091

Outdoor activities are by their very nature potentially hazardous. The publishers
and authors have done their best to ensure the accuracy of all the information in
New England Waterfalls, however, they can accept no responsibility for any loss,
injury, or inconvenience sustained by any traveler as a result of information or
advice contained in this guide. **Also, every effort was made to respect private
property. Users of *New England Waterfalls* are expected to respect notices of
private property.** Future editions of this guide will reflect any changes in land
ownership. If you believe any property-related information to be incorrect, please
let us know.

New England Waterfalls

ISBN 978-0-88150-874-1

Book design by Deborah Fillion
Page composition by Louise Bebeau
Cover and interior photographs by Greg Parsons and Kate B. Watson, except for
the photograph of Shin Falls, ME, which is the work of Brad Sullivan
Illustration on page XX by Dan Maleck

Published by The Countryman Press
P.O. Box 748, Woodstock, VT 05091

Distributed by W.W. Norton & Company, Inc.
500 Fifth Avenue, New York NY 10110

Printed in the United States of America
10 9 8 7 6 5

Contents

Acknowledgments

New England Waterfalls: A Guide to More Than 400 Cascades and Waterfalls could never have come into being without the help of many wonderful people who shared their time and expertise with us. Each person below, in his or her own way, helped develop this guidebook into something much more special than what the two of us could have done alone.

There were five individuals who sparked our initial inspiration: Jon Binder, Peter Chapin, David Ellis, Robert Glaubitz, and Dean Goss. Their enthusiasm and love for New England waterfalls really created a passion within us to write this book for readers like you. Jon Binder, the creator of the Web site "Jon's Waterfalls of the Eastern United States," deserves extra thanks for sharing his artistic vision in the area of waterfall photography.

Two professors at Babson College deserve a tremendous amount of recognition for donating their valuable time and words of wisdom to the first edition of the guide. Kerry Rourke, with her ideas on how to submit a book proposal, and our mentor, Martin Tropp, a professor with extraordinary passion for teaching, both made the process of the original construction of this book a great experience.

Both of us would like to thank our families—specifically our parents, Mark and Gail Watson, and Diane Parsons—for being so supportive throughout this process. It was an incredible experience to share these beautiful pieces of nature with our families.

This book could not have been written without the help of the following individuals who joined us as we traversed many miles of terrain: Matthew Arsenault, Rachael Barry, Michael Belleau, Katrina Brown, Anne Buckless, Christopher Bowser, Kaitlyn Clifford, Jessica Donahue, Michelle D'Souza, Grace Figueroa, Sylvia Fleming, Kyle Giaquinta, Adam Kavanaugh, Katie Kozin, Marita Lafontaine and her son, Evan, Brett LaFortune, Candice Mercier, Kristy Murphy, Garrett Parsons, Kyle Peterson, Brian Petroccione, Heather Sargent, Brad Sullivan, and Kasey Taylor. Last, but not least, Kate would like to thank her faithful K-9 companion, Timber Watson. He not only hiked to every waterfall, but also swam in nearly every place they stopped.

Major thanks are also due to editorial director Kermit Hummel, managing editor Lisa Sacks, and the rest of the staff at The Countryman Press. Thanks are also owed to Daniel Maleck, creator of the "types of waterfalls" image in this guide. All deserve our warmest gratitude.

Thank you to everyone who helped and supported us in this process, we truly could not have done it without you.

Introduction

～⌇～

Our passion for New England waterfalls developed years before we met during college. Our parents instilled a sense of respect and admiration for nature in us at a very young age. Greg was initially dragged kicking and screaming on daylong journeys through New England by his family. Travels during high school finally opened his mind to the wonders and attractions of the natural world. Meanwhile, Kate loved what New England had to offer from the beginning, and she pleaded to be taken on new trips continuously.

Soon after meeting at college, we began to take day trips all over New England, visiting a variety of places and, most important, a number of waterfalls. Day-trips with our friends turned out to become regular activities for us. It was not long before we realized that many of New England's waterfalls were known only to local residents. As we racked up miles and miles of hiking, we wondered why so many of these wonderful places could not be found in existing guidebooks.

And so the idea for *New England Waterfalls* was born. Our main focus, we decided, was to share all these great places with our readers in a way that minimized the amount of hassle a day-trip can bring. We wrote directions based on easily identifiable reference points, described trails in an easy-to-follow format, and snapped pictures that represent the actual beauty of these places. We also added detailed classifications to each waterfall trip, including an overall rating—intended to give you a sense of comparison—and information pertaining to the trail, such as the difficulty and altitude gain.

There you have it. *New England Waterfalls* is our contribution to the natural splendors of this region. We hope you enjoy our book.

THE SIX STATES

As you will begin to observe while sampling the waterfalls in this region, each New England state has its own unique beauties. A wide variety of experiences can be had as you move from state to state. As you will see below, the waterfalls of each state offer the enthusiast great variety in hiking terrain, geological structure, biological environments, and water characteristics.

CONNECTICUT

Connecticut's limited mountainous topography tends to result in falls that are more seasonal. To ensure a flowing waterfall, it is best to plan your visit before the dry spells of summer. The months of March, April, and May are your best bets.

Approximately half the Connecticut waterfalls described in this guide are under the protection of the state park system or other nonprofit organizations, such as The Nature Conservancy. As a result, these waterfalls are often located in parks that also have picnic facilities, complete with picnic tables, barbecue grills, bathrooms, and ample parking. The enforcement of state park rules and regulations has kept most areas well protected and very clean.

MAINE

Large sections of Maine remain relatively undeveloped. Vast expanses of wilderness can be found throughout the state, especially in the northern half. These wildernesses harbor dozens or even hundreds of remote waterfalls yet to be publicly documented or even discovered. The best chance for discovering your own private New England waterfall has to be in the state of Maine. Wildlife sightings are also more common in this state because of the lack of development.

Expect long backcountry roads when reaching some of the trailheads in this state. Low-clearance vehicles may not be able to access the formal trailhead parking areas. Make sure to carefully read the driving directions before beginning any trip. Some waterfalls do not even have a trailhead; more than a dozen popular waterfalls in Maine are accessible only by canoe. These waterfalls were largely omitted from this guide, but we still recommend visiting them if you enjoy lengthy canoe, kayaking, or white-water rafting trips.

Maine may be the northernmost state of New England, but its swimming holes can still manage to warm to tolerable temperatures with the sun's rays in summer. Some of these swimming spots are very popular, both with local residents and among visitors from other states.

Some waterfalls require you to pay entrance fees. Public reserved lands, such as the KI Jo-Mary Multiple Use Forest, require a modest entrance fee. Baxter State Park, the home of Mt. Katahdin and dozens of scenic waterfalls, also requires a fee for out-of-state residents.

MASSACHUSETTS

Highly rated waterfalls are few and far between in Massachusetts, making it difficult to visit more than two or three in a day. The Berkshire region, where the bulk of waterfalls in this state can be found, is your optimal location for visiting multiple waterfalls in a day.

You will find very few waterfalls in this state with swimming holes below them. Also, most waterfalls are either located within the state park system or managed by an organization. The Trustees of Reservations (www.thetrustees.org), a nonprofit group dedicated to preserving the Massachusetts landscape, has made a great effort to preserve several waterfall sites. They have succeeded well in their mission.

NEW HAMPSHIRE

It is no surprise that the majority of waterfalls in New Hampshire are found in or near the White Mountain National Forest. The high peaks of the White Mountains create hundreds of permanent and seasonal waterfalls. Within the last decade the White Mountain National Forest adopted a per-car fee for many of the trailhead parking lots. This fee, $3 in 2009 (but under review to be increased to $5), is used for maintenance of trails and roads, as well as related expenses. Other waterfalls in this region have become commercialized and are more costly to visit.

Most of this guide's longest and challenging hikes with the greatest elevation gains are found in New Hampshire. Unlike other states, many trips to waterfalls in New Hampshire can be extended by continuing farther on the trail to mountain summits, remote ponds and lakes, wilderness areas, and some of the finest scenic vistas in New England.

New Hampshire also offers backpacking opportunities to camp adjacent to waterfalls. The state also offers some of the coldest waterfall swimming holes, colorful foliage, and some of the tallest waterfalls in New England.

RHODE ISLAND

Rhode Island is not gifted with waterfalls like the other states. Our research indicates that Rhode Island only has one natural waterfall worthy of your attention. Perhaps there is still a natural waterfall or two to be discovered which may end up in future editions of this guide.

VERMONT

Avid hikers looking for long-distance hikes may be left somewhat unsatisfied with the waterfall trips in Vermont; the majority of falls are roadside attractions or require hikes of less than 0.5 mile. The waterfalls in this state are most likely to please swimmers and those who are unable to hike long distances.

Many of Vermont's waterfalls have been partially altered or diminished altogether by dams created through hydroelectric projects and power stations. As a result, locals are actively protective of the waterfalls left in their natural state. The Vermont River Conservancy is one organization fighting to purchase and protect the lands where waterfalls are found. They have succeeded in doing so on several projects so far and need our continued support.

Vermont is home to the finest swimming holes known among New England's waterfalls. Warm, refreshing, and clean, the swimming holes naturally attract a slew of visitors during summer months. The translucent emerald green color, so familiar in tropical waters, creates lovely pools. Some even argue that Vermont has the greatest swimming holes in the entire nation! Always carry a bathing suit and towel; you will surely need them.

DISCOVERIES ALONG THE WAY

- **Size does not matter.**
  There are no mathematical formulas to determine beauty based on height. Some of the most attractive and highly rated waterfalls in this guide are less than 30 feet in total drop.
- **Waterfall swimming holes are generally cold.**
  Swimming below waterfalls can be one of the most enjoyable outdoor activities. Always remember, however, that rushing mountain waters never really get a chance to warm up to comfortable temperatures. Expect chilly to cold pools in almost all cases, with many of Vermont's swimming holes being the exception.
- **Many waterfalls in New England are world-class in beauty and style.**
  New England offers some of the most picturesque falls in the country. If a photographic collection of the country's most scenic waterfalls were ever produced, some falls from New England would certainly be included.
- **Waterfalls are always endangered.**
  Plans for hydroelectric plants are occasionally proposed for sites at waterfalls. You will also find litter and even graffiti at some waterfalls in New England. Please do your part to ensure that waterfalls remain forever in their natural state. This includes traveling only on developed trails whenever possible, in order to prevent erosion. Try to support local organizations involved in land conservation efforts as well, if you can.

- **No two waterfalls are exactly alike.**
  New England has such a diversity of terrain that each waterfall found is sure to be a new experience. You will be hard-pressed to find two trails or falls that are comparable. Each new waterfall has its own geology, plant life, and style.
- **There are more waterfalls to be found and publicly documented.**
  Our original research for the first edition of the guide indicated that approximately 300 waterfalls existed in New England. We now have information on more than 1,100 waterfalls! We are positive there are even more waterfalls that are still yet to be documented. The forests of northern Maine certainly must harbor dozens more uncrowded and unspoiled gems of which we are currently unaware.
- **Waterfalls have a personality.**
  One visit to each waterfall is not enough. If you have visited a particular waterfall only once, you have not really grasped its personality. To see its true character you must visit in different seasons, and during different conditions. Check out the falls during dry and wet weather, when they're covered in snow, and during fall foliage. These ever-changing conditions create an unpredictable waterfall experience for each visit.
- **Bring the right equipment.**
  There is much to be said about being properly prepared for your waterfall day-trip. Food, water, adequate clothing, proper footwear, and a camera are standard items to bring along. Hiking poles and water shoes are other items that can add to your safe enjoyment of these places. Also make sure to check the weather forecast before starting any adventure.
- **Animals use trails, too.**
  Do not forget that we are merely visitors to wildlife habitats. Large animals such as black bears, white-tailed deer, and moose are not commonly seen on the trail, but in rare instances you may spot one. If you respect that you are visiting their home, they will likely scamper away and avoid close contact.

SEASONALITY

Seasonality is an issue of great importance to the falls of New England. It refers to the fluctuations in the volume of water. In an ideal world, each waterfall would always look the same, never losing any of its attractiveness or appeal. This just is not the case; seasonality is a factor to be considered before embarking on any trip described in this guide.

Our advice is simple: To reduce the likelihood of visiting a dried-up waterfall, visit it before the middle of June. Spring runoff from the previous winter can last throughout most of spring and, at times, even into summer. Unless a record-breaking drought has occurred, every waterfall in this guidebook will be flowing; we intentionally did not include other waterfalls we found to be extremely seasonal. Beyond the middle of June, however, each waterfall's character begins to change.

Here are some general guidelines that have proven themselves true in our travels.

- Mountain brooks are likely to dry up faster than lowland rivers.
- The waterfalls of northern New England remain powerful for longer in summer than do the falls of the south.
- Falls at the base of a mountain are likely to remain powerful longer than falls located halfway up a trail leading to a summit.
- Snowy winters mean longer waterfall seasons during the warmer months.
- If you are hiking along a stream to a waterfall and there is little water flowing, you run the risk of discovering a dried-up falls.
- If a wide stream with little running water is narrowed significantly enough, a waterfall can still become quite powerful and scenic. We have been pleasantly surprised many times over.
- You can expect a normally seasonal waterfall to be roaring with power for up to one week after a day of heavy rain (greater than 0.5 inch). You are essentially guaranteed a fine display if you visit within two or three days of a storm's passing.

Seasonality is not always a terrible thing; differences in water flow create new sparkling personalities and characteristic changes. Here are the benefits of seasonality:

- A trip to a dried-up falls can still be rewarding, especially if you have previously visited the waterfall when it was a thundering torrent of white water. You could witness the power of natural change and uncover beautiful rock formations behind the waterfall.
- A dangerous swimming hole at the base of a waterfall in May could be safe for all to visit by July.
- Less water can lead to photographs that are more artistic, when using proper technique.

- Each trip you make to the same waterfall will likely result in photographs with significant differences. It is quite rare to frame identical photographs taken on separate days.

WATERFALL PHOTOGRAPHY

Mastering the art of photographing falling water requires using the right equipment along with creative techniques. Although it may seem like an art best reserved for the professionals, photographing waterfalls can actually be quite simple to learn, and improvement can be immediate. After shooting thousands of photographs in just about every waterfall condition, we have come up with some straightforward guidelines for beginner and advanced photographers alike.

CAMERA AND LENSES

A camera with manual aperture and shutter-speed adjustments is essential for above-average quality pictures. Although some still use film or slide-based cameras, digital cameras have become the equipment of choice for most professional photographers who wish to capture water in motion. Medium-format and large-format cameras have taken many of the highest-quality pictures of falling water we have seen, but are not practical for many shutterbugs. This is attributable to the added costs of these cameras, both for the camera itself and for developing costs. The added weight and size of the larger-format cameras makes backpacking more of a challenge. Point-and-shoot cameras are inexpensive, reliable pieces of equipment, but do not allow much manual control. Digital single-lens reflex-type cameras (DSLRs), on the other hand, allow you the flexibility you will need to change shutter speed, aperture, and lenses. For all these reasons, for those seeking outstanding photographs we suggest purchasing and carrying a DSLR-type camera on all waterfall expeditions.

You may want to carry several different lenses to cover every shooting situation. Many waterfalls are located in gorges and narrow ravines, where a wide-angle lens (such as a 20mm one) is needed to encapsulate the entire falls into your picture. On the other hand, a telephoto zoom lens, such as a 100–300mm lens, is helpful to capture waterfalls located off in the distance. If carrying multiple lenses seems impractical or unjustifiable to you, a zoom lens such as a 28–90mm model—that starts at around $100—will suffice for the majority of waterfall situations. There are professional lenses available that are more expensive but can significantly add to your photo quality, as well.

SHUTTER SPEED AND TRIPODS

One of the best tips we can offer a waterfall photographer is always to carry a tripod. A tripod is essential for maintaining long shutter speeds (to eliminate camera shake, which can blur your picture). Also, tripods come in quite handy when you want to photograph yourself with these natural treasures and no one is around to snap the picture.

Long shutter speeds are essential to create the soft "angel-hair" or "silky" look so common to waterfall photographs. Generally, speeds of 1/15 second or longer will blur the water to create this artistic effect. Long shutter speeds are also essential if you are photographing in gorges or chasms, where, even on the sunniest days, the area around the falls receives little light. Shutter speed will also be longer if you are shooting at or around sunrise or sunset.

Long shutter speeds are not always the top choice for falls, though. With the traditional block-type waterfall, we suggest using shorter shutter speeds, such as 1/60 second, because longer shutter speeds on such falls often create a portrait of pure white water that lacks detail. You will find that long shutter speeds work much better for thin plunges or other weak-powered waterfalls. Most of the shots in this book were taken at shutter speeds between 1/15 of a second and 2 seconds using a DSLR set at a 100 ISO film equivalent. The trick with aperture and shutter speed is to keep experimenting.

SMALL APERTURE

Equally as important as shutter speed is proper exposure; aperture is often neglected in waterfall photography instructions. A small aperture is needed if you want to capture an entire waterfall landscape, including the wildflowers, trees, rocks, and any people around the falling water. We suggest experimenting with apertures between f/6.3 and f/13. Apertures of f/11 or f/13, for example, should capture everything in focus for most shots, from a boulder 6 feet in front of you to the trees and leaves that frame the waterfall. Many photographers focus on the shutter speed alone; do not forget to take aperture into account when composing pictures. Be aware that as you decrease the aperture (from f/13 to f/11, for example), you are decreasing the shutter speed (from 1/15 to 1/30 for example). It will take some trial and error to become familiar with this relationship and to figure out which apertures and shutter speeds provide you with the results you desire.

FILM SPEED

To create the soft, angel-hair water effect while keeping the foreground and background of the frame focused and sharp, slow-speed film (or the digital equivalent) is essential. Our personal favorite for waterfall photography is Fuji Velvia, which is rated ISO 50. Most DSLRS will allow you to select an ISO equivalent of 100. As you decrease the film speed, your camera requires more light for proper exposure, which means you can use the longer shutter speeds that you will need to achieve most of your desired effects. For enlarging your pictures, slow-speed films are also ideal, because they are typically very sharp. This translates into bigger enlargements as compared to "faster" film, such as those rated ISO 200 or ISO 400.

On sunny days, however, even the slowest films may not be able to get the long shutter speed you desire. For this, a circular polarizer filter can be very useful in extending the shutter speed to your desired level. These filters generally provide you with between one-and-a-half to two stops of extra light. For example, if you are set up with an aperture of f/13 and a shutter speed of 1/30 second, a polarizer will allow you to lengthen the shutter speed to 1/10 second or 1/8 second. Circular polarizers, which were used in nearly all the photographs contained in this guide, also reduce the glare that is reflected off water and wet rocks.

BRACKETING

Bracketing is a waterfall photographer's best friend. The meters inside your camera are affected by gleaming water and the dark walls of the gorges where many falls are found. To combat this problem, manually adjust the aperture or shutter speed around the suggested exposure from your camera's meter. We suggest taking exposures up to two stops in each direction to maximize your chance for a perfectly exposed picture. Although film and developing costs will increase, bracketing is often necessary in photographing falls. Very often, the correct exposure can be a full two stops away from the suggested exposure from your camera's meter. With a digital camera, the only cost of bracketing is of course the storage of data.

An alternative to bracketing is using cheap "gray cards" or partial metering to find a suggested exposure. With partial metering, compare your camera's suggested exposures of different parts of the scene, such as the falling water, the underlying rock, trees, or even the sky.

FOREGROUND AND COMPOSITION

By making minor changes in the composition of your picture, you can turn an average shot into a professional one. Just try incorporating some natural features positioned around the waterfall into the photograph. Boulders in a streambed, hikers climbing the rock wall of a waterfall, or wildflowers along the trail are three suggestions that can add quality to your photos.

Finding foreground objects becomes necessary with waterfalls that have abnormally large pools at their base. Take the time to observe the entire landscape around the falls, searching for anything else that can help fill your camera's frame. This will enhance the quality of your pictures and more accurately reflect the actual size of the waterfall.

WEATHER AND WATERFALL PHOTOGRAPHY

Mother Nature is very difficult to predict, but some facts are certain. The melting snow of early spring powers most waterfalls in New England well into June. After June, however, an understanding of the relationships among weather, waterfalls, and photography takes on great importance.

You can expect the waterfalls throughout all of New England to be at some of their highest volumes of the year in spring. You are not likely to find the thin veils of water you may see during summer. In spring months you can expect to photograph chaotic crashes of white water at most falls. Some waterfalls are yet to be obstructed by overhanging tree coverage, which will begin to occur as summer rolls around.

During summer, the greens of the trees and mosses surrounding the falls will add color to your pictures. Unfortunately, at many falls water flow is greatly reduced or even eliminated; photographs can look empty. Yet for some cataracts, this is the best time to compose a picture. Photos of waterfalls such as Bridal Veil Falls of New Hampshire and March Cataract Falls of Massachusetts radiate romantic feelings, as they capture thin veils of cascading water.

A true waterfall photographer will also return during autumn foliage and the winter season for new shots. If you want a typical postcard shot, capture the falls of northern New England during peak colors of foliage. Two of the best waterfalls to shoot during this season are Arethusa Falls and Silver Cascade. Both of these are located in the White Mountain National Forest, and just about every color of foliage is represented within yards of the falling water.

Peak times for New England vary by state, with foliage color usually near or at peak during the first two weeks of October for the northern states. The southern states often peak during the second and third weeks of the month.

Winter is the most difficult to photograph. The vibrant colors of spring and autumn are long gone, and your camera's meter is often fooled by the reflecting white of the snow. You will find that many waterfalls are closed for the season simply because they are too dangerous to visit. If the falls are reachable, be sure to bracket your exposures over a greater range to ensure that at least one photograph can make the scrapbook. A circular polarizer can be very helpful to reduce glare during this season.

For any season, it is a good idea to carry a trash bag or two in your backpack in case the weather turns bad. Cameras are easily damaged by water, and the combined protection of a backpack and a trash bag may save your equipment from the elements.

HOW TO USE THIS GUIDE

This guidebook aims to make your waterfalling experience as easy, safe, and enjoyable as possible. To help you decipher what you can expect with each trip and each waterfall, we have added simple characteristics to each chapter within this guide. They are useful in obtaining a quick summary of the adventures that lay ahead of you. Each of these characteristics is clarified below.

RATING

We have chosen to rate waterfalls on a scale of 1.0 to 5.0. A rating of 1.0 identifies a waterfall lacking in many categories. These waterfalls are not impressive, nor are they photogenic or scenic. A rating of 5.0, on the other hand, is for those special waterfalls that really deserve praise because they offer so much. If a particular waterfall has a rating of 5.0, you can expect an extraordinarily photogenic waterfall located in a wonderfully scenic setting. These waterfalls are bound to make a lasting impression on all who witness them. Each waterfall with its own chapter in this guide has at least a 2.0 for a rating; additional waterfalls that have earned less than a 2.0 for a rating, along with other waterfalls we are yet to visit, are detailed in Appendix F, the State-by-State and Additional Waterfalls List.

Each and every waterfall in this guide deserves your time and attention. If a waterfall carries a rating of 2.0, it does not mean that it should be excluded from your plans. It only suggests that you may want to supplement this particular waterfall with other falls or attractions in the area. For the dedicated enthusiast, every waterfall is a new and special place.

TYPE

After visiting waterfalls across the region, we have concluded that there are six distinguishable types.

Block—a cascade, wider than it is tall, that usually covers the entire distance across a stream and drops at a near vertical angle. Blocks are often referred to as being "classic" or "horseshoe" style falls.

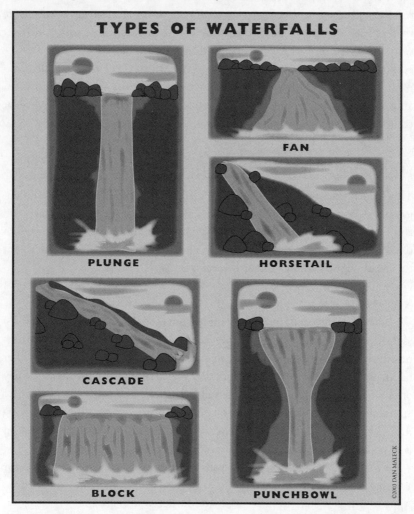

Cascade—a series of small drops, too many to count feasibly, that fall at a low angle of descent. Just about every type of waterfall usually has cascades shortly upstream or downstream from it.

Fan—a steep-angled cascade that fans out from a narrow width at the top to a larger base at the bottom. Most fans are also horsetails in that they maintain contact with underlying rock during their descent.

Horsetail—a nearly vertical drop characterized by waters maintaining constant or almost constant contact with the underlying rock that they are flowing over. This is essentially a very steep set of cascades.

Plunge—a waterfall in which water drops at an entirely vertical angle. Water flows over a broad ledge, usually an overhanging one, into a pool without making contact with the underlying rock during its descent.

Punchbowl—a special type of plunge characterized by water being forced to a very narrow width and being squeezed down into a pool. There are very few punchbowls found in this region.

HEIGHT

One of the first pieces of information people want to know about a waterfall is how tall it is. There is a tendency for individuals to believe that there is a direct correlation between height and beauty. We have found that this is just not the case. Some of our favorite waterfalls are less than 20 feet in total drop, and one is a mere 6-foot drop.

In determining the height of the falls, we either separated the major drops—if they were distinguishable—or lumped the entire formation into one total drop. Some heights have been accurately measured, but others have been reasonably estimated. In all cases, the height reflects the elevation drop and not the total horizontal distance over which the falls travel.

TRAIL LENGTH

All trail lengths listed are one-way, representing the distance from trailhead to the waterfall, unless otherwise noted. Some trails are loops, and they reflect the total hiking mileage covered on the trip. Before undertaking or deciding to skip a particular hike, consider other trail factors, such as altitude gain or loss, and trail difficulty. For instance: A 3-mile round trip with no altitude gain is much easier on your body than a 2-mile round trip with a 1,000-foot elevation change. A trail length of "less than 0.1 mile" indicates that the waterfall is very close to roadside but is not clearly visible from it.

WATER SOURCE

This defining characteristic informs you which brook, stream, creek, or river is feeding the formation. Several of the waterfalls described in this guide have water sources that are either unknown or so seasonal that they have never been assigned an official name.

ALTITUDE GAIN/LOSS

For the majority of waterfalls described in this guide, the altitude gain or loss on the trail was the prevalent factor in determining trail difficulty. For every 1,000 feet of elevation gain, average-paced hikers can expect to add about half an hour to their one-way trail time.

The trails that gain significant elevation in a short amount of distance can be hazardously slippery and muddy during the wet season. Unless you are prepared for the worst, in early spring avoid hiking trails that feature 500 or more feet of elevation gain over less than 2 miles of length. Examples include Beaver Brook Cascades of New Hampshire, Dunn Falls of Maine, and Race Brook Falls of Massachusetts—all three are sure to supply too many dangers to allow a pleasant overall experience during this season.

TRAIL DIFFICULTY

The trails described in this guide are categorized into one of five levels of difficulty: easy, easy side of moderate, moderate, moderate side of difficult, and difficult. To determine each hike's rating, we took into consideration trail distance, altitude gain, trail dangers such as the scale of muddy and slippery travel, and any other challenges present that must be overcome, like crossing a river. All of the ratings are conservative, based on family-friendly hiking. Travelers with years of hiking experience on rough trails can probably downgrade the hiking difficulty by one level.

Easy—generally flat, stable footing, with no significant obstacles or difficulties. These trails are perfect for families and safe for all. They may also be handicapped accessible, but this is not always the case.

Easy side of moderate—hikes that may involve a fair amount of navigating over rocks and roots on the trail. There also may be some elevation gain, mud in springtime, or sections of slippery travel after periods of rain, but nothing too difficult.

Moderate—trails offering some degree of challenge, whether it be significant altitude gain or steep and slippery stretches of terrain, or both. Moderate hikes may still be appropriate for families and children, but personal judgment should be used. Depending on the length of the trail, water and snacks should be carried, as these hikes are usually longer and more time consuming than trails with lower ratings of difficulty.

Moderate side of difficult—only a handful of New England's waterfall trails approach a difficult rating; we purposely chose waterfalls in this guide that were challenging but not extraordinarily so. For those trips rated as moderate side of difficult, you may face demanding altitude gains or short bushwhacks where no formal paths exist. You may be required to wade across a knee-deep river or scramble down a steep gorge wall. A hike need not be long in terms of distance to earn this rating. If you are embarking on such adventures, you should probably think about carrying some water, food, and other supplies with you. These hikes are generally not suitable for children or pets.

Difficult—any trail deemed difficult is reserved for the truly experienced. This type of trip may require extensive off-trail navigation or involve very steep or dangerous terrain. If you are not in great physical shape and familiar with such challenges, skip these hikes—there are scores of other waterfalls with less potential for problems. If you choose a difficult hike, you should consider bringing ample food, water, and even some company in case of emergency. These hikes are not suitable for children or pets, in our opinion.

HIKING TIME

The approximate hiking time is based on a commonly followed hiking formula: A mile can be covered in half an hour, and for every 500 feet of elevation gain, an additional half hour is added. Extras, such as the time required to cross a river, scale a steep embankment, or scramble down a riverbank, also add to the amount of approximate hiking time. As you might expect, our estimations can differ from the actual time it will take you to reach a waterfall. Our approximations are based on the average person's pace of travel: about 2 miles per hour. Experienced hikers may be able to cut down travel time by nearly half; conversely, a family with children might need nearly double the amount of time.

Take note that approximate hiking time is for one-way travel. If you are wondering what the entire trip might take you, double the hiking time given and allow some time for exploration and enjoyment at the waterfall. For loop trails, the hiking time reflects the entire trip.

DELORME ATLAS

We have provided the map coordinates for each waterfall as they appear in DeLorme's Atlas and Gazetteer series. The thought behind this is to make it simpler for you to plan your day outside; this in turn can allow you to visit multiple waterfalls in a day. Be aware that only about half of the waterfalls that we describe are actually marked by name on these maps. We have indicated in each chapter whether the waterfall is marked or unmarked based on the latest versions of each map (as of the summer of 2009).

BEST TIME TO VISIT

The best time to visit each waterfall is primarily determined by the seasonality of the waterfall, or how much water flow is present in each season of the year. Water flow alone is not always the determining factor; often, waterfalls are just plain inaccessible during certain times of the year, due to road closures, operating seasons (where an entry fee is charged), or trail hazards in winter. For those waterfalls designated seasonal, the best time to visit is typically from April to June, but be aware that some northern locations may not be snow-free until the middle of May.

I. Connecticut

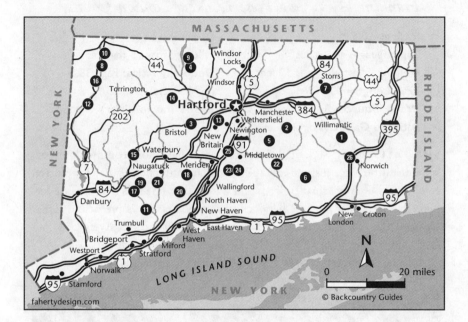

BAILEY'S RAVINE

Franklin, Ayers Gap Preserve, New London County

Rating: 3.0/5.0

Type: Plunges and slides

Height: Tallest plunge is 10 feet

Trail Length: 0.2 mile

Water Source: Bailey Brook

Altitude Gain/Loss: +20 feet

Difficulty: Easy

Hiking Time: 5 minutes

DeLorme Atlas: Page 38, A-1
(marked as Ayers Gap)

Best Time to Visit: Year-round

THE FALLS Ayers Gap, or Bailey's Ravine, as it is more commonly called, is a quiet little place just off CT 207. The main attraction, a 10-foot plunge, is followed by several smaller drops and waterslides. The falls here are not particularly spectacular, but the hemlock-surrounded ravine is pretty and rather secluded. The Nature Conservancy manages the 80 acres of Ayers Gap Preserve and requires that visitors come between sunrise and sunset.

TRAIL INFORMATION The parking area is not actually the trailhead.

Bailey's Ravine

To reach the ravine, you must walk back down CT 207, heading east for a few hundred feet, and turn left onto Ayer Road. Walk down Ayer Road for about 0.1 mile and the trailhead will be marked on your left. A well-used trail guides you to the top of the falls. Lesser-used trails navigate around the ravine and the rest of the nature preserve.

DIRECTIONS From I-395 in Norwich, take exit 83 for CT 97 north. Take CT 97 north for 3.1 miles to the village of Baltic. Take a left onto CT 207 west, which heads toward the village of North Franklin. Follow CT 207 west for 3.4 miles to a paved parking pull-off on the right marked with a sign for BAILEY'S RAVINE and THE NATURE CONSERVANCY. This parking area is across the street from Under The Mountain Road.

OTHER WATERFALLS NEARBY Yantic Falls

2

BLACKLEDGE FALLS
Glastonbury, Hartford County

Rating: 4.0/5.0
Type: Plunges
Height: 22 feet to 25 feet each
Trail Length: 0.5 mile
Water Source: Blackledge River
Altitude Gain/Loss: +50 feet, -30 feet

Difficulty: Easy
Hiking Time: 15 minutes
DeLorme Atlas: Page 45, J-18 (unmarked)
Best Time to Visit: March to June

THE FALLS Depending on the current water volume of the Blackledge River, this waterfall is either a set of two or three adjacent plunges. The plunges are similar in appearance, each being between 22 feet and 25 feet in height. Due to their low volume, you can stand directly underneath the middle waterfall and become instantly refreshed. Due to the overhanging ledge that the Blackledge River flows over, the middle plunge is also a completely vertical drop.

Several trees adjacent to the waterfall prevent this from being one of the most photogenic falls in the state. However, do not let that prevent you from enjoying the somewhat tropical appearance of Blackledge Falls. Be sure to check this one out in spring or after a rainstorm; during periods of dry weather, the rushing plunges can turn into small, unimpressive trickles of water. If not for being highly seasonal, Blackledge would certainly be one of Connecticut's best waterfalls.

TRAIL INFORMATION The trail begins at the parking area and heads immediately into the forest. After 0.1 mile of hiking, you will begin to notice an abundance of other trails on all sides of you. Keep straight, following blue and white trail markers all the way to the falls. Expect an easy 15-minute walk to reach this waterfall.

DIRECTIONS From Hartford, take CT 2 south to exit 8. Turn onto CT 94 east. Continue traveling on CT 94 east for 4.0 miles past the junction of CT 94 and CT 83. A sign and parking area for BLACKLEDGE FALLS is on the left.

OTHER WATERFALLS NEARBY Mill Pond Falls, Codfish Falls

Blackledge Falls

3

BUTTERMILK FALLS, PLYMOUTH

Plymouth, Buttermilk Falls Nature Preserve, Litchfield County

Rating: 4.0/5.0

Type: Horsetails, cascades and slides

Height: 55-foot total drop

Trail Length: 0.1 mile to base of falls

Water Source: Hancock Brook

Altitude Gain/Loss: -30 feet

Difficulty: Easy side of moderate

Hiking Time: 5 minutes

DeLorme Atlas: Page 33, A-21 (marked)

Best Time to Visit: Year-round

THE FALLS Over a half-dozen waterfalls in New England are named Buttermilk Falls. Buttermilk Falls of Vermont is perhaps the most favored of the bunch, being one of that state's premier swimming holes in terms of size and popularity. Other favorites include Buttermilk Falls of Gulf Hagas in Maine, Buttermilk Falls of Norfolk, Connecticut, and Buttermilk Falls of Plymouth, Connecticut, which is the highlight of this chapter.

From the top of this waterfall, onlookers are unable to get a full grasp of the height and beauty of 55-foot Buttermilk Falls. By scrambling to the bottom of the falls, viewers can finally see its elusive personality. The horsetails, which are surrounded almost entirely by hemlock trees, cut their way down to pools at your feet. There are plenty of flat trail sections adjacent to the brook that serve well for picnicking, photography, or for just gazing up at the falls. Small wildflowers and ferns also add to the beauty, as they grow in abundance around the rock-strewn river.

TRAIL INFORMATION This short, blue-rectangle marked trail can be as easy as you want to make it. From the parking lot to the top of the falls, the trail is flat and travel is quick. You will first reach a view from the top of the falls. Even though the well-worn trail ends here, the best views are to be had by descending to the base of the falls. There is a steep path that has been created over the years for such a reason.

DIRECTIONS From New Britain, take CT 72 west. Follow CT 72 west until you reach US 6. Take a left onto US 6 west and follow it for 1.7 miles and take a left onto Scott Road. Follow Scott Road for 0.3 mile and fork left onto Washington Road. After 0.9 mile on Washington Road, turn right

Buttermilk Falls, Plymouth

onto South Eagle Street. Follow South Eagle Street for 1.7 miles to its end. Take a left onto South Main Street, then an immediate right onto Lane Hill Road. After a steep incline there will be a dirt parking pull-off on the right.

OTHER WATERFALLS NEARBY Negro Hill Brook Falls, Nonnewaug Falls, Mill Pond Falls, Spruce Brook Falls

4

CARPENTER'S FALLS
Granby, McLean Game Refuge Wildlife Sanctuary, Hartford County

Rating: 2.5/5.0
Type: Horsetails
Height: 18-foot drop
Trail Length: Less than 0.1 mile
Water Source: Beach Brook
Altitude Gain/Loss: -30 feet

Difficulty: Easy
Hiking Time: Negligible
DeLorme Atlas: Page 52, G-6 (unmarked)
Best Time to Visit: March to June

THE FALLS George P. McLean, former governor of Connecticut and United States senator, left his property upon his passing in 1932 to trustees who formed the McLean Game Refuge in accordance with his will. Several additional purchases of adjacent tracts of lands since then have increased the size of the refuge. As a result of these conservation efforts, this waterfall should now be forever open to the public.

This 18-foot waterfall is gorgeous in high water but nearly lifeless for much of the summer when water is scarce. Under normal water conditions, the brook is split into two segments just below the lip of the waterfall. Both sides are heavily bordered by moss, which always adds a nice element to waterfall photography. Swimming is not an option here, as the pools are shallow and the water often retains an unattractive rust color.

There are many trails within the refuge available for hiking. Take note that despite what the phrase game refuge might imply to some, there is no hunting allowed in the park. Fishing and mountain bicycling are also prohibited, and dogs must be leashed. For additional information on the park, including a detailed trail map, visit www.mcleangamerefuge.org.

TRAIL INFORMATION From the parking area, head downstream on a trail that begins to the left of the bridge. The falls are just ahead. A spur path leads right to an observation point at the middle of the falls. If you travel downstream a few additional feet, another spur path will swing around to the base of the falls.

DIRECTIONS From the junction of CT 20, US 202, CT 189, and CT 10 in the town of Granby, take CT 20 west for 2.5 miles and take a left onto Day Street South. Follow Day Street South for 0.6 mile and take a right onto Simsbury Road. Follow Simsbury Road for 0.7 mile and take a left onto Broad Hill Road. Follow Broad Hill Road for 0.2 mile and you will reach a sign that says that the road is not maintained in winter. At this point, the road becomes a rough dirt road that should probably not be attempted by the average passenger car. For those with higher clearance (SUVs will most likely be fine), it is another 0.7 mile to the trailhead, which is just before a bridge over Beach Brook. A sign for the MCLEAN GAME REFUGE marks the trailhead. *To get to Granby,* take I-91 north from Hartford to exit 40 and follow CT 20 west.

OTHER WATERFALLS NEARBY Enders Falls

Carpenter's Falls

5

∽

THE CASCADE

East Hampton, Meshomasic State Forest,
Middlesex County

Rating: 2.5/5.0

Type: Horsetail

Height: 15 feet

Trail Length: 0.8 mile

Water Source: Carr Brook

Altitude Gain/Loss: +150 feet,
-75 feet

Difficulty: Easy side of moderate

Hiking Time: 25 minutes

DeLorme Atlas: Page 36, C-1
(unmarked)

Best Time to Visit: April to June

THE FALLS Meshomasic State Forest, created in 1903, is known as being the first official state forest in Connecticut. The forest is also known to hold a healthy population of timber rattlesnakes, although we have never seen one ourselves. What it is not known for, however, is for The Cascade, a heavily seasonal 15-foot horsetail that is one of the least-visited waterfalls in the state. There is an excellent chance you will be the falls' only visitor for the day.

Water slides gently over a near vertical wall into an inches-deep pool at this petite waterfall. A strong possibility exists that the brook will be completely dry unless recent rains have occurred; for that reason, we recommend visiting immediately after a prolonged series of April or May showers. Then again, since it is a horsetail, it will not take much water to create a dramatic effect and visiting more than once will help you decide as to which season is your favorite.

TRAIL INFORMATION The trail actually starts in front of the parking area, so do not cross the road. Begin the hike by heading north into the woods where you will reach a fork only 25 feet from your car. Fork right and begin a short climb while following trees marked with blue blazes. These blue blazes will guide you all the way to the falls and back. There are several potentially confusing trail intersections to contend with behind this point, so pay close attention to the turns you will have to make on the way to the falls. Here is a description of the intersections: About 0.2 mile from the parking area, you will come to a T-intersection. Take a left and in 200 feet you will reach a fork. Take the right fork, which leads slightly uphill (the left fork would take you downhill). From here, it is 0.1 mile to another T-intersection. Take a left here and 0.25 mile farther you will reach another fork. Take a left here onto a narrower trail. From this point, it's only another 0.25 mile to the falls, which are clearly visible from the trail. For the best view, find a safe spot above the falls to cross the brook and scramble down the opposite side of the river to the base of the falls.

DIRECTIONS From CT 9 in Middletown, take exit 16 and follow signs to CT 17 north and CT 66 east. Follow CT 17 north and CT 66 east as it crosses the Connecticut River and continue on this road until CT 17 north breaks away from CT 66 east. Take a left onto CT 17 north, travel for 1.6 miles, and take a right onto Cox Road. Follow Cox Road for 0.4 mile and take a left onto Rose Hill Road. Go 100 feet up this road and take a right back onto Cox Road. Continue for 0.4 mile on this new section of Cox Road and you'll reach a fork. Fork left to continue on Cox Road and go an additional 0.7 mile, at which point you will reach an intersection with Great Hill Road. Go straight here and continue for 0.7 mile and you will reach a fork. Take the right fork onto Wood Choppers Road, which is an unmarked road. Follow this road for 1.5 miles and the parking area will be on your left. The parking area is distinguishable by the fact that blue blazes are marked on several of the trees here.

OTHER WATERFALLS NEARBY Tartia-Engel Falls, Westfield Falls, Wadsworth Big Falls, Wadsworth Little Falls

6

CHAPMAN FALLS

*East Haddam, Devils Hopyard State Park,
Middlesex County*

Rating: 4.5/5.0

Type: Blocks

Height: 60-foot total drop

Trail Length: Less than 0.1 mile

Water Source: Eight Mile River

Altitude Gain/Loss: -60 feet

Difficulty: Easy

Hiking Time: 5 minutes

DeLorme Atlas: Page 37, J&K-13 (marked as Devil's Hopyard)

Best Time to Visit: April to November

THE FALLS (HIGHLY RECOMMENDED) Chapman Falls is almost as famous for a fascinating legend involving Satan as it is known as a popular state park day-trip destination. Posted on a billboard at the site is a Puritan belief that Satan once walked along the Eight Mile River and became infuriated as his tail became wet. To express his anger, he scampered up to the falls and stomped his hooves on each section of the falls, leaving scars in the boulders of the natural feature the falls descend over. This is where Chapman Falls derives its alternative name, Devil's Hopyard.

In addition to the interesting legend, the falls are quite scenic. The Eight Mile River drops about 60 feet in three bold drops. The waterfall is one of the most powerful in the state and is usually very crowded. This state park also calls for a picnic, so be sure to spend a combined few hours exploring the falls and the picnic area.

During extremely dry weather, the falls may lose their block formation and become weak-flowing horsetails. This should not ruin any plans for visiting, as the entire area is scenic regardless of the power of the river. Bring along your fishing rods as the odds are greatly in your favor for catching trout below the falls.

TRAIL INFORMATION The falls are located just across the street from the parking lot. An instantly apparent trail, lined with wooden fencing, guides you downstream a few steps to the base of the falls.

Chapman Falls

DIRECTIONS From Middletown, take CT 9 south to exit 7. Take CT 82 east through Haddam and into East Haddam. Continue traveling on CT 82 east for 100 feet past the junction of CT 82 and CT 151 north and take a left onto Mt. Parnassus Road. Follow Mt. Parnassus Road straight for 5.8 miles as it turns into Millington Road and then Haywardville Road, and take a right onto Hopyard Road. Follow Hopyard Road for 0.7 mile and take a left onto Foxtown Road. Immediately after, take another left into a large parking lot. There are several signs directing you to Devil's Hopyard State Park, beginning on CT 82 and guiding you all the way into the park. The falls are located near the entrance to the campground. Take note that the park is open from April 1 to December 1.

OTHER WATERFALLS NEARBY Tartia-Engel Falls, Yantic Falls

7

CODFISH FALLS
Mansfield, Tolland County

Rating: 3.0/5.0
Type: Plunges, cascades and a fan
Height: 20-foot total drop
Trail Length: Less than 0.1 mile
Water Source: Fishers Brook
Altitude Gain/Loss: None

Difficulty: Easy
Hiking Time: Negligible
DeLorme Atlas: Page 46, B-8 (unmarked)
Best Time to Visit: March to June

THE FALLS Although the brook was clogged by fallen trees during our recent visit, Codfish Falls should be worked into your waterfall-infused daytrip. Three separate drops of 2 feet, 5 feet, and 11 feet, along with several smaller cascades, combine to a total drop of about 20 feet within a fine-looking ravine. The most impressive of the lot is the upper falls, which consists of a 7-foot plunge immediately followed by a low-angle fan about 4 feet in height. Access is very straightforward and natural forces—such as ice during the winter and run-off during the spring—are likely to clear the trees stuck in the ravine by the time you get a chance to visit.

TRAIL INFORMATION To find the falls, continue upstream from the parking area with the river on your right and you will reach the falls in about 300 feet.

Codfish Falls

DIRECTIONS From Manchester, take US 44 east through Bolton and Coventry into Mansfield. Continue on US 44 east for 1.7 miles beyond the junction of US 44 and CT 195 and take a right onto Codfish Falls Road. Follow this road for 0.9 mile and pull into the small dirt parking spot on your right just after you cross a bridge over Fishers Brook. There is only parking for a car or two here, but visitation is light.

OTHER WATERFALLS NEARBY Blackledge Falls

8

DEAN'S RAVINE FALLS
Canaan, Litchfield County

Rating: 4.0/5.0

Type: Horsetails, cascades, and slides

Height: 50 feet

Trail Length: 0.4 mile

Water Source: Reed Brook

Altitude Gain/Loss: -100 feet

Difficulty: Easy side of moderate

Hiking Time: 15 minutes

DeLorme Atlas: Page 50, H-1 (marked as Dean Ravine)

Best Time to Visit: Year-round

THE FALLS The sister of New Hampshire's Ripley Falls resides in the small town of Canaan, Connecticut. Dean's Ravine Falls is a steep drop of Reed Brook. Similar in shape, location, and personality, both cascades fall at approximately the same vertical angle, about 65 degrees. Other similarities include their widths, being heavily exposed to the sun, and their trail features. The only major difference is that Dean's Ravine is about half the drop of Ripley Falls. Both are equally stunning in beauty and should not be missed.

TRAIL INFORMATION Starting from the parking lot, this easy trail begins immediately, enters the woods, and travels downstream along with the brook. Soon, the trail zigzags its way through steep terrain down to brook level. Instead of following the trail, many have skipped the switchbacks and trampled down the eroded short-cut trails. Please stay on the main trail to prevent further damage to the area. After about 0.4 mile you will reach the falls.

DIRECTIONS From West Cornwall, take US 7 north. Take a right onto Lime Rock Station Road just after you pass the CANAAN TOWN LINE sign, and 0.2 mile north of the junction of US 7 and CT 112. Travel for 1.0 mile on Lime Rock Station Road (crossing railroad tracks at mile 0.4) and take a left onto Music Mountain Road. Travel on Music Mountain Road for 0.8 mile and the large dirt parking lot will be on your left. The trail begins here. *To get to West Cornwall,* take US 7 north from Danbury.

OTHER WATERFALLS NEARBY Great Falls, Pine Swamp Brook Falls, Kent Falls, Race Brook Falls (MA), Campbell Falls (MA)

Dean's Ravine Falls

9

ENDERS FALLS
Granby, Enders State Forest, Hartford County

Rating: 4.5/5.0
Type: Plunges, horsetails, cascades and slides
Height: Tallest drop is 30 feet
Trail Length: 0.4 mile to lowest falls, including all spur trails
Water Source: Unknown
Altitude Gain/Loss: -150 feet to lowest falls

Difficulty: Easy to third set of falls; moderate thereafter
Hiking Time: 15 minutes to lowest falls
DeLorme Atlas: Page 52, F-5 (unmarked)
Best Time to Visit: Year-round

THE FALLS (HIGHLY RECOMMENDED) Enders Falls is an exceptional collection of five diverse waterfalls, several with popular swimmable pools. The first set of falls is a 6-foot cascade—commendable, but not a valid indication of what lies downstream. An easy jaunt farther along the trail brings you to the level of the river where the second falls can be partially seen upstream. The second falls, best seen by crossing the steam, are a 30-foot horsetail and plunge combination that fan widely down between rugged overhanging gorge walls. Fishing is popular in the pool below these falls, which are surrounded on all sides by hemlock trees and thick moss.

The third falls, probably the most heavily photographed of all here, are part horsetail, part plunge. The water gently slides sideways off a wide ledge only to plunge off a second ledge into a refreshing pool. Altogether, the third waterfall is about 18 feet in height, and also best seen from the opposite side of the stream bank.

The fourth falls are just a hop, skip, and jump downstream from the third falls. Here, the brook slips off an overhanging lip 12 feet down to a pool below. This is perhaps the least photogenic waterfall of the lot. The fifth falls should not be missed. This 15-foot two-segment plunge marks the end of the drops in fine style. A gathering of small boulders outlines the medium-sized pool at the base of the falls, which is likely to be less crowded than those above. Make sure to visit all five waterfalls to make the most of this remarkable destination.

TRAIL INFORMATION From the parking lot facing the woods, walk downhill on the trail to your right. In less than 500 feet, you will reach a very short spur path that leads to the top of a 6-foot cascade. This is the first set of falls. To reach the other falls here, head back to the main trail, which will swing left and continue down a nicely maintained gravel path. In less than 300 feet, you will arrive at another short spur path that leads down to several small cascades. Continue straight here, and in 50 feet take a right onto another trail that leads down to the river via a series of wooden steps. Soon you will reach the top of the third falls, where you can look upstream to spot the second set of falls, which are about 75 feet away. For the best views of both the second and third falls, you will want to find a safe place to cross the stream. The views and photographic opportunities are significantly improved on the opposite side of the stream for these two falls.

To reach the fourth set of falls, cross back over the stream and continue downstream with the water on your right for 350 feet past the third set of falls. The fifth set of falls is only 100 feet farther downstream from the fourth, but you will have to hike downhill a bit farther than that to find a spur trail. This spur trail will wind back upstream to the falls.

DIRECTIONS From the junction of US 20, CT 189, CT 10, and CT 202 in the town of Granby, take US 20 west for 3.6 miles to its junction with CT 219. Take a left onto CT 219 south (also called Barkhamsted Road), and drive 1.3 miles. The parking lot will be on your left, marked with a sign for ENDERS STATE FOREST.

OTHER WATERFALLS NEARBY Carpenter's Falls

Enders Falls

10

GREAT FALLS
Canaan & Salisbury, Litchfield County

Rating: 3.5/5.0

Type: Block and cascades

Height: 50 feet

Trail Length: Less than 0.1 mile

Water Source: Housatonic River

Altitude Gain/Loss: None

Difficulty: Easy

Hiking Time: 5 minutes

DeLorme Atlas: Page 49, F-23 (marked)

Best Time to Visit: March to June, or after heavy rains or dam releases

THE FALLS During the planned water releases in spring, the dam-controlled Great Falls of the Housatonic puts on a spectacular show for sightseers. This water flow is unsurpassed in power by any other waterfall in the region. When the water is flowing (and in the summer months it generally is not) white-water kayakers often take to the strong currents below the falls. From the upper viewpoint near the top of the falls, it is always interesting to watch them paddle the powerful currents of rapids below the falls.

The volume of water flowing over this 50-foot feature is impressive. If you are unable to make it to Niagara Falls in New York this summer, this waterfall might just be about as close as you can get in New England.

TRAIL INFORMATION The trail follows a short, worn, nearly flat path to an upper viewpoint of the falls. For better views, you can also hack your way downstream to river level, but this is moderately difficult, so take caution in doing so.

DIRECTIONS From the junction of CT 126 and US 7 in the section of Canaan known as Falls Village, take CT 126 north. Travel on CT 126 north for 0.3 mile, fork left, and follow a short road for 0.2 mile following signs toward Falls Village. At the end of the road, take a right at a sign for the RIVER AND FALLS. And then an immediate left onto Water Street. You will then drive through a bridge and need to fork right immediately thereafter in order to stay on Water Street. Continue on Water Street for 0.3 mile and then bear left and go over a one-lane bridge. Take a right just after the bridge and go 150 feet and take another right onto Housatonic River Road. Go 0.4 mile on Housatonic River Road and there will be a small parking area on the right. *To get to Falls Village,* take US 7 north from Danbury or US 7 south from Canaan.

OTHER WATERFALLS NEARBY Dean's Ravine Falls, Pine Swamp Brook Falls, Kent Falls, Campbell Falls (MA), Race Brook Falls (MA)

11

INDIAN WELL FALLS

Shelton, Indian Well State Park, Fairfield County

Rating: 4.0/5.0
Type: Plunge
Height: 15 feet
Trail Length: 0.2 mile
Water Source: Indian Hole Brook
Altitude Gain/Loss: Negligible

Difficulty: Easy
Hiking Time: 5 minutes
DeLorme Atlas: Page 24, G-2
(marked as Indian Well SP)
Best Time to Visit: Year-round

Indian Well Falls

THE FALLS Indian Well Falls is a 15-foot-tall slender horsetail that dumps into a circular pool nearly enclosed within a well-shaped circular gorge. The name Indian Well derives its name from this gorge, which greatly enhances the beauty of these falls.

Indian Well State Park closes at sunset, and make sure to leave the bathing suit at home—no swimming is allowed in the brook or at the falls, although as you will notice the temptation does exist. However, if swimming is what you desire, the state park also offers a nearby beach and swimming along the Housatonic River. Be aware that a parking fee is collected if you would like to visit the beach area. Parking for the falls is currently free.

TRAIL INFORMATION The trail begins across the street from the parking lot. There is a No CLIMBING sign with an arrow pointing toward the trail that will lead you to the falls. Wide and flat, reaching the base of the falls requires minimal effort. Climbing the steep walls around the falls is a different story. It can be quite difficult to access a birds-eye view of this waterfall, so you are better off enjoying the waterfall from below.

DIRECTIONS From Bridgeport, take CT 8 north to exit 14 in Shelton. Follow CT 110 north for 2.2 miles and take a right onto the road that leads into Indian Well State Park. After 0.4 mile on this road, pull into the parking area on the right.

OTHER WATERFALLS NEARBY Prydden Brook Falls, Southford Falls, Spruce Brook Falls, Sperry Falls

12

KENT FALLS
Kent, Kent Falls State Park, Litchfield County

Rating: 5.0/5.0
Type: Plunges, horsetails and cascades
Height: Approximately 250-foot total drop
Trail Length: 0.3 mile to top of falls
Water Source: Kent Falls Brook

Altitude Gain/Loss: +250 feet
Difficulty: Easy side of moderate
Hiking Time: 10 minutes
DeLorme Atlas: Page 40, E-8&9 (marked)
Best Time to Visit: Year-round

THE FALLS (HIGHLY RECOMMENDED) Grab the peanut butter and jelly sandwiches and head over to Kent Falls State Park, one of Connecticut's most popular state parks and one of New England's top places for a picnic. Here you will find 250 feet of cascades and plunges and one of the finest, well-maintained public parks in New England.

A trip to Kent Falls is one way to view just about every different classification of waterfall. There are plunges, horsetails, punchbowls, blocks, and fans. Many of the falls are also very photogenic, especially in the afternoon when the sun makes the water glitter.

The trail to the top of the falls is steep, but manageable. Although we feel that the view when you first see this waterfall is alone worth a trip, make sure to climb up the trail to see the rest of the variety this series of waterfalls has to offer. Schedule a few hours when you visit as there is also a small covered bridge, large grassy fields, and plenty of picnic tables and fire pits at this very popular park.

TRAIL INFORMATION From the large parking area you can see the beginning of the falls. Cross through the covered bridge and head toward the cascades. The rest of Kent Falls lies up the Kent Falls Trail, which is a short but steep climb that begins to the right of the lowest falls.

DIRECTIONS From Sharon, take US 7 south. Continue traveling on US 7 south for 0.4 mile past the KENT TOWN LINE sign and pull into the

Kent Falls

parking lot for Kent Falls State Park on your left. If you are traveling north on US 7 from New Milford, continue on US 7 north for 5.1 miles past the junction of US 7 and CT 341 in Kent. Both directions of US 7 have signs directing you to the state park, so you can't miss it.

OTHER WATERFALLS NEARBY Pine Swamp Brook Falls, Dean's Ravine Falls, Great Falls

13

MILL POND FALLS
Newington, Hartford County

Rating: 2.5/5.0

Type: Fan

Height: 12 feet

Trail Length: Roadside

Water Source: Mill Pond

Altitude Gain/Loss: None

Difficulty: Easy

Hiking Time: Not applicable

DeLorme Atlas: Page 44, J-2 (unmarked)

Best Time to Visit: March to June

THE FALLS Mill Pond Falls is formed from the outlet waters of Mill Pond, a flower-lined body of water with a paved walking route around its perimeter. The waterfall and pond have been made into a small park by the town of Newington.

The waterfall is surrounded by an iron fence. This fence slightly adds to or detracts from the beauty of the waterfall, the wildflowers, and the landscaped gardens here, depending on who you ask. A red wooden walking bridge is set just above the waterfall. The bridge, railing, and flowers can add significant character to a photograph or painting of the waterfall.

We do not suggest making a day out of this waterfall, as it is quite small and not all that impressive. If you are in the area, or looking for a spot to have a quick lunch, Mill Pond Falls is sure to please you.

TRAIL INFORMATION The falls are clearly visible from the parking area.

DIRECTIONS From Hartford, take I-84 west to exit 39a. Take CT 9 south into Newington. Take exit 29 off CT 9, and at the end of the off-ramp, take a left and follow the road signs toward CT 175. Take a right after 0.1 mile onto CT 175. Take CT 175 east 1.3 miles and take a right onto CT 173 south. After traveling on CT 173 south for 0.2 mile, take a left onto Garfield Street. The parking area is a few hundred feet on the right, marked by a sign for MILL POND FALLS.

OTHER WATERFALLS NEARBY Westfield Falls, Buttermilk Falls, Plymouth, Negro Hill Brook Falls, Blackledge Falls

14

~

NEGRO HILL BROOK FALLS

Burlington, Session Woods Wildlife Management Area, Hartford County

Rating: 2.5/5.0

Type: Plunges

Height: Three drops, each 20 feet tall

Trail Length: 2.9-mile loop

Water Source: Negro Hill Brook

Altitude Gain/Loss: +150 feet, -150 feet

Difficulty: Easy, but long

Hiking Time: 90-minute loop

DeLorme Atlas: Page 42, H-12 (unmarked)

Best Time to Visit: March to April

THE FALLS The Sessions Woods Wildlife Management Area is a 455-acre preserve in Burlington that introduces visitors to wildlife management through self-guided trails, various education programs, and an informative visitor center. The attractions of the management area include a beaver marsh, observation tower, and a set of three waterfall plunges on Negro Hill Brook. Each of the three plunges here is short in total drop, very narrow, and partially hidden between plates of rock.

Other published sources state that this waterfall is rather unimpressive. Negro Hill Brook Falls may not be tall, powerful, or particularly scenic, but it is still impressive to us, especially in high water. As an added bonus, the trail to the waterfall has many stops, where information is provided on the diverse biology of the park. There is also a beaver marsh, several beaver dams, and a boardwalk trail that leads out toward a beaver pond.

To make the most out of your visit, be sure to do the entire loop described below. This is one of the most rewarding easy hikes in the entire state.

TRAIL INFORMATION The falls are accessed by following the Beaver Dam Trail. If you are facing the visitor center, head right toward the dirt road on

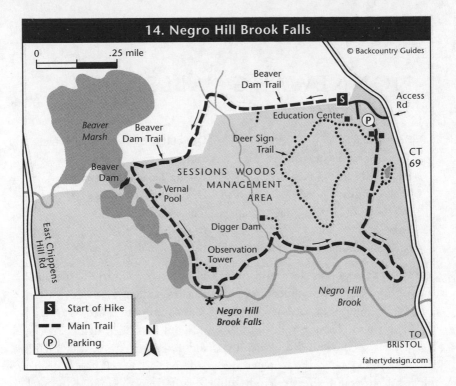

14. Negro Hill Brook Falls

0   .25 mile

© Backcountry Guides

Beaver Dam Trail

Access Rd

Education Center

Beaver Marsh

Beaver Dam Trail

Deer Sign Trail

CT 69

Beaver Dam

SESSIONS WOODS MANAGEMENT AREA

Vernal Pool

East Chippens Hill Rd

Digger Dam

Observation Tower

Negro Hill Brook

Negro Hill Brook Falls

S Start of Hike

– – – Main Trail

Ⓟ Parking

N

TO BRISTOL

fahertydesign.com

your right, where the trail begins. The Beaver Dam Trail follows a rolling and well-maintained dirt road for 2.6 miles. After about 1.4 miles of hiking, a WA-TERFALL sign will direct you onto a spur trail on your right. The falls are a short distance down that trail. When you return, continue the loop of the Beaver Dam Trail back to the visitor center and parking lot. Dogs are welcome on the trails, as long as they remained leashed at all times.

DIRECTIONS From the junction of CT 69 and US 6 in Bristol, take CT 69 north for 3.6 miles and the entrance for the Session Woods Wildlife Management Area will be on your left. Follow the park road to the large parking lot in front of the visitor center. *To get to Bristol,* take I-84 west from Hartford to exit 38. Take US 6 west.

OTHER WATERFALLS NEARBY Buttermilk Falls, Plymouth, Mill Pond Falls, Nonnewaug Falls

15

NONNEWAUG FALLS

Woodbury, Litchfield County

Rating: 3.5/5.0
Type: Horsetail and plunge
Height: 18 feet
Trail Length: 0.3 mile
Water Source: East Nonnewaug River
Altitude Gain/Loss: +30 feet

Difficulty: Easy to top of falls; moderate to base of falls
Hiking Time: 15 minutes
DeLorme Atlas: Page 32, C-11 (unmarked)
Best Time to Visit: Year-round

THE FALLS A popular local attraction, but unknown to most outsiders and absent from all known guidebooks and Web sites (at least that we are aware of), Nonnewaug Falls, or Leever Falls, as it is commonly called, is reached by an easy and pleasant walk through woods and past open fields.

The falls are surrounded by rich moss and other vegetation, which lends a bold green color to the hemlock-shrouded ravine. The 18-foot drop begins as a horsetail before gracefully spilling away from the underlying rock face for a final 7-foot plunge, landing in a waist-deep pool. Swimming is prohibited here, which is a bit of a shame. Exploration of the falls is limited to the side of the river you arrived at as the other side is marked private property. Although water is likely to flow over the falls year-round, high water showcases them best.

TRAIL INFORMATION From the parking area, continue on foot past the gate and up the dirt road. About 0.1 mile from the parking area, you will reach an intersection of several trails. Take the far right dirt road and begin climbing at a moderate pace. Follow this road as it passes by a pretty field on the right. About 0.25 mile from the road, you will reach a clearing and a fork in the trail. Take the right fork and head back into the woods after 100 feet of walking across an open area. The falls are just ahead.

DIRECTIONS From the junction of US 6 and CT 63 in Watertown, take US 6 west into Woodbury. Take a right onto CT 61 north. Follow CT 61 north for 0.7 mile and then take a right onto Nonnewaug Road. After 0.6 mile on Nonnewaug Road, take a right onto Hickory Lane. After 0.1 mile on Hickory Lane, continue straight onto Falls Road and park 300 feet farther on the right before a gate. The parking area is marked by a sign for the falls. *To get to Watertown,* take I-84 west to exit 17 and follow CT 63 north.

OTHER WATERFALLS NEARBY Spruce Brook Falls, Buttermilk Falls, Plymouth, Negro Hill Brook Falls, Southford Falls

16
~

PINE SWAMP BROOK FALLS
Sharon, Litchfield County

Rating: 2.5/5.0

Type: Horsetails and cascades

Height: 30-foot total drop

Trail Length: Less than 0.1 mile

Water Source: Pine Swamp Brook

Altitude Gain/Loss: None

Difficulty: Easy

Hiking Time: Negligible

DeLorme Atlas: Page 49, K&L-23 (unmarked)

Best Time to Visit: Year-round

THE FALLS This well-shaded waterfall, viewable only from the US 7 highway in Sharon, consists of two sections of small cascades tumbling down through tight chasm walls. The waters of Pine Swamp Brook pass beneath you, underneath the state highway, and then dump into the Housatonic River. It takes a true waterfall enthusiast to really appreciate this roadside attraction, as the falls are relatively unspectacular.

Pine Swamp Brook Falls is conveniently located on the route between Dean's Ravine and Kent Falls. For this reason, consider taking a break off the busy state highway to check out these small falls.

TRAIL INFORMATION From the parking area, walk carefully back up the road for a few yards, heading north, and the falls will be visible on your left. There is a sign on the road for PINE SWAMP BROOK.

DIRECTIONS From Canaan, take US 7 south. Continue traveling on US 7 south for 4.0 miles past the SHARON TOWN LINE sign and 0.6 mile beyond the junction of US 7 and CT 128. The parking area will be on your right just after a sharp curve in the road. If you are traveling north on US 7, the parking area is on your left, 2.0 miles north of the Housatonic Meadows Campground in Sharon. *To get to Canaan,* take US 7 north from Danbury.

OTHER WATERFALLS NEARBY Dean's Ravine Falls, Great Falls, Kent Falls

17
〜

PRYDDEN BROOK FALLS

Newtown, Paugussett State Forest, Fairfield County

Rating: 2.5/5.0

Type: Plunges and cascades

Height: 25-foot plunge and 40 feet of cascades

Trail Length: 1.5 miles

Water Source: Prydden Brook

Altitude Gain/Loss: +200 feet, -200 feet

Difficulty: Easy side of moderate

Hiking Time: 45 minutes

DeLorme Atlas: Page 23, B-21 (unmarked)

Best Time to Visit: March to April

THE FALLS The hike to Prydden Brook Falls is always a pleasure. For the majority of the trail, you walk along the west bank of the Housatonic River. As you walk, you pass several small sand and pebble river beaches. The climax of the trip is, of course, the waterfall itself.

This waterfall begins and ends as a plunge, with many sections of cascades between. The main attraction is a 25-foot horsetail, which is surrounded by a heavy growth of moss and plenty of tempting rocks for climbing. The entire feature receives little exposure to the sun, but on a clear day the sun sneaks its way through the trees onto the waterfall and illuminates the water and the vibrant greens of the moss.

Offering plenty of intimate explorations and a healthy 3.0-mile round-trip hike, Prydden Brook Falls is not a waterfall to be missed in high water. In low water, however, the falls become nearly dry, so try to plan your visit in the spring. During the fall months, be sure to wear colorful clothing, as hunting is permitted in the state forest.

TRAIL INFORMATION The Zoar Trail begins to the east end of the parking lot behind an information board with the rules and regulations of the state forest. Well traveled and marked by blue rectangles, the trail is mostly parallel to the Housatonic River for the entire way to the waterfall, sometimes as close as 5 feet to the river, and up to a few hundred feet west of it. After 1.4 miles, you will reach Prydden Brook and will need to take a right spur trail down to the falls. The trail is obvious and the falls are viewable a few hundred feet before you get there, so you should not experience any difficulties reaching the waterfall. Although the altitude gain is modest, there are several hills to ascend and descend.

DIRECTIONS From the junction of CT 34 and CT 111 in the village of Stevenson, take CT 34 west for 0.2 mile. Take a right onto Great Quarter Road and follow it for 1.0 mile to a fork. Take the left fork, and continue on Great Quarter Road for an additional 0.2 mile to the end of the road, where a circular parking area can be found. *To get to Stevenson,* take CT 25 north from Bridgeport to CT 111 north or take I-84 east from Danbury to exit 11 and follow CT 34 east.

OTHER WATERFALLS NEARBY Indian Well Falls, Southford Falls

18

ROARING BROOK FALLS

Cheshire, New Haven County

Rating: 3.0/5.0

Type: Horsetail and cascades

Height: 80-foot total drop

Trail Length: 0.5 mile

Water Source: Roaring Brook

Altitude Gain/Loss: +225 feet

Difficulty: Moderate

Hiking Time: 20 minutes

DeLorme Atlas: Page 34, J&K-1 (unmarked)

Best Time to Visit: Year-round

THE FALLS One of the tallest waterfalls in the state, Roaring Brook Falls is an 80-foot horsetail with several feet of cascades below the main drop. Similar in composition to Race Brook Falls of Massachusetts, the falls are surrounded by a variety of green plant life, causing the waterfall to play peek-a-boo with you from all viewing angles. This makes obtaining a prize-winning photograph very difficult here.

There is a small wooden seat between two trees just off the trail. Instead of trying to view or photograph the entire falls, we suggest accepting the best seat in the house.

TRAIL INFORMATION The trail begins as a continuation of Roaring Brook Road. Follow this dirt road for about five minutes and you will see a trailhead off to the left. Take this trail, which is often marked with orange and white markers on trees, to the falls.

The trail gets progressively steeper as you approach the falls. About 0.3 mile into the woods, you will reach the falls. You can choose to either enjoy the views already rewarded, or you can continue to the top of falls. We do not recommend continuing because the trail becomes hazardously steep and the views are no more spectacular. Getting to the base of the falls is completely out of the question, due to the danger of sliding down the ravine into the cascading brook; therefore we ask that you stay on the trail.

DIRECTIONS From I-84 in Waterbury, take exit 23. Take CT 69 south through Prospect until you reach the junction of CT 69 and CT 42. Take a left onto CT 42 east, and follow it for 2.6 miles. Take a left onto Mountain Road. Follow Mountain Road for 0.3 mile then take a left onto Roaring Brook Road. Travel along this road for 0.5 mile and park at a small pull-off on the right before a metal gate, which is the trailhead for the falls.

OTHER WATERFALLS NEARBY Spruce Brook Falls, Westfield Falls, Wadsworth Little Falls, Wadsworth Big Falls, Sperry Falls

19

SOUTHFORD FALLS

*Southbury & Oxford, Southford Falls State Park,
New Haven County*

Rating: 2.0/5.0

Type: Cascades and a small plunge

Height: 50-foot total drop

Trail Length: 0.3-mile loop

Water Source: Eightmile Brook

Altitude Gain/Loss: -75 feet, +75 feet

Difficulty: Easy

Hiking Time: 10 minutes

DeLorme Atlas: Page 32, L-12 (marked)

Best Time to Visit: Year-round

THE FALLS Your first impression of Southford Falls is that the falls are artificial. The remains of a mill are evident in the stonework around the top of the falls. Upon closer inspection, you realize that the rest of the cascades and small plunges below are completely natural. Despite the presence of a dam, Southford Falls seems to please the visiting picnickers of the park, and those fishing for trout in Papermill Pond, the body of water above the waterfall.

There is nothing scenic or anything out of the ordinary here—just another chain of small waterfalls surrounded by an area best suited for a family picnic.

TRAIL INFORMATION The falls are located on the opposite end of the pond from the parking lot. A short 0.3-mile loop trail walks along the riverbank, through a covered bridge, and back up the other side of the falls. This is a great place for a short relaxing stroll.

DIRECTIONS From Waterbury, take I-84 west to exit 16. Take CT 188 south for 2.7 miles as CT 188 joins with, and later splits away from, CT 67. The parking lot will be on your left on CT 188, marked by a sign for SOUTHFORD FALLS STATE PARK.

OTHER WATERFALLS NEARBY Spruce Brook Falls, Prydden Brook Falls, Indian Well Falls, Nonnewaug Falls

20

∽

SPERRY FALLS
Woodbridge, New Haven County

Rating: 3.0/5.0
Type: Small plunges
Height: 5 feet
Trail Length: 0.1 mile
Water Source: Sperry Brook
Altitude Gain/Loss: Negligible

Difficulty: Easy
Hiking Time: 5 minutes
DeLorme Atlas: Page 24, E10 (unmarked)
Best Time to Visit: March to December

THE FALLS If Sperry Falls were an inch or two shorter, it would have missed our 5-foot minimum requirement for a waterfall. This matters not, however; the falls are much more attractive than their height would lead you to believe. A rock outcrop splits the brook in two as the water drapes down into a medium-sized pool, which is unfortunately off-limits due to the fact that this is a public water supply.

Sperry Brook is certainly one of Connecticut's prettiest brooks, and Sperry Falls is likely to be the finest attraction along it.

TRAIL INFORMATION To reach the falls, follow the only path that stems from the parking area 0.1 mile to the falls.

DIRECTIONS From I-15 in New Haven, take exit 59 for CT 69. Follow CT 69 north for 3.9 miles and take a left onto Morris Road. Follow Morris Road for 0.5 mile and take a left onto Sperry Road. Follow Sperry Road for 0.6 mile and take a left onto a narrower dirt road and the

Sperry Falls

parking area will be only 100 feet up the road, marked by an engraved rock that says SPERRY PARK. This turn off Sperry Road is at a major curve and it can be easily missed.

OTHER WATERFALLS NEARBY Roaring Brook Falls, Indian Well Falls, Spruce Brook Falls

21

SPRUCE BROOK FALLS

Beacon Falls, Naugatuck State Forest,
New Haven County

Rating: 3.0/5.0

Type: Plunges and cascades

Height: Largest plunge is 15 feet

Trail Length: 0.3 mile

Water Source: Spruce Brook

Altitude Gain/Loss: +75 feet

Difficulty: Easy side of moderate

Hiking Time: 10 minutes

DeLorme Atlas: Page 33, L-17&18
(unmarked)

Best Time to Visit: Year-round

THE FALLS Spruce Brook Falls is one of only two waterfalls described in this guide that allows visitors to wander behind a waterfall. It is much easier to get behind the falling waters of Bartlett Falls in Vermont, but Spruce Brook Falls is the only other waterfall we are aware of where this is possible. For those who wish to take advantage of such a natural marvel, you will need to scramble down to and hop into the river. Once in the river, you can tuck yourself behind the falling water. This can only be safely done in low-water conditions, though.

At the base of the main falls, a 15-foot plunge, the rushing water is forced into rocks causing white foam to swirl around and look like a bubble bath. There are rust-colored pools, the deepest of which approaches 6 feet. There are cascades above and below, and farther downstream there is a petite-sized waterslide, and even a pool with a swirling eddy. Farther up the trail and beyond the main falls lies the last noteworthy waterfall—a segmented cascade over an egg-shaped boulder that sits in the center of the brook.

The entire fragment of Spruce Brook we are describing lies in a ravine that supports an unusually large variety of plant life. This adds much color to the area. We think it deserves to be a contender as one of the prettiest ravines in all of New England.

TRAIL INFORMATION From the end of the parking area, take the trail that leads slightly downhill into the woods on the right. Follow this trail for 300 feet and bear left onto a trail that parallels the brook. As you continue up the trail and begin passing the first cascades, expect more steep and slippery terrain. Continue upstream for a short distance for the second and third series of falls here. *Footing can become quite difficult, so be careful.*

DIRECTIONS From Waterbury, take CT 8 south to exit 24. Take a right at the end of the off ramp and after 0.1 mile, take another right onto Depot Street and drive over a bridge. Immediately after crossing over the bridge, take a right onto Lopus Road. Follow Lopus Road for 0.1 mile and take a right onto Cold Spring Road. Travel on Cold Spring Road for 1.0 mile and you will reach a fork. Take the left fork and park 200 feet farther at the parking area at the end of the road. Be aware that Cold Spring Road turns into a rather rough dirt road, but it should be passable in normal conditions by the average passenger car. Also, take note that exit 24 is only on the southbound side of CT 8.

OTHER WATERFALLS NEARBY Southford Falls, Roaring Brook Falls, Indian Well Falls, Prydden Brook Falls, Sperry Falls

22

~

TARTIA-ENGEL FALLS

East Hampton, Middlesex County

Rating: 3.0/5.0

Type: Horsetails and cascades

Height: Lower falls are 20 feet, upper falls are 6 feet

Trail Length: Lower falls are visible from roadside; 0.2 mile to upper falls

Water Source: Safstrom Brook

Altitude Gain/Loss: +50 feet to upper falls

Difficulty: Easy side of moderate

Hiking Time: 5 minutes

DeLorme Atlas: Page 36, G-5 (unmarked)

Best Time to Visit: Year-round

THE FALLS There are two waterfalls at Tartia-Engel Falls—a lower falls visible from roadside and an upper falls reached by a easy walk in the woods—but we must admit we are confused, as other visitors have likely been, as to which one is Tartia Falls and which one is Engel Falls. Or perhaps the full name is shared between both waterfalls? Until we resolve this matter, we will have to resort to referring to these two formations as lower and upper falls.

No effort is required on your part to see the 20-foot lower falls; they are clearly seen from the road. These falls begin and end as cascades, with several low-angle horsetails in between. The upper falls dart back and forth between a horsetail and a cascade, depending on how intense the water is flowing. During the summer, the falls take on more of a mild horsetail appearance, which allows for swimming in the pool below the falls. There is only room for a few people in this tiny pool, but it still is one of the state's finest natural swimming holes.

TRAIL INFORMATION The lower falls are visible from the bridge over the road. To reach the upper falls, cross the road and head upstream on the faint path with the river on your left. Take note that the opposite side of the stream is marked private property. Follow this path, which can be slightly difficult to follow at times, upstream for 0.2 mile to the upper falls. Although we found no indications that the public was not welcome at the upper falls, the possibility always exists. Please respect any landowner rights if the upper falls are marked private property on the day of your visit.

DIRECTIONS From Middletown, take CT 9 south to exit 7. Take CT 82 east through Haddam and across the Connecticut River into East Haddam. Take a left onto CT 149 north and follow that to a left onto CT 151 north.

Take CT 151 north to a right onto CT 196 north. Take CT 196 north for 0.3 mile and take a right onto Wopowaug Road. Follow Wopowaug Road for 1.2 miles as it turns into a dirt road and then returns to pavement. Take a right onto Tartia Road and follow that road for 0.3 mile. A parking pull-off will be on the right just after crossing a bridge over a stream.

OTHER WATERFALLS NEARBY The Cascade, Chapman Falls

Tartia-Engel Falls (lower falls)

23

WADSWORTH BIG FALLS

Middlefield, Wadsworth Falls State Park,
Middlesex County

Rating: 4.0/5.0

Type: Block

Height: 25 feet

Trail Length: Less than 0.1 mile

Water Source: Coginchaug River

Altitude Gain/Loss: -25 feet

Difficulty: Easy

Hiking Time: Negligible

DeLorme Atlas: Page 35, H-16 (marked)

Best Time to Visit: Year-round

THE FALLS One of the highest-volume waterfalls in New England, Wadsworth Big Falls is one of two notable falls within Wadsworth Falls State Park. Wider than it is tall, Wadsworth Big Falls is a stereotypical block-type waterfall. Wadsworth Big Falls earns its relatively high rating simply because you do not expect to find such a commanding waterfall in the heart of Connecticut. The currents of this river are astonishing given its location.

Do not expect to have any peace and quiet at this particular waterfall. The parking lot can begin to fill up, even on chilly, rainy days in the springtime. Its popularity can only be explained by its stunning volume and scale, especially considering how confined the area is. If seclusion and privacy is what you want, nearby Wadsworth Little Falls is there to fill your need—less than a mile away and accessed via a trail that starts at the same parking lot.

TRAIL INFORMATION From the parking lot, walk straight across a field and down the steps to the falls. There is also a cement overlook surrounded by safety fences at the top of the falls for a bird's-eye view of the falls.

DIRECTIONS From CT 9 in Middletown, take exit 16. Take CT 66 west until you reach the junction of CT 66 and CT 157 south. Take a left onto CT 157 south and follow it for 1.5 miles and a sign for WADSWORTH FALLS STATE PARK will appear on your left. Although there is a large parking lot here, and trails can be seen leading into the woods, the parking lot for the falls is not here. Continue farther on CT 157 for an additional 1.0 mile, and then take a left onto Cherry Hill Road. After traveling for 0.2 mile on Cherry Hill Road, take a left into a paved parking lot.

OTHER WATERFALLS NEARBY Wadsworth Little Falls, Westfield Falls, The Cascade

24

WADSWORTH LITTLE FALLS

Middlefield, Wadsworth Falls State Park,
Middlesex County

Rating: 3.0/5.0

Type: Small plunges

Height: 40 feet

Trail Length: 0.5 mile

Water Source: Wadsworth Brook

Altitude Gain/Loss: +50 feet,
-40 feet

Difficulty: Easy side of moderate

Hiking Time: 15 minutes

DeLorme Atlas: Page 35, H-16
(unmarked)

Best Time to Visit: March to
June

THE FALLS To our surprise, Wadsworth Little Falls turned out to be nearly two times taller than its neighbor, Wadsworth Big Falls. Wadsworth Little Falls must have earned its name from being much less powerful, and seasonal. Even though we visited the falls in spring after two previous days of heavy rain, Little Falls was still rather weak in power.

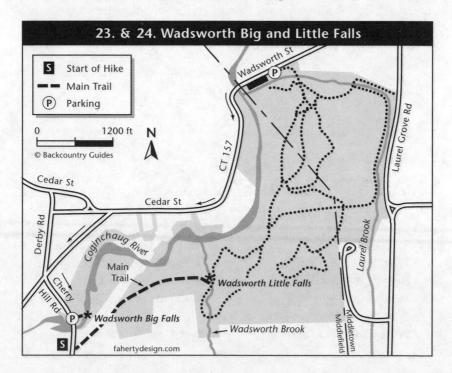

For structure, this waterfall is composed of about two dozen small-step plunges, none larger than 3 feet in height. Although weak, this waterfall is a fine example of a staircase falls, and is a nice alternative or supplement to the power and popularity of the Big Falls.

TRAIL INFORMATION From the parking lot facing the field, take a right and continue walking along Cherry Hill Road. Soon, you will cross a set of railroad tracks. Continue about 150 feet farther up the road past the tracks and the trailhead will be on your left. The trail you are now on is the Main Trail, an easily traveled trail that navigates through the center of the park. Hike this orange-blazed trail for 0.4 mile and you will see a faint trail that heads left into the woods just before the main trail starts climbing a bit. Take this left and the falls are only a few hundred feet away. The last 100 feet of the trail is somewhat steep and often muddy—this part may not be best for children.

DIRECTIONS From CT 9 in Middletown, take exit 16. Take CT 66 west until you reach the junction of CT 66 and CT 157 south. Take a left onto CT 157 south and follow it for 1.5 miles and a sign for WADSWORTH FALLS STATE PARK will appear on your left. Although there is a large parking lot here, and trails can be seen leading into the woods, the parking lot for the falls is not here. Continue further on CT 157 for an additional 1.0 mile, and then take a left onto Cherry Hill Road. After traveling for 0.2 mile on Cherry Hill Road, take a left into a paved parking lot.

OTHER WATERFALLS NEARBY Wadsworth Big Falls, Westfield Falls, The Cascade

25

WESTFIELD FALLS
Middletown, Middlesex County

Rating: 3.0/5.0
Type: Horsetail and plunge
Height: 18-foot plunge and 15-foot horsetail
Trail Length: Less than 0.1 mile
Water Source: Fall Brook

Altitude Gain/Loss: -30 feet
Difficulty: Easy
Hiking Time: 5 minutes
DeLorme Atlas: Page 35, E-15 (marked)
Best Time to Visit: Year-round

Westfield Falls

THE FALLS Westfield Falls is a set of two drops about 30 feet apart from each other. The falls on the left are an 18-foot-tall plunge, and the falls on the right are a 15-foot horsetail. The brook, which is separated by a rocky island just above the falls, rejoins about 80 feet downstream from the falls. There is also a long slide a few feet downstream from the falls worth noting.

Westfield Falls is a beautiful waterfall. Due to its residential location, however, the area around the waterfall has become victim to vandalism and litter. You can also hear the interstate highway. We hope this waterfall will be cleaned up in the near future. If it was, it would earn a higher recommendation from us in any future editions of this guidebook.

TRAIL INFORMATION Step over the cinder blocks, and walk along the trail in front of the parking lot for a few feet. To see the top of the falls first, continue straight down the trail. To get to the bottom of the falls, which we recommend you do, take an almost immediate left turn onto a trail that heads down into the woods. After a hundred feet, take the right trail at the fork that appears. You will shortly be able to see and hear the waterfall nearby.

DIRECTIONS From Middletown, take CT 66 west toward Middlefield. Take a right onto CT 217 north (also called Ballfall Road). Follow CT 217 north for 2.3 miles and take a left onto Miner Street. Follow Miner Street for 0.7 mile and park at the small parking area on the right. The parking area is outlined with cement blocks. You can also reach Miner Street by taking exit 21 off I-91, and following CT 372 east to a right onto CT 217 south.

OTHER WATERFALLS NEARBY Wadsworth Big Falls, Wadsworth Little Falls, Mill Pond Falls, Roaring Brook Falls, The Cascade

26

YANTIC FALLS
Norwich, New London County

Rating: 3.0/5.0

Type: Plunge and cascades

Height: 40-foot plunge

Trail Length: Less than 0.1 mile

Water Source: Yantic River

Altitude Gain/Loss: None

Difficulty: Easy

Hiking Time: Negligible

DeLorme Atlas: Page 38, G-4 (unmarked)

Best Time to Visit: Year-round

THE FALLS As the legend goes, Yantic Falls was a favorite camping spot and battleground for the Mohegan Indians in the 1640s. Uncas, Sachem of the Mohegans, led the Mohegans in a battle here against the Narragansetts, a major rival tribe. Legend states that during the battle, a group of Narragansetts chose to leap into the chasm of the Yantic River instead of surrendering to the Mohegans. All of the warriors supposedly met their death in the turbulent cascades of Yantic Falls.

Today, Yantic Falls is part dam and part natural. The main plunge is approximately 40 feet in height, and the volume of water is one of the most powerful in the state. The river continues through one of the most impressive gorges in the state before ending its descent and relaxing in calmer waters. Above the falls, a walking bridge and a railroad bridge have been constructed, but they do not detract from the scenery.

TRAIL INFORMATION From the parking area, walk back up Yantic Street and take a left at the sign for the YANTIC FALLS AND INDIAN LEAP. The falls are directly ahead. You can also take a short trail that leads directly from the parking lot to a different viewpoint of the falls.

DIRECTIONS From I-395 in Norwich, take exit 81 for CT 2. Follow CT 2 east toward Norwich and take exit 29 for Norwichtown. At the end of the off-ramp, take a right, and you will be on the New London Turnpike, heading south. After 1.3 miles on the turnpike, take a left onto New-

Yantic Falls

ton Street at a set of lights. Just after you take this left turn, you will be faced with a fork. Fork right and follow Newton Street for 0.5 mile to its end. At the end of Newton Street, take a left onto Asylum Street. Follow Asylum Street for 0.7 mile and take a right onto Sherman Street. Follow Sherman Street, making sure to follow the street as it takes a sharp right turn at 0.2 mile. At the end of Sherman Street, take a right onto Yantic Street. A dirt parking lot is 0.1 mile up the road, on your right just past a set of black fencing and a sign for the falls.

OTHER WATERFALLS NEARBY Bailey's Ravine, Chapman Falls

II. Maine

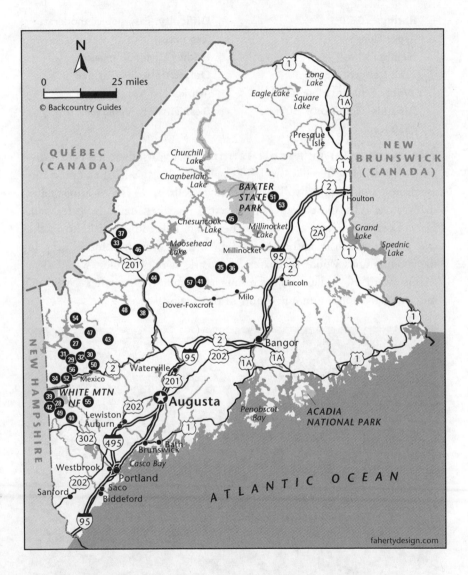

27

ANGEL FALLS
Township D, Franklin County

Rating: 5.0/5.0
Type: Plunge
Height: 90 feet
Trail Length: 0.8 mile
Water Source: Mountain Brook
Altitude Gain/Loss: -50 feet, +150 feet

Difficulty: Easy side of moderate (see notes)
Hiking Time: 30 minutes
DeLorme Atlas: Page 18, B-4 (marked)
Best Time to Visit: June to July

THE FALLS (HIGHLY RECOMMENDED) For years, there has been a dispute over which waterfall, Angel Falls or Moxie Falls, is Maine's tallest single drop. Some accounts will say that Angel Falls, at 90 feet, is a foot taller than Moxie Falls. Other sources have stated that they are both 90 feet tall. Dean Goss, maintainer of www.northeastwaterfalls.com, shed light on the true answer, which is neither! Katahdin Falls, a remote falls found deep in the mountainous woods of Baxter State Park, wins the tallest waterfall in Maine award. Regardless of which falls is the tallest, each offers a wild remote treasure not commonly found in this region.

Angel Falls

With surrounding cliff walls of up to 115 feet in height, Angel Falls is remarkably scenic. The 25-foot gap positioned on the top of the cliff wall can be explained by two theories, the first being erosion. Through the years it appears as if the water was slicing its way through the cliff walls, causing the sediments to flow downstream. The other theory suggests that the perfectly sized and shaped boulder at the base of the waterfall used to sit in the gap above. Perhaps it was knocked out during the last Ice Age or even by a great hurricane. We cannot say which theory is correct, but the gap on the cliff wall that the water flows through distinguishes Angel Falls from all others in the region.

What makes Angel Falls deserving of its name is the way the water lightly kisses the rocks upon its descent from the heavens. The light-flowing plunge has soft sounds as it sprays into the rust-colored water below. Given the difficulty of accessing this waterfall in winter, we can only assume that the strong early spring runoff offers a stronger and different perspective that limited viewers have the opportunity of seeing.

TRAIL INFORMATION From the parking pull-off, walk a few yards farther up Bemis Road to an unnamed road on your left. For the first 0.2 mile of the hike to the falls, the trail follows an old dirt road that stems from Bemis Road. It is currently only distinguishable from other roads by a sign prohibiting kindling fires in the area. Follow this dirt road as it descends past a gravel pit on the left and a large circular dirt lot on the right. You should soon see two obvious trails here. Take the red-blazed trail that is the farthest trail on the left. The parking area where the trail begins is identifiable by a large boulder.

About 0.5 mile from Bemis Road, you will have to cross Berden Stream, which, on our visits, was completed with minimal effort. We have heard of some difficulties of crossing this stream during periods of high water. After crossing the stream, continue for 0.3 mile farther, following the red markers as the trail skips back and forth across the brook before reaching the base of the falls.

DIRECTIONS From the junction of ME 17 and US 2 in Mexico, take ME 17 north for 17.3 miles. Take a left onto Houghton Road. Houghton Road is 1.5 miles south of the TOWNSHIP E TOWN LINE sign. Follow Houghton Road for 0.2 mile and take a right onto Bemis Road (marked as Bemis Track on some maps). Follow Bemis Road for 3.3 miles (staying straight at 1.2 miles at a junction to continue on the road) and several parking pull-offs will be on your left. *To get to Mexico,* take ME 17 north from Augusta or US 2 east from Bethel.

OTHER WATERFALLS NEARBY Coos Canyon, Rumford Falls, Ellis Falls, The Cataracts, Dunn Falls, Smalls Falls, Phillips Falls

28

BICKFORD SLIDES

Stow, White Mountain National Forest, Oxford County

Rating: 3.5/5.0

Type: Cascades and slides

Height: Lower slide is 50 feet, upper slide is 40 feet

Trail Length: To lower slide, 0.7 mile; to upper slide, 1.1 miles

Water Source: Bickford Brook

Altitude Gain/Loss: To lower slide, +300 feet; to upper slide, +500 feet

Difficulty: Moderate

Hiking Time: 50 minutes to upper slide

DeLorme Atlas: Page 10, C-1 (marked)

Best Time to Visit: May to October

THE FALLS Hidden in a deep ravine between Blueberry Mountain and Sugarloaf Mountain, Bickford Brook travels downstream toward its confluence with the Cold River. Along the way, hundreds of feet of cascades and slides adorn the brook, most accessible by connecting a few popular hiking trails.

The first slides of the trail, appropriately named Lower Slides, are reached just after your first contact with the brook. These slides are about 50 feet in height, and composed of cascades, slides, and delightful water chutes. Forget about exploring the Lower Slides; the sheer flume walls are very dangerous and too slippery to safely navigate.

Set in a heavily shaded glen, the Upper Slides have very low water throughout most of the year. The 40-foot-tall, medium-angle slides have a clear, dark green, attractive pool beneath them. Although the area is remote and access can be confusing, the pool, with depths up to 5 feet, receives moderate use. As the cold river waters warm up, visitors with swim shorts and towels can often be seen making their way to the Upper Slides.

TRAIL INFORMATION The trail to Bickford Slides begins at the parking lot to the right of Brickett Place when facing the entrance to the building. For the first 0.2 mile, the trail is a moderately steep climb. After climbing for about 10 minutes, the trail will reduce its intensity as you continue to hike the next 0.4 mile.

At this point in the hike (0.6 mile from the parking lot) you will reach a fork. The left fork is for the Bickford Brook Trail and the right fork, which you will be taking, is the Blueberry Ridge Trail. Follow the Blueberry Ridge Trail for 0.1 mile as it meanders down to the brook. Upon reaching the brook, a white sign will appear and point toward the Lower Slides and the trail that leads to the Upper Slides.

The Lower Slides are approximately 100 feet downstream, accessible by an overgrown path that parallels the brook. Take note that there are limited views of the slides from the trail, and scrambling off trail is not

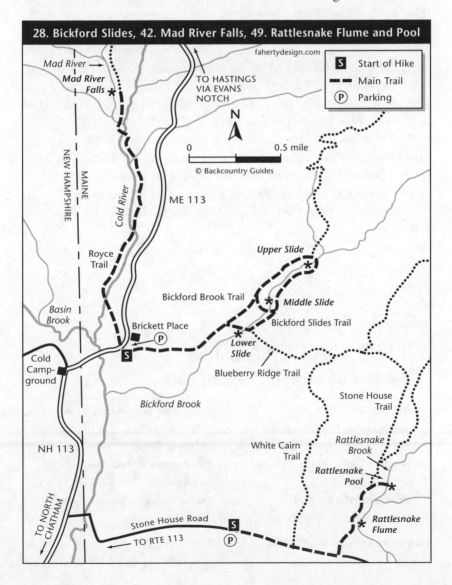

28. Bickford Slides, 42. Mad River Falls, 49. Rattlesnake Flume and Pool

faherty design.com

S Start of Hike

- - - Main Trail

P Parking

Mad River →
Mad River Falls ✳

TO HASTINGS VIA EVANS NOTCH

N ↑

0   0.5 mile

© Backcountry Guides

NEW HAMPSHIRE

MAINE

Cold River

ME 113

Royce Trail

Upper Slide ✳

Basin Brook

Bickford Brook Trail

✳ *Middle Slide*

Brickett Place

Bickford Slides Trail

P

S

✳ *Lower Slide*

Cold Camp-ground

Blueberry Ridge Trail

Bickford Brook

Stone House Trail

NH 113

White Cairn Trail

Rattlesnake Brook

Rattlesnake Pool

TO NORTH CHATHAM

Stone House Road

S

P

✳ *Rattlesnake Flume*

← TO RTE 113

recommended, as a fall from the river walls could cause serious injury. To reach the Upper Slides, continue back to where you first reached the brook and cross to the other side. There are two different trails that continue from the other side of the brook. The path on the right is the Blueberry Ridge Trail. The path on the left is the trail to the upper falls. Both are yellow-blazed, so be sure to take the left trail. Follow the aforementioned trail parallel to the brook for about 0.4 mile and you will reach a head-on view of the Upper Slides. If you are confident in your abilities, scramble down to the base of the slides, where you will find one of the more popular swimming holes of the White Mountains.

DIRECTIONS From the junction of ME 113 and US 302 in Fryeburg, Maine, take ME 113 north for 19.7 miles and take a right into the Brickett Place, where a hikers' parking lot can be found. If you are traveling on ME 113 south from US 2 in Gilead, Brickett Place will be on your right after driving 10.6 miles. *To get to Fryeburg,* take NH 113 east from NH 16 in Conway, New Hampshire into Maine.

Please be aware that this trailhead is part of the White Mountain National Forest parking fee program. The fee was $3 in 2009 but there is currently a proposal in review to raise this amount to $5.

OTHER WATERFALLS NEARBY Rattlesnake Flume and Pool, Mad River Falls, Kees Falls, Hermit Falls (NH), Eagle Cascade (NH), Brickett Falls (NH)

29

THE CATARACTS
Andover West Surplus, Oxford County

Rating: 3.5/5.0
Type: Lower falls are horsetails and cascades; upper falls is a fan
Height: Lower falls is 75 feet; upper falls is 25 feet
Trail Length: 0.5 mile
Water Source: Frye Brook

Altitude Gain/Loss: +150 feet
Difficulty: Easy side of moderate
Hiking Time: 20 minutes
DeLorme Atlas: Page 18, D-2 (marked)
Best Time to Visit: May to October

THE FALLS On our summer visits, The Cataracts consisted of many plunges dropping a total of 100 feet. The falls in the early spring are a behemoth of raging cascades, as the snow melt increases the water volume considerably during this wet season. On a positive note, with the cascades nearly disappeared in the summer months you can explore the small caves near the waterfall and between the precipitous gorge walls.

During the summer, The Cataracts are also a scrambler's delight, with opportunities for hours of exploration. The many swimming holes are refreshingly pleasing. We have seen pictures of people enjoying a natural waterslide in low-water conditions. Perhaps your multiple visits will reveal several of the many different personalities this waterfall has to offer throughout the seasons.

Anticipate big changes to the trail network to and around the falls as the state of Maine appears to be updating the park into a recreation area. There are currently picnic tables and there is evidence that additional facilities will be constructed. There is a dirt road that is under construction, which may ultimately allow for closer access to the upper falls in the near future.

TRAIL INFORMATION The Frye Brook Trail begins across the street from the parking area and to the right of Cataracts Road. There is a small sign referencing the recreation area as you enter into the woods. Continue along the blue-blazed trail, and about 0.5 mile from the parking lot, you will begin climbing at a more intense rate and the gorge will appear on your right, behind wooden fencing. The views are limited from the top, so backtrack a little and scout the easiest path down to the brook and hike upstream to the falls. Be careful as you hike upstream, as many rocks are covered in moss and others are weathered and very slippery.

To reach the tallest drop, you must pass through a narrow cave and hike upstream. Continue along the brook for as long as you feel safe, as the trail gets increasingly challenging as you begin to explore the cascades. If instead you continue up the trail to the middle and upper falls, you will notice that the trail strays back into the woods away from the river for a few tenths of a mile. When you come to a picnic area with the upper falls heard to your right, we recommend you scramble down the small embankment for a better view and access to a great swimming hole below.

DIRECTIONS From the junction of ME 120 and ME 5 in the center of Andover, head west on Newton Street (sometimes marked as East B Hill Road or Upton Road on maps). Follow Newton Street for 5.4 miles and a pull-off will be on your right across the street from a sign for CATARACTS ROAD. Use 5.4 miles as your reference and park to the right before a small bridge crossing Frye Brook. *To get to Andover,* take ME 5 north from Bethel or ME 120 west from Rumford.

OTHER WATERFALLS NEARBY Dunn Falls, Screw Auger Falls, Grafton, Step Falls, Ellis Falls, Coos Canyon, Angel Falls, Rumford Falls

30

〰

COOS CANYON

Byron, Oxford County

Rating: 3.5/5.0

Type: Horsetail

Height: 15-foot total drop

Trail Length: Roadside

Water Source: Swift River

Altitude Gain/Loss: None

Difficulty: Easy

Hiking Time: Not applicable

DeLorme Atlas: Page 18, C-5 (marked)

Best Time to Visit: Year-round

THE FALLS Coos Canyon is a great roadside park to stop for a swim or enjoy a picnic. The canyon is utterly beautiful. The rocks lining the canyon walls have uniquely carved lines in them due to erosion over the years. You will find this a hot spot to fit all ages. Some people jump off the canyon walls for a refreshing splash into the river below, while other families wade in the waters above. Overall, this is a great place to spend a warm day basking in the sun. What more could you ask for from a picnic area?

The Swift River is also known as one of Maine's prime places to pan for gold. The Ole Prospector Mineral & Gift Shoppe is located across the street

Coos Canyon

from the canyon and they rent inexpensive supplies. They also offer free demonstrations on how to correctly pan for these treasures.

TRAIL INFORMATION The canyon itself is rather large to explore. There is lots of green fencing protecting children from getting too close to the gorge walls. The picnic tables and grills at the parking area offer a great luncheon location. Not only are there views from the bridge over the river, but it is possible to walk around the fences and sit on the rim of the canyon.

DIRECTIONS From the intersection of ME 17 and US 2 in Mexico, take ME 17 west (which actually heads more north than west) for 13.2 miles. Turn right into a well-marked parking area for the canyon. *To get to Mexico,* take ME 17 north from Augusta or US 2 east from Bethel.

OTHER WATERFALLS NEARBY Angel Falls, Ellis Falls, The Cataracts, Dunn Falls, Rumford Falls, Smalls Falls, Phillips Falls

31

DUNN FALLS
Andover North Surplus, Oxford County

Rating: 5.0/5.0
Type: Upper Falls is horsetails and fans; lower falls is a plunge
Height: Lower Falls is 80 feet; Upper Falls is 70-foot total drop
Trail Length: 2.0-mile loop
Water Source: West Branch of the Ellis River
Altitude Gain/Loss: +350 feet, -350 feet

Difficulty: Moderate side of difficult
Hiking Time: 90 minutes
DeLorme Atlas: Page 18, D-2 (marked)
Best Time to Visit: July through October

THE FALLS (HIGHLY RECOMMENDED) The 2-mile loop trail that encircles Dunn Falls offers more than just two of the highest rated waterfalls in Maine. As you hike this trip, you will find swimming holes, travel a stretch of the 2,160-mile Appalachian Trail, and discover lower and upper Dunn Falls, plus a half-dozen smaller, unnamed cascades. With so many natural features, we would have to say that a trip to Dunn Falls is sure to leave a lasting impression on everyone.

Discovering the remote Lower Dunn Falls is as surprising as finding any waterfall in Maine. Before you reach the side trail to view Dunn Falls, only miniature horsetails and cascades will be spotted. How shocking and mind-boggling the nearly vertical 80-foot drop of lower Dunn Falls is to the virgin eye! With rock walls up to 100 feet in height on opposite sides of the falls, the area is outstandingly scenic. Take your camera for this waterfall, but beware that you will need to rock-hop upstream to earn the best view of the lower falls. The falls can also be seen safely from above, along the Appalachian Trail, but these views are limited.

As if the lower falls is not visually appealing and mentally satisfying enough, more gems lie ahead on the trail. Just before the upper falls lie two lovely rocky-bottom pools, each with small falls cascading into them. The first pool, about 80 feet in circumference, is surrounded by semi-circular rock walls, with the waterfall flowing through a gap in the wall. The second pool has a similar structure and almost equal dimensions, but behind the pool lies a 70-foot secret; the elusive upper falls. Although half-hidden by the forest, this fanning horsetail is beautiful and adds a perfect ending to the waterfalls on this trip.

TRAIL INFORMATION To find the trailhead, walk 200 feet downhill (heading east) along the road and look for where the white-blazed Appalachian Trail crosses the road. You will want to take the southbound section of the Appalachian Trail, which is across the street from the parking area.

The trail starts by descending 150 feet down to a junction just before a brook. Take a left onto the blue-blazed Cascade Trail instead of continuing across the brook on the Appalachian Trail. The Cascade Trail, which will guide you closer toward Lower Dunn Falls, eventually loops back to the Appalachian Trail at the top of the lower falls. From the junction, follow the Cascade Trail downstream (the brook will be on your right) for 0.5 mile, at which point you will have to cross the brook. Depending on water conditions, this can be an easy rock-hop or it can be a slightly more challenging affair that requires you to remove your boots and walk across the stream through the water. After crossing the brook, continue along the trail as it ascends and descends, steeply at times, several small ridges. You will reach a second water crossing 0.25 mile beyond the first. This crossing of the wide West Branch of the Ellis River can also be a challenge in high water, but it is almost always do-able.

About 200 feet beyond this second crossing, you will reach a fork in the trail. The left fork heads uphill and connects back with the Appalachian Trail in 0.2 mile at the top of the lower falls. To reach the base of Lower Dunn Falls, take the right fork and head closely along the riverbed upstream for 0.2 mile on another blue-blazed trail. This is a rougher section of trail than what you have encountered so far, and it requires some careful maneuvering along the way. This is not a family-friendly section of the trail and is constantly changing due to erosion. The trail ends at the base of the mighty lower falls.

After visiting Lower Dunn Falls, double back to the junction at the fork,

Dunn Falls

and continue climbing uphill along the Cascade Trail this time. After 0.2 mile beyond this junction, take a right onto the white-blazed Appalachian Trail. Only 50 feet later, cross the West Branch of the Ellis River at the top of the lower falls. If you are uncomfortable crossing the river so close to the plunge of the lower falls, it is possible to bushwhack upstream and cross where the danger is less imminent.

Just after crossing the river, the Appalachian Trail will continue straight, eventually leading you back to your vehicle. To reach the upper falls, take a left instead onto a new trail at a sign directing you toward the UPPER FALLS. This junction is only 10 feet beyond the river crossing above the top of the lower falls.

The trail to the upper falls also follows a blue-blazed trail. This section of trail is very straightforward and passes several small but interesting cascades before the magnificent 70-foot drop is unfolded before you. The trail does not end at the base of the upper falls; there is a very steep scramble that will bring you to the uppermost section of the falls, where you can practically reach out and touch the falling water. This is the best viewpoint, in our opinion, and completely conducive to outstanding photographs. A wide-angle lens is most useful here.

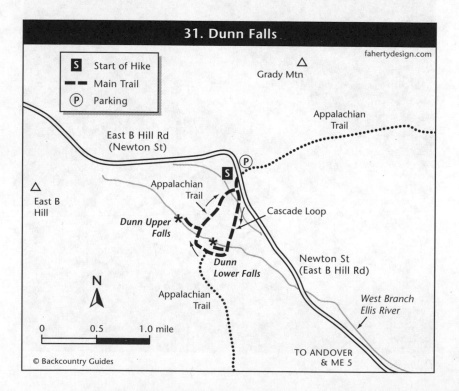

31. Dunn Falls

fahertydesign.com

S Start of Hike
- - - Main Trail
P Parking

Grady Mtn

Appalachian Trail

East B Hill Rd (Newton St)

East B Hill

Appalachian Trail

Dunn Upper Falls

Cascade Loop

Dunn Lower Falls

Newton St (East B Hill Rd)

N

Appalachian Trail

West Branch Ellis River

0   0.5   1.0 mile

© Backcountry Guides

TO ANDOVER & ME 5

After absorbing the moment at the upper falls, return downstream to the junction with the Appalachian Trail. Do not cross the West Branch of the Ellis River. Instead, take a left onto the Appalachian Trail and follow it northbound for 0.7 mile to complete the loop and return to the parking area. You will have to cross the same brook you saw only 150 feet from the road when you first started this loop. Cross the brook and climb uphill back to your vehicle.

DIRECTIONS From the junction of ME 120 and ME 5 in the center of Andover, head west on Newton Street (sometimes marked as East B Hill Road or Upton Road on maps). Follow Newton Street for 8.1 miles and park in a parking area on the right of the road. This parking area has room for three vehicles and is across from a HIKER sign, which can be difficult to spot. The parking area is primarily used for the Appalachian Trail. If you are traveling east along Newton Street from ME 26 in Upton, the parking area will be on your left after 5.9 miles. To get to Andover, take ME 5 north from Bethel or ME 120 west from Rumford.

OTHER WATERFALLS NEARBY The Cataracts, Screw Auger Falls, Grafton, Step Falls, Ellis Falls, Coos Canyon, Angel Falls, Rumford Falls

32

〜

ELLIS FALLS
Andover, Oxford County

Rating: 3.5/5.0
Type: Horsetails and a block
Height: 22-foot total drop
Trail Length: Roadside
Water Source: Ellis Meadow Brook

Altitude Gain/Loss: None
Difficulty: Easy
Hiking Time: Not applicable
DeLorme Atlas: Page 18, D-4 (marked)
Best Time to Visit: Year-round

THE FALLS Minutes away from other spectacular waterfalls in the area, Ellis Falls can be either the appetizer or the dessert for your waterfall day-trip. Its location, just over 2 miles east of Andover, and is likely to be central to the other natural attractions in your plan for the day.

At the top of the falls is a 5-foot-tall, 5-foot-wide block falling into an oblong-shaped pool. From here, the falls horsetail and cascade the additional 17 feet into a dark tea-colored pool below. The river, which was very flat both upstream and downstream, surprised us with a drop of this magnitude.

Not nearly as scenic as nearby Dunn Falls, and certainly not world-class in beauty, like nearby Angel Falls, Ellis Falls is outclassed by the local competition. Waterfall enthusiasts, however, should not shun Ellis Falls for its more impressive neighbors. This waterfall is in a covert location—only noticed if you have specific directions *and* if you are looking for it. The parking area is a simple pull-off, the type every road has a dozen of. For this reason, we suggest taking the few short minutes to pull over and check out these falls.

TRAIL INFORMATION The falls are difficult to see from the parking pull-off. To get close to the falls you can either walk right up to the ledge overlooking the falls or you can follow a short path that swings around to the base of the falls.

DIRECTIONS From the junction of ME 120 and ME 5 in the center of Andover, take ME 120 east for 2.5 miles. You will need to park on the left side of the road soon after driving over a small bridge. *To get to Andover,* take ME 5 north from Bethel or ME 120 west from Rumford.

OTHER WATERFALLS NEARBY The Cataracts, Dunn Falls, Coos Canyon, Angel Falls, Rumford Falls, Step Falls, Screw Auger Falls, Grafton

33

THE FALLS
Sandy Bay, Somerset County

Rating: 2.0/5.0
Type: Horsetails
Height: 45-foot total drop
Trail Length: Roadside
Water Source: Sandy Stream
Altitude Gain/Loss: None

Difficulty: Easy
Hiking Time: Not applicable
DeLorme Atlas: Page 39, A-4 (marked)
Best Time to Visit: Year-round

THE FALLS If you are traveling in the area north of the town of Jackman, make a quick pit stop at The Falls Rest Area, a small marked parking area off US 201. A fine road stop for a picnic or a break before crossing the Canadian border, the rest area is complete with picnic tables and a series of drops of Sandy Stream known simply as The Falls.

The Falls is far from spectacular or unique, but this is made up for with extremely easy road access and a rather original wildflower-lined rest area.

Supplementing this waterfall with nearby Heald Stream Falls and Parlin Falls makes for a fine tour of this quiet region of Maine.

TRAIL INFORMATION Proceed to the north end of the parking lot, where a good view of the falls unfolds. Obvious paths will quickly bring you to the brook below. Unfortunately, there really is limited reward in this; no pools for swimming, limited exploring, and the views are not significantly improved. It is perhaps better to appreciate the falls while having lunch at one of the picnic tables of the rest area.

DIRECTIONS From the junction of US 201, ME 6, and ME 15 in Jackman, take the combined highway US 201 north and ME 6 west. Travel on this highway for 8.9 miles and pull into the The Falls Rest Area on your right. The rest area is located 0.3 mile north of the SANDY BAY town line sign. *To get to Jackman,* take US 201 north from Skowhegan.

OTHER WATERFALLS NEARBY Heald Stream Falls, Parlin Falls, Moxie Falls

34

~

FRENCHMEN'S HOLE
Riley Township, Oxford County

Rating: 4.0/5.0	**Difficulty:** Easy
Type: Plunge	**Hiking Time:** Negligible
Height: 10 feet	**DeLorme Atlas:** Page 18, E-1
Trail Length: Less than 0.1 mile	(unmarked)
Water Source: Bull Branch River	**Best Time to Visit:** May to
Altitude Gain/Loss: Negligible	October

THE FALLS Tucked a few miles beyond the Sunday River Ski Resort, Frenchmen's Hole is now a well-known attraction. It used to be that the falls and the swimming hole were a closely guarded town secret. Now the secret is out; not only do the locals continue to visit regularly, but even guests from out-of-town take the time to enjoy this hot spot.

The highlight of this waterfall is the swimming pool created inside the giant pothole below the 10-foot-tall plunge. This pool is deep and inviting for swimmers. Some portions of the pool were too deep for us to determine the actual depth, but it did appear to be well over our heads. Cliff jumping

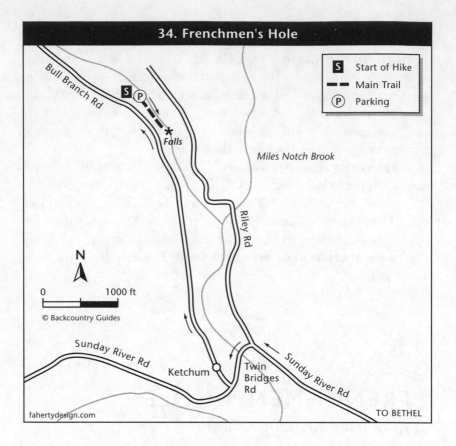

34. Frenchmen's Hole

is a real possibility here, but there is always an inherent risk in this activity. Always remember to scout the area before jumping; there could be currents and potential rocks that are not visible beneath the water.

Feel free to bring a picnic to this waterfall and enjoy one of several picnic tables on site.

TRAIL INFORMATION The main falls and swimming hole can be found by walking 100 feet back along the dirt road and scrambling down one of many paths to the river, where the falls and pool will become obvious. There are also some less-crowded smaller falls and shallower pools lying above the extremely popular main falls.

DIRECTIONS From the junction of ME 5, ME 26, and US 2 in downtown Bethel, take the combined highway ME 5 north, ME 26 north, and US 2 east, heading toward the Sunday River Ski Resort and the town of Newry. Travel on this highway for 2.7 miles and take a left onto Sunday River Road, which is the access road for the ski resort. Travel on Sunday

River Road for 2.1 miles and you will approach a fork in the road. Veer right and continue another 1.0 mile to another fork. Fork right again, and travel an additional 4.4 miles along Sunday River Road (turning into dirt at mile 3.1). Next you will want to take a left onto a dirt road that immediately travels over two old bridges. Just after the bridges, take a right and follow this new dirt road for 0.6 mile and the large parking pull-offs will be on the right.

OTHER WATERFALLS NEARBY Step Falls, Screw Auger Falls, Grafton

Frenchmen's Hole

35

~

GULF HAGAS

Bowdoin College Grant East, Piscataquis County

Rating: 5.0/5.0

Type: Plunges, horsetails, and cascades

Height: Varies (see notes)

Trail Length: 8.6-mile loop

Water Source: West Branch of the Pleasant River and Gulf Hagas Brook

Altitude Gain/Loss: To Screw Auger Falls, +300 feet, -75 feet; for entire loop, +700 feet, -700 feet

Difficulty: Moderate side of difficult

Hiking Time: 6 hours

DeLorme Atlas: Page 42, D-1 (marked as The Hermitage)

Best Time to Visit: July to October

THE FALLS (HIGHLY RECOMMENDED) In just under 9 miles of hiking, a visitor to Gulf Hagas can explore and take pleasure in about a dozen natural features, including four officially named waterfalls, dozens of unnamed cascades, tempting swimming pools, a gorge often referred to as The Grand Canyon of Maine, and two scenic rivers—Gulf Hagas Brook and the West Branch of the Pleasant River. Managed through the cooperative efforts of the National Park Service, the Maine Appalachian Trail Club, and KI Jo-Mary, Inc., Gulf Hagas offers an easy-to-follow trail system that allows hours of day-trip enjoyment. This is easily one of Maine's finest day-hikes.

With so many natural features (and so many chances for both exploration and swimming), it is no surprise that the waterfalls of Gulf Hagas rank among the most popular in the state. Luckily for you, the majority of the waterfall crowds remain at Screw Auger Falls, never bothering to venture along the rim of the gorge to the falls that lie upstream. All falls warrant the effort required, as each is beautiful and scenic in its own way.

Screw Auger Falls is our favorite falls on the hike. At the waterfall, Gulf Hagas Brook drops 25 feet in a punchbowl formation into a deep, dark pool encircled by a bowl-shaped rock wall. The pool, although relatively small compared to other classic swimming holes in Maine, still manages to be quite refreshing for the five or six visitors that can fit into it at any point in time. When visiting the falls, you should be aware that other unnamed waterfalls lie above and below Screw Auger Falls. Some of these additional falls also have swimming pools of their own, and are also recommended for their own properties.

Three more waterfalls are accessed by continuing past Screw Auger Falls along the rim of the gorge. The first waterfall, about 2.8 miles from the parking trailhead, is Buttermilk Falls, a 10-foot horsetail with a portion of its water diverting its way down a perpendicular slide to the right of the main route of the water. There is a large pool here that is often swum in by several people on any given summer day, but the water can have a slightly foamy appearance, forcing us to rate the pool as only somewhat attractive.

Beyond Buttermilk Falls lies Billings Falls, a 15-foot plunge with unobstructed views of the canyon, and Stairs Falls, an extensive system of little stairs cascading over jagged steps. Just 4 feet in height, Stairs Falls is short, but quite interesting and only feet from the main trail.

The final stop of the trip is the Head of the Gulf. At mile 4.0 from the parking lot, the Head is a good place to rest your legs as it is located at about the halfway point of the hike. There are several cascades and small pools to admire before setting out on the return trip back to the parking lot via the Pleasant River Road Trail.

TRAIL INFORMATION The gate station along the KI Road provides visitors a trail map handout to help guide you to all the destinations along Gulf Hagas. We highly recommended picking up a copy of this map. If we were to describe the trail in detail, we would most likely confuse you,

Gulf Hagas (Screw Auger Falls)

as other guidebook instructions have confused us. There are simply too many trail junctions and side paths to fit it all here into an easy-to-follow format. In all of our visits to this place, the gate station has always had a copy available. In the unlikely event that they are out of stock, one should consider asking to take a photograph of the trail map that they are sure to have on file (assuming you have a digital camera with a zoom feature).

Here is a summary of the adventure: Expect an 8.2- to 9.0-mile loop, depending on the number of side excursions you choose to take off the main trail. The trail is rated as moderately difficult, due to rough and often rocky terrain. There is also a significant river crossing of the West Branch of the Pleasant River, which can be impossible in early spring or after very heavy rains. Depending on the season, there may be extensive sections of muddy ground to maneuver. With that all said, this is a great introductory day-hike, but at the same time, a moderately challenging venture for any hiker.

DIRECTIONS From the junction of ME 11 and ME 157 in the center of Millinocket, take ME 11 south. Travel on ME 11 south for about 26 miles and take a wide right turn onto the Katahdin Iron Works Road (also

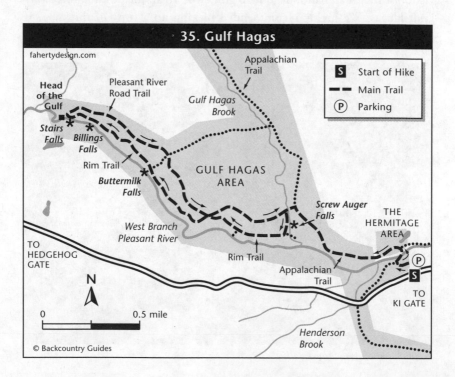

called the KI Road), which is a dirt road that leads to the Katahdin Iron Works. Follow the KI Road for 6.4 miles and you will reach the gate station, where you must register and pay the day use fee ($10/person for out-of-state residents and $6/person for Maine residents, when we visited in 2009). After registering, continue driving down the dirt road for 0.1 mile and you will reach the first fork of your journey. Take a right, following signs for Gulf Hagas Parking. Continue for 2.2 miles from the first fork and you will reach a second fork. Fork left this time, and continue 1.2 miles to a third fork. Take the left fork here and continue for a final 3.0 miles farther, where you will find a large parking area on your right. It is very common for this lot to fill up; parking alongside the road is allowed, but please allow enough space for passing logging trucks. *To get to Millinocket,* take exit 244 off I-95 in Medway and follow ME 157 west.

OTHER WATERFALLS NEARBY Hay Brook Falls, Nesowadnehunk Falls

36

$\backsim$

HAY BROOK FALLS
Bowdoin College Grant East, Piscataquis County

Rating: 4.5/5.0

Type: Horsetails

Height: 28-foot total drop

Trail Length: 0.2 mile

Water Source: Hay Brook

Altitude Gain/Loss: +20 feet, -10 feet

Difficulty: Easy

Hiking Time: 5 minutes

DeLorme Atlas: Page 42, D-1 (marked)

Best Time to Visit: June to October

THE FALLS (HIGHLY RECOMMENDED) Seldom is a natural feature found in New England that is truly still "off the beaten path." Sources have claimed that some of the waterfalls we visited were hidden gems, tucked away from the average traveler and sightseer. In reality, however, there were always at least a few people or traces of recent visitors at these waterfalls. Hay Brook Falls, buried deep in the KI Jo-Mary Multiple Use Forest, is one waterfall exception, remaining as nearly untouched and unspoiled as ever.

Equally magnificent and scenic in low or high water, the falls drop a total

Hay Brook Falls

of 28 feet in three distinguishable steps. The top drop is of particular interest; the waters of Hay Brook travel down a chute, hit an upward sloping slide, change direction by 90 degrees, and crash into a small pool. All drops are surrounded by varying species of moss—the colors of yellow, beige, and green are represented—creating a colorful opportunity for some photographs.

A friend that joined us on the trip summed up Hay Brook Falls in a simple sentence: "This is definitely one of my favorite waterfalls." We certainly agree with that and we believe you will enjoy this remote waterfall as much as we have. For the ultimate experience, you can reserve one of three campsites that are located a few hundred feet downstream of the falls. Inquire at the gate station along the KI Road for additional information.

TRAIL INFORMATION The difficulty in reaching Hay Brook Falls lies in the drive to the trailhead. Once at the trailhead, however, reaching the falls is pleasantly easy. Simply cross the dirt road and head up another dirt road while passing by the three primitive campsites at Hay Brook. The falls are 0.1 mile farther upstream of the campsites.

DIRECTIONS From the junction of ME 11 and ME 157 in the center of Millinocket, take ME 11 south. Travel on ME 11 south for about 26 miles and take a wide right turn onto the Katahdin Iron Works Road (also called the KI Road), which is a dirt road that leads to the Katahdin Iron Works. Follow the KI Road for 6.4 miles and you will reach the gate station, where you must register and pay the day use fee ($10/person for out-of-state residents and $6/person for Maine residents, when we visited in 2009).

After registering, continue driving down the dirt road for 0.1 mile and you will reach the first fork of your journey. Take a right, following signs for Gulf Hagas Parking. Continue for 2.2 miles from the first fork and you will reach a second fork. Fork left this time, and continue 1.2 miles to a third fork. Take the right fork here, marked with signs pointing you toward Hay Brook and the Hermitage. Follow this new road for 2.2 miles and reach the fourth fork. Fork left, immediately cross a bridge (the waterfall, High Bridge, is here; see appendix) and follow this new road for 0.2 mile to the fifth fork. You should now take a left when you see a sign marking HIGH BRIDGE CAMPSITE #3. Follow this new road for 0.4 mile and take another left at a sign for the HAY BROOK CAMPSITE. Follow this road for 1.4 miles to a gravel parking area on the left.

The parking area is just across the street from the campsites at Hay Brook. The network of dirt roads here may seem somewhat confusing, but there are signs directing you at most of the junctions. *To get to Millinocket,* take exit 244 off I-95 in Medway and follow ME 157 west.

SPECIAL NOTE We recommend this waterfall only if you have a sport-utility vehicle or truck. Low-clearance vehicles will likely not be able to travel safely on the dirt roads leading to the trailhead of Hay Brook Falls.

OTHER WATERFALLS NEARBY Gulf Hagas, Nesowadnehunk Falls

37

HEALD STREAM FALLS
Bald Mountain Township, Somerset County

Rating: 2.5/5.0
Type: Horsetails and cascades
Height: 18-foot total drop
Trail Length: Less than 0.1 mile
Water Source: Heald Stream
Altitude Gain/Loss: Negligible

Difficulty: Easy side of moderate
Hiking Time: Negligible
DeLorme Atlas: Page 39, A-4 (marked)
Best Time to Visit: May to October

THE FALLS Situated only a few miles from the Canadian border, Heald Stream Falls likely receives only a handful of visitors a month. Most day-trippers are either reluctant to go to this waterfall because of its remoteness, or simply because they do not know of its existence. If privacy is what you seek, this waterfall should provide you with exactly that.

There are several steps created by the ledges at the waterfall, and each step is visible from the base of the waterfall. The total drop is small, at only 18 feet. There are several dark, private pools for wading or swimming. It should be noted that the odds of encountering an animal along the drive to the trailhead or the hike in to the falls is higher than normal here, as this site is in prime moose habitat.

TRAIL INFORMATION The falls begin their descent beneath the bridge you just crossed. You have two options. You can either conclude your visit from the bridge or travel down several barely used paths on either side of the brook to explore the entire area. Expect privacy at this waterfall, especially if you bushwhack to the base of the falls.

DIRECTIONS From the junction of US 201, ME 6, and ME 15 in Jackman, take the combined highway US 201 north and ME 6 west. Travel on this highway for 9.4 miles and take a right onto Bald Mountain Road, a level dirt road marked with a sign for the BALD MTN TRAIL. This road is 0.4 mile north of the marked The Falls rest area. Travel on Bald Mountain Road for 2.3 miles, crossing the small bridge over Heald Stream. Parking is just after crossing the bridge on the right. *To get to Jackman,* take US 201 north from Skowhegan.

OTHER WATERFALLS NEARBY The Falls, Parlin Falls, Moxie Falls

38

HOUSTON BROOK FALLS
Pleasant Ridge, Somerset County

Rating: 4.5/5.0

Type: Horsetails and plunges

Height: 32-foot total drop

Trail Length: 0.25 mile

Water Source: Houston Brook

Altitude Gain/Loss: -75 feet

Difficulty: Easy

Hiking Time: 10 minutes

DeLorme Atlas: Page 30, D-3 (marked)

Best Time to Visit: May to October

THE FALLS (HIGHLY RECOMMENDED) Houston Brook Falls is another scenic splendor located minutes off the ME 201 highway, allowing for convenient and simple access. An easy, 10-minute walk through woods leads to the star of the show, a 32-foot nearly vertical drop of Houston Brook.

The falls are wild and rugged, with every outcrop of folded rock having a jagged appearance. There are a few notable swimming spots, the best being the shallow rectangular channel just below the falls. During low water it is a simple task to enter this pool, but in high water the difficulty multiplies. The mist of the falls often makes the surrounding rocks too dangerous to scramble across.

Just downstream, the brook terminates at Wyman Lake, which is visible from the waterfall. The entire area is scenic, with nothing blocking your views. The best time to visit this waterfall appears to be in the morning, as the views have eastern exposure and are lit up by the sun in the early hours of the day.

TRAIL INFORMATION First, locate and approach the roadside sign affixed to a tree for HOUSTON BROOK FALLS. At the sign, follow the trail down parallel to the transfer station. Expect some muddy areas along the trail in the springtime, and a few steps up and down near the brook to reach the falls. You will cross a deteriorating man-made log bridge and the falls will be visible through the trees. Continue downstream to the riverbed where the waterfall will become fully visible.

DIRECTIONS From the southern junction of ME 16 and US 201 in Bingham, take ME 16 south. Follow ME 16 south for only a few hundred yards as it crosses a bridge over the Kennebec River. Just after crossing the Kennebec River, only 0.2 mile from US 201, you will reach a T-junction. Take a right onto Ridge Road, which is currently marked. Follow Ridge Road northwest for 3.3 miles and pull into the parking lot on the right, at a transfer station. There will be a sign for HOUSTON BROOK FALLS masked by overgrown trees a few feet past the transfer station parking area. *To get to Bingham,* take US 201 north from Skowhegan.

OTHER WATERFALLS NEARBY Moxie Falls, Poplar Stream Falls, Tobey Falls

39

KEES FALLS

Batchelders Grant, White Mountain National Forest, Oxford County

Rating: 4.0/5.0
Type: Plunge
Height: 30 feet
Trail Length: 1.6 miles
Water Source: Morrison Brook
Altitude Gain/Loss: +300 feet

Difficulty: Easy side of moderate
Hiking Time: 1 hour
DeLorme Atlas: Page 10, B-1 (unmarked)
Best Time to Visit: May to October

THE FALLS Along this hike are many beautiful unnamed waterfalls that could be mistaken for Kees Falls. To ensure you are viewing the correct waterfall please note that Kees Falls is found at the third river crossing on the Caribou Trail. This waterfall can only be heard once you are within its immediate vicinity, so be sure to keep your eyes peeled. Though masked by many trees, Kees Falls is an impressive plunge of white water cutting into a dark narrow pool below.

After the water reconnects with the river below, the current travels through a narrow channel of moss green water. The frothy splashing at the base of the falls offers a fun addition to the surrounding area of the falls. This hike is very gratifying for a beautiful waterfall. For those wishing to continue hiking, the trail eventually leads to the summit of Caribou Mountain.

TRAIL INFORMATION The Caribou Trail will guide you the entire 1.6 miles to the falls. Along the trail you will observe multiple cascades, plunges, and horsetails that could be mistaken for Kees Falls. The true Kees Falls is found just before the third river crossing of Morrison Brook along the trail.

The best viewing of Kees Falls is obtained by bushwhacking down the very technical gorge walls to the riverbed below. Please note that this descent is dangerous and one should use the utmost caution if they choose to attempt this.

DIRECTIONS From the junction of ME 113 and US 2 in Gilead, take ME 113 south for 4.7 miles. Turn left into marked parking area for the CARIBOU MTN TRAIL. If you are traveling along ME 113 north from Fryeburg, the parking area will be on your right, 5.7 miles past Brickett Place. *To get to Gilead,* take US 2 west from Bethel or US 2 east from Gorham, New Hampshire.

OTHER WATERFALLS NEARBY Basin Trail Cascades, Hermit Falls (NH), Mad River Falls, Bickford Slides, Brickett Falls (NH), Eagle Cascade (NH), Rattlesnake Flume and Pool

40

KEZAR FALLS
Lovell, Oxford County

Rating: 2.5/5.0
Type: Cascades
Height: 30-foot total drop
Trail Length: Less than 0.1 mile
Water Source: Kezar River
Altitude Gain/Loss: -60 feet

Difficulty: Easy side of moderate
Hiking Time: Negligible
DeLorme Atlas: Page 10, D-3
(marked as Kezar Falls Gorge)
Best Time to Visit: May to October

THE FALLS Lying a few miles southeast of the White Mountain National Forest border, Kezar Falls is an unmarked local picnic spot with a modest-sized gorge and a few small waterfalls. The site has a dark rust-colored pool below the falls, which, when swam in, stirs up the murky sands below. Many fallen trees have long since made jumping off the gorge walls a dangerous activity. Kezar Falls is not really anything out of the ordinary, but it makes a fine place to read, picnic, or engage in any other relaxing activity. Locals have told us that this spot is a favorite party spot for young adults during the late hours of the day, but the site showed little evidence of this on our several visits.

TRAIL INFORMATION The crashing waters of the gorge can be heard from the parking lot. Follow the sound a few feet down to a slowly deteriorating fence that runs along the rim of the gorge.

DIRECTIONS From the junction of ME 35 and ME 118 in Waterford, take ME 35 south for 0.2 mile and take a right onto Five Kezar Road. Follow Five Kezar Road for 3.1 miles and you will come to a fork. Take the left fork and travel 0.2 mile farther, and the short road to the parking area will be on your right. Take note that the parking area is difficult to spot and there are three incorrect turn-offs along the way to skip. *To get to Waterford,* take the combined highway ME 5 south and ME 35 south from Bethel or US 302 west to ME 35 north from Portland.

OTHER WATERFALLS NEARBY Snow Falls

41

LITTLE WILSON FALLS

Elliotville Township, Piscataquis County

Rating: 4.0/5.0

Type: Horsetail

Height: 25 feet

Trail Length: Roadside

Water Source: Tributary of Little Wilson Stream

Altitude Gain/Loss: None

Difficulty: Easy

Hiking Time: Not applicable

DeLorme Atlas: Page 41, E-4 (marked)

Best Time to Visit: May to October

THE FALLS The 25-foot-tall lower falls of Little Wilson Falls offer a great pool for swimming and wading. This is where the locals go on a warm summer day. Between the scenic waterfall, free camping (tents only), and the fun swimming holes, visitors of all age groups are often seen here. There is a clear view of the falls from any one of the parking spots along the stream. The parking area and campground offer a few fire pits for those looking to spend some additional time at the falls.

Although we have yet to visit them, the upper falls of Little Wilson Falls are situated nearby. The falls are a popular rest stop on the Appalachian Trail, but we have been unable to locate them on two separate attempts. We know they are there—we have seen gorgeous pictures of the falls—but our luck finding them has so far been limited. For those looking for an adventure, finding the 40-foot upper falls is bound to be exciting.

TRAIL INFORMATION The falls are clearly visible from roadside.

DIRECTIONS From the junction of ME 15, ME 6, and ME 16 in Abbot Village, take the combined highway ME 15 north and ME 6 north into Monson. Just after passing through the center of Monson, take a right onto Elliotsville Road. Travel on Elliotsville Road for 7.6 miles and turn right onto an unmarked dirt road. After driving 0.5 mile on this road, fork right and travel for another 0.2 mile. The falls are viewable to the left and parking is available throughout the area. *To get to Abbot Village,* take ME 16 east from Bingham.

OTHER WATERFALLS NEARBY Tobey Falls

42

~

MAD RIVER FALLS

Batchelders Grant, White Mountain National Forest, Oxford County

Rating: 3.5/5.0

Type: Horsetails

Height: 100-foot total drop

Trail Length: 1.6 miles

Water Source: Mad River

Altitude Gain/Loss: +200 feet

Difficulty: Easy side of moderate

Hiking Time: 50 minutes

DeLorme Atlas: Page 10, C-1 (unmarked)

Best Time to Visit: June to October

THE FALLS From the overlook opposite the falls, you notice that Mad River Falls consists of several horsetails falling into a yellow-tinted pool. Aside from admiring the 100-foot total drop of the falls, there is not much to do here. Exploring is extremely limited as it would be dangerous to get closer to the falls, and photography is not an option because the falls lie under a heavy tree cover.

To a waterfall enthusiast, the sheer size of this waterfall makes the hike worth the visit. To justify the trail length for the obscured viewing of the falls, add Bickford Slides, another waterfall accessed via a trail from Brickett Place, and Rattlesnake Flume and Pool, a waterfall and swimming hole only a short drive and hike away.

TRAIL INFORMATION The actual trailhead for this waterfall is located across the street from Brickett Place. To reach the falls, you are going to follow the yellow-blazed Royce Trail for 1.6 miles. After hiking this trail for 0.3 mile, you will reach a field clearing and the trail will suddenly fork right. The trail markers can be difficult to spot here, so be on the lookout. From here, the rest of the 1.4-mile walk is normally fast and simple, but there are several water crossings that can be difficult in high water. During the warmer summer months, the Mad River is usually far from being *mad* in terms of rushing water. In early spring or during other times of abnormally high water, the river may be knee deep or so. In such situations, trekking poles may be helpful in getting you across. There is nothing too difficult about these crossings under most conditions, but we felt this was worth mentioning if you are contemplating this hike.

At the third river crossing, be sure to note that the trail continues between two sections of the river that merge together. The fourth and fifth river crossings are right before the trail starts to steeply climb. Just as you begin climbing, you will reach a junction with a spur trail about 1.6 miles into the hike. Take a left onto this 50-foot-long spur trail to reach the falls. This left turn is marked by a sign and an arrow for MAD RIVER FALLS.

DIRECTIONS From the junction of ME 113 and US 302 in Fryeburg, Maine, take ME 113 north for 19.7 miles and take a right into the Brickett Place, where a hikers' parking lot can be found. If you are traveling on ME 113 south from US 2 in Gilead, Brickett Place will be on your right after driving 10.6 miles. *To get to Fryeburg,* take NH 113 east from NH 16 in Conway, New Hampshire into Maine.

Please be aware that this trailhead is part of the White Mountain National Forest parking fee program. The fee was $3 in 2009 but there is currently a proposal in review to raise this amount to $5.

OTHER WATERFALLS NEARBY Bickford Slides, Rattlesnake Flume and Pool, Kees Falls, Hermit Falls (NH), Brickett Falls (NH), Eagle Cascade (NH)

43

∽

MOSHER HILL FALLS
Farmington, Franklin County

Rating: 4.5/5.0
Type: Horsetail
Height: 45 feet
Trail Length: 0.1 mile to top of the falls; 0.2 mile to base of falls
Water Source: Stream from Mosher Pond
Altitude Gain/Loss: -50 feet

Difficulty: Easy to the top of the falls, moderate side of difficult to base of falls
Hiking Time: 20 minutes
DeLorme Atlas: Page 20, C-1 (unmarked)
Best Time to Visit: May to June

THE FALLS (HIGHLY RECOMMENDED) This waterfall surprised us. After viewing it, we wondered how it escaped our initial research. It is an absolutely wonderful waterfall that is well known by local residents but outside the normal realm for visitors. If you are on a quest to find a great waterfall in central Maine, this is surely one of them.

Views of the waterfall from the easily obtained upper vantage point are minimal, but you can hear the sound of them clearly. With a moderately challenging bushwhack you can access the base of the falls for the best viewing. The water sprays over the granite rocks in a surprising display of beauty, especially given the limited power of the river.

This waterfall can be difficult to photograph as the base of the falls is within a confined and dark gorge. A wide-angled lens is very helpful in such conditions.

TRAIL INFORMATION The trail starts out as a flat wide walk along a small stream, which will be on your left. After only 0.1 mile, you will access the upper viewpoint, where an impressive gorge can be seen below. Even more thrilling is the quest to the views of the falls within the gorge itself. If you lightly bushwhack about 200 feet downstream through the woods, you will slowly make your way down to the stream's edge. Once you reach the stream, cross it and rock-hop your way upstream to the falls.

The gorge walls are covered with a dark green moss and dripping with moisture, so at times the trip upstream will be slippery. After you round a bend near the end of the gorge, the impressive waterfall will make the bushwhack you have completed more than worthwhile. There are steeper descents into the gorge, but these are not recommended due to the technical nature of the terrain and the erosion you would likely create.

DIRECTIONS From the junction of ME 4, ME 27, and ME 43 in the northern end of the center of Farmington, take the combined highway ME 4 north and ME 27 west. Follow ME 4 north and ME 27 west for 2.3 miles and take a right onto ME 27 west as ME 4 north breaks away. Follow ME 27 west for 4.3 miles and take a right onto Ramsdell Road. Follow Ramsdell Road for 1.7 miles (taking a sharp left after 0.5 mile to remain on this road) to a parking turnoff on the right. The parking turnoff is only large enough for two cars and there are no trail signs. Stick to the mileage we have provided and you should be able to find it. *To get to Farmington,* take ME 27 west from Augusta.

OTHER WATERFALLS NEARBY Poplar Stream Falls, Phillips Falls, Smalls Falls

44

〜

MOXIE FALLS

Moxie Gore, Somerset County

Rating: 5.0/5.0

Type: Plunge and cascades

Height: Tallest plunge is 90 feet

Trail Length: 0.6 mile

Water Source: Moxie Stream

Altitude Gain/Loss: -100 feet

Difficulty: Easy to initial viewpoints; difficult to base of falls

Hiking Time: 20 minutes

DeLorme Atlas: Page 40, E-3 (marked)

Best Time to Visit: May to October

THE FALLS (HIGHLY RECOMMENDED) One of the tallest single drops in the state of Maine, Moxie Falls is a scenic waterfall a few miles southeast of the famous white-water rafting river, the Kennebec. An equal mix of beauty and grandeur, the name Moxie Falls is given to a spectacular 30-yard drop of Moxie Stream. It offers a ruggedness matched by no other falls in New England.

Above and below the falls are several unnamed large, wide cascades with some pools. The best swimming holes here are 100 feet downstream from the main plunge, and another just above the main plunge, below a large set of cascades. Both pools require a moderately difficult level of scrambling and steep terrain, but they are worth every ounce of energy expended. Although scrambling down the gorge walls is a tiresome activity, the attempt is easily justified by the rugged, highly scenic gorge and the completely new perspective of the falls from below. Take caution if you decide to do this, and we do not recommend this for children.

Despite its remote location in mid-western Maine, Moxie Falls is heavily visited, mainly by those up for the weekend at the local white-water rafting outfitters. We have visited Moxie Falls on multiple occasions during less than ideal weather conditions, and there have always been at least a few people either along the trail, swimming in the pools, or resting at one of the many boardwalk vantage points. The popularity of this place attests to the fact that this is easily one of Maine's most unforgettable waterfalls.

TRAIL INFORMATION The trail begins at the center of the parking lot and follows a well-worn path to the falls. About halfway to the falls you will approach a sign for the falls and a warning of the suddenly changing, potentially dangerous currents of the dam-controlled rivers in the area.

The first views of the main plunge are head-on from the top of the gorge on a boardwalk trail. If you are confident in your ability to scramble down the side of a 100-foot gorge, you can reach the base of the falls and a pool suitable for swimming. There are multiple routes in which to complete such a task, but all are challenging and not recommended for children.

DIRECTIONS From Bingham, take US 201 north into the town of The Forks. Once you are in The Forks, take a right onto Old Canada Road just before crossing the Kennebec River Bridge. Follow Old Canada Road for 1.9 miles and a large sign for MOXIE FALLS will mark the parking area on your left. *To get to Bingham,* take I-95 to exit 133 in Fairfield. Follow US 201 north.

OTHER WATERFALLS NEARBY Parlin Falls, The Falls, Heald Stream Falls, Houston Brook Falls

45

NESOWADNEHUNK FALLS
Township 2, Range 10, Piscataquis County

Rating: 3.0/5.0
Type: Block
Height: 7 feet
Trail Length: Less than 0.1 mile
Water Source: West Branch of the Penobscot River
Altitude Gain/Loss: -25 feet

Difficulty: Easy
Hiking Time: Negligible
DeLorme Atlas: Page 50, D-4 (marked)
Best Time to Visit: May to October

THE FALLS A classic block-style waterfall (also known as a horseshoe falls), Nesowadnehunk Falls is a 7-foot drop of the West Branch of the Penobscot River. The falls are a well-known portage spot, often too dangerous for canoes and kayaks traveling down the river from the drop-in spot at Ripogenus Gorge. For white-water rafters, however, traveling over the falls is often the highlight of a journey down the Penobscot River. Often, outfitters will do multiple runs over the falls if time and conditions permit them to.

The powerful 100-foot-wide cascade drowns out the occasion logging trucks that are driving along Golden Road, only yards away. Fly-fishing is also common below the falls, and a decent view of Mt. Katahdin can be seen looking downstream. Also, since the falls are controlled by Ripogenus Dam upstream, and water is released throughout each day, expect to see a powerful waterfall any time of the year.

TRAIL INFORMATION The trail starts on the opposite side of the road from the parking lot and leads about 200 feet to the river, where the falls become blatantly obvious. There are limited scrambling opportunities around the falls.

DIRECTIONS From Bangor, take I-95 north to exit 244. Take a left onto ME 157, traveling west toward Millinocket. Continue traveling on ME 157 west into the center of the town of Millinocket. Just past where ME 157 ends in the town of Millinocket, where ME 11 comes in from the south, take a right onto Millinocket Avenue (sometimes called Katahdin Avenue or Baxter Park Road) while following signs toward Baxter State Park. As you approach Millinocket Lake on your right, about 8.5 miles beyond that junction of ME 157 and ME 11, you will need to switch over to the road running parallel to the left of the road you are traveling on. There are several paved lanes to do this, so be on the lookout when you see a sign pointing left toward AMBAJEJUS LAKE. The road you switched to is called the Golden Road. Travel north on the Golden Road as it eventually crosses the West Branch of the Penobscot River over the one-laned Abol Bridge. Continue traveling on the Golden Road for 3.1 miles past the Abol Bridge and park at the large pull-off on the left side of the road.

OTHER WATERFALLS NEARBY Gulf Hagas, Hay Brook Falls, Waterfalls of Baxter State Park

46

PARLIN FALLS
Parlin Pond, Somerset County

Rating: 3.5/5.0
Type: Horsetails and cascades
Height: Upper falls are 12 feet; lower falls are 45 feet
Trail Length: 0.1 mile to upper falls; 0.25 mile to lower falls
Water Source: Parlin Stream
Altitude Gain/Loss: -50 feet to upper falls; -100 feet to base of lower falls

Difficulty: Moderate to upper falls; difficult to lower falls
Hiking Time: 5 minutes to upper falls; 20 minutes to lower falls
DeLorme Atlas: Page 40, C-2 (unmarked)
Best Time to Visit: May to October

THE FALLS Of the six New England states, Maine has the largest amount of undeveloped land. This land, especially to the north of Augusta and Bangor, has a system of interconnected logging roads. For most of these roads the public is welcome, although a fee is often charged. Within these lands are dozens upon dozens of elusive waterfalls. Parlin Falls is one such falls. Without the knowledge of its existence and a set of clear directions, it is unlikely that you would ever stumble across it.

The upper falls are seen first; here, the stream cascades at a low angle in a zigzag formation. The lower waterfall showcases horsetails and cascades of various sizes totaling 45 feet. Access to both of these waterfalls is anything but easy—especially if you want to explore the more impressive lower falls. A challenging and potentially dangerous bushwhack or rock-hop downstream is required, as there are zero developed trails to be found along this section of the stream.

After hours of fruitless searching for Parlin Falls, we eventually learned of its location by succumbing to asking for directions. We stopped to discuss our intentions to find the falls with a local campground owner. Upon arrival to ask our questions, we inquired as to how he was doing on this particular day. He responded with a bold, "I am good everyday!" We suppose that we would be too if we had a waterfall like this in our backyard.

TRAIL INFORMATION From the parking area, head straight into the woods on a path that can be hard to spot. Follow this path for 0.1 mile toward the river. As you get close to the river, the trail becomes even less obvious and you must scramble down the last 100 feet to the river. When you reach the river, you can look upstream at the 12-foot upper falls. To get to the lower falls, you will have to rock-hop, bushwhack, or wade your way downstream for about 800 feet or so. This is difficult terrain and may not be safe in high water. An excursion to the lower falls is for the most adventurous only.

DIRECTIONS From Bingham, take US 201 north into the township of Parlin Pond, which is north of the town of The Forks. Continue traveling on US 201 north for 2.6 miles beyond the marked Parlin Pond rest area and take a right onto Parlin Mountain Road. This dirt road is 0.1 mile past the currently named Loon Echo Campground. After traveling only 200 feet on Parlin Mountain Road, stay right at a fork. Go 0.3 mile further and take a left onto a new dirt road. Follow this new road for 1.2 miles and take another left (this is the third left turn on this 1.2-mile section of road). The road becomes really rough here; the average car may not be able to continue. If your vehicle is able to, continue for 0.2 mile up this road to the parking area at its end. Otherwise, you will need to find a safe place to park and walk the additional 0.2 mile to the trailhead. *To get to Bingham,* take I-95 to exit 133 in Fairfield. Follow US 201 north.

As you travel along these private logging roads (or any other logging roads for that matter), always respect the trucks' right of way. Doing so should help ensure that the public access is continued.

OTHER WATERFALLS NEARBY Moxie Falls, Heald Stream Falls, The Falls

47

PHILLIPS FALLS
Phillips, Franklin County

Rating: 3.0/5.0
Type: Cascades
Height: 10-foot total drop
Trail Length: Roadside
Water Source: Sandy River
Altitude Gain/Loss: None

Difficulty: Easy
Hiking Time: Not applicable
DeLorme Atlas: Page 19, B-3
(unmarked)
Best Time to Visit: Year-round

THE FALLS There is a great view of Phillips Falls along the edge of the river. Swimming is not recommended due to the strong currents for most of the year, but a strong swimmer may be able to safely enjoy the pools found here in low enough water conditions. Even if you are not here for a dip, there are many boulders and flat rocks to sit on and enjoy the scenery around you.

The cascades themselves are framed by a unique bridge above that contains lots of etched detail. Although not the grandest waterfall we have ever seen by any means, the bridge and the park offer a nice spot to sit and have lunch if you are passing through the area.

TRAIL INFORMATION The falls are clearly visible from roadside.

DIRECTIONS From the junction of ME 149 and ME 142 in Phillips, take ME 149 east (marked as Main Street on some maps) toward the town of Strong. Travel on ME 149 east for 0.5 mile and take a right into a parking pull-off just after crossing a bridge over the Sandy River. There are a few picnic tables located here

OTHER WATERFALLS NEARBY Smalls Falls, Mosher Hill Falls, Poplar Stream Falls, Angel Falls, Coos Canyon

48

~

POPLAR STREAM FALLS
Carrabassett Valley, Franklin County

Rating: 4.5/5.0

Type: Horsetails

Height: 24 feet and 51 feet

Trail Length: 4.7-mile loop (see notes)

Water Source: Poplar Stream and South Brook

Altitude Gain/Loss: +450 feet, -450 feet (see notes)

Difficulty: Easy side of moderate

Hiking Time: 2 hours, 45 minutes (see notes)

DeLorme Atlas: Page 29, C-5 (marked)

Best Time to Visit: May to October

THE FALLS (HIGHLY RECOMMENDED) Poplar Stream Falls is located in Carrabassett Valley, a town famous for its ski resort, Sugarloaf USA. The falls lie a few miles east of the resort, accessible by either a short and uneventful hike or a long and enjoyable one. The falls can be accessed by mountain bicycles or hiking in summer, and cross-country skis or snowshoes in winter.

There are two drops here, each on a different water source. One set of falls, a 24-foot horsetail with a swimming pool below, is on Poplar Stream, just below a bridge on a private dirt road owned by the Penobscot Indian Nation. The other drop is a 51-foot horsetail on South Brook. These falls fan beautifully down a steep rock face into a wide sunny pool. These two streams merge only 0.1 mile downstream of each of the falls.

Once difficult to find, these falls are now easily accessible by the newly constructed Poplar Stream Falls Hut and its related trail network. This welcoming hut, which offers backcountry accommodations, hot meals, and hot showers year-round, is part of the grand vision of the Maine Huts and Trails organization. They hope to create a system of 12 rustic, yet comfortable backcountry huts stretching across 180 miles of trail from Bethel to Moosehead Lake. Two huts are already in service, and a third (Grand Falls Hut) is slated to begin construction in 2010.

Although you can reach these falls more easily by the private dirt road, we highly recommend using the trailhead on Gauge Road to create a memorable loop of the new trails, both sets of falls, and the fantastic Poplar Stream Falls Hut.

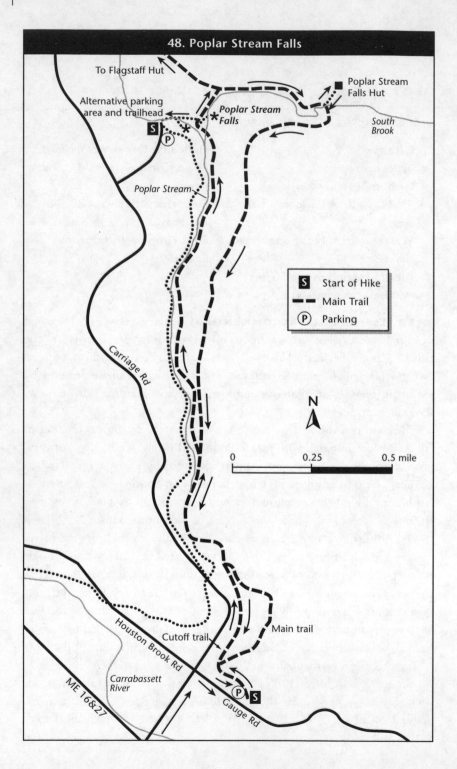

48. Poplar Stream Falls

To Flagstaff Hut

Alternative parking area and trailhead

Poplar Stream Falls

Poplar Stream Falls Hut

South Brook

Poplar Stream

Carriage Rd

S   Start of Hike

— —   Main Trail

P   Parking

N

0   0.25   0.5 mile

Houston Brook Rd

Cutoff trail

Main trail

Carrabassett River

ME 16&27

Gauge Rd

TRAIL INFORMATION Due to the construction of a Maine Huts and Trails hut facility near the falls, several new trails have been constructed to the falls. As such, the following trail information will be significantly different from the first edition. The trails described below depict the most enjoyable route to visit both waterfalls and the new hut. There is an easier and shorter way to visit just the falls—see the Special Note section within the driving directions.

The starting point of this hike is now the new Gauge Road trailhead. There is a large billboard display here with a detailed trail map to help you attain your bearings. The trail begins behind this display and immediately enters the woods on a wide, well-maintained path. After only 0.1 mile, you will reach a junction; take a left onto the Cut-Off Trail, which will merge back with the main trail after an easy 0.3 mile. Taking this cut-off trail is optional, but it does reduce the hike by 0.2 mile. When you connect back with the main trail, take a left to continue heading north toward the falls and the hut. Hike for 0.1 mile along the main trail and you will reach a junction with the Narrow Gauge Trail. Take a right and in 0.2 mile you will reach another junction, this time with the Falls Loop Trail. Take a left and hike along this blue-blazed trail for 1.1 miles as it closely parallels Poplar Stream for the majority of its distance. When you reach a hikers' bridge over South Brook, follow the trail as it heads right toward the magnificent 51-foot falls.

To find the other waterfall, which is on Poplar Stream, follow the blue-blazed trail uphill on a well-designed rock staircase. This staircase is about 100 feet away from this first waterfall. Just beyond the top of the staircase, look for a slightly less obvious trail on your left. This is the spur trail that will guide you 0.1 mile to the falls. Once you are done visiting this second set of falls, backtrack to this junction.

At this point, you will have a choice to make. *If you wish to visit the new Poplar Stream Falls Hut and make a large loop out of your hike* (which we highly recommend), take a left and hike onward for 0.4 mile while passing two signed junctions along the way to the hut. When you are done visiting the hut, take a left at the trail junction that is 0.1 mile south of the Hut. Follow this new trail for 1.4 miles and you will arrive back at the junction with the Falls Loop Trail, which you passed much earlier. From here, follow the original trails you took at the start of your hike to return back to your vehicle. Helpful signage posted at every conceivable junction assures that you should not get lost returning to your car. Just make sure you follow signs to the Gauge Trailhead and do not confuse it with the Narrow Gauge Trail! *If you wish to skip the hut and return to the parking area,* take a right and head back down the rock staircase to the first set of falls. Cross the bridge downstream of the falls, and follow the trails that originally guided you here.

DIRECTIONS From the junction of ME 27, ME 16, and ME 142 in the center of Kingfield, take the combined highway ME 27 north and ME 16 west. Travel on this highway for 9.2 miles and take a right onto Carriage Road. After 0.2 mile on Carriage Road, take a right onto Gauge Road at a sign stating TRAILHEAD PARKING. You will find a large parking area about 750 feet down this road. *To get to Kingfield,* take ME 27 north from Farmington.

SPECIAL NOTE There is an easier and shorter way to reach these two waterfalls. Instead of taking a right onto Gauge Road, continue 1.8 miles farther down Carriage Road (assuming the access gate is open, as it often is) and take a right onto an unmarked road. Follow this bumpy dirt road for 0.2 mile to a parking area on the right, just before the road curves left and crosses a bridge over Poplar Stream. The 24-foot horsetail waterfall described above is located just below this bridge.

To reach the more impressive waterfall on South Brook, find the blue-blazed trail that runs parallel to Poplar Stream and hike along it with the river on your right. Follow this trail for 0.1 mile and you will reach a T-junction. A left would direct you toward the Poplar Stream Falls Hut. Instead, take a right to descend a lengthy rock staircase and the 45-foot falls will be presented to you on your left.

OTHER WATERFALLS NEARBY Houston Brook Falls, Mosher Hill Falls, Smalls Falls, Phillips Falls

49

~

RATTLESNAKE FLUME AND POOL

Stoneham, Oxford County

Rating: 4.0/5.0

Type: Plunge, slides, and a pool

Height: 10-foot plunge

Trail Length: To Rattlesnake Flume, 0.7 mile; to Rattlesnake Pool, 1.1 miles

Water Source: Rattlesnake Brook

Altitude Gain/Loss: +150 feet to Rattlesnake Pool

Difficulty: Easy side of moderate

Hiking Time: 35 minutes to Rattlesnake Pool

DeLorme Atlas: Page 10, C-1 (unmarked)

Best Time to Visit: May to October

Rattlesnake Pool

THE FALLS We have a confession to make; the high rating we gave this waterfall is not solely attributable to the cascading waters of Rattlesnake Brook, but rather skewed by the dazzlingly attractive swimming hole created inside a giant pothole, commonly known as Rattlesnake Pool.

This pool attracts visitors from all over, not just local residents. This is surprising, because the pool is quite small, barely large enough for one family of swimmers. The pool also offers frigid waters year-round, due to the overhanging hemlock trees above the pool and the already chilly mountain water. The drawing feature of the pool is the exceptionally clean, teal green water and the moss-surrounded slide that feeds the pool. Visualize a lagoon-like pool with a romantic spirit and you will picture something similar to Rattlesnake Pool. Maine is truly blessed to have such a treasure.

For waterfalls, Rattlesnake Brook offers two small attractions. The first is at Rattlesnake Flume. The flume consists of a 10-foot plunge dumping down into narrow gorge walls. The falls above the pool are small cascades only 3 or 4 feet in height.

Please take note that both the Flume and the Pool are located on private property. In order to keep public access to these special places, we must all do our part to not abuse the private trail system. For starters, visitors must stay on the CTA trails at all times. The owners have allowed Rattlesnake Flume and Pool to remain available to the public for many years, and we hope it will always remain that way. Please be respectful and skip hiking any trails that are marked NO TRESPASSING.

TRAIL INFORMATION Start your hike by continuing up the dirt road beyond the gate. After an easy 0.5-mile walk along the road, enter the woods on your left at a sign for the STONE HOUSE TRAIL. Follow the Stone House Trail as it slowly gains in elevation for 0.2 mile and you will reach a fork. Fork right and you will find Rattlesnake Flume a few feet down the trail, visible from a wooden bridge by looking upstream. Fork left and you can visit the stunning Rattlesnake Pool. To reach the pool, continue for 0.2 mile beyond this fork and you will reach a lonely arrow and a sign for the STONE HOUSE TRAIL, just after going across a small bridge. Take a right here follow the trail for a final 0.1 mile to the pool. To swim in the pool, you must scramble down a moderately steep, although short, embankment.

DIRECTIONS From the junction of ME 113 and US 302 in Fryeburg, Maine, take ME 113 north for 18.5 miles and take a right onto Stone House Road. Follow Stone House Road to its end approximately 1 mile, where you will reach a gate. Parking is reserved to the right shoulder just before the gate only. *To get to Fryeburg,* take NH 113 east from NH 16 in Conway, New Hampshire into Maine.

OTHER WATERFALLS NEARBY Brickett Falls (NH), Eagle Cascade (NH), Bickford Slides, Mad River Falls, Hermit Falls (NH), Kees Falls

50

RUMFORD FALLS
Rumford, Oxford County

Rating: 3.0/5.0

Type: Cascades

Height: 176-foot total drop

Trail Length: Middle Falls are visible from roadside; 0.2 mile to upper falls

Water Source: Androscoggin River

Altitude Gain/Loss: None

Difficulty: Easy

Hiking Time: Not applicable for middle falls; negligible for lower falls; 5 minutes to upper falls

DeLorme Atlas: Page 19, E-1 (marked)

Best Time to Visit: Year-round

THE FALLS Originally referred to as Pennacook Falls or New Pennacook Falls, Rumford Falls is a chain of massive drops of the Androscoggin River. Although the waterfall drops a total of 176 feet, dams have split the once-continuous cascading waters into several distinct sections.

The beauty of the scenic upper falls ensured it a spot in this guide. Worthy of drawing the attention of any form of artist, Rumford Falls is quite spectacular in strength and setting. The artificial lake below offers popular fishing for landlocked salmon and three species of trout. The best view of this area is after snowmelt, as the water flow often slowly reduces during the summer months because of the dams.

TRAIL INFORMATION The total drop of the falls is 176 feet, but this is split up among several segments. No single view along the river will encompass all segments of the falls. The main visitor parking lot on US 2 offers the best view of the middle falls.

To view the upper falls, follow the directions below to a parking area on Hartford Street. There is a small dirt path about 4 feet wide that leaves from the back of the parking area. After a few hundred feet, you will cross ME 108 and continue hiking upstream alongside the Androscoggin River (the river will be on your right). The best view of the upper falls can be found just ahead.

To view the lower falls, follow the trail over the blasted rock beneath a bridge, downstream from the lower lot of the public library. This short trail will take you from the library to large rock ledges adjacent to the falls, where you can bask in the sun or enjoy an afternoon of good fishing.

DIRECTIONS The middle segment of Rumford Falls, which is the most popular vantage point, is viewable from the roadside only 20 feet south of the US 2 and ME 108 junction in Rumford. Pull into the parking lot marked with a sign for the SCENIC FALLS VIEWING AND TOURIST INFORMATION on US 2. The parking lot is just west of the ME 108 bridge over the Androscoggin River.

To access the parking area for the upper falls, drive east on ME 108 from the primary parking lot on US 2. Cross a bridge over the Androscoggin River and take a left onto Canal Street after passing through a set of traffic lights. Take your first right onto Hartford Street and drive over a bridge. At the end of the bridge there is a dirt parking area in front of you. The trail begins in the back of this parking area.

A locally known hot spot from which to view the lower falls can be found by parking in the lower lot of the Rumford Library, which is close to the rotary on US 2 that connects with Portland Street and York Street.

OTHER WATERFALLS NEARBY Ellis Falls, Dunn Falls, Coos Canyon, Angel Falls

51

SAWTELLE FALLS
Township 6, Range 7, Penobscot County

Rating: 2.5/5.0
Type: Horsetails
Height: 12 feet
Trail Length: 0.5 mile
Water Source: Sawtelle Brook
Altitude Gain/Loss: Negligible

Difficulty: Easy
Hiking Time: 15 minutes
DeLorme Atlas: Page 51, A-4
(marked)
Best Time to Visit: May to
October

THE FALLS Why should you visit Sawtelle Falls, you ask? It is simple— very few people know about it. Part of the reason is obviously its location in northern Maine. Most vacationers in New England simply never get the chance to travel this far north. As a result, this 12-foot, two-tiered horsetail will likely be all yours to enjoy on your visit. The falls drop into a gorge, where the river continues flowing lazily for as far as you can see downstream. Swimming within the gorge is possible, but the dark, sometimes foamy appearance of the water is less tempting than many other swimming holes we have come across.

TRAIL INFORMATION Before starting your hike, take note of the direction of the flow of the brook from the bridge just before the parking area. You will now need to find the trail near the parking area that travels downstream along an old logging road. The river will be on your right, although it will not be visible from the actual trail for a while. Follow this logging road for 0.5 mile as it progressively narrows into a hiking trail. You will be able to hear the falls just before the trail curves right to the top of the falls. It is somewhat dangerous to do so, but it is possible to scramble down to the river, where the best view of the falls is obtained. We feel that the view from the top of the falls is worthwhile enough.

DIRECTIONS From Bangor, take I-95 north to exit 264 in Sherman. Take ME 11 north into the town of Patten and take a left onto ME 159 west (often marked as Shin Pond Road). Follow ME 159 west for 9.8 miles until it ends at Shin Pond. At Shin Pond, ME 11 continues straight as the paved Grand Lake Road. From Shin Pond, drive 6.8 miles on Grand Lake Road and take a right onto Scraggly Lake Road (marked as Sawtelle Road on some maps), a dirt road. Follow this road for 1.6 miles (bearing right at mile 1.0) and park on a pull-off on the right just after crossing a bridge over Sawtelle Brook.

OTHER WATERFALLS NEARBY Shin Falls, Waterfalls of Baxter State Park

52

SCREW AUGER FALLS, GRAFTON

Grafton Township, Grafton Notch State Park, Oxford County

Rating: 4.5/5.0

Type: Plunge and cascades

Height: Plunge is 30 feet

Trail Length: Less than 0.1 mile

Water Source: Bear River

Altitude Gain/Loss: None

Difficulty: Easy

Hiking Time: Negligible

DeLorme Atlas: Page 18, E-2 (marked as Screw Auger Falls Gorge)

Best Time to Visit: May to October

THE FALLS (HIGHLY RECOMMENDED) One of two Grafton Notch waterfalls described in this guide, Screw Auger Falls, not to be confused with the Screw Auger Falls of Gulf Hagas Brook, also located in Maine, is a 30-foot plunge over the lip of a broad granite ledge into a gorge. A transparent curtain of white water is created by the plunge. Below the main plunge, the Bear River travels through a curvaceous gorge, dropping an additional 30 feet in a series of cascades past giant potholes, shallow pools, and grottos.

This waterfall is arguably Maine's most heavily visited. On a hot day in early July, we shared the falls and gorge with approximately a hundred others. Although the waterfall is far from remote, the breadth of sunny ledges and sunbathing spots, together with the ability to explore above and below the gorge, will allow you to enjoy this site immensely. Wooden fencing marks the gorge walls with stone steps to an upper wading area.

As you walk along the gorge to the best viewpoint of the waterfall, historical information boards add to the fun experience. Here you will learn about settlers in the 1800s who built a sawmill directly over the falls in the 1850s. The mill was run by the power of the current and produced lumber until it burned in the 1860s. You also have the opportunity to learn about how the falls were initially formed. As glaciers began to melt thousands of years ago, excessive amounts of water flowed into the Bear River, carrying rocks and sand along with the current. The consistent abrasion of these sediments smoothed away the gorge walls to create potholes that are still visible today.

There are several picnic tables, bathrooms, and a large parking area at the site that is known to fill up on hot sunny days in midsummer. As of 2009, the area is open daily from 9 AM to sunset, allowing plenty of time to visit.

TRAIL INFORMATION The path to the falls begins by paying the parking fee ($2/person for Maine residents and $3/person for non-residents, in 2009) at the center of the parking lot. The trail first passes a 5-foot-tall cascade and then heads left to the larger drop, several other cascades, and the gorge. It is dangerous, but possible, to scramble into the gorge during periods of low water. We watched as several people waded in the pools inside the gorge on our visit. Others even swam between the gorge walls up to the lower plunge, but unless you fully understand and can handle the dangers present, this is not recommended.

DIRECTIONS From the junction of ME 26, ME 5, and US 2 in Newry, take ME 26 north. Continue along ME 26 north for 9.5 miles and the parking area will be on your left shortly after crossing into Grafton Notch State

Park. *To get to Newry,* take the combined highway ME 5 north, ME 26 north, and US 2 east from Bethel.

OTHER WATERFALLS NEARBY Step Falls, Dunn Falls, The Cataracts, Ellis Falls, Frenchmen's Hole

53

SHIN FALLS

Township 6, Range 7, Penobscot County

Rating: 4.0/5.0

Type: Plunges and horsetails

Height: Main falls are 30 feet; total drop is 44 feet

Trail Length: 0.3 mile to upper or lower falls; 0.7-mile loop to visit both

Water Source: Shin Brook

Altitude Gain/Loss: -60 feet to upper falls; -100 feet to lower falls

Difficulty: Easy side of moderate to upper falls and top of lower falls; moderate side of difficult to lower falls.

Hiking Time: 10 minutes to upper or lower falls; 15 minutes for entire loop

DeLorme Atlas: Page 51, A-4 (marked)

Best Time to Visit: May to October

THE FALLS Shin Falls is an unforgettable waterfall and one of the finest in Maine. Despite its remoteness, the falls do see a fair share of visitors. Three drops can be found here, but the final spectacular drop of 30 feet is, without a doubt, the highlight. This horsetail spreads diagonally as it bobbles over row after row of rock shelves. Above the main drop is a pair of 7- or 8-foot plunges, which we should add, cannot be seen from the base of the main falls.

The fishing is excellent below the falls, and swimming is good, too. One warning, though: The trail to the base of the main falls is sheer in places and not recommended for children. The good news is that part of the trail network here includes a relatively easy spur to the upper falls, where you can also stare down at the main falls.

You will want to get right into the brook if you are here for a photoshoot. The stream is wide and fully exposed to the sun, so the morning or afternoon hours are going to boost your chances for a winning photograph. We also suggest complementing this waterfall with nearby Sawtelle Falls, a smaller but more secluded falls.

Shin Falls   ©Brad Sullivan

TRAIL INFORMATION The trail begins to the right of the parking area, and it starts off mostly flat and easy. You will reach a fork after only 0.1 mile. Take the left fork and in only 300 feet look for a narrower trail leading off deeper into the woods on your right.

At this point, you will have to make a decision. *To visit the base of the lower falls,* take this right onto the narrower trail, and after about 25 feet of flat terrain, the path will begin to descend on a very steep and rough trail. The base of the lower falls is about 500 feet away from here. This down-climb can be difficult, requiring some cautious maneuvering. *To visit the upper falls and the top of the lower falls,* do not turn right; instead, continue straight for another 300 feet and take a right onto another trail just before you reach the brook. From here, travel downstream on this trail for about 300 feet to the upper falls and, soon after, the top of the lower falls. There is one section of this part of the trail with a steep drop-off on your left side, so please be cautious.

A very steep and rough trail connects the top of the lower falls with its base. This can enable you to make a nice loop out of both waterfalls here, although this connecting trail is not recommended for children.

DIRECTIONS From Bangor, take I-95 north to exit 264 in Sherman. Take ME 11 north into the town of Patten and take a left onto ME 159 west (often marked as Shin Pond Road). Follow ME 159 west for 9.8 miles until it ends at Shin Pond. At Shin Pond, ME 11 continues straight as the paved Grand Lake Road. From Shin Pond, drive 5.1 miles on Grand Lake

Road and take a left onto Shin Falls Road, a dirt road. Follow Shin Falls Road for 0.2 mile and there will be a parking area straight ahead of you before the road curves to the right.

OTHER WATERFALLS NEARBY Sawtelle Falls, Waterfalls of Baxter State Park

54

SMALLS FALLS
Township E, Franklin County

Rating: 5.0/5.0
Type: Horsetails and cascades
Height: 54-foot total drop
Trail Length: 0.1 mile to top of falls
Water Source: Sandy River
Altitude Gain/Loss: +50 feet

Difficulty: Easy
Hiking Time: 5 minutes
DeLorme Atlas: Page 19, A-1 (marked)
Best Time to Visit: May to October

THE FALLS (HIGHLY RECOMMENDED) Just south of the town of Rangeley, the Smalls Falls Rest Area attracts more than just travelers looking for a driving break. Smalls Falls, with its scenic waterfall, colorful gorge, and fine swimming holes, welcomes all, often including visitors from all over New England.

It does not take much water flow to make this waterfall impressive enough to please all its visitors. Just a tiny stream can create a false sense of white-water power. This is attributable to the fact that the river upstream is considerably wider than the width of water that flows over the four sets of falls at Smalls Falls.

The bottom of Small Falls consists of a 3-foot cascade falling into a 20-foot-wide circular pool. The next waterfall up is a 14-foot fanning horsetail with a deep oblong-shaped pool people tend to jump into from above, a stunt that is highly dangerous. Even farther up the trail, you will find a 25-foot segmented waterfall, with a plunge on the left and segmented horsetail on the right. The top waterfall is a 12-foot horsetail and slide. Beyond the final falls of Small Falls lies tiny plunges and cascades with equally clear and beautiful water. The only potential detraction from these great views are the chain-link fences keeping you safe from falling over the rock walls, an acceptable price to pay for a dangerous alternative.

All four sets of falls are found within one of most colorful and beautiful gorges in the region. Its colors consist of beiges, oranges, greens, blacks, browns, golds, and ivories. There are plenty of places to sit along the gorge walls and bask in the beauty of the wide-open area.

Other features that make this waterfall so popular are the pools to swim in and the numerous places to picnic. At the base of each plunge, cascade, and horsetail is a pool to either wade or swim in. At the base of the lowest fall is a rocky beach leading to the pool. There are also bathrooms, picnic tables, and fire pits—altogether, a place as accommodating as any picnic spot you can find.

TRAIL INFORMATION A short boardwalk trail begins at the far end of the parking lot. After descending a set of stairs, the bottom pool and lower falls will come into view. Cross the bridge over the river and climb up the left side of the gorge along a metal fence, if you wish to continue exploring upstream. Within 0.1 mile, you will observe four distinct sets of falls, and eventually reach the top of the gorge and other popular swimming areas.

DIRECTIONS From the junction of ME 4 and ME 142 just west of the center of Phillips, take ME 4 north for 8.1 miles. Pull into the marked Small Falls Rest Area parking lot on your left. The rest area is 3.4 miles west of the MADRID TOWN LINE sign on ME 4. *To get to Phillips,* take ME 4 north from Farmington.

OTHER WATERFALLS NEARBY Phillips Falls, Angel Falls, Coos Canyon, Mosher Hill Falls, Poplar Stream Falls

55

∽

SNOW FALLS
West Paris, Oxford County

Rating: 4.0/5.0
Type: Plunge and cascades
Height: 25-foot total drop
Trail Length: Roadside
Water Source: Little Androscoggin River
Altitude Gain/Loss: None

Difficulty: Easy
Hiking Time: Not applicable
DeLorme Atlas: Page 11, C-1 (marked as Snow Falls Gorge)
Best Time to Visit: April to November

Snow Falls

THE FALLS The Little Androscoggin River cuts its way through a narrow gorge at Snow Falls in West Paris. At this special rest stop, the state of Maine has constructed a fine picnic area complete with trails on both sides of the gorge, picnic tables, restrooms, and plenty of parking.

There are four distinctive cascade sets at Snow Falls, with the last being our favorite. It is a thin plunge flowing into a dark pool just below the footbridge over the river. The gorge, with walls up to 30 feet in height, is surrounded by fencing, making this place family friendly and safe for the little ones. The water may be sometimes dark and slightly foamy, but the gorge is interesting and beautiful, and the falls are right off the road, so include a visit to Snow Falls if you are close by.

TRAIL INFORMATION This waterfall is located only a few feet from the road. There are plenty of log fences providing many viewpoints of different angles of the gorge. There are also picnic tables where you can sit and admire the falls, as well as a water pump in case you get thirsty.

DIRECTIONS From the junction of ME 26, ME 117, and ME 119 in South Paris, take ME 26 north for 6.0 miles, heading toward West Paris. Take a left into the marked Snow Falls Rest Area. *To get to South Paris,* take ME 121 west to ME 26, north from Auburn.

OTHER WATERFALLS NEARBY Kezar Falls

56

STEP FALLS
Newry, Step Falls Preserve, Oxford County

Rating: 4.5/5.0
Type: Horsetails, cascades, slides and pools
Height: Approximately 250-foot total drop
Trail Length: 0.6 mile
Water Source: Wight Brook

Altitude Gain/Loss: +300 feet
Difficulty: Easy side of moderate
Hiking Time: 20 minutes
DeLorme Atlas: Page 18, E-2 (marked)
Best Time to Visit: May to October

THE FALLS (HIGHLY RECOMMENDED) Step Falls is a spectacular long chain of descending horsetails and cascades that lies a few miles outside the eastern border of Grafton Notch State Park. Situated on a 24-acre property managed by the Nature Conservancy, an influential organization dedicated to preserving "the plants, animals and natural communities that represent the diversity of life on Earth by protecting the lands and waters they need to survive," Step Falls was acquired in 1962 and has been a popular attraction for waterfall fanatics and swimming-hole lovers for decades.

At Step Falls, Wight Brook, a wide mountain stream, meanders its way down several hundred feet of sunny granite slabs. During spring runoff, the water volume can supposedly reach up to 500 cubic feet per second. In the summer months, however, horsetails and plunges transform into skinny, nearly powerless slides, and dozens of water-sculptured paths that existed in spring often dry up.

As if being one of the tallest falls in Maine is not enough, Step Falls also has numerous shallow pools, many of which offer fine places to wade and, in the slightly deeper of the pools, swim. The yellow-tinted water in the pools has a very clear and clean appearance. The largest pool at the site, approximately 40 feet long by 12 feet wide, is surrounded by several moss-edged horsetails that empty into the pool. Along the edges of the pools are broad, mostly flat, sunny granite slabs that meet every requirement for a relaxing picnic. Be aware that signs at the falls indicate that pets are not welcome here.

TRAIL INFORMATION From the parking area, walk north on the obvious trail into the woods. Soon after entering the woods, the Nature Conservancy has set up a self-registration box with information describing the geology, history, and a description of Step Falls. After registering, continue up the yellow-marked trail to all sections of the falls. There are cascades and plunges for a few hundred yards, all easily accessed by many spur paths created by traveling visitors over the years.

DIRECTIONS From the junction of ME 26, ME 5, and US 2 in Newry, take ME 26 north. Travel along ME 26 north for 7.9 miles and a short dirt road leading to the parking area will be on your right just before crossing a bridge over Wight Brook. Note that there is not a sign on ME 26 indicating the dirt access road or parking area for the falls. *To get to Newry,* take the combined highway ME 5 north, ME 26 north, and US 2 east from Bethel.

OTHER WATERFALLS NEARBY Screw Auger Falls, Grafton, Frenchmen's Hole, Dunn Falls, The Cataracts, Ellis Falls

57

TOBEY FALLS
Willimantic, Piscataquis County

Rating: 4.0/5.0
Type: Horsetail
Height: 8 feet
Trail Length: 0.2 mile
Water Source: Big Wilson Stream
Altitude Gain/Loss: Negligible

Difficulty: Easy
Hiking Time: 5 minutes
DeLorme Atlas: Page 31, A-4&5 (marked)
Best Time to Visit: May to October

THE FALLS Tobey Falls is normally a slide-type waterfall, but during high water it looks more like a horsetail as water speeds over and down a smooth, 45-degree angle slate rock. Big Wilson Stream is normally a 30- to 50-foot-wide river, but at the waterfall the stream condenses to a fraction of that—usually about 8 feet under normal conditions. A stream being condensed to such a degree ensures a waterfall with torrents of white water, even when other falls that can be found along Big Wilson Stream have lost much of their visual appeal.

Tobey Falls is another waterfall that is much more impressive than its size would indicate. You will be quite surprised, as we were, of just how scenic an 8-foot-tall waterfall can be.

TRAIL INFORMATION Walk straight from the parking lot, passing three boulders, and onto the obvious trail that enters the woods. Continue down this very easy and short dirt road for about five minutes and the falls will be on your left as you approach a cleared out area. This hike can be avoided if you have a four-wheel drive vehicle and are able to drive down the road.

DIRECTIONS From the junction of ME 150, ME 16, ME 6, and ME 15 in Guilford, take ME 150 north for 8.7 miles. When you reach Goodell Corner, ME 150 will swing right. You should instead fork left onto Elliotsville Road and continue straight for 0.1 mile until you reach a stop sign. Take a right here onto Norton Corner Road (marked as Elliotsville Road on some maps). Travel on Norton Corner Road for 1.3 miles and take a left onto Tobey Falls Road just after passing Titcomb Road. Follow Tobey Falls Road for 0.7 mile, pass through a yellow gate and parking will be immediately on the right just after crossing a bridge over Leeman Brook. The parking area is distinguishable by three boulders along its edge that have overgrown grass and underbrush surrounding them. *To get to Guilford,* take ME 150 north from Skowhegan.

OTHER WATERFALLS NEARBY Houston Brook Falls, Little Wilson Falls

III. Massachusetts

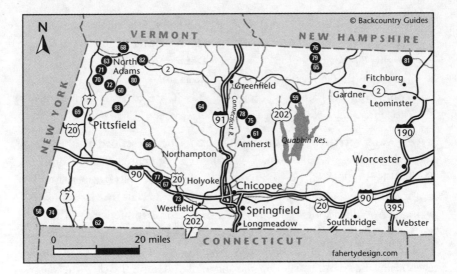

© Backcountry Guides

N

VERMONT   NEW HAMPSHIRE

NEW YORK

68

63 North 82
71 Adams
70 80
72 60

7

69 83

20 Pittsfield

66

64

Greenfield

Connecticut R.

91

78 75

61

Amherst

Northampton

90 77 67
67
20 Holyoke

73

7

58 74

62

202

Westfield

U.S. 202

CONNECTICUT

Springfield
Longmeadow

Chicopee

76
79
65

81

Fitchburg

Gardner 2 Leominster

59

202

Quabbin Res.

190

Worcester

90
20

Southbridge

395

Webster

0   20 miles

fahertydesign.com

58

BASH BISH FALLS

Mt. Washington, Bash Bish Falls State Park, Berkshire County

Rating: 5.0/5.0

Type: Plunge

Height: 80-foot total drop

Trail Length: 0.4 mile

Water Source: Bash Bish Brook

Altitude Gain/Loss: -300 feet

Difficulty: Easy side of moderate

Hiking Time: 25 minutes

DeLorme Atlas: Page 43, I-26 (marked)

Best Time to Visit: April to November

THE FALLS (HIGHLY RECOMMENDED) Often described as "the state's most dramatic waterfall," Bash Bish Falls is a segmented 80-foot drop of Bash Bish Brook. Worthy of our highest rating, the falls are perhaps the most well known and frequently photographed waterfall in Massachusetts. A mighty boulder splits the falls into two sections. Immediately after, the walls surrounding both sides of the falls ricochet the water back together just before crashing into a pool below. With a little imagination, you could even claim that the falls take on the shape of a diamond. Below the waterfall is a deep pool, with clear and inviting water, but, unfortunately, dangerous currents have forced state park officials to prohibit swimming.

Bash Bish Falls is one of the most publicized waterfalls in the state. Just about every hiking guide to Massachusetts, whether online or in print form, mentions this waterfall. There is a downside to this immense popularity; we have heard accounts of as many as three thousand people a day visiting the falls during the warmest of summer days. On the upside, Bash Bish Falls sees very few visitors on the cooler days of early spring.

Those looking for more difficult terrain might consider adding nearby Race Brook Falls to complement Bash Bish Falls. Only a few miles apart, both falls combined provide an excellent sample of the waterfalls southwestern Massachusetts has to offer.

TRAIL INFORMATION The trail, marked with blue triangles, travels downhill for its entirety. Full of roots and rocks to maneuver across, the trail crosses two small streams that often dry up during the summer, but can be very muddy after a heavy rainstorm. As you hike down to the falls, the powerful crashing sound of the waterfall increases. Near the falls is a nicely constructed rock stairway complete with handrails to provide you easy access down to the best viewpoint. Altogether the trail is just under a half-mile in length, very easy to follow, and requires only a small amount of careful scrambling.

SPECIAL NOTE Although technically located in New York, there is an additional noteworthy set of falls that can be accessed from the lower parking area of Bash Bish Falls in New York (see directions, below). To access these falls, which are on Cedar Brook, walk across Bashbish Road and follow a blue-blazed trail as it parallels the brook. The last falls are about 0.5 mile up this trail.

DIRECTIONS From the junction of MA 23, MA 41, and US 7 in Great Barrington, take the combined highway MA 23 west and MA 41 south into Egremont. After crossing into Egremont, take a left onto MA 41 south. After 0.1 mile on MA 41, take a right onto a road that is marked with a sign for MT. WASHINGTON/MT. EVERETT. Follow this road for 7.5 miles until you reach a white sign that says BASH BISH 4. Take a right here onto Cross Road, and follow this road for 0.7 mile and turn right onto West Street. Follow West Street for 1.0 mile and take a left onto Bashbish Falls Road. Follow Bashbish Falls Road for 1.4 miles to the upper parking lot for the falls, on your left. There are several signs along the way directing you to the park. If this parking lot is full, or if you would like to extend your hike to the falls, continue 1.0 mile down Bashbish Falls Road to the lower and larger parking area on the left, just after crossing over the NY/MA border. The hike will now be 0.75 mile one-way. *To get to Great Barrington,* take exit 1 off I-90 and follow MA 41 south.

OTHER WATERFALLS NEARBY Race Brook Falls, Campbell Falls

59

BEAR'S DEN FALLS
New Salem, Bear's Den Reservation, Franklin County

Rating: 3.5/5.0

Type: Cascades

Height: 12-foot total drop

Trail Length: 0.2 mile

Water Source: Middle Branch of the Swift River

Altitude Gain/Loss: -30 feet

Difficulty: Easy

Hiking Time: 5 minutes

DeLorme Atlas: Page 24, M-6 (unmarked)

Best Time to Visit: Year-round

Bear's Den Falls

THE FALLS The Middle Branch of the Swift River drops about 12 feet in a 70-foot-tall gorge while on its way to the Quabbin Reservoir. This drop, formally known as Bear's Den Falls, is a segmented set of almost equally sized cascades. The two falls are split by massive boulders in the middle of the brook, lying between the gorge walls. On the right side of the falls, a cascade turns into a fan before landing in a shallow pool.

This area is rich with history and legend. The property was named after a black bear that was shot in the area by a settler. Also interesting is the legend of how King Philip met here in 1675 with neighboring chieftains to plan Indian attacks on the white settlers of nearby villages, specifically Hadley, Deerfield, and Northampton. It is believed that these Native Americans celebrated their victories, and hid during their defeats, at the waterfall within the gorge.

Bear's Den Falls is one of several waterfalls located on property managed by the Trustees of Reservations, a Massachusetts nonprofit, member-supported land conservation organization that manages more than 100 properties throughout the state. Several of the properties managed by this organization include some of Massachusetts' best waterfalls, such as Chapel Falls, Glendale Falls, Doane's Falls, Royalston Falls, and Spirit Falls. The Trustees place their focus on "conserving the Massachusetts landscape," and because of their dedication these waterfalls should never be threatened by development.

TRAIL INFORMATION From the parking lot, follow the obvious path down into the woods. After about 75 feet, cross a dirt road and bear slightly left into the woods on the other side. About 0.1 mile farther into the woods, take the faint path on your left just before reaching the river to access the falls. Some light scrambling is required to get to the base of the falls.

DIRECTIONS From MA 2 in Orange, take exit 16 for US 202. Follow US 202 south into New Salem. Follow US 202 south for 2.1 miles and take a right onto Elm Street. After 0.7 mile on Elm Street, turn left onto Neilson Road. A small pull-off for the park is 0.4 mile down the road on the right, marked by a sign for the reservation. *To get to Orange,* take MA 2 west from Leominster or MA 2 east from Greenfield.

OTHER WATERFALLS NEARBY Doane's Falls, Spirit Falls, Royalston Falls

60

BELLEVUE FALLS
North Adams, Berkshire County

Rating: 2.5/5.0
Type: Plunge
Height: 6 feet
Trail Length: Less than 0.1 mile
Water Source: Dry Brook
Altitude Gain/Loss: -20 feet

Difficulty: Easy
Hiking Time: Negligible
DeLorme Atlas: Page 21, I-18 (unmarked)
Best Time to Visit: Year-round

THE FALLS Bellevue Falls barely meets our 5-foot minimum requirement to be classified as a waterfall. At only 6 feet of height, the falls are split into two segments by a large thumb-shaped rock. The falls are by no means spectacular, but the pool you will find at the base of the falls is one of the state's best, as it could easily fit a party of 20 swimmers. The entire stream is attractive and you will find cliff jumping possible off an 8-foot ledge. Always use common sense before engaging in such an activity, and never jump into white water near the falls until you at least scout its depth.

Be aware that dogs are not welcome here and parking is within a cemetery, which, according to the entrance sign, is open from 8 AM to 9 PM daily.

TRAIL INFORMATION From the parking area, head downhill on the trail that is just a few feet ahead of the parking area. This easy trail reaches the falls in just a few hundred feet. Also, do not miss the excellent view of Mt. Greylock from the parking area.

DIRECTIONS From Pittsfield, take MA 9 east to MA 8 north. Continue traveling on MA 8 north for 1.2 miles past the ADAMS TOWN LINE sign and take a right onto Leonard Street. After 200 feet on Leonard Street, stay left to remain on this road. Travel for 0.2 mile further and take a right onto Bellevue Avenue. Follow Bellevue Avenue for 0.2 mile and you will reach the Bellevue Cemetery. Enter the cemetery, and travel along its roads for 0.2 mile, taking a right at every possible junction until you see a very small parking turnoff in front of a very small section of white fence. From the parking area, you should be able to spot a path leading into the woods.

OTHER WATERFALLS NEARBY Pecks Falls, Hudson Brook Chasm, The Cascade, Money Brook Falls, March Cataract Falls, Tannery Falls

6 |

BUFFAM FALLS

Pelham, Buffam Falls Conservation Area, Hampshire County

Rating: 3.0/5.0
Type: Cascades and slides
Height: 25-foot total drop
Trail Length: 0.4 mile to lowest falls
Water Source: Buffam Brook
Altitude Gain/Loss: -75 feet

Difficulty: Easy
Hiking Time: 15 minutes
DeLorme Atlas: Page 35, H-28 (unmarked)
Best Time to Visit: March to June

THE FALLS A trip to Buffam Falls includes a relatively flat and peaceful walk to three main sets of cascades and slides. No more than 10 feet in height apiece, Buffam Falls is small, but still worth the visit, mainly because of the lowermost fall, a fanning slide about 7 feet in height. Buffam Brook takes its last major drop at this fanning slide before connecting with Amethyst Brook a few feet downstream. The town of Pelham maintains the network of trails around the falls, so the area is easy to navigate. Be sure to explore and enjoy the two small brooks as they merge below the falls.

TRAIL INFORMATION Do not take the trail that begins at the parking lot and immediately climbs a staircase. This is *not* the trail used to access the falls. The real trailhead for Buffam Falls is actually 0.1 mile back up the road. After walking east along the road, you will see a trail entering the woods on your right. Enter the woods and shortly after crossing a bridge you will see a sign for the BUFFAM FALLS CONSERVATION AREA. Take a right, and hike parallel to Briggs Brook past little falls to all three segments of the larger cascades and slides. The trail you are on is actually part of the 117-mile Metacomet-Monadnock Trail (M&M trail) that runs from Connecticut to southern New Hampshire.

Once you reach the lowest falls—easily identifiable by the joining of two brooks a few feet farther down the trail—take note of which trail you have been following. The Metacomet-Monadnock Trail becomes quite confusing near this lowermost falls, and it would be unsettlingly easy to continue traveling on the M&M trail, heading south instead of heading north. Remember to take the trail that runs closest to Briggs Brook, the brook you followed down to the falls originally.

DIRECTIONS From MA 2 in Orange, take exit 16 for US 202. Follow US 202 south through New Salem and Shutesbury. Continue traveling on US 202 south for 1.8 miles after crossing the PELHAM TOWN LINE sign. Take a right turn onto Amherst Road and follow it for 0.8 mile, and take a right onto North Valley Road. Follow this road for 2.6 miles, passing a cemetery on your left. The parking area is a paved shoulder to the right of the road.

Buffam Falls

The trailhead can be found by turning around and walking back 0.1 mile up the road you originally arrived on. *To get to Orange,* take MA 2 west from Leominster or MA 2 east from Greenfield.

OTHER WATERFALLS NEARBY Roaring Falls, Slatestone Brook Falls

62

CAMPBELL FALLS

New Marlborough, Campbell Falls State Park, Berkshire County

Rating: 5.0/5.0
Type: Plunge and cascades
Height: 50-foot total drop
Trail Length: 0.2 mile
Water Source: Whitney River
Altitude Gain/Loss: -150 feet

Difficulty: Easy
Hiking Time: 10 minutes
DeLorme Atlas: Page 44, M-11&12 (marked)
Best Time to Visit: Year-round

THE FALLS (HIGHLY RECOMMENDED) Within Campbell Falls State Park, the Whitney River drops 50 feet in a magnificent thundering display at Campbell Falls. The river falls through a tight gorge where the direction of the water flow changes twice, first to the left, then to the right. This zigzagging waterfall, as it can best be described, has a rugged form not often found in New England waterfalls. Its power in early spring is a thunderous surprise, considering the gentle terrain of the trail and the surrounding forest.

Make sure to pack all your photographic equipment when hiking to this waterfall. The falls have both an upper and lower section, which can be easily framed into one photograph. There is plenty of opportunity to view Campbell Falls because it is open to the public year-round from dawn to dusk.

TRAIL INFORMATION From the parking area, follow the white-square-marked trail down on easy terrain for about 0.2 mile and the falls will be unveiled.

DIRECTIONS From Great Barrington, take the combined highway MA 23 east and MA 183 south heading toward Monterey. Take a right onto MA 57 east and MA 183 south when MA 23 continues left. Continue traveling on MA 57 east and MA 183 south until you reach a right turn for the New Marlborough-Southfield Road, just after arriving in the town of New Marlborough. This turn is 3.9 miles beyond where you pass the New MARLBOROUGH TOWN

Campbell Falls

LINE sign on MA 57 and MA 183. Travel on New Marlborough-Southfield Road for 1.2 miles and take a left onto Norfolk Road. Take Norfolk Road south for 5.8 miles to a right onto Campbell Falls Road (a dirt road), just before the Connecticut-Massachusetts border. Take this dirt road for 0.4 mile and park at the trailhead, marked by a sign for the falls.

OTHER WATERFALLS NEARBY Race Brook Falls, Bash Bish Falls

63

THE CASCADE
North Adams, Berkshire County

Rating: 3.5/5.0

Type: Horsetail

Height: 45 feet

Trail Length: 0.6 mile

Water Source: Notch Brook

Altitude Gain/Loss: +150 feet

Difficulty: Easy side of moderate

Hiking Time: 20 minutes

DeLorme Atlas: Page 21, D-18 (unmarked)

Best Time to Visit: April to June

The Cascade

THE FALLS Mt. Greylock State Reservation is not the only park in north-western Massachusetts known to embrace waterfalls. The Cascade, or Notch Brook Cascade, as it has also long been known, lies in a small town park in North Adams. The Cascade is partially hidden in an almost completely enclosed gorge with towering walls, and the only way to get a full look at the falls is to hike into the gorge. The reward is a sometimes powerful, sometimes gentle 45-foot horsetail, depending on the water conditions.

The Cascade is highly seasonal and is also affected by a dam upstream, which is not visible. The months of April to June should present you with the best of what the falls are capable.

TRAIL INFORMATION From the parking area, hike upstream on an easy trail that parallels the brook. After 0.25 mile, you will cross a bridge over the brook. About 0.1 mile beyond this point, you are presented with a somewhat tricky section of trail. You have two options; you can *either* stay on the right side of the stream and scramble along the riverbank *or* cross the stream, hike 30 feet upstream, and re-cross back over the stream. Once this tricky section is completed, continue hiking upstream with the stream on your left for about 0.25 mile farther to the falls. The trail ends just before the falls, so you will have to scramble closer for the best views. Be aware that the ledges in the stream are very slippery. Shoes with excellent grip will be an enormous help here.

DIRECTIONS From the junction of MA 2 and MA 8 in North Adams, take MA 2 west for 1.1 miles and take a left onto Marion Avenue. Follow Marion Avenue for 0.3 mile and park on the right just before the end of the road. There is only room for two or three cars here.

OTHER WATERFALLS NEARBY Money Brook Falls, March Cataract Falls, Hudson Brook Chasm, Pecks Falls, Bellevue Falls, Tannery Falls, Twin Cascades

64

CHAPEL FALLS
Ashfield, Chapel Brook Reservation, Franklin County

Rating: 3.5/5.0
Type: Cascades, slides, and a block
Height: 10 feet, 15 feet, and 20 feet
Trail Length: 0.2 mile to lowest falls
Water Source: Chapel Brook
Altitude Gain/Loss: -50 feet to lowest falls

Difficulty: Easy
Hiking Time: 5 minutes
DeLorme Atlas: Page 34, A&B-10 (unmarked)
Best Time to Visit: March to June

THE FALLS Managed by the Trustees of Reservations, Chapel Brook Reservation was a gift of Mrs. Henry T. Curtis, in memory of her husband, who passed away in 1964. Within this reservation lies Chapel Falls, a set of three drops totaling 45 feet, and Pony Mountain, a summit overlooking a nearby valley.

The first waterfall is a 10-foot-tall medium-angle cascade. This section of falls is categorized as a fan because Chapel Brook expands from 8 feet to 15 feet as it travels down the falls. The next waterfall is slightly wider, and travels at a lower angle than the first set of falls. The entire formation is more a slide than a cascade, as the waters maintain close contact with the rock as it descends farther downstream.

The final set of falls at the Chapel Brook Reservation drops a total of 20 feet in a block-style formation. This block waterfall ends as a 5-foot-tall slide. For the hearty explorer, smaller pools and cascades can be found downstream. The pools are inviting in summer when the brook is flowing more gently and the warm weather invites a cool dip in the brook.

Also located at Chapel Brook Reservation is Chapel Ledge, a sheer 100-foot granite cliff of Pony Mountain accessible only to skilled rock climbers, or to those interested in watching the experts master their abilities.

TRAIL INFORMATION The trail begins on the other side of the road after crossing the bridge. It is about a hundred feet farther up the road from the parking lot. The trail is marked by a sign and you should be able to hear the falls from the parking lot. Continue down the trail 0.2 mile to the lowermost falls.

DIRECTIONS From the junction of MA 2 and I-91 in Greenfield, take I-91 south. Take exit 25 off I-91 and follow MA 116 north toward Ashfield (take note that MA 116 travels more west than it does north). Continue traveling on MA 116 north for 1.9 miles after passing the ASHFIELD TOWN LINE sign. Take a left onto Creamery Road, and immediately after, take another left onto Williamsburg Road. Travel on this road for 2.2 miles and the marked parking area will be on your right just before a small bridge. The falls are found by hiking down a trail on the other side of the road.

OTHER WATERFALLS NEARBY Slatestone Brook Falls, Roaring Falls

Chapel Falls

65

DOANE'S FALLS

Royalston, Doane's Falls Reservation, Worcester County

Rating: 4.0/5.0

Type: Plunges, cascades, and a block

Height: Approximately 175-foot total drop

Trail Length: 0.3 mile to lowest falls

Water Source: Lawrence Brook

Altitude Gain/Loss: -175 feet

Difficulty: Easy side of moderate

Hiking Time: 15 minutes

DeLorme Atlas: Page 24, F&G-13 (unmarked)

Best Time to Visit: Year-round

THE FALLS The town of Royalston offers three well-known waterfalls. There is Royalston Falls, a remote plunge toward the northern end of the town line; Spirit Falls, in the Jacob's Hill Reservation; and Doane's Falls, a nearly 200-foot-tall chain of wide cascades and plunges on a 46-acre preserve managed by the Trustees of Reservations.

Doane's Falls is split into three easily distinguishable sections. With a stone bridge as a backdrop, the first section is a pair of plunges. Following a well-marked trail downstream for a few minutes, you come to the other sections of Doane's Falls. You will pass a few sets of cascades before reaching a 20-foot block waterfall falling over a ledge. The river continues on with small cascades and pools, eventually meeting up with the East Branch of the Tully River.

As you explore the brook, please stay on the trail as there has been substantial erosion over the years. Several water-related fatalities have also occurred here, so the property is now off-limits to swimming and wading.

TRAIL INFORMATION Starting directly in front of the parking lot, the trail descends parallel with the brook. The trail, which should not be deviated from for safety reasons, is marked by yellow blazes. About 0.1 mile on the trail from the parking area, another trail heads right toward Tully Lake and connects with the Tully Trail, a 22-mile loop trail that can be used to explore all three waterfalls in Royalston.

DIRECTIONS Take MA 2 west from Leominster to exit 17 in Athol. Take MA 32 north as it joins with MA 2A west. Once you are in Athol, take a right to continue on MA 32 north as MA 2A west breaks off and heads straight. Almost immediately after, leave MA 32 north by taking a right at a sign for ROYALSTON onto Chestnut Hill Avenue. Follow Chestnut Hill Avenue for 4.1 miles to the marked parking area for the falls on the left.

Doane's Falls

OTHER WATERFALLS NEARBY Spirit Falls, Royalston Falls, Bear's Den Falls

66

GLENDALE FALLS

Middlefield, Glendale Falls Reservation, Hampshire County

Rating: 3.0/5.0

Type: Cascades

Height: Approximately 160-foot total drop

Trail Length: 0.2 mile to base of falls

Water Source: Glendale Brook

Altitude Gain/Loss: -160 feet to base of falls

Difficulty: Easy to initial viewpoint; moderate to base of falls

Hiking Time: Not applicable to initial viewpoint; 15 minutes to base of falls

DeLorme Atlas: Page 33, J-27&28 (unmarked)

Best Time to Visit: Year-round

THE FALLS Glendale Falls earns our recommended rating through its sheer size and volume. The drop, which is over 160 feet, is Massachusetts' third tallest cascade chain. The waters of Glendale Brook crash thunderously and haphazardly over endless ledges and boulders strewn in the brook over this long drop. At the base of the falls is a deep pool with some swimming appeal. However, the current is rarely gentle enough to safely allow this. This is not really the best place for children, as it takes a certain level of skill in scrambling techniques to access this pool.

The Trustees of Reservations, which manages the 60-acre preserve at Glendale Falls, have placed a sign at the parking lot outlining other interesting natural attractions in the area. Parking at this particular property is free, and the reserve is open year-round, sunrise to sunset.

TRAIL INFORMATION Although there are limited views of the falls from the top of them, many visitors will probably choose to scramble down the side of the falls for additional views. If you do scramble down, be aware that this is steep and slippery terrain, with no formal paths guiding you along the way. There are places that will require you to use your hands to scramble over wet sections of roots and rocks. Please take caution if you decide to do this.

DIRECTIONS From I-90 (Mass Pike) in Westfield, take exit 3 and follow the combined highway MA 10 and US 202 south. After crossing the Westfield River, turn onto MA 20 west which heads toward Huntington. When you arrive in Huntington, take a right onto MA 112 north. Soon after turning onto MA 112 north, cross a bridge and take a major left turn immediately after onto Basket Street. After driving on Basket Street for 0.2 mile, you will come to a fork in the road. Take the left fork onto Old Chester Road. Travel on Old Chester Road for 1.3 miles and you will reach another fork and a sign for the SKYLINE TRAIL. Take the right fork here and continue on this road for 2.5 miles, eventually reaching a third fork in the road. There will be a sign indicating that a right turn will lead you toward N. Chester and W. Worthington. Take this right fork onto East River Road. Travel on this road for 7.0 miles and take a left onto Clark Wright Road just before crossing a small bridge. Follow Clark Wright Road for 0.4 mile and a sign will mark the parking area on your right.

OTHER WATERFALLS NEARBY Sanderson Brook Falls, Goldmine Brook Falls, Wahconah Falls

67

~

GOLDMINE BROOK FALLS

Chester, Chester-Blandford State Forest,
Hampden County

Rating: 4.0/5.0

Type: Plunge and horsetails

Height: 40-foot total drop

Trail Length: 0.1 mile

Water Source: Goldmine Brook

Altitude Gain/Loss: +100 feet

Difficulty: Moderate

Hiking Time: 5 minutes

DeLorme Atlas: Page 45, A-30 (unmarked)

Best Time to Visit: Year-round

THE FALLS If you are not specifically looking for it, you would never stumble across Goldmine Brook Falls. Despite being just 0.1 mile deep in the woods off a major state highway, the waterfall feels worlds away. Perhaps that is why it took us two visits to this area before we could even find it ourselves.

Once you find the falls, by carefully following the directions below, you will be rewarded with an ultra-photogenic and seldom-visited 40-foot waterfall set in a splendid gorge. There is a fairly tempting pool for swimming here, but very little of the sun's rays actually reach it and it is therefore quite cold. This waterfall is an excellent off-the-beaten path attraction.

Goldmine Brook Falls

TRAIL INFORMATION From the parking area, continue west on foot along US 20 for 30 feet and look for a very obscure set of rock stairs on your left on the opposite side of the road. Take these stairs and begin bushwhacking through thin woods toward the brook on your right. This bushwhack is very short, lasting only 100 feet. Once you reach the brook, the trail becomes more well defined. Hike upstream and you will reach the main falls only about 0.1 mile from the parking area. Although this waterfall does require bushwhacking, it is really not that difficult and the reward is quite satisfying in our opinion.

DIRECTIONS From Springfield, take I-90 (Mass Pike) west to exit 3 in Westfield. Turn onto the combined highway US 202 and MA 10 south. Travel on US 202 and MA 10 south and take a right within downtown Westfield onto MA 20 west. Travel on MA 20 west through Russell and Huntington and into Chester. Continue traveling on MA 20 west for 0.8 mile past the CHESTER TOWN LINE sign to an unmarked dirt parking area on the right. This parking area is 1.5 miles east of the parking area for Sanderson Brook Falls off MA 20.

OTHER WATERFALLS NEARBY Sanderson Brook Falls, Pitcher Falls, Glendale Falls

68

∽

HUDSON BROOK CHASM

North Adams, Natural Bridge State Park, Berkshire County

Rating: 2.5/5.0
Type: Cascades and small plunges
Height: 25-foot total drop
Trail Length: 0.1 mile (see notes)
Water Source: Hudson Brook
Altitude Gain/Loss: Negligible
(see notes)

Difficulty: Easy
Hiking Time: Not applicable
(see notes)
DeLorme Atlas: Page 21, C-20
(marked as Natural Bridge State
Park)
Best Time to Visit: May to October

THE FALLS Hudson Brook Chasm does not contain any major waterfalls. What it does have is a 100-foot-long chasm and plenty of petite but powerful cascades. To see the gorge and the cascades contained within, the park

Hudson Brook Chasm

has constructed a maze of boardwalk trails following chain-link fences that let you see just about every possible viewpoint you would want to.

The geology of the area is fascinating. The marble rock formations are worth the visit alone, with many circular pools and small caves carved out in the chasm. There is also a natural bridge after which the park is named. Some may find the extensive fencing placed in and around the chasm to be damaging to the natural environment, but it allows you to witness viewpoints that would otherwise be inaccessible.

Although there are not any specific waterfalls worth noting, this site is still worth visiting because it does have some small cascades, it is a great place for a picnic, and the chasm is fascinating. There is a visitor center with restrooms, and wide fields well suited for a family gathering or picnic.

TRAIL INFORMATION Starting from the parking lot, follow the clear trail to the falls. There is a sign for NATURAL BRIDGES. If the gate to the state park is closed, you will have to walk up the road for 0.2 mile until you see a staircase on your left leading uphill into the woods. The chasm is just up these stairs. There is also a viewpoint of the bottom of the chasm just to the left of this staircase. If the gate is closed, the total walk for you will be 0.3 mile each way, with an elevation gain of approximately 100 feet.

DIRECTIONS From the eastern junction of MA 8 and MA 2 in North Adams, take MA 8 north. Drive on MA 8 north for 0.4 mile and take a left onto McCauley Road. If the gate to Natural Bridge State Park is open, drive 0.3 mile to the parking lot. If it is not open, find a place to park near the gate and walk up the road to the center of the park.

OTHER WATERFALLS NEARBY The Cascade, Money Brook Falls, March Cataract Falls, Pecks Falls, Bellevue Falls, Tannery Falls, Twin Cascades

69

LULU CASCADE
Pittsfield, Pittsfield State Forest, Berkshire County

Rating: 2.0/5.0
Type: Plunge and cascades
Height: 8-foot total drop
Trail Length: 0.1 mile
Water Source: Lulu Brook
Altitude Gain/Loss: Negligible

Difficulty: Easy
Hiking Time: 5 minutes
DeLorme Atlas: Page 32, A-7&8
(unmarked)
Best Time to Visit: May to June

THE FALLS Pittsfield State Forest, on the western edge of the state, is a state park with much to offer. There are waterfalls, some of the finest scenic vistas in the state, ponds, a large network of trails, as well as inexpensive camping opportunities.

Lulu Cascade

The most visited of the several waterfalls in Pittsfield State Forest are the two small cascades that comprise Lulu Cascade. The falls, which lie in a pretty ravine containing exceptionally clear water, are found via a short walk from the Lulu Day Use Parking Area. They may not be the most interesting falls in New England, but they are visually charming. After visiting the falls, however, your trip to the state forest is not complete.

From the falls, continue down the main park road (Berry Pond Circuit Road) in your vehicle and complete the scenic drive as it loops back to the park entrance. Along the way, you will be pleased by vistas, Berry Pond—a natural body of water with the highest elevation in the state—and lots of trailhead parking for the various trails within the park. For information on trails, obtain a map at the visitor center. There is a nominal fee for entering the park. Some motorized vehicles (such as ATVs) are allowed here, as are bicyclists and equestrians. Just about any type of outdoor enthusiast can find a way to enjoy themselves in this large state park.

For added adventure, three other small waterfalls exist within the park's boundary: Daniels Brook Chasm, Hawthorne Falls, and Parker Brook Cascade. Although they are not described here due to space limitations, dedicated waterfall hunters will enjoy researching and finding these additional falls. Of the three, Daniels Brook Chasm is the least seasonal and most scenic.

TRAIL INFORMATION From the Lulu Day Use Parking Area, continue farther up the park road and take a right onto the Lulu Brook Trail just before crossing a small bridge over the brook. The falls are 0.1 mile up this trail. The main plunge lies a few feet beyond the first set of cascades. The best views and photographic opportunities of the cascade are achieved by hiking down into the circular basin just below the falls.

DIRECTIONS From I-90 in Lee, take exit 2. Follow US 20 west toward Pittsfield. Soon US 7 north will join with, and later split from, US 20 west. Continue traveling on US 20 west for 0.75 mile past where US 7 breaks away and take a right onto South Merrium Street. Follow South Merrium Street for 0.4 mile and take a left onto West Street. Follow West Street for 1.9 miles and take a right onto Churchill Street. After driving 1.6 miles on Churchill Street, take a left onto the northern end of Cascade Street. Travel on Cascade Street for 0.5 mile and you will need to take a right. About 0.1 mile from this point, you will reach the contact station for Pittsfield State Forest. Pay the daily parking fee ($5 in 2009) and continue straight for 0.6 mile farther and park at the very large Lulu Day Use Parking Area on the left.

OTHER WATERFALLS NEARBY Wahconah Falls, March Cataract Falls

70

∽

MARCH CATARACT FALLS

Williamstown, Mt. Greylock State Reservation,
Berkshire County

Rating: 3.5/5.0

Type: Fan

Height: 30 feet

Trail Length: 1.5 miles

Water Source: Hopper Brook

Altitude Gain/Loss: +50 feet,
-325 feet

Difficulty: Moderate

Hiking Time: 50 minutes

DeLorme Atlas: Page 20, G-14
(unmarked)

Best Time to Visit: Late May to
July

THE FALLS March Cataract Falls is the premier waterfall of Mt. Greylock State Reservation, and one of the must-see waterfalls of northwestern Massachusetts. The falls are a continuous 30-foot fan of water dancing down the western slopes of Mt. Greylock. The trail allows you to safely come within inches of the falls, making this an intimate place. It is considered a seasonal waterfall though, as it can reduce to merely a trickle during the summer dry months. However, it does not take much water to reveal the true beauty of this place.

To add more to your trip to this waterfall, be sure to check out Deer Hill Falls, a waterfall accessed by the same camping area you will pass through on your hike. There is also Money Brook Falls and the summit of Mt. Greylock to consider, both accessible by nearby park roads. At the summit of Mt. Greylock, there is a paved parking area ($2 parking fee in 2009) and beautiful views of several New England states as well as New York.

TRAIL INFORMATION Access to this waterfall has significantly changed since the first edition of this guide. From the parking area, continue on foot down Sperry Road for 0.6 mile until you reach a small ranger station and a fork in the road. Take the right fork and after you pass several campsites on your left, you will reach the trailhead for the falls on your right in about 0.1 mile. From this point, it is 0.8 mile to the falls along a blue-blazed, fairly well used, and easy to follow trail.

SPECIAL NOTE If you would like to visit Deer Hill Falls, which is another pretty but seasonal waterfall located close by, return back to the fork near the ranger station on Sperry Road. This time, take the left fork, and in 200 feet, take another left and walk past a few different campsites and restrooms, all the while following signs toward the Deer Hill Trail. After walking a few hundred feet on this dirt road, bear right and cross a wooden bridge. In just a few more feet, you should fork right at the next junction and continue hiking for about five more minutes. You will then reach a T-junction; turn left here and follow the Deer Hill Trail to the base of the falls. Starting from the campground on Sperry Road, there are signs at all significant trail junctions to help guide you along this walk.

DIRECTIONS From Pittsfield, take US 7 north. Continue traveling along US 7 north for 3.2 miles past the LANESBOROUGH TOWN LINE sign

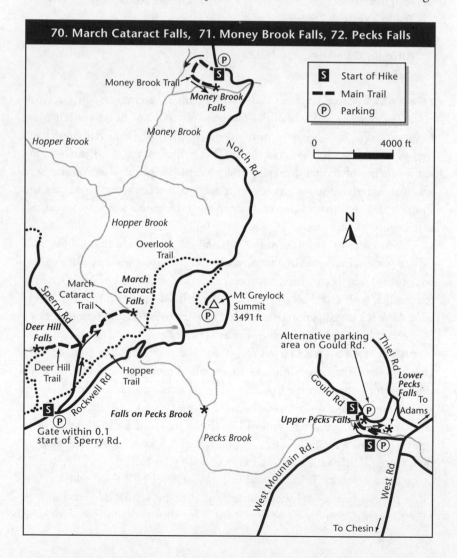

70. March Cataract Falls, 71. Money Brook Falls, 72. Pecks Falls

and take a right onto North Main Street. Follow North Main Street for 0.7 mile and take a right onto Rockwell Road, marked only by a sign for State Reservation. Follow Rockwell Road for 6.6 miles (bearing left at mile 0.4 to stay on this road) and take a left onto Sperry Road when you see several signs listing the park attractions and features. Follow Sperry Road for 0.1 mile and park at a small pull-off on the right just in front of the gate preventing farther travel down the road. If this parking area is full, there is more parking back on Rockwell Road across from the start of Sperry Road. Take note that Sperry Road also accesses March Cataract Falls and that the road is 2.3 miles south of the summit parking area.

OTHER WATERFALLS NEARBY Money Brook Falls, The Cascade, Hudson Brook Chasm, Pecks Falls, Bellevue Falls, Lulu Cascade

71

MONEY BROOK FALLS

North Adams, Mt. Greylock State Reservation, Berkshire County

Rating: 3.0/5.0

Type: Cascades

Height: 70-foot total drop

Trail Length: 0.75 mile

Water Source: Money Brook

Altitude Gain/Loss: -200 feet, +20 feet

Difficulty: Moderate

Hiking Time: 30 minutes

DeLorme Atlas: Page 21, F-16 (unmarked)

Best Time to Visit: Late May to July

THE FALLS Although the trailhead for this waterfall is a clearly marked parking area along the popular auto road to the summit of Mt. Greylock, Money Brook Falls receives little attention. That is a shame because the 80-foot-tall horsetail located here is quite a spectacular sight, especially in high water. Similar to the other waterfalls within the park, this set of falls is seasonal and best viewed in late spring or early summer.

If time allows, consider combining a visit to these falls with other highlights of the park, such as March Cataract Falls, Deer Hill Falls, and the summit of Mt. Greylock. An excursion to these worthwhile destinations can make quite an eventful day for you and your family.

TRAIL INFORMATION Follow the trail from the parking area to the blue-blazed Money Brook Trail. You will reach two forks on this trail. Take a left at the first fork after 0.25 mile and a left at another fork only 0.1 mile from the falls. There are signs directing you toward the falls at all junctions.

DIRECTIONS From the junction of MA 2 and MA 8a in North Adams, take MA 2 west for 1.3 miles. Take a left onto Notch Road. Follow Notch Road for 5.1 miles (making sure to take a left after 1.2 miles and bearing right at mile 2.3 to stay on this road) to a small parking area on the right. The parking area for the falls is 4.0 miles north of the summit of Mt. Greylock.

OTHER WATERFALLS NEARBY March Cataract Falls, The Cascade, Pecks Falls, Bellevue Falls, Hudson Brook Chasm, Twin Cascades

72

PECKS FALLS
Adams, Berkshire County

Rating: 2.5/5.0

Type: Plunges, horsetails and cascades

Height: Lower falls, 50-foot total drop; upper falls, 12-foot total drop

Trail Length: Less than 0.1 mile to lower falls; 0.2 mile to upper falls

Water Source: Pecks Brook

Altitude Gain/Loss: +40 feet, -20 feet to lower falls; +40 feet, -20 feet to upper falls

Difficulty: Easy

Hiking Time: 5 minutes to lower falls; 10 minutes to upper falls

DeLorme Atlas: Page 21, H-17 (unmarked)

Best Time to Visit: Year-round

THE FALLS Many waterfalls are spread along Pecks Brook as it drains the eastern side of Mt. Greylock. A set of seasonally dramatic upper falls, called Falls on Peck's Brook by the guidebook *Berkshire Region Waterfall Guide,* is not described in detail here as access is difficult and the falls are typically weak in flow for much of the warmer months.

Several more waterfalls with easier access are found downstream within close proximity to the town of Adams. Pecks Falls, a name commonly used to describe the two distinct waterfalls that lie between Gould Road and West Mountain Road, consist of a 50-foot lower fall, a set of horsetails and cascades that fall mostly through a slender chasm, and a 12-foot upper fall, consisting of two consecutive tiers of plunges. The upper falls include a pool suitable for wading, and most summer visitors appear to be parents and their children here for such a purpose.

TRAIL INFORMATION From the parking area, head into the woods on the only unmistakable trail that does so. Immediately after entering the woods, you will reach a junction. *To get to the lower falls,* take a right and follow a trail downhill for about 300 feet to the falls. *To get to the upper falls,* take a left at the junction and follow a trail uphill for 0.2 mile and

Pecks Falls (lower falls)

the falls will appear. If you would like to get the base of the upper falls, cross the stream above the upper falls and follow the paths downstream on the opposite side of the brook.

DIRECTIONS From the junction of MA 8 and MA 116 in Adams, take MA 8 south for 0.3 mile and take a right onto Prospect Street. Follow Prospect Street for 0.1 mile and take a left onto Harmony Street. Follow Harmony Street for 0.1 mile and bear left onto Fisk Street (do not take a complete left onto Martin Avenue). Follow Fisk Street for 0.5 mile and take a right onto West Road. Follow West Road for 0.1 mile and take a left onto West Mountain Road. Follow West Mountain Road for 0.2 mile and park on the side of the road. There is no official parking area here, so look for a place to park near the only trail that leads into the woods. This trail, which accesses both the lower and upper falls, can be somewhat challenging to spot.

SPECIAL NOTE There is a somewhat easier alternative approach to the upper falls. They can be accessed by a parking area and trail off Gould Road, which connects with West Road about 0.1 mile north of West Mountain Road. The parking area is 0.3 mile up Gould Road on the right. This easy 0.1-mile trail to the falls starts on the opposite side of the road.

OTHER WATERFALLS NEARBY Bellevue Falls, Hudson Brook Chasm, The Cascade, Money Brook Falls, March Cataract Falls, Tannery Falls

73

PITCHER FALLS

Russell, AMC Noble View Outdoor Center, Hampden County

Rating: 4.0/5.0

Type: Plunge, cascades and a punchbowl

Height: Tallest is 12 feet

Trail Length: 0.8 mile to the base of Pitcher Falls

Water Source: Pitcher Brook

Altitude Gain/Loss: +100 feet, -250 feet

Difficulty: Easy to top of Pitcher Falls; moderate side of difficult to base of falls

Hiking Time: 30 minutes

DeLorme Atlas: Page 46, G-4 (unmarked)

Best Time to Visit: May to November

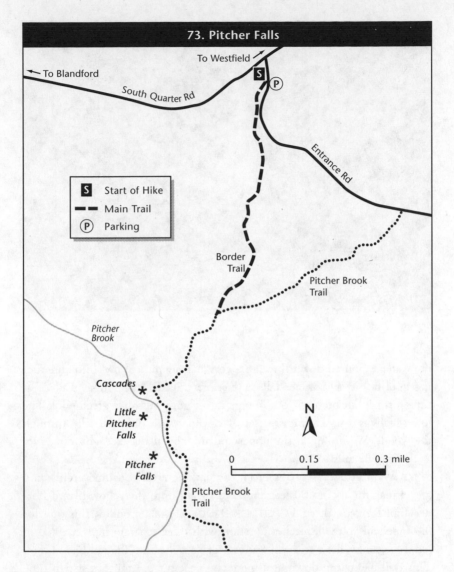

73. Pitcher Falls

To Westfield

S P

To Blandford

South Quarter Rd

Entrance Rd

S Start of Hike

▬ ▬ Main Trail

P Parking

Border
Trail

Pitcher Brook
Trail

Pitcher
Brook

Cascades ✳

Little ✳
Pitcher
Falls

✳
Pitcher
Falls

Pitcher Brook
Trail

N

0   0.15   0.3 mile

THE FALLS The Boston-based Appalachian Mountain Club continues to purchase large tracts of land in the Northeast as part of their mission to promote "the protection, enjoyment and stewardship of the mountains, forests, waters, and trails of the Appalachian region." The Noble View Outdoor Center of Massachusetts is one of their more recent acquisitions. The Pitcher Falls, however, are on private property and access is restricted to AMC members only; they are not open to the general public.

You will find three sets of falls over the course of a tenth of a mile. The name Pitcher Falls was most likely derived by the 12-foot middle falls, as

Pitcher Falls

the water is poured down through a very narrow punchbowl into an enticing pool below. The upper falls, sometimes called Little Pitcher Falls, features a small but pretty 5-foot plunge into a gorgeous olive green pool. The lowest falls is a less impressive set of cascades seen only partially through the woods. Swimming at the upper and middle falls is excellent, especially at the middle falls.

TRAIL INFORMATION From the parking area, continue uphill on a gravel road for about 400 feet and take a right onto the yellow-blazed Border Trail at a sign that says PITCHER BROOK 0.4 MILE. Follow this trail for 0.4 mile and you will reach a junction with three separate trails marked in red, blue, and yellow. You will want to take a right onto the red-blazed trail. This trail will climb down at a moderate pace for 0.3 mile, at which time you will begin paralleling the river. Once you see the river, the first set of falls will be just ahead.

To get to Pitcher Falls, which is the second set of falls of this trip, continue downstream on the trail, staying very close to the river, for about 300 feet. The trail will place you at the top of the falls. From this point on, the trail gets steeper and rougher, especially if you wish to scramble down to the base of Pitcher Falls. There is also another set of cascades about 100 feet farther downstream as well, but they are less impressive and more obstructed than what you have seen thus far.

DIRECTIONS From Springfield, take I-90 (Mass Pike) west to exit 3 in Westfield. Turn onto the combined highway US 202 and MA 10 south. Travel on US 202 and MA 10 south and take a right within downtown Westfield onto MA 20 west. Travel on MA 20 west into the village of Woronoco and take a left onto MA 23 west. Travel on MA 23 west for 1.6 miles and take a left onto General Knox Road. Follow General Knox Road for 1.2 miles and take a right onto South Quarter Road. Follow South Quarter Road for 1.2 miles and pull into a large parking area marked AMC NOBLE VIEW on the left. There is an informational display marking the parking area as well.

OTHER WATERFALLS NEARBY Goldmine Brook Falls, Sanderson Brook Falls

74

RACE BROOK FALLS
Sheffield, Mt. Everett State Reservation, Berkshire County

Rating: 4.5/5.0
Type: Horsetails and cascades
Height: Approximately 300-foot total drop
Trail Length: 0.7 mile to lowermost falls; 1.1 miles to uppermost falls
Water Source: Race Brook
Altitude Gain/Loss: +450 feet, -30 feet to lower falls; +900 feet, -50 feet to upper falls

Difficulty: To the lowest falls, moderate; to the upper falls, moderate side of difficult
Hiking Time: 20 minutes to lower falls; 60 minutes to visit all five falls
DeLorme Atlas: Page 43, J-30 (marked)
Best Time to Visit: May to November

THE FALLS (HIGHLY RECOMMENDED) Race Brook Falls offers five distinct and very scenic sets of waterfalls. If that is not enough to entice you into visiting, you can continue past the falls up to the nearby summits of Mt. Everett or Mt. Race as an added bonus.

The lowermost falls drops nearly 100 feet and is surrounded by dozens of hemlock trees, creating a nice frame. The second falls, a pretty horsetail, is more exposed to the sun, and presents improved photographic opportu-

nities. This is our favorite of the five waterfalls here. This one fans gracefully down a steep ledge before splashing in a shallow pool below. Braving
the slippery process of wading across the brook, it is possible to wade right
up and lean against the rugged, nearly vertical wall that the water tumbles
down.

Most waterfall types, including horsetails, plunges, cascades, slides, and
fans, can be found by continuing up the steep trail past the second falls. The
third and fourth falls consist of plunges, horsetails, and cascades. You will
probably want to avoid the third falls in the early spring; constant mud is
likely to be a common nuisance between the second and fourth falls for hikers during this season. The fifth and final falls has very low water flow as it
is found high on the mountainside. Viewing the upper, fifth falls requires a
short bushwhack, which almost ensures you privacy here.

TRAIL INFORMATION Start your hike by checking the informational
billboard to see if they have current trail maps of the Mt. Everett State
Reservation available for your use. There is a network of potentially confusing trails here and there have been significant trail changes over the years
that have altered access to the five waterfalls.

Begin your hike at the left end of the parking lot where the Race Brook
Trail, marked with blue triangles, starts out relatively flat until you reach a
fork after 0.3 mile. Take a left and you will reach Race Brook in 0.1 mile
farther, which you will have to cross. Once you cross the brook, continue
hiking upstream on a trail for an additional 0.2 mile and you will reach a
fork, marked by a sign for VIEW OF LOWER FALLS LOOP TRAIL. Take a right
at this fork and hike a few hundred feet to a T-junction, currently marked
by a small sign pointing right saying FALLS VIEW.

Here is where things can get a little confusing. *To get to the base of the
lowermost falls,* take a right at this sign and head downhill for less than 0.1
mile to witness the nearly 100-foot horsetail. Return back to this junction
to visit the remaining four other waterfalls as there is no safe passage directly between the lowermost falls and the other falls along the brook. *To
visit the rest of the falls,* take a left at the FALLS VIEW sign and continue hiking uphill for 0.1 mile and you will approach the top of the falls you just
visited, visible on your right, and the base of the 30-foot second falls, visible just upstream. To safely reach the third falls, you will need to find the
trail that leads steeply uphill starting between the top of the lowermost falls
and the base of the second falls. The third falls, a 30-foot drop of horsetails and cascades, are only about 200 feet up this trail.

After the third falls, the trail climbs higher across even rougher and
somewhat difficult terrain for about 250 feet before connecting back up

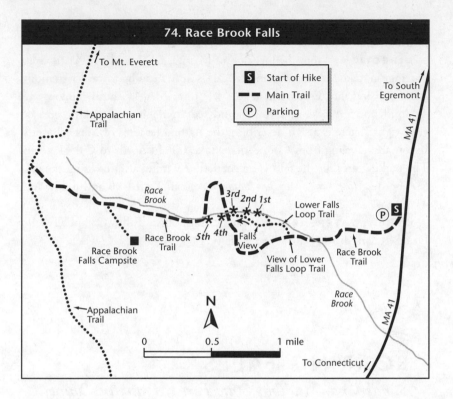

74. Race Brook Falls

To Mt. Everett

Appalachian Trail

S Start of Hike
- - - Main Trail
P Parking

To South Egremont

MA 41

Race Brook

3rd 2nd 1st

Lower Falls Loop Trail

P **S**

Race Brook Trail 5th 4th Falls View

Race Brook Falls Campsite

View of Lower Falls Loop Trail

Race Brook Trail

Appalachian Trail

N

Race Brook

0   0.5   1 mile

To Connecticut

with the Race Brook Trail. The fourth set of falls, a 60-foot set of gorgeous horsetails in high water, is located at this junction.

For many, this will be a good turnaround point to their trip. For those wanting to skip the seasonal fifth waterfall, you can either follow the blue-blazed Race Brook Trail back to your car, or you can return down the way you came past the waterfalls. For those who want to visit the upper falls, cross Race Brook below the fourth falls and follow the Race Brook Trail for 0.3 mile as it leads away from and then back toward the brook. When you arrive back at the brook, you will need to bushwhack about 75 feet downstream to see the 15-foot-tall fifth falls, about 1.1 miles from your car. To make this task as easy as possible, we recommended crossing the brook and heading down with the brook on your left. This section of trail is quite treacherous and is not recommended for children.

SPECIAL NOTE The Race Brook Trail continues above the falls to a junction with the white-blazed Appalachian Trail, about 2.1 miles from the parking area. By linking the Race Brook Trail with the Appalachian Trail, you can complement the waterfalls of Race Brook with the peaks of Mt. Race or Mt. Everett, both of which offer equally compelling views of the surrounding countryside. If you are looking for a little privacy, Mt. Race is the mountain to head to, as there is an auto road to the top of Mt. Everett.

DIRECTIONS From the junction of MA 23, US 7, and MA 41 in Great Barrington, take MA 23 west and MA 41 south, heading toward Egremont. After crossing into Egremont, take a left onto MA 41 south. Follow MA 41 south for 5.1 miles and you should see a semicircular parking area on your right. There is a sign describing the natural features of Massachusetts. If you are traveling from Connecticut, take CT 44 north to CT 41 north. The parking area for the falls is on the left, 2.9 miles after crossing the CT-MA border. *To get to Great Barrington,* take exit 1 off I-90 and follow MA 41 south.

OTHER WATERFALLS NEARBY Bash Bish Falls, Campbell Falls, Dean's Ravine Falls (CT), Great Falls (CT)

75

ROARING FALLS

Sunderland, Mt. Toby State Forest, Franklin County

Rating: 2.5/5.0
Type: Punchbowl and a plunge
Height: 18-foot total drop
Trail Length: 1.2 miles
Water Source: Roaring Brook
Altitude Gain/Loss: +300 feet

Difficulty: Moderate side of difficult
Hiking Time: 35 minutes
DeLorme Atlas: Page 35, A-24 (unmarked)
Best Time to Visit: April to June

THE FALLS This lightly visited waterfall is split into two sections by a flat base that contains an oddly positioned boulder, perhaps the result of a tumble down one of the sides of the gorge walls years ago. The water here is exceptionally clear and the rock formations and vertical potholes are of great interest. A small pool at the base of the falls is good for wading.

A final tip: look for delicious wild blackberries in early August about halfway into the hike!

TRAIL INFORMATION The trail starts behind the gate at the parking area. Immediately after passing by the gate, continue straight on a well-used dirt road (called the Summit Road). Follow this road for 1.1 miles, making sure to bear left at a fork after 0.7 mile, as it gently begins to climb Mt. Toby.

After 1.1 miles, you will reach a sign for the ROARING FALLS TRAIL on your left just after ascending a short hill. Take this left onto the newly constructed path, which will lead you 0.1 mile to the base of the falls. This new path has replaced the old hazardously steep and slippery trail that hikers previously used. There is a potential for getting lost on this short 0.1-mile section of trail as there are several confusing junctions. The key is to bear right and not to follow any of the trails that descend deep down into the woods. There are a few blue blazes to help guide you along here, but they are sporadic and hard to spot. If the river is flowing well, you can follow the sound of the falls. When the trail reaches the river, you can see the falls a few feet upstream.

Summit Road leads to the summit of Mt. Toby, which contains a watchtower with good views of the surrounding area. At the point where you turned onto the Roaring Falls Trail, you are approximately halfway to the summit. The rest of the trail to the summit is similar to the´ trail traveled to the falls, although it climbs more moderately. This trip to the summit makes a nice addition to your day-trip.

DIRECTIONS From Springfield, take I-91 north to exit 24. Follow US 5 and MA 10 north and take a quick right turn onto MA 116 south (although the road travels more east than south here). Follow MA 116 south to the junction of MA 116 and MA 47 in Sunderland. Turn left onto MA 47 north and travel on MA 47 for 3.9 miles. Turn right onto Reservation

Roaring Falls (in low water)

Road 100 feet past the MONTAGUE TOWN LINE sign. The trailhead will be on your right after 0.5 mile on Reservation Road. The parking lot is on the right, marked by a large sign for MOUNT TOBY STATE FOREST.

There is an alternative parking area off MA 63 that reduces this trip to just a 0.25-mile hike, but it crosses private property. A donation box is rumored to exist here. We believe that you will enjoy the full hike from the trailhead we have described more than this shortcut. We have chosen to exclude directions to this parking area for these reasons.

OTHER WATERFALLS NEARBY Slatestone Brook Falls, Buffam Falls, Chapel Falls

76

ROYALSTON FALLS

Royalston, Royalston Falls Reservation, Worcester County

Rating: 3.5/5.0

Type: Plunge

Height: 45 feet

Trail Length: 0.5 mile, plus road walk (see notes)

Water Source: Falls Brook

Altitude Gain/Loss: -150 feet

Difficulty: Easy side of moderate

Hiking Time: 20 minutes

DeLorme Atlas: Page 24, C-11 (unmarked)

Best Time to Visit: Year-round

THE FALLS The most interesting part of this waterfall may be the cylinder-shaped gorge that the water flows down into. Some have speculated that the gorge was created by a retreating glacier from the last Ice Age. It seems doubtful that the normally calm waters of Falls Brook could have created such a rugged place through erosion, but streams and rivers change over time and therefore this is the most viable explanation.

The falls themselves are also quite a treat. This 45-foot plunge drops off a flat rock ledge. You can either view the falls from behind safety-cable wire fences or by standing on a firmly planted rock at the top of the falls. You can also cross the brook and scramble downstream for wonderful new views of the gorge and falls if you are comfortable in doing so.

Royalston Falls is one of three waterfalls located on properties within the town of Royalston that are managed by the organization called The Trustees

Royalston Falls

of Reservations. The other two waterfalls, Doane's Falls and Spirit Falls, should be added to your itinerary if time permits.

TRAIL INFORMATION Yellow markers guide you on this easy to follow trail. Although generally a pleasurable and easy walk, the trail becomes steep once you get within 0.1 mile of the falls. A very small amount of scrambling is required, but there are many trees to help stabilize you. Although the trail is 1.0 mile round-trip, you must add mileage based on how far you travel on the unimproved dirt road that leads to the trailhead. For those who must hike up the road, do not despair; the trailhead is obvious and marked with a sign for the falls.

DIRECTIONS From the junction of MA 68 and MA 2 in Gardner, take MA 68 west. Continue traveling on MA 68 west for 6.0 miles past the ROYALSTON TOWN LINE sign. Take a right onto Falls Road. Falls Road is 1.3 miles north of the town center of Royalston. The distance from the beginning of Falls Road to the trailhead is 3.2 miles. However, after 2.3 miles, the road becomes unimproved and contains many puddles, rocks, and potholes. There is a SEASONAL LIMITED USE HIGHWAY sign letting you know right before when the road turns really bumpy. Lower-clearance vehicles will experience great difficulty on this road very early after the road transitions and high-clearance vehicles, such as SUVs and trucks, will most likely encounter problems soon as well.

Continue as far as you are comfortable driving, park on the side of the road, and begin walking farther on up the road until you reach the trailhead. A Trustees of Reservations sign for ROYALSTON FALLS marks the trailhead on the left. *To get to Gardner,* take MA 2 west from Boston or MA 2 east from Greenfield.

There is an alternative approach to the falls off MA 32 (Athol-Richmond Road) that is more appropriate for low-clearance vehicles. Directions for this alternative parking area can be found on the Web site of The Trustees of Reservations, www.thetrustees.org. The round-trip hike from this trailhead is 1.5 miles. We have not visited the falls from this trailhead ourselves, but we have heard it is an easier alternative to the long walk up Falls Road required for those who cannot drive their vehicles along a substantial portion of that road.

OTHER WATERFALLS NEARBY Spirit Falls, Doane's Falls, Bear's Den Falls

77

~

SANDERSON BROOK FALLS

Chester, Chester-Blandford State Forest,
Hampden County

Rating: 3.0/5.0

Type: Horsetails and cascades

Height: 60-foot total drop

Trail Length: 1.0 mile

Water Source: Sanderson Brook

Altitude Gain/Loss: +100 feet, -30 feet

Difficulty: Easy

Hiking Time: 30 minutes

DeLorme Atlas: Page 45, A-28 (unmarked)

Best Time to Visit: April to June

THE FALLS The waters of Sanderson Brook travel down a 60-foot face of rock wall, called Sanderson Brook Falls. Plunges adorn the top of the wall, followed by cascades of different structures. The force of the plunge smashes into a flat obstructing rock, causing the water to shoot upward before landing into the cascades below. At the base of the falls are pools, small cascades, and plenty of picnic-approved ledges. The shallow pools are child-safe. Although they may be slightly chilly, children will love splashing around in them on a hot day. There are also large boulders scattered everywhere to climb on, which also provide opportunities for exploration.

TRAIL INFORMATION The trail to the falls follows a wide dirt road (Sanderson Brook Road), maintained by the Chester-Blandford State Forest. There is minimal elevation gain, and the road is well marked with blue triangles. At mile 0.9, take a right off the road and follow the trail the rest of the way down to the brook, where the scale of the falls will surely surprise you.

DIRECTIONS From Springfield, take I-90 (Mass Pike) west to exit 3 in Westfield. Turn onto the combined highway US 202 and MA 10 south. Travel on US 202 and MA 10 south and take a right within downtown Westfield onto MA 20 west. Travel on MA 20 west through Russell and Huntington and into Chester. Continue traveling on MA 20 west for 1.6 miles past the main entrance of the Chester-Blandford State Forest and there will be a small parking lot on the left with a sign for SANDERSON BROOK FALLS. The trail to the falls continues up Sanderson Brook Road, which is closed to car travel.

OTHER WATERFALLS NEARBY Goldmine Brook Falls, Pitcher Falls, Glendale Falls

78

SLATESTONE BROOK FALLS
Sunderland, Franklin County

Rating: 2.5/5.0

Type: Fan

Height: 40-foot total drop

Trail Length: Roadside

Water Source: Slatestone Brook

Altitude Gain/Loss: None

Difficulty: Easy

Hiking Time: Not applicable

DeLorme Atlas: Page 23, O-22 (unmarked)

Best Time to Visit: April to June

THE FALLS There lies a house in the town of Sunderland that either one of us would love to live in. Imagine that you own a small, quaint little house in a town, and in your backyard, only 30 feet from your back door and porch, is a picturesque 40-foot fanning waterfall. How relaxing life must be listening to a waterfall all day long! We admit our jealousy, and you probably will as well once you see Slatestone Brook Falls for the first time.

The entire scene is picture-book perfect, with the Connecticut River on your left and a dazzlingly pretty cascade surrounded by sea green moss on your right. Visit in spring when water levels are at their highest and you will have a fine day of waterfall sightseeing.

TRAIL INFORMATION Being on private property, the only view to be had of this waterfall is from the road. Please be sure to respect these landowners and enjoy this natural spectacle from a distance.

DIRECTIONS From the junction of MA 47 and MA 116 in Sunderland, take MA 47 north for 1.4 miles and take a left onto Falls Road. After traveling on Falls Road for 2.0 miles, you should see the falls on your right as you drive across a small bridge. *To get to Sunderland,* take I-91 north from Springfield or I-91 south from Greenfield to exit 24 in Whately. Follow signs to MA 116 south and follow MA 116 south to its junction with MA 47.

OTHER WATERFALLS NEARBY Roaring Falls, Buffam Falls, Chapel Falls

79

SPIRIT FALLS

Royalston, Jacob Hill Reservation, Worcester County

Rating: 2.5/5.0

Type: Cascades

Height: 150-foot total drop

Trail Length: 1.0 mile

Water Source: Outflow from Little Pond

Altitude Gain/Loss: -250 feet

Difficulty: Easy side of moderate

Hiking Time: 35 minutes

DeLorme Atlas: Page 24, E-12 (unmarked)

Best Time to Visit: April to June

THE FALLS Spirit Falls is a two-tiered waterfall in the Jacob Hill Reservation—yet another waterfall lying on property managed by The Trustees of Reservations. No single part of the falls is over 10 feet, but collectively the outflow from Little Pond drops a total of 80 feet. Not really worthy as a single-destination trip, as this waterfall is seasonal and limited in its beauty, but Spirit Falls can be added with other strongly recommended natural features in the area—specifically, Doane's Falls and Royalston Falls.

There are several areas of poison ivy close to the trail, and every time we have visited, we have been attacked by swarms of biting black flies. Also,

Spirit Falls

be aware that some steep scrambling is required if the entire falls are to be explored.

TRAIL INFORMATION From the parking lot, follow the trail in front of you, which will occasionally change back and forth from a yellow-blazed trail to a blue-blazed trail. After 5 or 10 minutes, you will come to a small and muddy body of water. Make sure to bear right here and continue following the yellow and blue blazes, which will guide you the rest of the way to the falls.

The first set of falls is about 40 feet tall, and it would be easy to assume your trip is complete here. However, you can continue scrambling downstream over the next 0.1 mile to additional falls that are just as impressive, or perhaps more so than the falls above.

DIRECTIONS From the junction of MA 68 and MA 2 in Gardner, take MA 68 west. Continue traveling on MA 68 west for 5.4 miles past the ROYALSTON TOWN LINE sign. Take a left into the small parking area for the Jacob Hill Reservation. This parking area is 0.7 mile north of the center of Royalston. The parking area for Spirit Falls is also located 0.8 mile south of Falls Road, which leads to nearby Royalston Falls. *To get to Gardner,* take MA 2 west from Boston or MA 2 east from Greenfield.

OTHER WATERFALLS NEARBY Royalston Falls, Doane's Falls, Bear's Den Falls

80

TANNERY FALLS
Savoy, Savoy Mountain State Forest, Berkshire County

Rating: 5.0/5.0
Type: Plunges, cascades, and slides
Height: 60 feet, 80 feet, others ranging 5 to 20 feet
Trail Length: 0.4 mile to the base of Tannery Falls
Water Source: Ross Brook and Parker Brook

Altitude Gain/Loss: -200 feet
Difficulty: Easy side of moderate
Hiking Time: 20 minutes
DeLorme Atlas: Page 21, H-25 (unmarked)
Best Time to Visit: April to November

THE FALLS (HIGHLY RECOMMENDED) Tannery Falls and the various other waterfalls and cascades in the general vicinity make up what we would like to call a section of waterfall country. Within a square mile almost a dozen waterfalls, several worthy of their own pages in this guide, lie on the trail network at Tannery Falls. The main attraction, officially known as Tannery Falls, is an 80-foot series of tall plunges and curving horsetails. The upper 35 feet of this falls are a thundering curtain of white water, always impressive, even with little water flow. The bottom half of the falls is a series of narrowing horsetails that end in a shallow pool.

The second largest falls, Parker Brook Falls, lies only feet from Tannery Falls. It can be seen from the main trail as you walk back up, but you have to look carefully. This multi-section plunge waterfall falls down through an angular gorge. The water remains only 4 to 5 feet in width throughout the long formation. There is also a small set of cascades that is inches from the parking lot, accessible by bushwhacking on a primitive path to the left of the main trail.

Altogether, Tannery Falls, Parker Brook Falls, and the nearly dozen other unnamed plunges and cascades that adorn Ross Brook and Parker Brook, offer one of the top "off-the-beaten-path" treasures in the region. Try to budget several hours when you plan a trip to this special place.

TRAIL INFORMATION From the parking lot, head straight down the wide trail that is marked with blue blazes. This trail will bring you to the bottom of the largest waterfall, passing many small waterfalls along the way. After about 8 to 10 minutes, wooden stairs will lead you to metal wire fencing and a view from the top of the falls. Continue right and follow the trail to the bottom of the falls for a much different view. About 100 feet before you reach the bottom of the falls, take a right and walk off the main trail for about 50 feet and you will see 60-foot-tall Parker Brook Falls, first viewed as you come around a corner.

There is a small narrow trail to the left side of the parking lot that leads to another small waterfall, only a hundred feet or so down the trail. This is the waterfall you can hear from the parking lot. Although smaller in size than the main attractions here, this minor addition, along with the other cascades and small plunges on the trail to the main falls, can add much to the enjoyment factor of your visit.

DIRECTIONS From Greenfield, take MA 2 west head toward Savoy. Continue traveling on MA 2 west for 1.7 miles beyond the SAVOY TOWN LINE sign and take a left turn onto Black Brook Road just before you reach the FLORIDA TOWN LINE sign. The sign for this road is hard to spot, but it should be there. If you are traveling east on MA 2 from North Adams, take a right onto Black Brook Road just after you pass the SAVOY TOWN LINE sign. Travel on Black Brook Road for 2.5 miles, forking right after 1.3 miles, and take a right onto Tannery Road, an unmaintained dirt road. After traveling for 0.7 mile on Tannery Road, take a right onto another dirt road and the parking lot, marked by a sign for TANNERY FALLS, will soon appear. Be aware that although Tannery Road is unmaintained, it is often drivable in the average car. However, it is possible that you may not be able to drive the entire route, and this would add a short walk to your hike.

OTHER WATERFALLS NEARBY Twin Cascades, Hudson Brook Chasm, The Cascade, Bellevue Falls, Pecks Falls

81

TRAP FALLS

Ashby, Willard Brook State Forest, Middlesex County

Rating: 3.0/5.0
Type: Plunges
Height: 10 to 12 feet each
Trail Length: 0.1 mile
Water Source: Trapfall Brook
Altitude Gain/Loss: None

Difficulty: Easy
Hiking Time: 5 minutes
DeLorme Atlas: Page 26, E-9
(unmarked)
Best Time to Visit: Year-round

THE FALLS A favorite hangout spot for local residents, Trap Falls is sure to please anyone who ventures into Willard Brook State Forest. Set in an extremely picturesque setting, Trap Falls is much more impressive than its size would indicate. In the right water conditions, it consists of three plunges lined up side by side. The center fall is slightly higher than the others, and is shaped like a punchbowl. To help visualize the waterfall, picture a mini-golf hole with three paths leading to the golf hole below. This waterfall would definitely be one of the attractions on the course. In higher water, the three plunges merge into two.

We suggest spending a few hours here. Bring a picnic (there are plenty of picnic tables near the falls) or start a barbeque in one of the many fire pits. Although probably crowded in the summer, this is one family-friendly waterfall you will not want to miss. Your children will love this waterfall; remember a camera to capture the smiles on their faces.

TRAIL INFORMATION From the parking lot, walk parallel to the river on a level wooded road for 0.1 mile to the falls. You should be able to hear the falls from the parking lot.

DIRECTIONS From MA 2 in Leominster, take exit 32 for MA 13 north. Travel on MA 13 north for 10.1 miles and you will reach the town of Townsend, where you will want to take a left onto MA 119 west. Travel on MA 119 west 3.8 miles and the parking lot for the falls will be on your right. The parking area is 0.2 mile past the Willard Brook State Forest ranger station and 1.4 miles east of the junction of MA 119 and MA 31.

OTHER WATERFALLS NEARBY None

82

TWIN CASCADES
Florida, Berkshire County

Rating: 4.0/5.0

Type: Plunges and cascades

Height: 80 feet and 60 feet

Trail Length: 0.3 mile

Water Source: Cascade Brook

Altitude Gain/Loss: +80 feet

Difficulty: Moderate side of difficult

Hiking Time: 15 minutes

DeLorme Atlas: Page 21, E-25&26 (unmarked)

Best Time to Visit: April to November

THE FALLS Twin Cascades, as the name suggests, is composed of two waterfalls. The falls collectively tumble down in the shape of a Y. The waterfall on the right is a 60-foot multi-tiered plunge with rows of cascades at the bottom; the waterfall on the left is similar, except it's 20 feet taller. Even from the best viewpoints, with your head fully tilted upward, you cannot see the top of the falls because the water comes from around a bend and the steepness of the gorge blocks your view. From your relative position it is hard to imagine that a substantial water source could exist above these falls. Even from the trailhead, there is not a mountain to be seen that could generate a brook with such water volume or a falls of such great height. It is as if the waters are cascading from the heavens and is a wonderful stretch for the imagination.

Trail difficulties and dangers prevent this waterfall from receiving a higher rating. The trail is narrow in spots; your feet could slip—sending you down toward the brook—if you are not careful enough. You will also have to clamber up and over an always-slippery dam to attain the best views. We must stress that good hiking shoes or boots with solid traction are required equipment in order to enjoy this place to its full potential.

Twin Cascades

TRAIL INFORMATION From the parking lot facing the train tracks, walk over the tracks and take a left. Walk in the woods parallel to the tracks. The area immediately adjacent to the tracks is private property, so do not walk along or near the tracks. The trail, which is a mere 0.3 mile in length, begins to the right of the train tunnel. Take note that the trail may not be appropriate for amateur hikers, as it is often steep, muddy, and slippery.

There is also a 3-foot rock wall near the start of the trail that must be climbed over.

Also, be particularly careful around the waterfalls. You will be tempted to find alternate viewpoints upstream of the dam that sits at the base of the falls. If you do, take note that the surrounding riverbanks are heavily covered with moss and therefore very slippery. Many trees on the mountainside are loosely rooted, ready to be ripped out with a small amount of force; do not trust all of your weight on them. Based on the water flow at the time of your visit, it may be possible to climb up the dam on the left side. However, this involves a significant amount of risk, and therefore we cannot recommend that you try to do this.

DIRECTIONS From North Adams, take MA 2 east, heading toward Charlemont. Continue traveling on MA 2 east for 3.0 miles past the CHARLEMONT TOWN LINE sign and take a left onto Zoar Road. It is a wide turn and the street sign is rather small. There is also another sign here pointing toward Rowe/Monroe. If you are traveling from Greenfield, take MA 2 west, heading toward Charlemont. Continue on MA 2 west for 1.6 miles past the junction of MA 2 and MA 8a south and take a right onto Zoar Road. Follow Zoar Road for 2.5 miles and take a left onto River Road. Travel on River Road for 4.6 miles and the parking will be on your left just before a set of railroad tracks. There is plenty of space to park, but do not park near the train tracks as they are private property.

OTHER WATERFALLS NEARBY Tannery Falls, Hudson Brook Chasm, The Cascade, Money Brook Falls, March Cataract Falls

83

WAHCONAH FALLS
Dalton, Wahconah Falls State Park, Berkshire County

Rating: 4.0/5.0
Type: Cascades
Height: 40-foot total drop
Trail Length: 0.2 mile
Water Source: Wahconah Falls Brook

Altitude Gain/Loss: -30 feet
Difficulty: Easy
Hiking Time: 5 minutes
DeLorme Atlas: Page 33, A-18 (marked)
Best Time to Visit: Year-round

THE FALLS The state of Massachusetts has several waterfalls deemed worthy enough to be conserved under the protection of the state park system, including Bash Bish Falls, located in the southwestern corner of the state, Campbell Falls, located near the Connecticut-Massachusetts state line, and Wahconah Falls, the highlight of this chapter.

Wahconah Falls lies in the heart of the Berkshires, a central location to the waterfalls of Mt. Greylock State Reservation, as well as Tannery Falls, Glendale Falls, and Lulu Cascade. Because of its central location to these other waterfalls, Wahconah's picnic facilities provide for an ideal lunch rest stop before finishing out the rest of your day-trip. There are picnic tables, rest room facilities, and charcoal grills available for visitors. Also, as an added bonus, the small pools in the clean waters of Wahconah Falls Brook offer refreshing wading and even swimming. We expect this state park to be quite popular on sunny summer weekends, judging by the size of the parking lot.

TRAIL INFORMATION From the parking lot, walk past the gate, head down the embankment, and walk on an easy gravel path past the picnic area to the falls.

DIRECTIONS From the junction of MA 9 and US 7 in Pittsfield, take MA 9 east. Continue traveling on MA 9 east for 2.2 miles beyond where MA 8a joins with MA 9 in Dalton. Take a right onto North Street. Follow North Street for 0.1 mile and fork right onto Wahconah Falls Road. Travel on Wahconah Falls Road for 0.3 mile and a large parking lot will be on your right.

OTHER WATERFALLS NEARBY Tannery Falls, Lulu Cascade, Glendale Falls

IV. New Hampshire

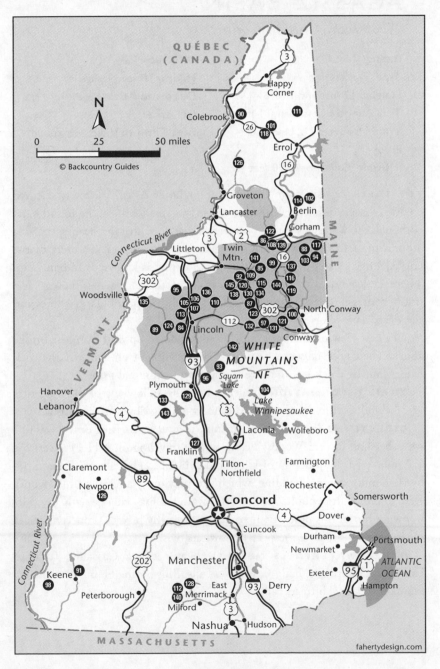

QUÉBEC (CANADA)

3

Happy Corner

Colebrook 90 111
26 101
118
Errol
126 16

Groveton 114 102
Lancaster Berlin
Gorham
122
3 2 86 108 139 88 117
Littleton 141 16 103 94
Twin Mtn. 85 99 137
92 109 116
145 120 115 144
95 138 130 134 119
136 87
105 110 123 302 100 North Conway
135 107 113 132 97 121 100
89 124 84 112 131
Lincoln Conway
142 WHITE
MOUNTAINS
93 NF
93
96 Squam Lake
Plymouth 129 104
133 Lake Winnipesaukee
143
Laconia Wolfeboro
Hanover
Lebanon 4 127
Franklin Farmington
Tilton-Northfield
Claremont Rochester Somersworth
Newport 126
89 4 Dover
Concord
Suncook Durham
Newmarket Portsmouth
202 Manchester ATLANTIC OCEAN
Keene 91 128 Derry 1 95
98 112 East 93 Exeter
140 Merrimack Hampton
Milford
Peterborough Nashua Hudson
3

MASSACHUSETTS

faheritydesign.com

VERMONT

MAINE

Connecticut River

Connecticut River

N

0   25   50 miles

© Backcountry Guides

Woodsville

302

135

112

141

84

AGASSIZ BASIN

Woodstock, Grafton County

Rating: 2.5/5.0
Type: Plunges
Height: 12 feet and 7 feet
Trail Length: Less than 0.1 mile
Water Source: Mt. Moosilauke Brook
Altitude Gain/Loss: -20 feet

Difficulty: Easy
Hiking Time: Negligible
DeLorme Atlas: Page 43, J-11 (unmarked)
Best Time to Visit: Year-round

THE FALLS Agassiz Basin is named after Louis Agassiz, a Swiss scientist credited for the discovery of the Ice Ages. Two small falls can be found here. Although the waterfalls are by no means large or of striking beauty, the area around the falls is of historical and geological interest. The waters of the curved gorge created a gap about 6 feet wide that is known as Indian Leap. There are legends that Native Americans used to jump across the gap as a test of courage. Also of particular interest are the deep, circular potholes and the deep, dark pools in the river.

The best view of the lower falls is looking down upon it from the bridge above. The upper falls can be viewed by scrambling on some of the rock ledges, but be careful as they are slippery with minimal grip.

TRAIL INFORMATION To get to the falls, follow any of the trails that lead behind a currently abandoned white building down to the brook.

DIRECTIONS From I-93 in Lincoln, take exit 32. Turn onto NH 112 west, heading toward Woodsville. Continue traveling on NH 112 west for 1.7 miles past the junction of US 3 and NH 112. The falls are located behind an unused white building, which was previously a restaurant (Govoni's Restaurant). Future public access of this waterfall may change with any shift in ownership of this property. If you encounter any private property notices during your visit, please respect the owners' wishes.

OTHER WATERFALLS NEARBY Beaver Brook Cascades, Paradise Falls, Swiftwater Falls, Bath, Georgiana Falls, Falls on the Flume–Pool Loop, Franconia Falls, Thirteen Falls

85

AMMONOOSUC RAVINE

Sargents Purchase, White Mountain National Forest, Coos County

Rating: 4.5/5.0

Type: Plunges, horsetails, and cascades

Height: 100 feet of upper falls viewable from the trail

Trail Length: 2.1 miles to Gem Pool; 2.3 miles to upper falls

Water Source: Ammonoosuc River

Altitude Gain/Loss: +950 feet to Gem Pool; +1,300 feet to upper falls

Difficulty: Moderate to Gem Pool; moderate side of difficult to upper falls

Hiking Time: 1 hour, 30 minutes to Gem Pool; 1 hour, 50 minutes to upper falls

DeLorme Atlas: Page 44, A&B-5 (unmarked)

Best Time to Visit: May to October

THE FALLS (HIGHLY RECOMMENDED) The Ammonoosuc Ravine Trail passes two picturesque sets of falls before clambering above tree line and landing at the doorstep of the AMC Lakes of the Clouds Hut, one of eight backcountry huts offering hiking accommodations and meals in the White Mountains. For most hikers, the falls and hut will be used as places to catch their breath before tackling the mighty Mt. Washington.

The first falls reached are seen directly from the trail. This small set of cascades is seen on your right at the distant end of a frigid pool named Gem Pool. Farther up, a spur trail will lead you right and slightly downhill to a commanding view of the upper falls, which are split into two sections about 50 feet apart. From this position, the upper falls appear to consist of a 100-foot drop into deep pools of water. The true total drop of the falls is hundreds more, but scrambling to find them is just not an option here; starting at Gem Pool, the terrain along the trail is notoriously steep. Some estimate the total drop to be 600 or 700 feet.

Although we have not experienced all routes to the summit of Mt. Washington, we doubt we will find another access trail to this mountain that we will enjoy more than the waterfall-packed Ammonoosuc Ravine Trail.

TRAIL INFORMATION The trail to the falls begins near the restrooms and immediately enters the woods. Follow the gently climbing trail for 1.0 mile and you will reach a junction with a path that leads left to the Cog Railway base station. Stay straight here and continue hiking, mostly uphill, for

Ammonoosuc Ravine (Gem Pool)

1.1 additional miles and you will see Gem Pool, a pretty emerald pool at the base of a small cascade on your right. The trail to this point has been moderate, but in order to reach the more impressive upper falls, you will have to travel on rougher and steeper terrain. To continue, cross the stream in front of Gem Pool and continue climbing for 0.2 mile farther, at which point you will reach a spur trail on your right. Take this spur trail, and in about 200 feet, you will reach the upper falls, often called The Gorge.

DIRECTIONS From the junction of US 302 and US 3 in the village of Carroll known as Twin Mountain, take US 302 east for 4.5 miles and take a left onto Base Road, which is marked by a sign for the COG RAILWAY. Follow Base Road for 5.6 miles and pull into the large, well-marked hiker parking lot for the Ammonoosuc Ravine Trail on the right. This parking area is 1.1 miles beyond the intersection of Base Road and Mt. Clinton Road. If you have reached the Cog Railway station, you have gone too far. *To get to Twin Mountain,* take US 3 north from Lincoln.

Please be aware that this trailhead is part of the White Mountain National Forest parking fee program. The fee was $3 in 2009 but there is currently a proposal in review to raise this amount to $5.

OTHER WATERFALLS NEARBY Upper Ammonoosuc Falls, Gibbs Falls, Beecher and Pearl Cascades, Thoreau Falls, Zealand Falls

86

~

APPALACHIA WATERFALLS

Randolph, White Mountain National Forest, Coos County

Rating: 4.0/5.0

Type: Horsetails and cascades

Height: Varies (see notes)

Trail Length: 2.6-mile loop

Water Source: Cold Brook and Snyder Brook

Altitude Gain/Loss: +300 feet, -300 feet

Difficulty: Easy side of moderate

Hiking Time: 90 minutes

DeLorme Atlas: Page 48, I-6 (unmarked)

Best Time to Visit: May to October

THE FALLS This chapter describes four waterfalls fed by two mountain streams that drain waters from Mt. Adams and Mt. Madison. Gordon Fall is the first stop on the 2.6-mile loop. A fanning 18-foot low-angle cascade, Gordon Fall is a well-shaded treat just downstream from where the Maple Walk meets Snyder Brook. There are several shallow pools for wading here.

The next waterfall of your journey is Salroc Falls, a two-part waterfall. Lower Salroc Falls consists of many small cascades, a long slide, and, finally, a short plunge into a large, cold, and clear pool. Upper Salroc Falls is a few feet upstream. Here, Snyder Brook horsetails down moss-covered rocks and then slides down into a calm pool. Be sure to rock-hop across the brook to the table rock in front of the falls for the best view of the falls and the greatest chance for a fine photograph.

Tama Falls, the third waterfall of the trip, is just upstream from Salroc Falls. The final fall on Snyder Brook to be described here, Tama Falls is a 40-foot-tall combination of a block and a set of steep cascades. The view from the trail is not sufficient for this waterfall. Be sure to follow one of several paths down the riverbank to the brook. From here, you witness a much more visually appealing waterfall, and as an added bonus, very often you can find yourself hidden from the crowded trail above.

Cold Brook Falls marks the last stop of the hike, yet is the first and only waterfall of Cold Brook on this trip. Cold Brook crashes down a wide terraced wall 30 feet tall into a dark pool. Although there are several modest swimming holes at the other falls of this trip, swimming is prohibited at Cold Brook Falls, as the water is Randolph's water supply.

In addition to Gordon, Salroc, Tama, and Cold Brook Falls, over half a dozen other waterfalls can be found farther up the trails that travel parallel to Cold Brook and Snyder Brook on the way to Mt. Madison and Mt. Adams. Although these are not described in this guide, many of these falls are quite impressive and provide excellent challenges for experienced hikers. For those interested, this route is described more comprehensively in Bolnick's *Waterfalls of the White Mountains*. Waterfalls to be found higher on the mountainside include Canyon Fall, Duck Fall, Chandler Fall, Marian Fall, Spur Brook Fall, Mossy Fall, Salmacis Fall, and Thorndike Fall. Some of these are lost waterfalls in that they are seldom visited and currently require bushwhacks of varying degrees of difficulty.

TRAIL INFORMATION The trail begins at the center of the large parking lot for Appalachia. Follow the path beyond the trail information boards, cross the remnants of a set of railroad tracks, and arrive at the Air Line junction. The Air Line Trail will continue right, but you must continue straight onto Valley Way for a short distance until you reach a sign for the MAPLE WALK. At this junction, the Valley Way Trail forks right and the Maple Walk forks left. Veer left and continue along the Maple Walk until you reach Snyder Brook and several trail signs.

To reach Gordon Falls, you will need to proceed downstream 100 feet where the falls are marked with a small white sign. After visiting Gordon Falls, backtrack 100 feet upstream to the junction you were just at. From here, proceed upstream on the Fallsway Trail, which is marked with a sign stating FALLSWAY TOWARD TAMA FALL. Marked yellow, the Fallsway Trail will lead you 0.25 mile to Lower and Upper Salroc Falls (both of which are marked with small signs). After passing Upper Salroc Falls, continue climbing along the Fallsway for about 200 feet and you will reach another junction. Turn left uphill on Valley Way and in less than 100 feet fork left onto the Tama Fall Loop and Tama Falls will be a short distance ahead, not marked by a sign.

After visiting Tama Fall, return back to the junction you were just at and this time, fork left onto the Valley Way Trail. The right fork will lead you back to Salroc and Gordon Falls. Travel along the blue-blazed Valley Way Trail for 0.3 mile and take a left onto the Sylvan Way. The sign for this trail is currently placed on a tree behind you, so be sure to stop at each trail junction to spot the inconspicuous trail signs. Continue on the yellow-blazed Sylvan Way, crossing two very skinny brooks and hiking straight through two irrelevant trail junctions. Soon, you will reach Cold Brook and the last waterfall of the trip will be just to your left, a few feet upstream.

To get back to the parking lot from Cold Brook Falls, follow the yellow-blazed trail directly downstream (do not cross Cold Brook at any time). In

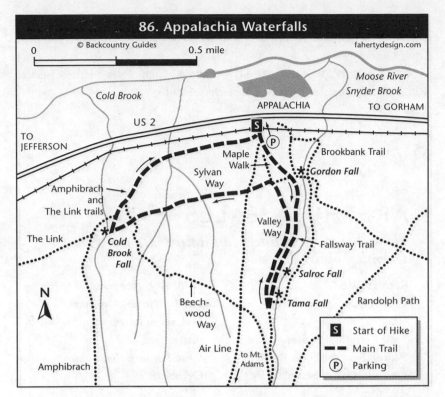

86. Appalachia Waterfalls

0   © Backcountry Guides   0.5 mile   fahertydesign.com

Moose River
Snyder Brook
Cold Brook
APPALACHIA
TO GORHAM
US 2
TO JEFFERSON
Maple Walk
Brookbank Trail
Gordon Fall
Sylvan Way
Amphibrach and The Link trails
Valley Way
The Link
Fallsway Trail
Cold Brook Fall
Salroc Fall
N
Beech-wood Way
Tama Fall
Randolph Path
Air Line
to Mt. Adams
Amphibrach

S	Start of Hike
– – –	Main Trail
P	Parking

a few seconds you will reach an interestingly constructed bridge on your left, half wooden, half stone. Instead of crossing the bridge, take a right turn onto the Amphibrach Trail. This trail will parallel the highway, which you will only be able to hear but not see. Be sure to stay on the yellow-blazed Amphibrach trail as there are some private property trails that merge on this section of the trail. If you follow the white signs and arrows pointing the way, you are sure to keep to the correct path. After a 15-minute trek along the Amphibrach Trail, you will reach a T-junction. Take a left and a minute later take another left onto the Valley Way Trail. The parking lot is just ahead and the 2.6-mile loop will be completed.

SPECIAL NOTE The trails used to visit the four waterfalls of Appalachia are located in one of the most complex and confusing trail networks we have found in our travels. For this reason, we urge you to purchase the *AMC White Mountain Guide* (28th edition), which contains an excellent trail map for this area.

DIRECTIONS From the junction of US 2 and NH 16 in Gorham, take US 2 west for 4.5 miles and take a left into a large parking lot, marked with a sign for APPALACHIA and several US Forest Service HIKING signs. This parking area is 0.8 mile past the Pinkham B Road (which leads to Dolly

Copp Campground and several other waterfalls described in this book) and 2.1 miles east of Lowe's Store on US 2. *To get to Gorham,* take NH 16 north from Conway.

OTHER WATERFALLS NEARBY Mossy Glen, Falls on the Howker Ridge Path, Triple Falls, Giant Falls, Dryad Fall

87

〜

ARETHUSA FALLS

Harts Location, White Mountain National Forest, Carroll County

Rating: 5.0/5.0

Type: Plunge

Height: 160 feet

Trail Length: 1.5 miles

Water Source: Bemis Brook

Altitude Gain/Loss: +900 feet, -100 feet

Difficulty: Moderate

Hiking Time: 60 minutes

DeLorme Atlas: Page 44, F-4 (marked)

Best Time to Visit: May to October

THE FALLS (HIGHLY RECOMMENDED) Discounting the seasonal waterfalls, our research indicates that Arethusa Falls is the single longest drop in New England. However, its height is of great controversy. We have come across sources stating that Arethusa is anywhere from 125 feet tall to "well over 200 feet in height." Several other sources believe the falls to be about 160 feet, with which we agree.

This multi-tiered plunge appears to fall from the sky. From the trail and the bottom viewpoints, you cannot see anything above the falls, aside from a few trees on the side of the river. What you do see is a peaceful and heavenly expression of Bemis Brook. The streams of water range from extremely powerful during high-water runoff times to hundreds of trickles during prolonged droughts. The gracefulness of the falls for most of the summer is what makes this waterfall a must-visit.

Over the years, we have seen many inexperienced hikers struggle on the trail just to have the chance to see Arethusa Falls. They may be exhausted along the trail, but we have never seen anything short of a relieved smile at the waterfall. Everyone appears deeply content when they finally reach the falls. Arethusa Falls becomes, in a nutshell, a job well done for all who witness its elegant beauty. This is also one waterfall you will not want to miss during peak fall foliage.

TRAIL INFORMATION Start your hike by crossing a set of railroad tracks and you should notice a signed trailhead to the left of a private residence. The blue-marked Arethusa Falls Trail will lead you all the way to Arethusa Falls. About 0.1 mile after entering the woods, the Bemis Brook Trail will fork left and loop you past Fawn Pool, Coliseum Falls, and Bemis Brook Falls. This yellow blazed-trail rejoins the trail to Arethusa Falls about 0.5 mile from the parking area, so it is worth your while to take this route either on the way to Arethusa Falls or on the way back down. Given that this trail is more difficult than the Arethusa Falls Trail, we both agreed that hiking up the Bemis Brook Trail and using the Arethusa Falls Trail to return to the parking area was the best approach to visiting these additional falls.

Just after the Bemis Brook Trail rejoins the Arethusa Falls Trail, you will need to turn right to continue. The trail will swing left soon after. About 1.0 mile into the hike, you will cross two bridges; the first one is named the Kingsway Bridge. Once you are within 0.2 mile of the falls, you will reach a junction with the Arethusa-Ripley Falls Trail. A sign points left toward Arethusa Falls. Take this left and you will soon reach the falls.

Although recently re-routed in order to avoid the more difficult terrain found along the edge of Bemis Brook, the Arethusa Falls Trail can still have sections of muddy ground to cross, largely depending on the season. We have also noticed that ice can remain on this trail deep into spring. This hike requires about 60 minutes of walking in each direction, but the reward of spectacular Arethusa Falls is sure to justify such efforts.

It is also possible for strong hikers to connect Arethusa Falls with Ripley Falls, another outstanding Crawford Notch attraction, as part of a long loop. Although Ripley Falls can be reached by a much shorter and easier trail stemming from US 302 (see Ripley Falls chapter), this can make for an excellent full-day journey in the mountains. If you would like to do this loop, backtrack to the junction with the Arethusa-Ripley Falls Trail. Follow the Arethusa-Ripley Falls Trail north for 2.3 miles (making sure to take a left after 1.1 miles at a junction with the Frankenstein Cliff Trail) and you will arrive at the base of Ripley Falls after crossing Avalanche Brook. To return to your car, return 1.5 miles to the junction of the Arethusa-Ripley Falls Trail and the Frankenstein Cliff Trail. Take a left onto the Frankenstein Cliff Trail and follow this moderately difficult trail 2.1 miles, passing several excellent viewpoints along the way, back to a parking lot on Arethusa Falls Road. You will need to hike back up the short road if you parked at its end. The total distance of this loop is approximately 7.3 miles with approximately 2,250 feet of cumulative elevation gain (and loss).

DIRECTIONS From the junction of US 302 and NH 16 in the section of Bartlett known as Glen, take US 302 west for 14.5 miles. Turn left onto Arethusa Falls Road, drive past the first parking lot on the left, and continue up the hill to the parking lot at the end of the road. Arethusa Falls Road is 3.3 miles east of the Willey House Historical Site on US 302. If the parking lot at the end of the road is full, there is additional parking in the lot just off US 302. *To get to Glen,* take NH 16 north from Conway.

OTHER WATERFALLS NEARBY Ripley Falls, Nancy Cascades, Kedron Flume, Silver Cascade, Flume Cascade

88

BASIN TRAIL CASCADES

Beans Purchase, White Mountain National Forest, Coos County

Rating: 4.0/5.0

Type: Horsetail and cascades

Height: 30 feet (left waterfall), 20 feet (right waterfall)

Trail Length: 1.3 miles

Water Source: Blue Brook

Altitude Gain/Loss: +200 feet

Difficulty: Easy side of moderate

Hiking Time: 35 minutes

DeLorme Atlas: Page 45, A-12 (unmarked)

Best Time to Visit: May to October

THE FALLS We had the pleasant surprise of discovering two waterfalls merging into one brook along this hike. As we arrived at the small, sandy beach viewing area, we saw a beautiful wide horsetail to our right about 20 feet high. This waterfall was split into two sections and a hidden pool was in between the two segments.

As you turn your head to look around the area you see another 30-foot waterfall to your left. This cascade cuts its way through the rock face down to a lime green pool below. The water is quite cool in temperature as these two waterfalls are constantly oscillating the water farther down the brook. This is definitely a nice spot to take a break and cool off if you are continuing your hike deeper into the Wild River Wilderness.

TRAIL INFORMATION From the parking area, begin hiking on the Basin Trail, which is not to be confused with the nearby Basin Rim Trail. After 0.3 mile of hiking the Basin Trail along a logging road, you will need to fork left to follow a yellow-blazed path. From here, the remaining 1.0 mile on the trail will be very muddy at times, and even the helpful wooden walkways that are here to assist you are at times covered in swampy waters. About 1.3 miles from the parking area, the trail will cross the brook below the falls.

Upon inspection of a trail map, you may be tempted to continue along the Basin Trail to Hermit Falls. This is certainly a feasible plan for strong hikers, but it will require two substantial climbs over the pass between Mt. Meader and West Royce Mountain; once to reach Hermit Falls and again on the return hike back to your original trailhead. A car-spot between both trailheads of the Basin Trail (the other being off ME 113) would eliminate the return climb. Walking between the two trailheads is inadvisable as the distance is considerable.

DIRECTIONS From the junction of ME 113 and US 302 in Fryeburg, Maine, take ME 113 north for 27 miles and take a left onto Wild River Road, which leads to the Wild River Campground. Take note that during our visit in 2009, this road was unmarked but still obvious. Drive on Wild River Road for 5.5 miles and turn left into the parking area for the Basin Trail. Do not get confused by another parking area along Wild River Road for the Basin Rim Trail. This is not the trail that you need. *To get to Fryeburg,* take NH 113 east from NH 16 in Conway, New Hampshire into Maine.

OTHER WATERFALLS NEARBY Kees Falls (ME), Dryad Fall, Giant Falls

89

BEAVER BROOK CASCADES
Woodstock, White Mountain National Forest, Grafton County

Rating: 4.5/5.0

Type: Plunges, horsetails, cascades and slides

Height: Approximately 600-foot total drop

Trail Length: To the lower falls, 0.4 mile; to the upper falls, 1.1 miles

Water Source: Beaver Brook

Altitude Gain/Loss: +1,200 feet to the upper falls

Difficulty: Moderate side of difficult

Hiking Time: 20 minutes to lower falls; 60 min to upper falls

DeLorme Atlas: Page 43, I-9 (marked as Beaver Brook Trail)

Best Time to Visit: May to October

THE FALLS (HIGHLY RECOMMENDED) The Beaver Brook Trail, a challenging section of the Appalachian Trail, runs past set after set of unnamed cascades as it climbs several thousand feet to its termination at the summit of 4,223-foot-tall Mt. Moosilauke. As you climb this steep and moderately difficult trail, the cascades seem to become more impressive, with the final cascade being our favorite. Nearly every classification of waterfall is represented along this chain of cascades, including horsetails, plunges, cascades, and slides. It is for this reason, and more, that we highly recommend this hike.

With the right combination of good weather, physical ability, and time, you should also considering venturing farther up the Beaver Brook Trail to the heavily windblown summit of Mt. Moosilauke, where outstanding 360-degree views await you. This 8-mile round trip hike is a true White Mountains classic.

TRAIL INFORMATION Enter the woods behind the White Mountain National Forest billboard and the parking fee pay station. Begin following the white-blazed Beaver Brook Trail, which is a rugged, steep stretch of the Appalachian Trail. About 0.1 mile from the parking area, you must cross over Beaver Brook twice over solidly constructed footbridges. Continue along the trail for 0.3 mile to the bottom of the first falls. Once you reach these first falls, do not give up on this killer energy climb; more falls, with wonderfully differing character lie farther ahead. Keep hiking uphill, very steeply at times, for as long as you are comfortable. Some of the most impressive cascades are those at the highest elevation. The cascades end 1.1 miles from the parking area.

The entire trail is quite a calorie-burner. In just over a mile of hiking, you gain over 1,200 feet of altitude. This may sound too difficult for your tastes, but as long as you do not attempt the hike in early spring, when the trail is soaked with waterfall mist and snow runoff, your trip to this waterfall should be manageable, especially to those familiar with the challenging terrain of the White Mountains.

SPECIAL NOTE Instead of just visiting the lovely cascades on Beaver Brook, venture to the summit of Mt. Moosilauke, where outstanding views of New Hampshire, Vermont, even New York on clear days, can be enjoyed.

Expect rugged, steep terrain for the entire 3.8 miles from the trailhead to the 360-degree views of the 4,802-foot-tall mountaintop. The altitude gain is 3,100 feet and the expected round-trip time is about six hours for the average hiker. The final stretch of the trail is above treeline, meaning you will be exposed to potential weather hazards any time of the year, including the notoriously strong wind currents. This is a large and demanding mountain that should only be climbed during good-to-great weather conditions.

DIRECTIONS From I-93 in North Woodstock, take exit 32. Follow NH 112 west. Continue traveling on NH 112 west for 6.0 miles beyond the US 3 and NH 112 junction. Pull into the parking lot marked with a TRAIL-HEAD PARKING sign on your left. The parking lot is 0.4 mile west of the Lost River Reservation. *To get to North Woodstock,* take I-93 north from Concord, or I-93 south from Franconia.

OTHER WATERFALLS NEARBY Paradise Falls; Agassiz Basin; Swift-water Falls, Bath; Georgiana Falls; Falls on the Flume–Pool Loop

90

BEAVER BROOK FALLS, COLEBROOK

Colebrook, Beaver Brook Falls Natural Area, Coos County

Rating: 4.5/5.0
Type: Horsetail
Height: 80-foot total drop
Trail Length: Roadside
Water Source: Beaver Brook
Altitude Gain/Loss: None

Difficulty: Easy
Hiking Time: Not applicable
DeLorme Atlas: Page 50, A-2
(marked as Beaver Brook Falls
Wayside Park)
Best Time to Visit: May to June

THE FALLS (HIGHLY RECOMMENDED) As you are driving along NH 145 past the center of the town in Colebrook, you will travel up and down gently rolling hills, although nothing of significant elevation change. The land is nearly flat and it is difficult to imagine that a waterfall over 80 feet in height could be located here. Just as you come around a bend in the road, you look to your right and you are instantly mesmerized by the sheer size of the dribbling horsetails at Beaver Brook Falls.

Also surprising is the number of visitors to a waterfall located in northern New Hampshire, well past the White Mountain National Forest region and within close range of the Canadian border. The area is popular enough that the state has declared it as an official Scenic Area and has thus equipped the park with several covered picnic tables and bathrooms.

TRAIL INFORMATION To view this waterfall, you have the option of sitting in your car, relaxing at the picnic tables, or taking a short gravel trail closer to the falls. The short gravel trail brings you to a tilted head view at the base of the falls. There are steep, loose dirt trails that climb the falls on both sides, but this is very dangerous and is therefore discouraged.

DIRECTIONS From the junction of NH 145 and US 3 in Colebrook, take NH 145 north for 2.4 miles, and the parking lot will be on the right. The falls can be easily seen from the road. *To get to Colebrook,* take US 3 north from Lincoln.

OTHER WATERFALLS NEARBY Dixville Flume, Huntington Cascades, Pond Brook Falls

91

BEAVER BROOK FALLS, KEENE
Keene, Cheshire County

Rating: 3.0/5.0
Type: Horsetail and cascades
Height: 12-foot total drop
Trail Length: 0.6 mile
Water Source: Beaver Brook
Altitude Gain/Loss: +50 feet

Difficulty: Easy to top of falls; moderate to base of falls
Hiking Time: 15 minutes
DeLorme Atlas: Page 19, B-12 (unmarked)
Best Time to Visit: Year-round

THE FALLS Beaver Brook Falls is a double plunge that will be barely visible to casual visitors. The view that earns this waterfall its recommended rating requires a short bushwhack downstream. From the edge of the brook, you will clearly see that the lower plunge is 6 feet wide and 12 feet high. The mossy green surroundings, thick tree cover, and the dark gorge that the falls pass through create challenges to the photographer but add to the rich atmosphere of the location. Please note the falls themselves are not visible from the trail above; only the sound of rushing water and a gentle stream above make you aware that there is something worthy of note below.

TRAIL INFORMATION The trail to Beaver Brook Falls is actually an old highway that has been gated off for the walking pleasure of locals and visitors of the falls. From the parking area, walk past the gate and continue up an old paved road for 0.6 mile and the falls will peek through the woods on your right. When you view the falls from above, you are actually standing in an overgrown highway overlook that was intended for parking purposes when the road was drivable. Given that the trail is an old highway, it is paved with faded yellow lines and guardrails along the side and is therefore handicap accessible, although viewing the falls is a bit more difficult.

There is no official path to the base of the falls, but the best way to do so is to backtrack about 40 feet on the road and scramble down the riverbank. Take caution, though, as the embankment is steep and slippery. There is a memorial located here, and it is a lesson of how the trail came to be. Per the memorial: BEAVER BROOK CANYON WAS DONATED TO THE CITY OF KEENE IN 1969 BY DR. JAMES AND MRS. RUTH WESTON BALLOU. IT PROVIDED A MAJOR STEP IN THE CITY'S PRESERVATION OF SCENIC CONSERVATION LAND.

DIRECTIONS From the northern junction of NH 9, NH 10, and NH 12 in Keene, take the combined NH 9 east and NH 10 north for 1.3 miles and take the Washington Street exit off the highway. Follow Washington Street south for 0.3 mile and take a left onto Concord Road. Immediately thereafter, take a left onto Washington Street Ext. Follow this road for 0.25 mile to its end, marked with a white gate and a sign for BEAVER BROOK FALLS.

OTHER WATERFALLS NEARBY Chesterfield Gorge

Beaver Brook Falls, Keene

92

~

BEECHER AND PEARL CASCADES

Bethlehem, White Mountain National Forest, Grafton County

Rating: 3.5/5.0

Type: Horsetail, cascades, and a fan

Height: Beecher Cascade is 35 feet; Pearl Cascade is 20 feet

Trail Length: To Beecher Cascade, 0.4 mile; to Pearl Cascade, 0.5 mile

Water Source: Crawford Brook

Altitude Gain/Loss: +200 feet to Pearl Cascade

Difficulty: Easy

Hiking Time: 20 minutes

DeLorme Atlas: Page 44, C-3 (unmarked)

Best Time to Visit: May to October

THE FALLS Beecher and Pearl Cascades are two falls located on Crawford Brook, a mountain steam that drains the waters of Mt. Field. The first fall, Beecher Cascade, a 35-foot horsetail hidden under heavy tree cover, is encompassed by gorge walls of pink brown Conway granite. Opportunities for exploring and photography are extremely limited at Beecher Cascade as the water has carved itself a path into the rock face over the years. Make sure to hike a few hundred feet farther up the trail to Pearl Cascade, a 20-foot-tall fan. Below the fan, water enters a gorge and becomes trapped in a jagged-edged pothole, creating one of the most delightful small swimming pools in the White Mountains. About 4 to 5 feet in depth, this colorful pool—with hues of brown, pink, yellow, green, and black—is the perfect cool refreshing treat for two or three people.

TRAIL INFORMATION The trail to both falls begins across the railroad tracks behind the Crawford Depot Station at the AMC's Highland Center. After entering the woods, you will reach a billboard and a trail junction. The trail to the left climbs Mt. Willard, and is one of the best short hikes in the White Mountains. To reach the falls, continue straight about 200 feet farther and take a left onto the Cascade Loop Trail. About 100 feet up the loop trail, take a left at the white sign for BEECHER CASCADE. This waterfall will be just ahead, visible through a thick growth of trees. If you keep hiking beyond Beecher Cascade you will reconnect with the Cascade Loop Trail. To see Pearl Cascade, it is instead recommended that you turn around after viewing Beecher Cascade and continue climbing on the Cascade Loop Trail an additional 0.1 mile and you will reach a white sign for PEARL CASCADE. Take a left and follow a short path down to the brook. Scramble up the brook a few feet for the best view of the falls and to discover a lovely wading spot.

If you wish to extend your hike, consider continuing up to the summit of Mt. Avalon and Mt. Field. To do this, keep on climbing to the end of the Cascade Loop. The Avalon Trail will continue climbing and reward you with outstanding views at each of these fine summits.

DIRECTIONS From the junction of US 302 and NH 16 in the section of Bartlett known as Glen, take US 302 west for 20.5 miles and take a left into the AMC's Highland Center at Crawford Notch. The AMC's Highland Center at Crawford Notch is 0.3 mile west of the sign marking the CRAWFORD NOTCH STATE PARK boundary and 0.3 mile east of Mt. Clinton Road. *To get to Glen,* take NH 16 north from Conway.

OTHER WATERFALLS NEARBY Gibbs Falls, Flume Cascade, Silver Cascade, Kedron Flume, Ripley Falls, Arethusa Falls

93

BEEDE FALLS
Sandwich, Sandwich Notch Park, Carroll County

Rating: 4.5/5.0
Type: Horsetail and small plunge
Height: 35-foot total drop
Trail Length: 0.2 mile
Water Source: Bearcamp River
Altitude Gain/Loss: -30 feet

Difficulty: Easy
Hiking Time: 5 minutes
DeLorme Atlas: Page 40, F-2
(marked)
Best Time to Visit: May to October

THE FALLS (HIGHLY RECOMMENDED) What makes this waterfall unique and worthy of its rating is the fun outdoors experience you get while visiting. There is a large, clean, and sandy pool perfect for taking a dip on a hot day. The slow-moving water circles around the pool and then escapes into the lazy river below. This is an excellent natural playground for children.

The waterfall itself is a 35-foot-wide horsetail cascading down a smooth rock face before plunging into a 50-foot-wide pool below. The pool is calf- to knee-deep and it is possible to squeeze behind the falls. The pool is drained by two lazy rivers that merge back together shortly downstream,

Beede Falls

where more small pools await you. The trees are spaced wide enough apart that exploration up and downstream is simple and fun. Allot several hours to truly enjoy this park.

TRAIL INFORMATION From the parking area, head downhill on the Bearcamp River Trail, which has yellow blazes. The falls are only an easy and flat five-minute walk away. Other than a few roots and a few short sections of mud after rainstorms, this trail provides the ease of access for locals to bring a picnic to enjoy the surrounding area of the falls. We even saw children playing in water tubes during one visit. There are additional smaller waterfalls a short distance upstream of the main falls to explore as well.

DIRECTIONS From I-93 in Ashland, take exit 24. Take the combined highway US 3 south and NH 25 east into Holderness. In Holderness, take a left onto NH 113 north. Follow NH 113 north for 11.6 miles and take a left onto Grove Street when you reach Center Sandwich and just before the junction of NH 113 and NH 119. Follow Grove Street for 0.4 mile and bear left as the road turns into Diamond Ledge Road. Follow Diamond Ledge Road for 2.0 miles and you will reach a fork. You will want to fork left and travel on Sandwich Notch Road for 0.7 mile, where there will be a large parking area on your right. Take note that Sandwich Notch Road is a dirt road that is not maintained during the winter. It should be passable by the average car from late May until early October, though.

OTHER WATERFALLS NEARBY Rainbow Falls, Campton Falls, Fall of Song

94

BRICKETT FALLS
Chatham, White Mountain National Forest, Carroll County

Rating: 4.0/5.0

Type: Horsetails, cascades and slides

Height: Tallest falls is 8 feet; 75-foot total drop

Trail Length: 1.1 miles

Water Source: Mill Brook

Altitude Gain/Loss: +100 feet

Difficulty: Easy

Hiking Time: 30 minutes

DeLorme Atlas: Page 45, B-12 (marked)

Best Time to Visit: May to June

THE FALLS As we hiked to this waterfall we were reminded of Step Falls in Maine. Although not as grand, there are many similarities. This waterfall consists of short horsetails and slides that snake their way around ledges and rocks in the riverbed. There are lots of refreshing wading areas, and the potential to sit in some of the slides. High water levels are optimal at these falls, so time your visit for the springtime.

To add to the fun, be sure to continue along the Mt. Meader Trail to ledges found just below the summit of Mt. Meader. There are great views of Evans Notch that await your visit here.

TRAIL INFORMATION Start your trip to Brickett Falls by hiking up a private logging road that begins near the parking area. This road is open to hikers but it is not very well marked. After only 200 feet, you will need to fork left to stay on the primary logging road. As you continue walking along the road, you will notice other roads and trails spurring off on each side. Continue straight through each of these junctions to stay on the correct route. As you continue hiking you will begin to see yellow blazes. The trail will narrow and you will pass a WHITE MOUNTAIN NATIONAL FOREST sign, and a few feet later, a MT. MEADER TRAIL sign. At 0.1 mile past this sign, you will reach another junction where the Mt. Meader Trail continues straight and a path heads left at a sign for BRICKETT FALLS. Take this left and follow the path for 0.1 mile to the falls. A yellow blaze in the form of a T signifies the end of the trail.

DIRECTIONS From the junction of ME 113 and US 302 in Fryeburg, Maine, take ME 113 north for 13 miles and park on the right side of the road only 10 feet after you pass Meader Road on the left. The Mt. Meader Trail begins directly across the street from the parking area. The trail sign is affixed to a telephone pole and only visible when heading southbound on ME 113. *To get to Fryeburg,* take NH 113 east from NH 16 in Conway, New Hampshire into Maine.

OTHER WATERFALLS NEARBY Eagle Cascade, Rattlesnake Flume and Pool (ME), Hermit Falls, Mad River Falls (ME), Bickford Slides (ME), Kees Falls (ME)

95

BRIDAL VEIL FALLS

Franconia, White Mountain National Forest, Grafton County

Rating: 4.5/5.0

Type: Plunge and slides

Height: 80-foot total drop

Trail Length: 2.5 miles

Water Source: Coppermine Brook

Altitude Gain/Loss: +1,100 feet

Difficulty: Moderate

Hiking Time: 1 hour, 45 minutes

DeLorme Atlas: Page 43, E-10 (marked)

Best Time to Visit: May to October

THE FALLS (HIGHLY RECOMMENDED) Many visitors may feel they have been to this waterfall before. In actuality, it is one of the most commonly photographed waterfalls in the White Mountain National Forest. Pictures of Bridal Veil Falls are scattered across dozens of publications pertaining to the attractions of this area. Many of these publications hold high praise for this scenic waterfall, and they have good reason to.

The major attraction of Bridal Veil Falls is the 30-foot-tall main plunge that has the characteristics of a bride's veil. Water elegantly flows at a right angle down to a small pool below. Below this plunge is a large waterslide over flat, polished granite.

With so many other natural attractions in the National Forest with shorter and easier trails, many will be turned off by the 5-mile round trip hike that Bridal Veil Falls requires. We encourage you to undertake this invigorating hike; Bridal Veil Falls is an extra special place to relax, sunbathe, and of course, have a picnic.

For those looking for an exciting challenge, there are two rumored waterfalls upstream: Holden Falls and Noble Falls. Access to these smaller and likely less impressive falls is likely to be extremely difficult as there is no trail and the woods are rumored to be quite thick.

TRAIL INFORMATION From the parking pull-off on Coppermine Road, continue farther along the road on foot for about 0.4 mile until you reach a US Forest Service HIKER sign. Take a left off the road and continue up this yellow-blazed trail all the way to the falls. Although the altitude gain is gradual, the nearly continuous incline of this trail makes a visit to these falls a demanding one for some. The trail does become slightly more steep and difficult as you near the falls, especially if you choose to advance beyond the first waterslide to the bridal-veil plunge. This is moderately difficult to do, but the falls are much more intimate and camera-friendly up close.

DIRECTIONS From Lincoln, take I-93 north to Franconia. Take exit 38 for Franconia/Sugar Hill. At the end of the off-ramp, take a left and follow signs toward NH 116. Continue straight and you will begin to travel on NH 116. Follow NH 116 south for 3.4 miles and take a left onto Coppermine Road. Continue up Coppermine Road and park on the left shoulder of the road just before the sign that states NO PARKING BEYOND THIS POINT.

Bridal Veil Falls

OTHER WATERFALLS NEARBY Falls on the Falling Waters Trail, Falls on the Basin-Cascades Trail, Falls on the Flume–Pool Loop, Swiftwater Falls, Bath

96

~

CAMPTON FALLS
Campton, Grafton County

Rating: 3.5/5.0

Type: Block

Height: 15 feet

Trail Length: Less than 0.1 mile

Water Source: Beebe River

Altitude Gain/Loss: -35 feet

Difficulty: Moderate side of difficult

Hiking Time: Negligible

DeLorme Atlas: Page 39, F-12 (unmarked)

Best Time to Visit: April through November

THE FALLS Campton Falls is a traditional block waterfall on the Beebe River. Within a backdrop of pine and hemlock trees, Campton Falls evokes feelings of ruggedness and seclusion, all despite being only about 50 feet from the road.

Catch this waterfall if you are ever in the Campton area. You should be surprised to see such a stout and powerful waterfall here, as the road is rather flat and the falls cannot be seen from the road. When you do reach the waterfall, observe the two sounds emanating from the waterfall; the crash of the block and the gurgling and splashing of the small cascades downstream.

TRAIL INFORMATION The trail begins at the north end of the small parking area. Follow this short trail with caution, as it is slippery and narrow at times. There is also a 3-foot-tall cement wall to climb down to reach the base of the falls. Be aware that the trail has greatly succumbed to erosion and access has been getting progressively more difficult over the years. If the trail erodes any further, we may consider removing this waterfall from future editions of this guide—at least until safer access becomes available.

DIRECTIONS From Plymouth, take I-93 north to exit 28 in Campton. Turn onto NH 49 west, heading toward Waterville Valley. Soon you will reach the junction of NH 49 and NH 175. Take a right onto NH 175 south and continue for 2.9 miles, where the unmarked dirt parking area can be found on the left.

OTHER WATERFALLS NEARBY Waterville Cascades, Beede Falls, Rainbow Falls

97

~

CHAMPNEY FALLS

Albany, White Mountain National Forest, Carroll County

Rating: 3.5/5.0

Type: Plunges, horsetails and cascades

Height: 70-foot total drop

Trail Length: 1.7 miles

Water Source: Champney Brook

Altitude Gain/Loss: +600 feet

Difficulty: Easy side of moderate to the initial falls; moderate to top of falls

Hiking Time: 1 hour, 30 minutes

DeLorme Atlas: Page 44, K-6 (unmarked)

Best Time to Visit: May to October

THE FALLS With waterfalls that are as well known as Champney Falls, finding historical information comes with ease. At the trailhead, you will have the pleasure of reading an informative sign stating that these particular falls were named after Benjamin Champney, a famous White Mountains landscape painter during the second half of the 19th century. He romanticized many nearby waterfalls, including Glen Ellis Falls, Ripley Falls, and Thompson Falls.

Champney Falls is broken into several major sections. The first drop you approach is the lower falls and this is 10 feet wide with a 20-foot drop. Please note that this width does depend on the season and the earlier you visit in the springtime, the wider the falls will be. Above this plunge is an impressive 60-foot drop made up of a series of cascades, plunges, and a 12-foot horsetail. Comparatively speaking, this waterfall is less rewarding than others, considering the efforts needed to get there. Perhaps the best way to visit the falls is to enjoy them as a break on a day-trip up to the rocky and open summit of Mt. Chocorua.

TRAIL INFORMATION The trailhead begins on the left end of the parking lot when facing the woods. Start your journey to the falls by hiking 0.1 mile into the woods along the Champney Falls Trail, where you will come to a junction in which the Bolles Trail splits off to the right. Continue straight and keep climbing along the Champney Falls Trail. After passing a few arrow signs, which can be difficult to spot, you will reach a trail junction. Take a left onto the loop trail that guides you past Pitcher Falls and Champney Falls. Soon after turning onto the loop, you will see a series of seasonal plunges to the left. Hike farther upstream from this point and you will arrive at Pitcher Falls first, identifiable by larger cascades than what you have seen up to this point, along with several small pools.

The trail climbs steeply above Pitcher Falls for a short distance to Champney Falls. Once you arrive at Champney Falls, the trail ascends dramatically alongside the waterfall via stone steps before it reconnects back with the Champney Falls Trail at the end of the loop. From this junction above the falls, you can either head down 1.7 miles to the parking lot or continue to the summit of Chocorua, 2.1 miles and 1,600 feet of elevation gain away.

DIRECTIONS From the junction of NH 112 and NH 16 in Conway, take NH 112 (the Kancamagus Highway) west for 10.6 miles and the marked parking area will be on your left. If you are traveling from I-93 in Lincoln, take exit 32 and follow NH 112 east for 24.6 miles and the parking area will be on your right. A sign marks the parking area for CHAMPNEY FALLS TRAIL. This parking area is 1.6 miles west of the Rocky Gorge Scenic Area and 1.6 miles east of Bear Notch Road.

Please be aware that this trailhead is part of the White Mountain National Forest parking fee program. The fee was $3 in 2009 but there is currently a proposal in review to raise this amount to $5.

OTHER WATERFALLS NEARBY Rocky Gorge, Lower Falls, Sabbaday Falls

98

~

CHESTERFIELD GORGE

Chesterfield, Chesterfield Gorge State Wayside Area, Cheshire County

Rating: 2.5/5.0

Type: Horsetails, cascades, slides and small plunges

Height: Tallest falls is 18 feet; 120-foot total drop

Trail Length: 0.7-mile loop

Water Source: Wilde Brook

Altitude Gain/Loss: -200 feet, +200 feet

Difficulty: Easy side of moderate

Hiking Time: 30 minutes

DeLorme Atlas: Page 19, D-9 (marked)

Best Time to Visit: May to October

THE FALLS The falls at Chesterfield Gorge are not nearly as impressive as the height of the gorge itself. It is a geological wonder that just happens to have a series of horsetails, cascades, slides, and plunges in its midst. The upper falls, a 10-foot-tall narrow plunge, is at first seen from a bridge at the head of the gorge. Continuing downstream you will find the middle falls, a series of small cascades, with no particular cascade really distinguishing itself as more scenic than another. The lower falls are the most impressive of the lot; a 20-foot horsetail falling into a murky, dark pool below.

The best views on this loop are along the rim of the gorge that is closest to the road. If you are like most hikers here, you will return to your vehicle along this side of the gorge. On the return trip, we rediscovered what we originally thought was an insignificant cascade from the opposite side of the gorge. Directly in front of us now was a 75-foot horsetail barreling down through the gorge—instantly earning Chesterfield Gorge a high enough rating for placement within this guide. We believe your experience will be similar, unless you visit in the early spring before trees obscure some of the views from the rim of the gorge.

TRAIL INFORMATION From the parking area, bear right and head down the obvious red-blazed trail marked with a sign for the GORGE TRAIL. You will pass by a few picnic tables and about 200 feet from the road, take a left and begin following a red-blazed trail. About 0.2 mile farther down the trail, you will cross a wooden bridge over the brook. Only 100 feet farther,

Chesterfield Gorge

continue hiking downstream along a chain-link fence past several series of falls and cascades. About 0.4 mile from the road, the trail will cross back over the brook. Climb back upstream on the opposite side of the brook and continue straight once you reach the top of the falls, to stay on the path that will lead you back to the parking area.

This loop trail makes off-trail exploration unnecessary as it offers views from every side and aspect of the gorge. Well-maintained bridges and fences provide the safety necessary for viewing such a steep gorge; they also give you something to hold on to when catching your breath over the hilly terrain.

DIRECTIONS From the southern junction of NH 9, NH 10, and NH 12 in Keene, take NH 9 west. Follow NH 9 west for 5.7 miles toward Vermont and take a right into the signed CHESTERFIELD GORGE STATE WAYSIDE AREA. The parking area is 2.0 miles beyond the CHESTERFIELD TOWN LINE sign on NH 9.

OTHER WATERFALLS NEARBY Beaver Brook Falls, Keene, Jelly Mill Falls (VT)

99

CRYSTAL CASCADE

Pinkham's Grant, White Mountain National Forest, Coos County

Rating: 5.0/5.0
Type: Horsetails and a block
Height: 100-foot total drop
Trail Length: 0.3 mile
Water Source: Ellis River
Altitude Gain/Loss: +250 feet

Difficulty: Easy
Hiking Time: 15 minutes
DeLorme Atlas: Page 44, B-7
(unmarked)
Best Time to Visit: May to October

DESCRIPTION (HIGHLY RECOMMENDED) Crystal Cascade is an often-overlooked waterfall in Pinkham Notch. Too many hikers get caught up tackling Mt. Washington to take a short break off the Tuckerman's Ravine Trail to view Crystal Cascade. As a result, the falls are visited by only a fraction of the trail's hikers. Enough traffic is generated, however, for the Forest Service to post signs prohibiting off-trail hiking, to prevent erosion.

Directly ahead of a rock-wall outlook, Crystal Cascade drops a total of

100 feet in two uneven segments that are split by a platform with a shallow dark pool. The upper segment is a horsetail of approximately 70 feet in height, and the lower section is a 30-foot-tall block.

Whether you are visiting, dining, or staying the night at the AMC Pinkham Notch Visitor Center, or driving along NH 16, stop and give Crystal Cascade a few moments of your time. Your goal of hiking Mt. Washington should not be to summit as quickly as possible, but rather to enjoy the entire journey up this magnificent mountain.

TRAIL INFORMATION Head past the front entrance of the Pinkham Notch visitor center and take a right, following signs for the TUCKERMAN'S RAVINE TRAIL. Directly behind the center are bathrooms and another sign

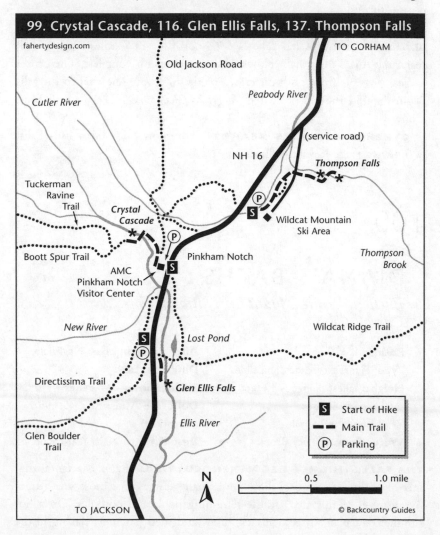

99. Crystal Cascade, 116. Glen Ellis Falls, 137. Thompson Falls

fahertydesign.com

TO GORHAM

Old Jackson Road

Peabody River

Cutler River

(service road)

NH 16

Thompson Falls

Tuckerman Ravine Trail

Crystal Cascade

Wildcat Mountain Ski Area

Boott Spur Trail

Pinkham Notch

Thompson Brook

AMC Pinkham Notch Visitor Center

New River

Lost Pond

Wildcat Ridge Trail

Directissima Trail

Glen Ellis Falls

Glen Boulder Trail

Ellis River

S Start of Hike

— — Main Trail

(P) Parking

N

0   0.5   1.0 mile

TO JACKSON

© Backcountry Guides

for the trail. From here, follow this modest uphill trail 0.3 mile to a rock staircase on your right. The only safe spot to view the falls is at the stop of the staircase.

SPECIAL NOTE If you are in decent physical shape, have at least eight hours to spare, and, most important, the weather forecast is in your favor, consider continuing the additional 3.7 miles beyond Crystal Cascade to the 6,288-foot summit of the northeast's tallest mountain, Mt. Washington. From the waterfall to the summit, you will gain approximately 4,000 feet of altitude. This significant climb should not be underestimated.

As a safety precaution, always check with the visitor center for current information regarding the trail and the weather conditions before setting out on this hike.

DIRECTIONS From the junction of NH 16 and US 302 in the section of Bartlett known as Glen, take NH 16 north for 11.7 miles and you will reach the AMC's Pinkham Notch Visitor Center on your left. The center is clearly visible from both directions of the highway. The trail to the falls begins behind the visitor center. *To get to Glen,* take NH 16 north from Conway.

OTHER WATERFALLS NEARBY Thompson Falls, Glen Ellis Falls, Winniweta Falls, Jackson Falls

100

DIANA'S BATHS
Bartlett, White Mountain National Forest, Carroll County

Rating: 4.5/5.0
Type: Plunges, cascades, and slides
Height: Tallest plunge is 12 feet; total drop is 60 feet
Trail Length: 0.6 mile
Water Source: Lucy Brook

Altitude Gain/Loss: Negligible
Difficulty: Easy
Hiking Time: 20 minutes
DeLorme Atlas: Page 45, H-9 (unmarked)
Best Time to Visit: Year-round

THE FALLS (HIGHLY RECOMMENDED) Diana's Baths is a tantalizing mix of potholes, cascades, slides, and small plunges. For most, the attractive features of this area are the refreshing pools and potholes. On a hot summer day, plan to see many children (and their parents) relaxing in the

Diana's Baths

swimming holes of Diana's Baths. Do not worry too much about the popularity, though; there is always enough space to relax and cool off.

During high water, the entire area, swimming holes included, can be engulfed with hammering cascades and plunges. During normal conditions, however, there is only one major waterfall, a 20-foot plunge over granite. In addition to being highly photogenic, this plunge is structured in such a way to allow you to stand below its falling waters. This plunge can be too powerful in the spring, but in the drier months of the year, it becomes much more people-friendly.

To make the most out of your visit, bring your family, swimsuit, and camera. As a local additional sight, check out nearby Cathedral Ledge, where technical rock-climbers can often be seen working their way up its broad face.

TRAIL INFORMATION The Moat Mountain Trail begins at the end of the parking lot and will guide you to the falls. Identified by yellow markers, the trail to the falls is fairly flat and wide, and very well maintained. The trail is handicap accessible to the initial viewpoint of the falls. There are several benches to rest along this easy trail.

DIRECTIONS From the junction of NH 16 and US 302 in Conway, take the combined highway NH 16 north and US 302 west, for 2.7 miles into the village of North Conway. Take a left onto River Road at a set of traffic lights. Travel on River Road for 0.9 mile and the road will become West Side Road. Travel on West Side Road for 1.3 miles and the parking area will be on the left.

Please be aware that this trailhead is part of the White Mountain National Forest parking fee program. The fee was $3 in 2009 but there is currently a proposal in review to raise this amount to $5.

OTHER WATERFALLS NEARBY Jackson Falls, Winniweta Falls, Lower Falls, Rocky Gorge

101

DIXVILLE FLUME

Dixville, Dixville Notch State Park, Coos County,

Rating: 3.0/5.0
Type: Plunges and cascades
Height: 18-foot total drop
Trail Length: Less than 0.1 mile
Water Source: Flume Brook
Altitude Gain/Loss: Negligible

Difficulty: Easy
Hiking Time: Negligible
DeLorme Atlas: Page 50, C-6
(unmarked)
Best Time to Visit: Year-round

THE FALLS Dixville Notch State Park has two waterfall picnic areas. Huntington Cascades is located near the southern tip of the park and is described in this guide in a separate chapter. The other waterfall, Dixville Flume, is a set of three drops in a narrow flume whose maximum width is 12 feet.

The total height of the three drops is about 18 feet, considerably smaller than its neighbor to the south. Because the vertical walls allow for little sunlight to reach the pools, the flume can appear somewhat dreary. Perhaps the lack of sunshine is the reason why this area always seems to be bug infested, even when other trails in the area are flying-insect free. Do not skip this one though; it makes for a nice quick rest stop—just remember to bring some bug spray.

TRAIL INFORMATION Although the flume is very close to the parking area, it cannot be seen from there. To view the falls, pass the sign at the parking lot that explains the geology of Dixville Notch, and walk a short distance to the flume, which will be on your left. During periods of low water, the scope of exploring within the flume is increased.

DIRECTIONS From the junction of NH 26 and US 3 in Colebrook, take NH 26 east. Travel on NH 26 east for 11.6 miles and take a left into Baby Flume Picnic Area, marked by a sign for DIXVILLE NOTCH STATE WAYSIDE AREA. *To get to Colebrook,* take US 3 north from Lincoln.

OTHER WATERFALLS NEARBY Huntington Cascades, Beaver Brook Falls, Colebrook, Pond Brook Falls

Dixville Flume

102

~

DRYAD FALL

Shelburne, Coos County

Rating: 4.0/5.0

Type: Horsetails and slides

Height: Falls of 15 feet and 40 feet are visible from trail; approximately 300-foot total drop

Trail Length: 0.8 mile or 2.9 miles, depending on trailhead used (see notes)

Water Source: Dryad Brook

Altitude Gain/Loss: +650 feet or +1,100 feet, depending on trailhead used (see notes)

Difficulty: Moderate

Hiking Time: 35 minutes or 2 hours, depending on trailhead used (see notes)

DeLorme Atlas: Page 49, G-11 (marked as Dryad Fall)

Best Time to Visit: May to June

THE FALLS This waterfall was a complete shock to us. We had heard reports of Dryad Fall being far too seasonal. This may be true, but this is a must-see during high runoff times. When water is flowing well, there is a steady stream of water that starts out as a horsetail before fanning into a slide below. As an additional benefit, there are impressive views of the Presidential Range of the White Mountains seen from the base of the falls.

Some say that Dryad Fall is in excess of 300 feet, and given the drops visible from the trail and the steep terrain above, we believe this to be true. Please note only 55 feet of this impressive waterfall is visible—hence the reason as to why this waterfall has not earned our highest level of recommendation. There are two trailheads that serve this waterfall. Our personal opinion is that this waterfall is definitely worth the 0.8 mile-hike from the trailhead at Mill Brook Road, but perhaps less rewarding if you are traveling the 2.9 miles from North Road. As a final note, Dryad Fall can be difficult to photograph, but a wide-angle lens can certain help.

TRAIL INFORMATION The trail length and altitude on your hike will depend upon at which of the two trailheads you have parked (see directions, below). Be aware that Austin Brook and Mill Brook are different names in common use for the same water source.

If you have parked on North Road your hike will be 2.9 miles with 1,100 feet of elevation gain. To begin, walk across the street and pass through the hikers' turnstile. Continue hiking for 1.1 miles and you will reach Mill Brook Road, a dirt road that the trail begins to follow. Some maps and guidebooks often call this road the Austin Brook Trail (instead of Mill Brook Road) from this point forward. Turn left and hike along the road for 0.1 mile where you will need to bear left at a fork. Hike for another 0.1 mile and you will reach a second fork after crossing a bridge; take the right option this time. From here, continue hiking along the road until you reach several large boulders, which actually outline the alternative trailhead described below. At this point, you are about 2.1 miles into the hike. Refer to the trail information below to reach the falls from this alternative parking area.

If you have parked on the alternative trailhead off Mill Brook Road, your hike will be 0.8 mile with 650 feet of elevation gain. To start this hike, walk past the boulders and across a small brook. Do not take the skidder road to the left before the boulders; be sure to continue up Mill Brook Road. After a few hundred yards the road turns left at a well-marked junction. Continue hiking for 0.3 mile beyond this point and you will come to a fork with the yellow-blazed Dryad Fall Trail. Fork left and follow this trail for 0.4 mile, where you will find a small sign currently pointing left to Dryad Fall. Hike down less than 100 feet to the exposed waterfall in front of you. There is a commanding view of the White Mountains to the left of here, as well.

DIRECTIONS From the junction of US 2 and NH 16 in Gorham, take US 2 east for 3.4 miles and take a left onto North Road. How far you drive on North Road will depend upon where you choose to park. There are two available trailheads.

One of the trailheads is a parking pull-off on the right, after driving 3.2 miles west on North Road. This is the parking area for the start of the Austin Brook Trail, and it is used if the alternative trailhead is not available for public use (due to a road gate that may be locked). Across the street from this pull-off is a turnstile indicating that the area is private property but that hiker access is allowed. Although this section of the Austin Brook Trail is a fine hike, you may want to consider using the alternative trailhead as it reduces the amount of hiking considerably.

To reach this alternative trailhead, continue 0.5 mile farther east along North Road from the first trailhead (heading toward Bethel) and take a left onto Mill Brook Road. You are now 3.7 miles from where you left US 2. *If the gate on Mill Brook Road is open and public access appears allowed,* drive on Mill Brook Road for 1.5 miles and fork left. There is a currently a small sign saying AMC TRAIL at this fork. Drive another 0.1 mile and fork right onto the Austin Brook Trail, which is an actual road here. There is currently a carved sign here for the AUSTIN BROOK TRAIL as well, but it is difficult to find signs along the road. Drive along the Austin Brook Trail road until you can drive no farther, as it is blocked by boulders, and park on the shoulder of the road. *If the gate on Mill Brook Road is closed,* return back to the original Austin Brook Trail parking pull-off on North Road, 0.5 mile west of Mill Brook Road.

To get to Gorham, take NH 16 north from Conway.

OTHER WATERFALLS NEARBY Giant Falls, Basin Trail Cascades, Mossy Glen, Appalachia Waterfalls, Falls on the Howker Ridge Trail, Triple Falls

103

EAGLE CASCADE

Beans Purchase, White Mountain National Forest, Coos County

Rating: 4.5/5.0
Type: Fan
Height: 40 feet visible from trail
Trail Length: 2.3 miles
Water Source: Charles Brook
Altitude Gain/Loss: +500 feet

Difficulty: Moderate
Hiking Time: 1 hour, 25 minutes
DeLorme Atlas: Page 45, B-12 (unmarked)
Best Time to Visit: May to October

THE FALLS (HIGHLY RECOMMENDED) This beautiful fan-shaped waterfall immediately makes you feel that you have discovered something special. The length and altitude gain of the hike may have you wondering if this cascade will be worth it or not, but it absolutely is. The falls, which skip and slide down a steep rock face, are dazzling.

Not only is the waterfall worth the effort, but nearby North and South Baldface offer some of the most fascinating views in Evans Notch. A difficult but highly rewarding loop can be formed that combines both of these open summits with Eagle Cascade. With all these cool features, it is no wonder why this site is so well traveled. This is a definite must-hike when you are in the area!

TRAIL INFORMATION Cross the road from the parking area and walk 150 feet north up ME 113, where you will see the Baldface Circle Trail breaking into the woods on the left. Hike along the trail as it gradually climbs for 0.7 mile and you will come to an intersection of several trails.

If you would like to visit Emerald Pool, the finest swimming hole in the area in our opinion, turn right and follow a spur trail 0.1 mile down to the pool. There is a miniature waterfall here as well.

To continue to Eagle Cascade, continue straight onto the northern loop of the Baldface Circle Trail, heading toward Eagle Crag and North Baldface (a left would guide you along the southern end of the loop toward South Baldface). Continue for 0.7 mile farther and you will come to a fork. The Bicknell Ridge Trail will head left and begin climbing toward North Baldface. You will want to take the right fork and stay on the Baldface Circle Trail. Continue hiking for 0.7 mile and you will reach a third junction. At this point you are 2.1 miles from the trailhead. Take a left this time onto the Eagle Cascade Link Trail, This trail eventually reconnects with the Bicknell Ridge Trail above the cascade, but you do not need to go that far to reach the waterfall. After hiking about 0.25 mile along the Eagle Cascade Link Trail, the breathtaking cascade will be exposed through the trees. A short trail brings you closer to the falls.

DIRECTIONS From the junction of ME 113 and US 302 in Fryeburg, Maine, take ME 113 north for 17.3 miles and turn right into a parking area for the Baldface Circle Trail. *To get to Fryeburg,* take NH 113 east from NH 16 in Conway, New Hampshire into Maine.

OTHER WATERFALLS NEARBY Brickett Falls, Rattlesnake Flume and Pool (ME), Hermit Falls, Mad River Falls (ME), Bickford Slides (ME), Kees Falls (ME)

104

FALL OF SONG

Moultonborough, Castle in the Clouds Conservation Area, Carroll County

Rating: 4.0/5.0
Type: Plunge
Height: 40 feet
Trail Length: 0.1 mile
Water Source: Shannon Brook
Altitude Gain/Loss: Negligible

Difficulty: Easy
Hiking Time: 5 minutes
DeLorme Atlas: Page 40, I-6
(marked as Castle in the Clouds)
Best Time to Visit: May to October

THE FALLS Fall of Song is a quick and surprising detour off the winding auto road that leads to the famous mountaintop estate known as Castle in the Clouds. With tours of the magnificent castle being offered, and a restaurant open for lunch that has an outdoor patio with grand views of the Lakes Region, we can understand why these falls may not necessarily be the highlight of a trip to this property. Of course, we enjoy the 40-foot-tall, 2-foot-wide freefalling waterfall the most, but we are clearly biased!

The recently reopened 0.8-mile-long Brook Walk continues upstream beyond Fall of Song, passing at least four other historically named waterfalls: Bridal Veil Fall, Roaring Falls, Twin Falls, and Whittier Falls. Each of these falls struggles to match the innate beauty of the Fall of Song, but where else can you find five waterfalls in such a short distance?

There are 45 miles of additional trails located on the property, but some of these abruptly end at the borders of the castle's property. Up until 2009, many of these continued on to private lands, leading to several excellent views on nearby mountain ledges and summits. However, these connecting trails are currently closed because of illegal trail maintenance that was performed without landowner permission. This complicated issue has many significant parties involved; we hope a resolution is found soon so that these trails may be reopened to use by respectful public visitors.

TRAIL INFORMATION From the parking area, cross the road and follow the easy trail upstream to the falls. Viewing of the falls is limited to the boardwalk and observation platform. No swimming is allowed here.

DIRECTIONS From the junction of NH 171 and NH 28 in Ossipee, take NH 171 west for 11.3 miles and take a right into the Castle in the Clouds main entrance. This property is located 2.1 miles east of the junction of NH 25 and NH 171 in Moultonborough. Immediately upon entering, stop at the gate station to pay the required Grounds Fee ($5/person in 2009). Take note that you do not need to purchase the full admission to the Castle in order to visit the waterfalls here. From the gate station, drive 0.4 mile to a large and popular parking lot on the left. Hours for the property vary greatly from season to season, so always check their Web site, www.castleintheclouds.org, or give them a call (1-603-476-5900) before driving there. *To get to Ossipee,* take NH 16 north from Rochester or NH 16 south from Conway.

OTHER WATERFALLS NEARBY Beede Falls

105

FALLS ON THE BASIN-CASCADES TRAIL

Lincoln, White Mountain National Forest, Grafton County

Rating: 4.5/5.0

Type: Cascades, slides, and small plunges

Height: Varies (see notes)

Trail Length: 0.1 mile to The Basin; 0.6 mile to Kinsman Falls; 1.1 miles to Rocky Glen Falls

Water Source: Cascade Brook

Altitude Gain/Loss: Negligible to The Basin; +300 feet to Kinsman Falls; +500 feet to Rocky Glen Falls

Difficulty: Easy to the Basin; easy side of moderate to Kinsman Falls; moderate to Rocky Glen Falls

Hiking Time: 5 minutes to The Basin; 25 minutes to Kinsman Falls; 45 minutes to Rocky Glen Falls

DeLorme Atlas: Page 43, F&G-11 (marked as The Basin)

Best Time to Visit: May to October

Falls on the Basin-Cascades Trail (Rocky Glen Falls)

THE FALLS (HIGHLY RECOMMENDED) Imagine a mile-long stretch of brook with several named waterfalls and dozens of large, unnamed cascades. This is Cascade Brook as seen from the Basin-Cascades Trail. Over a stretch about 1 mile in length, the wide brook drops a total of 600 vertical feet. Even though the trail that runs parallel to the brook is one of the most popular in the White Mountains region, there are enough sun-exposed cataracts, cascades, and slides for everyone to be able to claim themselves a private spot for hours.

The major tourist attraction is a small waterfall located in The Basin. Only a few feet tall, the small drop travels sideways down through a narrow chute into a deep whirlpool. There is almost always at least one visitor to the Falls at the Basin during all hours of sunlight. This high visitation is far from surprising; access to the Basin could not be easier. The area is marked by large signs on a major interstate, there is ample parking, and it is located just south of the other highly visited features of Franconia Notch State Park, such as The Flume and Cannon Mountain.

Kinsman Falls, Rocky Glen Falls, and a mile of the Basin-Cascades Trail lie beyond the waterfall at the Basin. Kinsman Falls, a narrow 15-foot plunge into a swimmable pool, is the first officially named waterfall of the Basin-Cascades Trail. Before Kinsman Falls, the trail is blessed with unnamed cascades and plunges, many worthy of their own name and recognition.

Rocky Glen Falls is the final waterfall of the trip. Here, Cascade Brook falls roughly 35 feet over two segments of jagged steps between narrow gorge walls into deep, yellow pools. Of all the falls along this trip, Rocky Glen is our top pick.

For a complete day in the sun with waterfalls, add the waterfalls of the Basin-Cascades Trail to the Falls of the Flume-Pool Loop and the less popular Georgiana Falls (see separate chapters). All are within several driving minutes of each other. Also consider trekking beyond Rocky Glen Falls an additional 1.8 miles to Lonesome Lake. This small but beautiful lake is very well regarded and also has an AMC backcountry hut.

TRAIL INFORMATION *If you are parked on the southbound side of I-93,* walk down the paved path to a set of waterslides and a bridge. If you wish to view the area referred to as The Basin, take a left before the bridge and follow the crowds a few feet down a flat dirt trail to a staircase.

If you are parked on the northbound side of I-93, you will need to follow signs to THE BASIN and cross under I-93 via a tunnel. After you cross through the tunnel, take a right and continue following a well-defined path for a few hundred feet and the The Basin will soon become evident.

105. Falls on the Basin-Cascades Trail

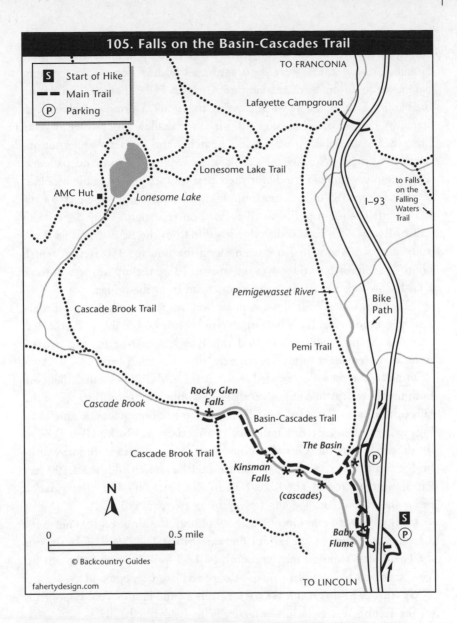

S Start of Hike

Main Trail

P Parking

TO FRANCONIA

Lafayette Campground

Lonesome Lake Trail

AMC Hut

Lonesome Lake

to Falls
on the
Falling
Waters
Trail

I–93

Pemigewasset River →

Bike
Path

Cascade Brook Trail

Pemi Trail

Rocky Glen Falls

Cascade Brook

Basin-Cascades Trail

Cascade Brook Trail

The Basin

P

Kinsman Falls

(cascades)

N

Baby Flume

S

P

0   0.5 mile

© Backcountry Guides

fahertydesign.com

TO LINCOLN

Both the Baby Flume and the cascades and waterfalls of the Basin-Cascades Trail can be accessed from The Basin. If you wish to visit the 6-foot drop of Baby Flume, continue downstream along the river for 0.25 mile along the Pemi Trail and the cascades will be on your left. If you wish to visit the cascades and waterfalls of the Basin-Cascades Trail, look for a large sign about 125 feet west of The Basin for the BASIN-CASCADES

TRAIL. This sign is visible from The Basin, but it can be somewhat difficult to spot. This trail will steadily climb in elevation past many sets of lovely unnamed cascades, to a very short spur trail leading down a 25-foot embankment to an unobstructed view of Kinsman Falls, about 0.6 mile from the parking area. Take care when crossing the brook. During periods of high water, we have seen several people slip into the shallow brook when making this crossing and end up with a few scratches and bruises. While not abnormally difficult, crossing the brook often requires balance and patience. Trekking poles come in handy for such a task. Once you cross the brook, it is an additional 0.5 mile of moderate hiking before you reach a view of the last waterfall of the trip, Rocky Glen Falls, on your right. Only the bottom half of Rocky Glen Falls is directly viewable from the Basin-Cascades Trail. You must continue hiking upstream along the trail for 150 feet, at which point you will reach a bridge over the stream. To see the top segment of these falls, bushwhack a short distance downstream from the bridge.

The Basin-Cascades Trail is a popular, well-marked, moderate uphill walk past dozens of cascades. The farther you continue on the trail, the less crowded the trail will become, and this is especially true for the last 0.6 mile, as most visitors turn back after reaching Kinsman Falls.

SPECIAL NOTE Lonesome Lake and the AMC Hut located there are both highly worthwhile objectives that are within reasonable distance of the falls of the Basin-Cascades Trail. To reach these remote places, keep climbing up the Basin-Cascades Trail for 0.1 mile beyond Rocky Glen Falls to its junction with the Cascade Brook Trail. Cross Cascade Brook over a bridge and from here, it is 1.6 miles to the lake and an additional 500 feet left along the Around-The-Lake Trail to the Hut. This hut offers snacks, meals (in season), and lodging (reservations are required).

DIRECTIONS From Lincoln, take I-93 north. Continue on I-93 north for 2.1 miles past exit 34a, the exit for the waterfalls at The Flume. Take the exit for The Basin. If you are traveling south on I-93 from Franconia, the exit for The Basin will be 1.3 miles past the Lafayette Place Campground.

OTHER WATERFALLS NEARBY Falls on the Flume–Pool Loop, Falls on the Falling Waters Trail, Georgiana Falls, Bridal Veil Falls

106

~~~

FALLS ON THE FALLING WATERS TRAIL

Lincoln & Franconia, White Mountain National Forest, Grafton County

Rating: 5.0/5.0

Type: Plunges and cascades

Height: 20 feet, 60 feet, and 80 feet

Trail Length: To Swiftwater Falls is 0.9 mile; to Cloudland Falls is 1.4 miles (see notes)

Water Source: Dry Brook

Altitude Gain/Loss: To Swiftwater Falls, +450 feet; to Cloudland Falls, +1,000 feet

Difficulty: To Swiftwater Falls, easy side of moderate; to Cloudland Falls, moderate side of difficult

Hiking Time: 75 minutes to Cloudland Falls

DeLorme Atlas: Page 43, F-12 (unmarked)

Best Time to Visit: May to October

THE FALLS (HIGHLY RECOMMENDED) The Falling Waters Trail is a popular 3.25-mile trail to the summit of Little Haystack Mountain. Along the way are several waterfalls, each with its own personality. Stairs Falls, where Dry Brook plunges down small granite steps into a shallow pool, is the first waterfall seen on this trip. Of the three waterfalls on the Falling Waters Trail, this waterfall is the least crowded, mainly because hikers must venture off the main trail to get a good grasp of this waterfall, whereas the others can be seen directly from the trail.

Just a few hundred feet above Stairs Falls is Swiftwater Falls, a 60-foot-tall mix of cascades and small plunges. The trail crosses in front of this waterfall, so if the crowds are thick on the day of your visit, it can be tough to spend quality time here.

The last waterfall, and by far the main attraction of this trail, is 80-foot Cloudland Falls, a picturesque fan-type horsetail. Like the other two, this waterfall can be seen from the trail, but the best views are afforded by side-stepping off the main trail and getting closer. The fanning structure of this waterfall is its most impressive aspect, with the width at the top at about 2 feet, while the width at the bottom is about 25 feet during periods of high water.

TRAIL INFORMATION The Falling Waters Trail begins at the center of the northbound parking area for the Lafayette Campground. Follow the paved road slightly uphill and east for 0.1 mile and then enter the woods. Only 0.2 mile from the parking area, you will reach a fork. The left fork is for the Old Bridle Path Trail, which leads to the summit of Mt. Lafayette via the Greenleaf Trail. The right fork is for the Falling Waters Trail. Follow this blue-marked trail to the three waterfalls.

The first waterfall, Stairs Falls, is approached after 0.8 mile and slightly less than 400 feet of elevation gain. The second falls, Swiftwater Falls, lies about 75 feet upstream from Stairs Falls. Until now, the trail has been an uphill battle with very few trail dangers present. Accessing Cloudland Falls, which is an additional 0.6 mile from Swiftwater Falls, demands more effort. In just over a half-mile, you will climb nearly 600 feet vertically, cross the Dry Brook, and negotiate many steep, often muddy sections of terrain.

SPECIAL NOTE If you are in good shape, the weather forecast is promising, and you have a full day available, follow the rest of the crowd on the Falling Waters Trail to the Franconia Ridge Trail and ultimately to the 5,260-foot summit of Mt. Lafayette, for a clockwise-loop round trip of 8.8 miles. It is possible to do this loop counterclockwise, but we have always enjoyed this method better. Make sure to assess your stamina before considering this optional hike.

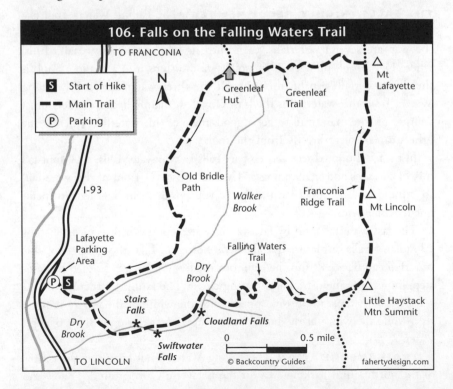

106. Falls on the Falling Waters Trail

TO FRANCONIA

S Start of Hike
Main Trail
P Parking

N

Greenleaf Hut

Greenleaf Trail

Mt Lafayette

Old Bridle Path

I-93

Walker Brook

Franconia Ridge Trail

Mt Lincoln

Lafayette Parking Area

Falling Waters Trail

Dry Brook

P S

Stairs Falls

Dry Brook

Cloudland Falls

Little Haystack Mtn Summit

Swiftwater Falls

0   0.5 mile

TO LINCOLN

© Backcountry Guides

fahertydesign.com

This loop has sections of steep and often slippery trail, often for long stretches at a time, and can be snowy and icy until late spring. The winds along the ridge can be deadly—be absolutely sure the weather forecast is in your favor before you attempt this rigorous hiking loop. With a hefty elevation gain of nearly 4,000 feet, it will take the average hiker about six to eight hours to complete this exhausting endeavor.

Before tackling any hike of this caliber, make sure that you are properly prepared and have done additional research as to what lies ahead of you.

DIRECTIONS From Lincoln, take I-93 north. Continue traveling on I-93 north for 1.5 miles past the parking area for The Basin. Take a right into the parking area for the Lafayette Campground, which also has a TRAILHEAD PARKING sign. If you are traveling south on I-93 from Franconia, the Lafayette Campground exit will be on your right approximately 3.2 miles south of the WELCOME TO FRANCONIA NOTCH STATE PARK sign.

OTHER WATERFALLS NEARBY Falls on Basin-Cascades Trail, Falls on the Flume–Pool Loop, Georgiana Falls, Bridal Veil Falls

107

FALLS ON THE FLUME– POOL LOOP

Lincoln, Franconia Notch State Park, Grafton County

Rating: 5.0/5.0
Type: Plunges, horsetails and cascades
Height: Avalanche Falls is 45 feet; Liberty Gorge Cascade is 70 feet
Trail Length: 2.0-mile loop
Water Source: Flume Brook, Cascade Brook, and the Pemigewasset River.

Altitude Gain/Loss: +250 feet, -250 feet
Difficulty: Moderate
Hiking Time: 1 hour, 15 minutes
DeLorme Atlas: Page 43, G-11&12 (marked as Flume Gorge)
Best Time to Visit: May to October

THE FALLS (HIGHLY RECOMMENDED) This just may be the most popular waterfall hike in New England. A trip to the Flume–Pool Loop, or The Flume, as it is known to so many, has long been a favorite for families, hikers, photographers, and sightseers. This is no surprise to us, considering the variety of natural features offered on the 2-mile loop trail. Along the way, you will get your daily dose of waterfalls, covered bridges, glacial boulders, a long flume, and one of the deepest pools below a waterfall in the region.

The first waterfall you visit, Table Rock, is more of a slide than a waterfall. At Table Rock, granite has been weathered by Flume Brook for thousands of years. This waterslide is quite large—about 500 feet long and 75 feet wide.

The next is Avalanche Falls, located at mile 0.7 of the trip and the climax of the boardwalk within the Flume gorge. The falls were supposedly formed during the great storm of 1883. This waterfall is a major highlight of the hike, and is therefore extremely crowded. We had difficulty in taking a picture of the falls without fellow visitors in the frame. You will most likely be pushed along the boardwalk trail due to the crowds. Continue hiking to the top of the falls, where you can enjoy a less-crowded birds-eye view of this 40-foot-tall plunge.

After Avalanche Falls, continue along the loop to a short spur trail that leads to a view of Liberty Gorge Cascade. This waterfall is a 70-foot clearwater horsetail. Considerably sunnier than its nearby neighbor, Liberty Gorge Cascade is a more appropriate place for a photograph. The gorge is highly exposed to the sun and although there is only one viewpoint of the falls from an observation point, you really should not miss this. It is perhaps the prettiest of all the waterfalls here.

The final scenic wonder of the trip is called The Pool. Very large in size—40 feet deep and 150 feet in diameter—The Pool is located in a deep basin of the Pemigewasset River. Viewpoints from the trail extend around the pool, offering just about every perspective possible. If swimming were allowed, we would have to say this pool would be one of the top five swimming pools in New England. However, The Pool is off limits, probably due to both the intense popularity of the loop, and to the difficulty one would have entering and exiting the area.

TRAIL INFORMATION Before you begin your hike, you must stop in the visitor center and pay the admission fee, which was $13 for adults and $9 for children in 2009. The trail actually starts behind this center. For the first 0.2 mile of this loop trail, you cross relatively flat, easy terrain. Once you reach the Glacial Boulder, take a right onto a trail heading toward The Flume. Walk through a covered bridge and the flume boardwalk trail will soon begin. About 0.7 mile past the visitor center, Avalanche Falls will appear just before the flume boardwalk ends. After relishing in the different viewpoint perspectives offered of the falls, continue farther along the trail until you reach a fork. Fork right here onto the Ridge Path, which will bring you to Liberty Gorge Cascade, The Pool, and finally back to the visitor center. A left here would bring you directly back to the visitor center, but you would miss the other attractions of the Flume-Pool Loop.

Take the Ridge Path and in about 0.6 mile you will reach a marked spur trail that leads down a 100-foot-long dead-end trail to a heads-on view of the Liberty Gorge Cascade. After observing the cascade, continue farther along the Ridge Path to The Pool. After The Pool, follow signs back to the visitor center, again passing the Glacial Boulder along the way.

The entire 2.0-mile trail is meticulously maintained and well marked, which makes for a pleasant family outing. You should not encounter any problems along the entire length of the trail.

DIRECTIONS From Lincoln, take I-93 north to exit 34a. Follow the signs to the FLUME VISITOR CENTER. Both sides of I-93 will have large signs directing you toward THE FLUME.

OTHER WATERFALLS NEARBY Falls on the Basin-Cascades Trail, Falls on the Falling Waters Trail, Georgiana Falls, Agassiz Basin, Franconia Falls, Thirteen Falls

Falls on the Flume–Pool Loop (Liberty Gorge Cascade)

108

~

FALLS ON THE HOWKER RIDGE TRAIL

Randolph, White Mountain National Forest, Coos County

Rating: 3.0/5.0

Type: Horsetails, cascades, fans, and small plunges

Height: Stairs Falls is 10 feet; Coosauk Falls is 15 feet; Hitchcock Falls is 30 feet

Trail Length: To Stairs Falls is 0.6 mile; to Coosauk Falls is 0.7 mile; to Hitchcock Falls is 1.0 mile

Water Source: Bumpus Brook

Altitude Gain/Loss: +500 feet to Hitchcock Falls

Difficulty: Moderate

Hiking Time: 45 minutes to Hitchcock Falls

DeLorme Atlas: Page 48, I-7 (marked as Coosauk Falls and Hitchcock Falls)

Best Time to Visit: May to July

THE FALLS The brooks and streams draining water from the northern end of the Presidential Range Mountains are rich in cascades and falls. There are the Triple Falls on Town Line Brook, the waterfalls of Appalachia, as well as many unnamed cascades and falls. Three more waterfalls exist just east of Triple Falls—also off Dolly Copp Road—along the Howker Ridge Trail. This includes Stairs Falls, Coosauk Falls, and Hitchcock Falls, all of which are accessible via a mile-long trail located in the small town of Randolph.

The steps of Stairs Falls are blatantly obvious, and increase the expansion of the fan as the water travels down it. Heavily shaded and located on the other side of the brook from the trail, Stairs Falls is unfortunately too hidden for a photograph or even a closer inspection.

Coosauk Falls is a 15-foot-tall set of cascades and slides that dump into the Devil's Kitchen Gorge. There are old, bumpy paths leading into the gorge for closer views if you just so happen to see water flowing.

Hitchcock Falls is the concluding feature of the trip. Here, waters pigtail past boulders in the streambed into clear, green-tinted pools. Located in a secluded ravine that probably sees only a handful of visitors each week, Hitchcock Falls is a place best suited for intimate exploration. Many angular boulders are scattered in and around the brook, creating many opportunities to survey the area. Out of the three falls on the trip, Hitchcock is our favorite stop, more for the thrill of being alone in a rocky playground than for the actual impressiveness of the waterfall.

TRAIL INFORMATION From the parking area, follow the combined Howker Ridge Trail and Randolph Path through a field and into the forest. About 0.1 mile from the parking lot, take a left and continue on the Howker Ridge Trail. About a 0.1 mile farther, cross an old logging road and continue straight. After a total of about 20 minutes, you will reach Stairs Falls, visible across the brook from the trail and currently marked by a small, carved, white sign. Continue climbing upstream along the trail for another 0.1 mile and you will reach Coosauk Falls. A small, not immediately obvious, white sign will let you know that you have reached this waterfall.

Up to this point, the trail has been an easy-to-follow moderate uphill climb of 0.7 mile. For the rest of the way to Hitchcock Falls, however, things are not so simple. The trail is hardly ever used, very narrow in some stretches, steep, and often has muddy sections.

If you are seeking a waterfall offering the potential for hours of seclusion, Hitchcock Falls is one of your best bets. If you make the decision to

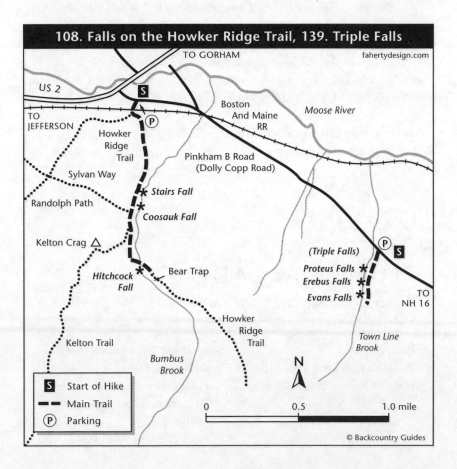

continue to this final waterfall, fork left just past Coosauk Falls and continue climbing along the Howker Ridge Trail. About 0.1 mile beyond Coosauk Falls, fork left again as the Kelton Trail forks right. The falls are a few minutes ahead and are clearly identifiable from the trail.

Upstream of Hitchcock Falls is the lost waterfall of Muscanigra Falls. Years ago, a spur trail led to the base of this elusive falls. These days, there is no trail and the bushwhack is said to be very difficult.

It is also possible to connect Hitchcock Falls with the Appalachia Waterfalls (see separate chapter). You will need a good trail map of the area to connect these two series of waterfalls.

DIRECTIONS From the junction of NH 16 and US 302 in the section of Bartlett known as Glen, take NH 16 north. Continue traveling on NH 16 north for 3.4 miles past the entrance to the Mt. Washington Road and take a left onto Dolly Copp Road. Follow Dolly Copp Road for 0.5 mile, passing the entrance to the campground on the left, and you will reach a fork in the road. Take the left fork onto Pinkham B Road. Follow Pinkham B Road for 3.8 miles to a US Forest Service parking area on the left. On Dolly Copp Road, there is a large parking area for the Presidential Range Rail Trail before the trailhead parking area, so be sure to look for the US Forest Service HIKER logo sign. The trailhead parking area is 0.1 mile south of US 2 on Dolly Copp Road. *To get to Glen,* take NH 16 north from Conway.

OTHER WATERFALLS NEARBY Triple Falls, Mossy Glen, Appalachia Waterfalls, Thompson Falls, Crystal Cascade, Giant Falls, Dryad Fall

109

∽

FLUME CASCADE

Harts Location, Crawford Notch State Park, Carroll County

Rating: 4.0/5.0

Type: Cascades and small plunges

Height: Approximately 300-foot total drop

Trail Length: Roadside

Water Source: Unknown

Altitude Gain/Loss: None

Difficulty: Easy

Hiking Time: Not applicable

DeLorme Atlas: Page 44, C&D-4 (marked)

Best Time to Visit: May to June

THE FALLS Flume Cascade is the less-visited sister of nearby Silver Cascade, which lies a few hundred feet southeast of these falls. Flume Cascade is often confused with The Flume, which is actually part of the Falls on the Flume–Pool Loop in this guide.

At Flume Cascade, small cascades and plunges end up in the Saco River below the highway. Be sure to scramble up alongside the falls for additional and improved views that are not seen from the highway.

The falls are even more beautiful in early spring when some of the water is still frozen. During this time, the waterfall not only looks larger and bolder, but the ice formations created here over the rock face can be quite dazzling.

TRAIL INFORMATION The falls are across the highway from the parking areas. A few worn paths lead their way up the side of the falls, where new views await you. Increase the scope of your explorations by visiting Silver Cascade, a similar stretch of cascades a few feet down the road.

DIRECTIONS From the junction of US 302 and NH 16 in the section of Bartlett known as Glen, take US 302 west for 19.8 miles and the parking area will be on the left. The parking lot is 0.4 mile east of the sign marking the entrance to CRAWFORD NOTCH STATE PARK BORDER, and 2.0 miles west of the Willey House Historical Site. *To get to Glen,* take NH 16 north from Conway.

OTHER WATERFALLS NEARBY Silver Cascade, Beecher and Pearl Cascades, Gibbs Falls, Kedron Flume, Ripley Falls, Arethusa Falls

110

∽

FRANCONIA FALLS

Lincoln, White Mountain National Forest, Grafton County

Rating: 4.0/5.0

Type: Cascades and slides

Height: 30-foot total drop

Trail Length: 3.2 miles

Water Source: Franconia Brook

Altitude Gain/Loss: +300 feet

Difficulty: Easy

Hiking Time: 90 minutes

DeLorme Atlas: Page 43, G-14 (marked)

Best Time to Visit: May to October

THE FALLS Franconia Falls is located at the end of one of the flattest long-distance strolls in the White Mountains. In just over 3 miles, you will gain a mere 300 feet of altitude, with no real noticeable ups or downs. For comparison, consider nearby Beaver Brook Cascades, which gains 1,200 feet of altitude in only 1.1 miles, or the waterfalls along the Falling Waters Trail, which gains 1,000 feet in 1.3 miles. The lack of elevation gain is the big reason why Franconia Falls is a favorite hike for families. Another reason is that the falls can be easily accessed year-round by foot, mountain bike, snowshoe, or cross-country ski.

Franconia Falls lacks any single waterfalls of striking natural elegance or style. It makes up for this deficiency with sunny slabs of rock, swimming pools that widely vary in size, depth, and current, and the possibilities of roving around the falls for hours of refreshing pleasure.

There are several good waterslides here when the water is running low enough. The best slide in the house is near the base of the most significant falls. Roughly 20 feet long, but not continuous, this slide will propel you into a 5-foot deep pool. Before we began writing in our waterfall journals, we felt the urge to chute down the slide first ourselves!

TRAIL INFORMATION The trail to the falls begins near the ranger station cabin. Proceed down a wooden staircase, cross a wooden bridge, and follow signs to the trailhead for the LINCOLN WOODS TRAIL. A few hundred feet beyond the visitor center, you will cross a suspension footbridge over the East Branch of the Pemigewasset River.

After crossing the bridge, you will reach a junction with a large sign. Take a right and continue hiking along the wide and nearly completely flat Lincoln Woods Trail, which is an old railroad bed. After hiking for 1.5 miles, a junction with the Osseo Trail will appear. The Osseo Trail is a gateway to the Franconia Ridge Trail, a trail considered by many to be one of the finest hikes in the northeast. Continue straight at this junction to stay on the Lincoln Woods Trail for an additional 1.2 miles and you will reach a stone wall where you will find sign for FRANCONIA FALLS. Take this left and hike the final 0.4 mile to the falls on a narrower, slightly rougher trail. Before or after visiting the falls, we also recommend passing 20 feet beyond the stone wall to enjoy a scenic bridge over Franconia Brook. The blue and green cascading waters of the river are stunning and worth the little extra hiking effort.

Depending on recent snowfall, this hike can make for an excellent cross-country ski or snowshoe in the winter, but expect heavy traffic. As a final note, be aware that the permit system that once restricted the area to only 60 visitors per day is no longer in effect.

DIRECTIONS From I-93 in Lincoln, take exit 32. Take NH 112 west for 5.2 miles and take a left into the Lincoln Woods parking area just after

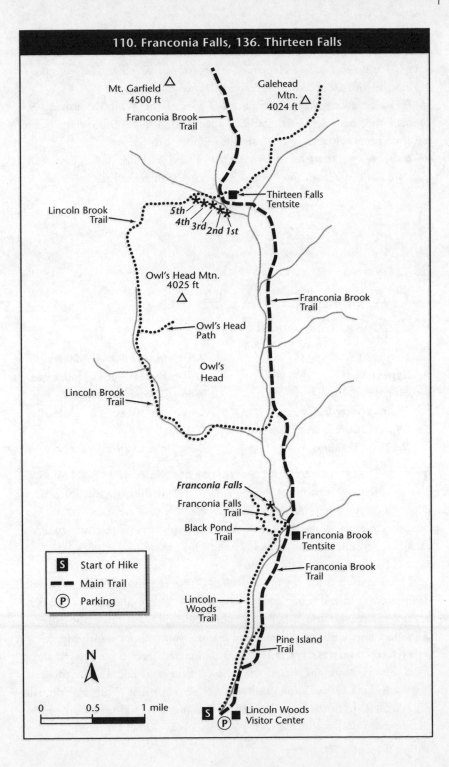

110. Franconia Falls, 136. Thirteen Falls

Mt. Garfield
4500 ft

Galehead
Mtn.
4024 ft

Franconia Brook
Trail

Thirteen Falls
Tentsite

Lincoln Brook
Trail

5th
4th 3rd 2nd 1st

Owl's Head Mtn.
4025 ft

Franconia Brook
Trail

Owl's Head
Path

Owl's
Head

Lincoln Brook
Trail

Franconia Falls

Franconia Falls
Trail

Black Pond
Trail

Franconia Brook
Tentsite

Franconia Brook
Trail

Lincoln
Woods
Trail

Pine Island
Trail

S Start of Hike

— — — Main Trail

P Parking

N

0   0.5   1 mile

S Lincoln Woods
P Visitor Center

crossing a bridge over the East Branch of the Pemigewasset River. The Lincoln Woods parking area is 2.1 miles west of the Big Rock Campground and 0.3 mile east of the Hancock Campground. *To get to Lincoln,* take I-93 north from Concord or I-93 south from Franconia.

Please be aware that this trailhead is part of the White Mountain National Forest parking fee program. The fee was $3 in 2009 but there is currently a proposal in review to raise this amount to $5.

OTHER WATERFALLS NEARBY Thirteen Falls, Georgiana Falls, Agassiz Basin, Falls on the Flume–Pool Loop, Sabbaday Falls

| | |

GARFIELD FALLS
Pittsburg, Coos County

Rating: 4.5/5.0
Type: Plunge
Height: 40 feet
Trail Length: 0.25 mile
Water Source: East Branch of the Dead Diamond River

Altitude Gain/Loss: -100 feet
Difficulty: Easy side of moderate
Hiking Time: 10 minutes
DeLorme Atlas: Page 53, H-10 (marked)
Best Time to Visit: June to October

THE FALLS (HIGHLY RECOMMENDED) Northern New Hampshire has an extensive network of logging roads and untamed lands. Located in these lands are a few highly rated waterfalls. Several are located on Dartmouth College-owned property, and can only be visited by students, faculty, or alumni of the school. Luckily for the rest of us, gems such as Garfield Falls are very welcoming.

This waterfall is the premier waterfall of the region. At 40 feet, the falls drop into a wild and scenic gorge—one of New Hampshire's best and a photographers' playground. Smaller cascades and rapids continue downstream. Allocate a few hours for this waterfall because you will not want to leave.

TRAIL INFORMATION From the parking area, continue straight ahead for a few feet and you should spot the trail on your left. Follow this relatively easy trail for 0.25 mile and you will get your first glimpse of the falls on your left, from the opposite end of the gorge. A well-used trail continues down to the base of the river and passes other small cascades.

DIRECTIONS From the junction of US 3 and NH 145 in Pittsburg, take US 3 north heading toward the Canadian border. Continue traveling on US 3 north for 4.8 miles past the dam on the First Connecticut Lake and take a right onto Magalloway Road, which is marked by a sign for the MAGALLOWAY TOWER. You will have to follow this normally well-maintained dirt road for a total of 10.7 miles, but be aware that there are several potentially confusing intersections along this road. In order to stay on the correct course, you will need to stay straight at mile 1.1, bear left at mile 2.9, stay straight at mile 8.5, and bear right at mile 9.6. At mile 10.7, there should be a small sign for the falls on the right. From here, head straight an additional 1.4 miles farther and an obvious parking pull-off will be on the left, surrounded by several large boulders. There is an outhouse across the road from the parking area that will help you identify the correct spot. *To get to Pittsburg,* take US 3 north from Lincoln.

OTHER WATERFALLS NEARBY None

Garfield Falls

112

GARWIN FALLS

Wilton, Hillsborough County

Rating: 3.0/5.0

Type: Horsetails and cascades

Height: 40 feet

Trail Length: 0.25 mile to base of falls

Water Source: Unknown

Altitude Gain/Loss: -125 feet

Difficulty: Easy

Hiking Time: 10 minutes

DeLorme Atlas: Page 21, F-9 (unmarked)

Best Time to Visit: May to June

THE FALLS In high water, Garwin Falls—sometimes called Barnes Falls—is a clear winner. When water is rushing over the dam just upstream, you will see this waterfall in all its glory—and it is indeed impressive. The river is just as wide as the falls are tall, and in high water, a huge curtain of water covers most of it, giving the appearance of a block-style waterfall.

Town history indicates Garwin Falls was an immensely popular picnic spot in the days before the invention of the automobile. Fishing and swimming were popular pastimes as well. Popularity appears to have waned a bit since then, but Garwin Falls is just as enjoyable and welcoming as it has ever been. The only difference is that you should try to time your visit during high water due to the presence of the dam.

TRAIL INFORMATION From the parking area, begin by walking down an old dirt road. After about 0.1 mile, a spur trail will lead left about 100 feet to a small but pretty 3-foot cascade. To reach the main falls, continue farther along the old road for 0.1 mile and you will reach a small reservoir and a dam. Garwin Falls is only about 300 feet farther downstream, accessible by an easy trail that swings left and down to the base of the falls.

DIRECTIONS From the western junction of NH 101 and NH 101a in Milford, take NH 101 west into Wilton as it joins with, and later splits from, NH 31. Continue traveling on NH 101 west for 0.3 mile beyond where NH 31 splits and heads south and take a right onto the Isaac Frye Highway. Travel on this road for 1.2 miles, making sure to stay straight through two different intersections along the way. At the end of the 1.2 miles, bear right at a sign for the BENNINGTON BATTLE TRAIL and go 0.1 mile farther. You will then reach a fork. Take the left option as Sand Hill Avenue comes in on the right and then take an almost immediate right onto Davisville Road. Travel on Davisville Road for 0.2 mile, passing the Vale

End Cemetery along the way, and the parking pull-off will be on the right. The parking area is large enough for four or five cars. *To get to Milton,* take NH 101a west from Nashua.

OTHER WATERFALLS NEARBY Purgatory Falls, Tucker Brook Falls

113

~

GEORGIANA FALLS
Lincoln, Grafton County

Rating: 2.5/5.0

Type: Plunges, cascades, and a fan

Height: Georgiana Falls is 30 feet; Harvard Falls is 60 feet

Trail Length: To Georgiana Falls, 0.7 mile; to Harvard Falls, 1.3 miles

Water Source: Harvard Brook

Altitude Gain/Loss: +250 feet to Georgiana Falls; +750 feet to Harvard Falls

Difficulty: To Georgiana Falls, easy side of moderate; to Harvard Falls, moderate side of difficult

Hiking Time: 25 minutes to Georgiana Falls; 45 minutes to Harvard Falls

DeLorme Atlas: Page 43, H-11 (marked)

Best Time to Visit: May to October

THE FALLS Many visitors to Georgiana Falls only reach the lower half of this waterfall. They are simply unaware of the quiet isolation provided by the set of falls lying upstream. This is not surprising at all, considering the rough and poorly marked trail beyond the Lower Falls.

The lower falls consists of a 30-foot-high set of cascades spread across a 20-foot-wide ledge. At the base of this waterfall is a deep, dark pool, as well as a very spacious ledge for sunbathing and picnicking. Although this waterfall is regularly visited, you can still find a spot to claim as your own at this highly photogenic, delightful spot.

Upper Georgiana Falls, which has been referred to as Harvard Falls in the past, has a different personality than the Lower Falls. Here Harvard Brook splits in two and plunges over 60 feet into a long chasm below. The plunge on the right is particularly fascinating; the plunge actually fans out, then reverse-fans back in before landing, somewhat resembling the shape of a diamond. The plunge on the left is rather difficult to see from the trail, and we could not find a reasonably safe approach to the bottom of the gorge. It is worth noting that to view the falls head-on from a cliff on the trail can

Georgiana Falls (lower falls)

be thrilling and dangerous, so watch your footing. You can also continue bush-whacking to the top of these falls for an additional perspective.

TRAIL INFORMATION From the parking area, follow the yellow-blazed trail that passes through a fence opening and passes underneath I-93 shortly thereafter. A few feet beyond I-93, take the right fork at the sign for GEORGIANA FALLS. After about 0.3 mile, you will reach small cascades and the yellow markers that have guided you thus far will begin to turn red. At first the blazes are both yellow *and* red, but in a few hundred feet the rest of the trail becomes marked only with red trail blazes.

About 0.1 mile below Georgiana Falls (or 0.6 mile from the parking area), the trail partially leaves the woods and becomes more of a moderate rock scramble along the side of the brook. You will know when you have reached the falls when you find a wide-open area with a large pool separating you and the 30-foot falls. To get to Harvard Falls, continue hiking upstream to the right of the falls. From here to the upper falls, the trail is difficult to follow; trail markers are faded and sparsely found. We wandered off-trail several times, constantly peeping into the woods looking for the blazes. Although you may find yourself off-trail, if you simply stay close to the brook you should eventually spot Harvard Falls. If you can reach it, the views from the top of Harvard Falls are said to be lovely. While the trail to Georgiana Falls is only moderately used, the trail to Harvard Falls is considerably even less so, meaning you will probably want a healthy sense of adventure to find these elusive falls.

DIRECTIONS From I-93 in Lincoln, take exit 33. Follow US 3 north for 0.3 mile toward North Lincoln and take a left onto Hanson Farm Road. After following Hanson Farm Road for 0.1 mile, continue straight onto Georgiana Falls Road. Continue straight to the parking area at the end of the road.

OTHER WATERFALLS NEARBY Falls on the Flume–Pool Loop, Falls on the Basin-Cascades Trail, Falls on the Falling Waters Trail, Agassiz Basin, Paradise Falls, Beaver Brook Cascades, Franconia Falls, Thirteen Falls

114

GIANT FALLS
Shelburne, Coos County

Rating: 5.0/5.0
Type: Horsetail
Height: 110 feet visible from trail; approximately 350-foot total drop
Trail Length: 1.5 miles
Water Source: Peabody Brook
Altitude Gain/Loss: +850 feet, -100 feet

Difficulty: Easy side of moderate
Hiking Time: 45 minutes
DeLorme Atlas: Page 49, G-10 (marked)
Best Time to Visit: May through October

THE FALLS (HIGHLY RECOMMENDED) Not expecting much while navigating the confusing network of trails to find this waterfall, we were greatly surprised as Giant Falls opened up before us. This waterfall has the potential to have many different personalities. During our visit in late summer, the absence of strong waters created a picturesque drizzle of water kissing the rock face as it dropped in a fan-like formation. The sheer height of the rock wall in front of you makes this waterfall worthy of multiple visits. During snowmelt in early spring, water must come crashing down the vast rock walls with tremendous force. This waterfall is a definite must-see and on our personal top 20 list!

TRAIL INFORMATION Cross the street to begin the Peabody Brook Trail, which starts off as a grassy logging road. You must first pass a gate that prevents vehicles from driving up this road. A few hundred feet later, the trail forks right, identifiable by a small cairn. From here, continue hiking as the trail crosses over an old logging bridge and soon you will have to fork left to continue on this blue-blazed trail. From this point on you will not cross the brook again. The trail continues relatively flat, with overgrown grass in some areas. At a point about 0.8 mile from the road, the trail will fork left into the woods and become more of a recognizable hiking trail. From this point, hike another 0.4 mile to a small, unmarked trail that spurs downhill on your left. This unmarked trail is identifiable by turning around and spotting a trail sign for the PEABODY BROOK TRAIL. Instead of continuing on the Peabody Brook Trail, take this spur trail for 0.3 mile as it leads downhill to the riverbed and then begins climbing upstream to the falls. Only a portion of the true size of the falls is viewable from the trail.

DIRECTIONS From the junction of US 2 and NH 16 in Gorham, take US 2 east for 3.4 miles and take a left onto North Road. Drive for 1.3 miles on North Road, crossing the Androscoggin River along the way, and there will be a small parking pull-off on the right. There is a trail sign across the street for the PEABODY BROOK TRAIL, but it is partially obscured by trees. If you get to Evans Road, you have gone too far. *To get to Gorham,* take NH 16 north from Conway.

OTHER WATERFALLS NEARBY Dryad Fall, Basin Trail Cascades, Mossy Glen, Appalachia Waterfalls, Falls on the Howker Ridge Trail, Triple Falls

115

GIBBS FALLS

Beans Grant, White Mountain National Forest, Coos County

Rating: 4.0/5.0
Type: Horsetail
Height: 35 feet
Trail Length: 0.6 mile
Water Source: Gibbs Brook
Altitude Gain/Loss: +300 feet

Difficulty: Easy side of moderate
Hiking Time: 20 minutes
DeLorme Atlas: Page 44, C-4
(marked as Gibbs Brook Scenic Area)
Best Time to Visit: May to
October

THE FALLS This waterfall flows into a gorgeous, rocky-bottomed clear pool, great for soaking your tired feet. Due to its sunny southern exposure, this wading pool is one of the warmer swimming holes in New Hampshire. Note that there are currently fallen trees in the way that will need to be crossed in order for you to swim.

The waterfall fans out for the last 2 or 3 feet of this 35-foot horsetail. It is in a wide-open area, although a large rock near its base prevents you from seeing the whole fall at one time. The waterfall scoops down around this rock, ending with a final plunge onto a series of small rocks.

Gibbs Falls makes for a great early resting place on a day-trip hike up Crawford Path to Mt. Pierce, but it is also worthwhile on its own merit. It is a nice destination away from the nearby crowds of other waterfalls in Crawford Notch State Park, as well.

TRAIL INFORMATION The hike to the falls begins by following the Crawford Connector for 0.4 mile to a bridge over Gibbs Brook. You will find some unnamed cascades just upstream of the bridge, along with yellow-tinted pools. This is a relaxing spot to take a break before you finish hiking to the main waterfall. There is also a diversion worth noting; right before the bridge is a path to Crawford Cliff, which provides great views.

When you are ready to continue to the falls, cross the bridge over the brook, walk a very short distance farther, and take a left onto the Crawford Path. Follow the Crawford Path uphill (north) for 0.2 mile and there will be a short trail that descends to the falls. The falls can be seen and heard momentarily.

DIRECTIONS From the junction of US 302 and NH 16 in the section of Bartlett known as Glen, take US 302 west for 20.8 miles. Turn right onto Mt. Clinton Road, which is across the street from the AMC's Highland Center at Crawford Notch, and follow it 0.1 mile to a left into a hiker's parking lot. *To get to Glen,* take NH 16 north from Conway.

OTHER WATERFALLS NEARBY Beecher and Pearl Cascades, Flume Cascade, Silver Cascade, Kedron Flume, Ripley Falls, Arethusa Falls, Ammonoosuc Ravine, Upper Ammonoosuc Falls

116

GLEN ELLIS FALLS

Jackson, White Mountain National Forest, Carroll County

Rating: 5.0/5.0
Type: Plunge
Height: 64 feet
Trail Length: 0.3 mile
Water Source: Ellis River
Altitude Gain/Loss: -100 feet

Difficulty: Easy
Hiking Time: 10 minutes
DeLorme Atlas: Page 44, B-7 (unmarked)
Best Time to Visit: May to October

THE FALLS (HIGHLY RECOMMENDED) The most popular waterfall of the Pinkham Notch area is the 64-foot plunge known as Glen Ellis Falls. With a fine spray of water throughout the warmer months, this waterfall attracts thousands of vacationers from all over.

Being situated minutes from other long-time favorite attractions of the area, along with its ease of access, makes this waterfall another White Mountain National Forest attraction that can be crowded even in the lousiest weather conditions. However, as unattractive as a crowded waterfall can be, it is crowded for a reason.

This waterfall is quite distinctive, with its exceptionally deep, green pool and the leftward angle at which the water plunges. It is too bad that the waterfall is off-limits to swimming, as this would be one of the more enjoyable swimming holes in the state.

Just about anyone that can walk down stairs can visit this waterfall. The trail is short and well worth it. Just do not expect to be alone at this waterfall.

TRAIL INFORMATION From the parking lot, follow the Glen Ellis Falls Trail to the falls. The trail will pass underneath NH 16 and then proceed down several staircases, passing several unnamed cascades with clear and clean pools. These are not the main attractions—continue to the trail's end and be sure to check out the upper, middle, and bottom viewpoints, as each offers its own stunning perspective.

DIRECTIONS From the junction of NH 16 and US 302 in the section of Bartlett known as Glen, take NH 16 north for 11.0 miles. Take a left at the sign for GLEN ELLIS FALLS. The parking area will be down this road. This turnoff is 0.6 mile south of the AMC Pinkham Notch visitor center. *To get to Glen,* take NH 16 north from Conway.

Please be aware that this trailhead is part of the White Mountain National Forest parking fee program. The fee was $3 in 2009 but there is currently a proposal in review to raise this amount to $5.

OTHER WATERFALLS NEARBY Crystal Cascade, Thompson Falls, Winniweta Falls, Jackson Falls

117

~

HERMIT FALLS

Chatham, White Mountain National Forest, Carroll County

Rating: 3.0/5.0

Type: Horsetail

Height: 30-foot total drop

Trail Length: 1.3 miles

Water Source: Basin Brook

Altitude Gain/Loss: +100 feet

Difficulty: Easy side of moderate

Hiking Time: 35 minutes

DeLorme Atlas: Page 45, A-12 (marked)

Best Time to Visit: May to July

THE FALLS Hermit Falls is located in near the North Chatham/Beans Purchase town border. It is tucked a mile northwest of the Basin Campground, which is operated by the U.S. Forest Service.

A seasonal falls, the best time to visit Hermit Falls is before the end of June, or after a substantial rainstorm. In high-water conditions, Hermit Falls is a pretty 30-foot horsetail within a remote, moss-surrounded ravine. In low water, the falls turns into a powerless slide down dark, wet rock.

The falls are an easy walk from either the campground or from the picnic area at Basin Pond. Do not go out of your way to visit the falls, unless, of course, you are a waterfall fanatic. Rather, check out Hermit Falls if you happen to be vacationing at the campground, or if you are visiting other nearby waterfalls. The falls may not be spectacular enough to visit on their own, but it makes a fine addition to other local attractions.

You can add to the fun of visiting this waterfall by combining it with Basin Trail Cascades, also accessible by the Basin Trail. The best way to do this is to do a car-spot between both trailheads of the Basin Trail (the other one being along Wild River Road; see chapter on Basin Trail Cascades for additional information).

TRAIL INFORMATION The trip to Hermit Falls follows the Basin Trail, a yellow-marked trail that first parallels the southern edge of Basin Pond. The trail begins near the parking area restrooms behind a brown sign for the BASIN TRAIL. For the first 0.5 mile, you will hike along the southern edge of Basin Pond, with several gaps providing scenic views to the north. Soon after passing the eastern edge of the pond, the trail markers will become less obvious and, in several stretches, the trail becomes narrow due to overgrown plants. Continue to look aggressively for trail blazes, and the trail will soon return to its original width after crossing several streams. The remainder of this 1.3-mile walk is rated easy but watch out for occasional muddy patches.

DIRECTIONS From the junction of ME 113 and US 302 in Fryeburg, Maine, take ME 113 north for 19.4 miles and take a left into the signed BASIN RECREATION AREA. This turn is 7.7 miles past the southern junction of ME 113 and NH 113b in the village of Stow. Follow the access road toward the Basin Campground for 0.6 mile and turn right before the campground into the Basin Pond parking area. *To get to Fryeburg,* take NH 113 east from NH 16 in Conway, New Hampshire into Maine.

OTHER WATERFALLS NEARBY Rattlesnake Flume and Pool (ME), Bickford Slides (ME), Mad River Falls (ME), Brickett Falls, Eagle Cascade, Kees Falls (ME)

118

~

HUNTINGTON CASCADES
Dixville, Dixville Notch State Park, Coos County

Rating: 3.5/5.0

Type: Horsetails and cascades

Height: Lower falls are 18 feet; upper falls are 50 feet

Trail Length: 0.25 mile to upper falls

Water Source: Cascade Brook

Altitude Gain/Loss: +150 feet to upper falls

Difficulty: Easy to lower falls; moderate to upper falls

Hiking Time: 5 minutes to lower falls; 10 minutes to upper falls

DeLorme Atlas: Page 50, C-6 (unmarked)

Best Time to Visit: May to October

THE FALLS Located in the Dixville Notch State Park, less than a half-mile from the Dixville Flume, Huntington Cascades, often referred to as Huntington Falls, offers two servings of slim horsetails. Lower Huntington Cascades is the formation described in Bolnick's *Waterfalls of the White Mountains.* It consists of a segmented horsetail in the center of a ravine, about 18 feet tall in height and surrounded by the luscious greens of various species of moss.

The upper falls are markedly different from their sister below. With visibility restricted by hemlock trees, the upper falls appear quite small and insignificant from the lower section of cascades. The true height and beauty of the upper falls can only be seen by continuing up the Huntington Cascades Trail. Although the slender horsetails of the upper falls are mostly hidden under heavy tree cover and surrounding steep gorge walls, this section of the falls is the least crowded, and several rock ledges are conveniently located at great vantage points.

TRAIL INFORMATION Travel up the Huntington Cascades Trail from the parking area. About 300 feet after entering the woods, fork right and cross a brook a few feet later. The lower falls are 100 feet upstream from here, and can be seen on either side of the brook. The upper waterfall is a few hundred feet farther up the trail, which can only be accessed by a moderate climb up the trail with the river on your right. Accessing the upper falls is slightly more difficult than what you have navigated so far, but this should not prevent you from at least getting a satisfying view of the falls.

Huntington Cascades

DIRECTIONS From the junction of NH 26 and US 3 in Colebrook, follow NH 26 east. Travel on NH 26 east for 11.9 miles and take a right into the Cascade Brook Picnic Area, marked by a sign for the DIXVILLE NOTCH WAYSIDE AREA. This parking area is only 0.2 mile east of the Dixville Flume. After you pull into the picnic area, you will need to continue farther down this rough road, bearing left at a fork, until you reach a trailhead with a sign for HUNTINGTON FALLS. *To get to Colebrook,* take US 3 north from Lincoln.

OTHER WATERFALLS NEARBY Dixville Flume, Beaver Brook Falls, Colebrook, Pond Brook Falls

119

JACKSON FALLS
Jackson, Carroll County

Rating: 4.0/5.0
Type: Cascades and small plunges
Height: Approximately 100-foot total drop
Trail Length: 0.1 mile to lower falls; upper falls are roadside
Water Source: Wildcat Brook

Altitude Gain/Loss: Negligible
Difficulty: Easy
Hiking Time: 5 minutes to lower falls; none to upper falls
DeLorme Atlas: Page 45, E-9 (unmarked)
Best Time to Visit: Year-round

THE FALLS During the summer, the small town of Jackson attracts hundreds of visitors to its swimming holes at Jackson Falls. Early runoff in the springtime offers impressive masses of water crashing over endless boulders and rock ledges. Although Jackson Falls lacks any magnificent drops, it does contain many cascades, slides, and plunges of differing sizes. When viewing Jackson Falls from below, you are likely to have the best photo opportunity, but be aware that your photos are most likely going to have some people lounging on the rocks above.

For generations, this special place has been a favorite picnic place. Families often let their children roam free in the chilly waters and splash in the various pools and potholes for hours. It does not matter if it is springtime, summer, or fall, Jackson Falls always has more than a few contented visitors.

If you want a part of Jackson Falls to enjoy to yourself, try the lower half of the falls by walking up the path that starts across from The Wentworth

Hotel. The crowds are much thinner here, and there are several large plunges that usually photograph well. Pay close attention to your personal safety in this area, as the current is stronger and the drops are larger on these lower falls. Always play it safe when scrambling around such places.

TRAIL INFORMATION Access to the lower falls has recently changed. To reach the lower falls, follow a public way upstream directly alongside the river that begins across from the Wentworth Hotel. The falls will be easily reached in 0.1 mile. It is no longer safely possible to get to the upper falls from this point. To view the middle and upper falls, you must walk back to the road and either drive or walk 0.3 mile up Carter Notch Road. The middle and upper falls are clearly visible from the road.

DIRECTIONS From the junction of US 302 and NH 16 in the section of Bartlett known as Glen, take NH 16 north for 2.7 miles, past Storyland, and take a right onto NH 16a (Take note that NH 16a is a loop with two NH 16 junctions—you want to take the northernmost one). Follow NH 16a for 0.3 mile to a left onto Carter Notch Road.

There are separate trailheads for the upper and lower segments of the falls. *To visit the lower falls,* park immediately on the dirt shoulder on your right just after making the turn onto Carter Notch Road. *To visit the middle and upper falls,* drive 0.3 mile up Carter Notch Road and several dirt pull-offs will begin on your right and continue up the road. *To get to Glen,* take NH 16 north from Conway.

OTHER WATERFALLS NEARBY Winniweta Falls, Glen Ellis Falls, Diana's Baths, Crystal Cascade, Thompson Falls

120

KEDRON FLUME
Harts Location, Crawford Notch State Park, Carroll County

Rating: 3.0/5.0

Type: Cascades and slides

Height: Approximately 150 feet of vertical drop viewable from trail

Trail Length: 0.75 mile

Water Source: Kedron Brook

Altitude Gain/Loss: +500 feet

Difficulty: Moderate

Hiking Time: 40 minutes

DeLorme Atlas: Page 44, E-4 (unmarked)

Best Time to Visit: May to October

THE FALLS Just north of the two famous waterfalls of Crawford Notch State Park—Ripley Falls and Arethusa Falls—lies a relatively unknown third waterfall, Kedron Flume. Here, the mountain waters of Kedron Brook surge through a narrow flume, slide for a long distance through a narrow chute, and eventually begin their steep descent toward the highway below.

Exploring the flume is a dangerous business. The rocks on the trail and around the falls are deceptively slippery. Although most of the time the water volume is quite low, perhaps only a few inches deep, mist and condensation makes exploring the terrain hazardous. If you take extra caution, walk 20 feet downstream from the trail crossing and you can stand atop a waterfall ledge, with views of Mt. Webster to the north opening up.

The waters of Kedron Brook can run throughout summer, but we expect you will enjoy the flume more during times of rushing waters. Beginning at the end of the snowmelt season—usually early May to the middle of June— you are pretty much guaranteed a good show. In midsummer, the waterfall becomes progressively more difficult to see due to ever-growing leaves and tree coverage. We urge you to visit this place soon; over time, this waterfall has the potential to become lost to the woods as the underbrush continues to thicken.

TRAIL INFORMATION From the southernmost parking lot at the Willey House Picnic Area (the first parking lot reached if coming from Glen), start climbing up the Kedron Flume Trail to the falls. There is a small sign for the trail above the PICNIC AREA roadside sign at the end of the parking lot, just before the Willey House historic building.

This blue-marked trail is a continuous uphill hike. After about 15 minutes of hiking, you will cross a set of railroad tracks, just before the halfway mark. From the parking area to this set of tracks, the trail gradually weaves its way toward the flume via switchbacks. From the railroad tracks to the flume, the trail transforms to a rather steep, slippery, and muddy trail. About a half-mile beyond the tracks, the trail will level out and the narrow flume will appear on the right and continue underneath your feet before dropping again in a horsetail formation. Only about 150 feet of the falls is visible along the trail. The total drop of the falls is probably hundreds more, but there is no safe access to witness other sections not seen from the trail.

DIRECTIONS From the junction of US 302 and NH 16 in the section of Bartlett known as Glen, take US 302 west for 17.9 miles. Turn left into the parking area for the Willey House Picnic Area, which is adjacent to the Willey House Historical Site. The Willey House Picnic Area is 0.9 mile west of the access road to Ripley Falls and 1.9 miles east of Silver Cascade. *To get to Glen,* take NH 16 north from Conway.

OTHER WATERFALLS NEARBY Ripley Falls, Arethusa Falls, Silver Cascade, Flume Cascade, Beecher and Pearl Cascades, Gibbs Falls, Thoreau Falls

121
~

LOWER FALLS
Albany, White Mountains National Forest, Carroll County

Rating: 3.0/5.0
Type: Cascades
Height: 10-foot total drop
Trail Length: Roadside
Water Source: Swift River
Altitude Gain/Loss: None

Difficulty: Easy
Hiking Time: Not applicable
DeLorme Atlas: Page 44, J-7
(marked as Lower Falls Picnic Area)
Best Time to Visit: Year-round

THE FALLS Located just feet off the Kancamagus Highway, Lower Falls is a legendary White Mountains National Forest attraction. This is *the* waterfall of the White Mountains that so many travelers will recall immensely enjoying during childhood. Hot summer weekends can bring thousands of visitors per day.

Although none of cascades are large or particularly powerful, it does not really matter; the many cascades and pools to swim and splash in make this place special. With simple and easy access you can understand why this waterfall may be the most heavily visited in New England.

There are bathrooms, drinking water, and a covered picnic area with a grill—all to provide more enjoyment while visiting the falls. Lower Falls is definitely worth your attention, as it is photogenic, and historically, one of the most cherished falls of the White Mountains. Just down the road are additional beloved waterfalls: Sabbaday Falls, Rocky Gorge, and Champney Falls. Of all these Kancamagus Highway waterfalls, Lower Falls is the best for swimming. Make sure to bring your bathing suit!

TRAIL INFORMATION From the parking lot, follow the river downstream 200 feet to the main cascades. For a complete view of the falls, considering walking alongside NH 112 a few hundred feet downstream of the parking area where you can take an unobstructed photograph of the entire formation. Be very careful doing so as the highway is very popular.

DIRECTIONS From the junction of NH 112 and NH 16 in Conway, take NH 112 (the Kancamagus Highway) west for 6.9 miles and the marked parking lot for the LOWER FALLS will be on your right. If you are traveling from I-93 in Lincoln, take exit 32 and follow NH 112 east for 28.5 miles and the parking lot will be on your left. The falls are located 2.0 miles east of the Rocky Gorge Scenic Area and 0.6 mile west of the Blackberry Crossing Campground.

Please be aware that this trailhead is part of the White Mountain National Forest parking fee program. The fee was $3 in 2009 but there is currently a proposal in review to raise this amount to $5.

OTHER WATERFALLS NEARBY Rocky Gorge, Champney Falls, Sabbaday Falls, Diana's Baths

122

MOSSY GLEN
Randolph, Coos County

Rating: 3.0/5.0

Type: Cascades and slides

Height: 40-foot total drop

Trail Length: 0.3 mile

Water Source: Carlton Brook

Altitude Gain/Loss: +100 feet

Difficulty: Easy

Hiking Time: 10 minutes

DeLorme Atlas: Page 48, I-6 (unmarked)

Best Time to Visit: May to October

THE FALLS A short stroll from the road will bring you to Mossy Glen; a series of pools, slides, and cascades set among heavy growth of several moss species. Thin sheets of water drop at low angles here. There is also a pool with a whirlpool current, and a nicely crafted pine bridge, which adds much visual appeal to the hike.

Be sure to read the historical sign affixed to the ceiling of this pine bridge. For additional fun on your return hike, cross back over the bridge and take the trail on the left to the moss-covered stone steps of the Mossy Glen Amphitheatre. The Randolph Mountain Club, a volunteer-based organization deeply involved in trail work and backcountry lodging in the area, continues to use this location on occasion for meetings and gatherings.

TRAIL INFORMATION The trail to the falls begins by traveling up a dirt road marked by a sign for the GROVEWAY. After passing by two houses on your left, take a right onto the trail. You will pass a mossy amphitheatre and shortly thereafter cross a nicely constructed pine bridge. The bridge was built in 1968 and is "a New England copy of one seen in Nepal by Louise Baldwin and Miriam Underhill." After crossing the small bridge, take a left onto a trail marked by a sign for GLENSIDE TO BEE LINE VIA MOSSY GLEN. The upper falls are only 100 feet up this trail. On our visits to Mossy Glen, the trail connecting the lower and upper falls has been very muddy.

DIRECTIONS From the junction of US 2 and NH 16 in Gorham, take US 2 west. Travel on US 2 west for 5.8 miles and take a right on Durand Road East. This road is 1.3 miles past the RANDOLPH TOWN LINE sign on US 2. Take a left after 0.1 mile to continue on Durand Road East. From here, continue 0.4 mile farther and the trailhead, marked by a sign for the GROVEWAY, will appear. The trail begins before the Randolph Public Library. Parking is available in the grass across the street. *To get to Gorham,* take NH 16 north from Conway.

OTHER WATERFALLS NEARBY Appalachia Waterfalls, Falls on the Howker Ridge Trail, Triple Falls, Giant Falls, Dryad Fall

123

~

NANCY CASCADES

Livermore, White Mountain National Forest, Grafton County

Rating: 5.0/5.0
Type: Horsetails and cascades
Height: Approximately 300-foot total drop
Trail Length: To lower falls, 2.4 miles; to upper falls, 2.8 miles
Water Source: Nancy Brook
Altitude Gain/Loss: +1,700 feet to upper falls

Difficulty: Moderate side of difficult
Hiking Time: 2 hours
DeLorme Atlas: Page 44, G-4 (marked as Nancy Brook)
Best Time to Visit: May to October

THE FALLS (HIGHLY RECOMMENDED) The sum of the height of the cascades that adorn Nancy Brook is estimated at 300 feet, making Nancy Cascades undeniably one of the tallest in New England. Nancy Brook is fed by the waters of Nancy Pond. Both the cascades and the pond have been held in high regard for over a century, and rightfully so.

A rust-colored pool below the 45-foot fanning horsetail marks the lowest segment of the cascades. The waters of Nancy Brook cascade down gray gneiss bedrock before hopping over a ledge, causing the water to plunge the remaining distance into the pool below. By the time you reach the lower falls, at mile 2.4 on the trail, you may be tired of the continuous climbing effort already demanded of you. For that reason, the spectacular lower falls are a rewarding relief.

Above the main falls are hundreds of feet of chutes, slides, horsetails, and small plunges equally as stunning and charming as the bottom falls. About 0.7 mile above the uppermost falls, Nancy Pond, also accessed by the same trail, is a remote, peaceful body of water just southeast of Mt. Nancy.

The brook, pond, falls, and a nearby mountain are named after a passionate servant woman, known only as Nancy, who entered Crawford Notch during a White Mountain winter, trying to reach the camp where her lost fiancé was. Failing to catch up with her lover, who left Nancy to go on a trip without saying goodbye (why he left is not known), Nancy crossed the Saco River and quickly become exhausted by the chilly waters, and was found dead from hypothermia the next day.

TRAIL INFORMATION The Nancy Pond Trail starts from the parking area on US 302 and immediately enters into the woods, traveling at first along a yellow-blazed forest road. For the first two-thirds of the trail, the elevation gain is modest. The final third of the trail is markedly steeper. This final section is not as well marked or easy to follow, so pay attention to the trail. One stretch of the upper section has experienced heavy erosion, and it is difficult to ramble through this area.

Once you reach the bottom set of cascades, continue climbing to the left of the falls to view the two additional segments of horsetails and cascades above. Beyond the lower falls, expect a steeper, tough trail. We expect that during the spring months, the trail to the upper falls is extraordinarily slippery and sullied with muddy stretches.

DIRECTIONS From the junction of US 302 and NH 16 in the section of Bartlett known as Glen, take US 302 west for 11.3 miles and the parking area for the Nancy Pond Trail will be on the left. The trailhead is located 2.8 miles west of the sign marking the WHITE MOUNTAIN NATIONAL FOREST border and 3.1 miles east of the sign marking the CRAWFORD NOTCH STATE PARK border. *To get to Glen,* take NH 16 north from Conway.

OTHER WATERFALLS NEARBY Arethusa Falls, Ripley Falls, Kedron Flume, Silver Cascade, Flume Cascade, Diana's Baths

124

∽

PARADISE FALLS

Woodstock, Lost River Reservation, Grafton County

Rating: 3.5/5.0

Type: Plunges and small cascades

Height: Tallest plunge is 20 feet

Trail Length: 0.8-mile loop

Water Source: Lost River

Altitude Gain/Loss: -300 feet, +300 feet

Difficulty: Easy side of moderate

Hiking Time: 60 minutes

DeLorme Atlas: Page 43, I-9 (marked as Lost River)

Best Time to Visit: May to October

THE FALLS The first question a visitor to the Lost River Reservation may ask is, "Where was this place when I was a child?" Not only does the Lost River Reservation have two waterfalls, one of which is particularly scenic, it also has about a dozen different small caves open for exploration. While some caves are large enough to walk straight into, others require passing through tight squeezes, where your agility and upper-body strength will be put to the test.

The prime waterfall within the reservation is Paradise Falls, and it is located near the middle of the 0.8-mile boardwalk loop trail. From the trail, you are provided both a head-on view and a bird's-eye vantage point. Although viewing this waterfall is limited to the boardwalk due to fencing, there are enough spots to encapsulate the beauty of this waterfall.

The Falls of Proserpine are the second falls you can find here. This waterfall is more elusive than its neighbor; you must enter the Judgment Hall of Pluto to obtain any sort of view. Photography will be difficult here due to the small size of the cave and the fact that the falls are for the most part hidden behind a huge boulder.

This waterfall is one of the most visited in New England, simply because it is seen by all who visit the reservation. We suggest joining the crowds, especially if you (or your children) enjoy caves or waterfalls. An accurate rating system is in place to let you know which caves along the loop are more difficult than others. This information is printed on the trail map provided to each guest upon paying the entrance fee. This fee was $14.00 for adults and $10.00 for children in 2009, and well worth it in our opinion.

TRAIL INFORMATION The trail begins at the visitor center and follows a boardwalk loop trail 0.8 mile past Paradise Falls and various small caves before bringing you back to the visitor center. You will easily be able to spot Paradise Falls on the boardwalk about 0.3 mile from the visitor center.

There is another waterfall within this property that was just recently opened to the public for viewing after being closed for 20 years. About 0.5 mile from the visitor center, enter the cave known as the Judgment Hall of Pluto, where you can obtain a partially obstructed view of the underground waterfall known as the Falls of Proserpine.

Take note that you will be required to maneuver through one cave toward the end of this loop. While it is not a tight squeeze, as many of the other optional caves you can explore along this route are, you may find yourself having to walk on your knees or at the very least, removing and carrying your backpack as you navigate through it.

DIRECTIONS Paradise Falls is located within the Lost River Reservation. To get to the Lost River Reservation, take exit 32 off I-93 in North Woodstock. Turn onto NH 112 west. Continue traveling on NH 112 for 5.7 miles west of the junction of NH 112 and US 3. There are several large signs for the LOST RIVER RESERVATION on the highway, so it is hard to miss.

OTHER WATERFALLS NEARBY Beaver Brook Cascades, Agassiz Basin, Georgiana Falls, Falls on the Flume–Pool Loop, Swiftwater Falls, Bath

125

POLLARDS MILLS
Newport, Sullivan County

Rating: 3.0/5.0
Type: Cascades
Height: 18-foot total drop
Trail Length: Roadside
Water Source: South Branch of the Sugar River

Altitude Gain/Loss: None
Difficulty: Easy
Hiking Time: Not applicable
DeLorme Atlas: Page 33, K-14 (unmarked)
Best Time to Visit: Year-round

THE FALLS If our rating system was based on overall experience and not solely on the waterfalls themselves, this location would earn our top recommendation. The waterfall itself is a simple but pretty 18-foot cascade that shoots into a large pool below that is excellent for swimming. In fact, this is likely to be the prime swimming hole in the region. The falls are surrounded by beautiful gardens, picnic tables, chairs, and a small nature trail.

The land is private property, but the current landowner encourages visitors to enjoy the area and go swimming for the day. Based on a discussion with this landowner, this very spot has been where many locals first learned how to swim.

The property used to be the site of three mills along the river; a lumber mill, a gristmill, and a peg mill. The old mill below the falls was built in 1797 and was washed out by a flood in 1919. The remnants of the foundations of these mills can be found by exploring around the waterfall and hiking the small nature walk that is maintained by the property owner.

In order to prevent the loss of this special place to the general public, we must all respect the landowners' requests. Pollards Mills deserves to be enjoyed by all but as visitors we are responsible for keeping it open. Please do not litter or cause any sort of harm to the natural environment. Overall, you will find this waterfall to be charming, but the entire experience to be incredible!

TRAIL INFORMATION The falls are clearly visible from roadside.

DIRECTIONS From the southern intersection of NH 10, NH 103, and NH 11 in Newport, travel on NH 10 south for 1.9 miles. Turn right onto Pollards Mill Road. Drive 0.3 mile and turn left onto Falls Road. The small parking pull-off is just up ahead on the left.

OTHER WATERFALLS NEARBY None

126

POND BROOK FALLS

Stratford, Nash Stream Forest, Coos County

Rating: 3.5/5.0
Type: Cascades and slides
Height: 100-foot total drop
Trail Length: 0.1 mile
Water Source: Pond Brook
Altitude Gain/Loss: +150 feet to top of falls

Difficulty: Easy
Hiking Time: 5 minutes
DeLorme Atlas: Page 50, I-3 (unmarked)
Best Time to Visit: May to October

THE FALLS Pond Brook Falls is a concealed chain of sparkling cascades and slides in New Hampshire's Coos County. Before the Bolnicks' *Waterfalls of*

Pond Brook Falls

the White Mountains, Pond Brook Falls was absent from practically all other guidebooks of the area. The identity may now be revealed, but Pond Brook Falls remains just as private and untouched as it was before.

Just north of the popular day-hike summits of Percy Peaks, the individual cascades of Pond Brook Falls are not exceptionally spectacular or mystifying. The pleasing appeal is derived from the broad slabs of rock that nature constructed for your picnicking and sunbathing pleasure. As an added bonus, there are plenty of cascades and other nooks and crannies to explore upstream. This is the waterfall for those of you wishing to avoid the crowds at the waterfalls located south in the White Mountains region.

TRAIL INFORMATION Continue to the end of the parking lot where you will cross over a few boulders and enter the woods on a soft dirt path. After 0.1 mile, you will approach the lower cascades. The official path ends and you must continue climbing cautiously upstream among rocks and boulders to the right of the falls.

DIRECTIONS From the junction of NH 110 and US 3 in Groveton, take NH 110 east for 2.6 miles. Take a left onto Emerson Road. Follow this road for 1.4 miles and you will come to a fork. Take the right fork and continue on Emerson Road for an additional 0.7 mile farther. Take a left onto Nash Stream Road. Follow Nash Stream Road, a well maintained logging road, for 5.7 miles and the parking area will be on your right just after crossing a culvert over Pond Brook The parking area is not well marked, but if you look closely enough, you should be able to spot a POND BROOK FALLS sign on a tree here. Be aware that Nash Stream Road may be impassible during the early spring mud season. *To get to Groveton,* take US 3 north from Lincoln.

OTHER WATERFALLS NEARBY Beaver Brook Falls, Colebrook, Dixville Flume, Huntington Cascades

127

PROFILE FALLS
Bristol, Merrimack County

Rating: 4.0/5.0

Type: Fan

Height: 30 feet

Trail Length: 0.2 mile

Water Source: Smith River

Altitude Gain/Loss: Negligible

Difficulty: Easy

Hiking Time: 10 minutes

DeLorme Atlas: Page 35, C-10

(unmarked)

Best Time to Visit: Year-round

THE FALLS Despite being located so close to the road and being part of a town park, this waterfall was very surprising. Who knew that this section of central New Hampshire had such a mighty river with a dominant waterfall? This waterfall, a horsetail that fans dramatically across an elongated ledge, is just a portion of the park, which offers lots of trails to explore (some suitable for mountain biking), picnic tables, and barbecue grills.

Profile Falls

Profile Falls is one of our favorite waterfalls for fishing, so be sure to bring your rod as you are very likely to catch some trout or even salmon if the season is right. One downside to the falls: on two separate visits we noticed an bad odor in the air. We are unsure if the smell is from the river or not, but it prevented us from going for a swim, which is normally popular here in the summer months.

TRAIL INFORMATION From the parking area, follow the signs upstream 0.2 mile to the falls. It is an easy and pleasant walk in the woods along a wide, well-maintained trail. After some trial and error, we believe that the best place for a photograph is from the island in the middle of the Smith River.

DIRECTIONS From I-93 in New Hampton, take exit 23. Follow NH 104 west into Bristol. Once you reach the center of Bristol, take a left onto NH 3a south. Follow NH 3a south for 2.1 miles and take a left onto an unmarked paved road (Profile Falls Road) just before crossing a bridge. Follow this road for 0.2 mile and take a right onto a new unmarked road at a sign for the falls. Follow this road for 0.1 mile and there will be a parking lot on the right. *To get to New Hampton,* take I-93 north from Concord or I-93 south from Lincoln.

OTHER WATERFALLS NEARBY Welton Falls, Sculptured Rocks

128

~

PURGATORY FALLS

Mont Vernon & Lyndeborough, Purgatory Falls Conservation Area, Hillsborough County

Rating: 3.5/5.0

Type: Cascades and a small plunge

Height: 25-foot total drop

Trail Length: 1.2 miles

Water Source: Purgatory Brook

Altitude Gain/Loss: +75 feet, -175 feet

Difficulty: Moderate

Hiking Time: 40 minutes

DeLorme Atlas: Page 21, E-11 (unmarked)

Best Time to Visit: May to October

THE FALLS If you are in the area of Mont Vernon, jump on over to secluded Purgatory Falls, a short series of cascades traveling through a narrow gorge, accessible by horseback, by mountain bike, or by foot. No matter your transportation, expect to get a little muddy, as we always have when we visit. Several local residents informed us that for most of the year the trail has giant muddy puddles that must either be traveled through or passed by. Every section is manageable if you take the time to scout the best way through or around these puddles.

The total drop of the falls is short, about 25 feet, but worth the visit as many other waterfalls do not offer the seclusion that this one does. Although we have not visited any of the additional cascades downstream, they are rumored to be a nice bonus to this hike.

TRAIL INFORMATION The trail to the falls begins by continuing on foot along Upton Road for 0.9 mile. If Upton Road is washed out, which it usually is, use the paths to the side of the road to avoid stepping in any large puddles. When you reach a trail junction, Purgatory Brook and a small swamp, take a left and continue on another old dirt road 0.3 mile south to the falls, which will be on your right. Scramble down the embankment for the best view of the falls.

There are additional cascades (sometimes called Lower Purgatory Falls) that can be reached by continuing downstream an additional 3.0 miles from the main falls. We have not personally visited these cascades, but they do look slightly promising based on pictures found during our research.

DIRECTIONS From the western junction of NH 13 and NH 101a in Milford, take NH 13 north for 3.7 miles. Take a left onto Purgatory Road. Follow Purgatory Road for 0.8 mile and take a right onto Wilton Road. Drive along Wilton Road for 0.6 mile, and take a left onto Upton Road, a

Purgatory Falls

dirt road. Follow Upton Road for 0.3 mile and the parking lot will be on the left. *To get to Milton,* take NH 101a west from Nashua.

OTHER WATERFALLS NEARBY Garwin Falls, Tucker Brook Falls

129

RAINBOW FALLS
Plymouth, Walter/Newton Natural Area,
Grafton County

Rating: 3.5/5.0

Type: Horsetail

Height: 25-foot total drop

Trail Length: 0.75 mile

Water Source: Glove Hollow
Brook

Altitude Gain/Loss: +100 feet

Difficulty: Easy

Hiking Time: 30 minutes

DeLorme Atlas: Page 39, I-11
(unmarked)

Best Time to Visit: May to
October

THE FALLS This well-maintained nature preserve offers benches to sit on and view the falls, which is a series of horsetails falling over a broad granite face. The top drop is especially scenic and photographs well. Unfortunately, over the last few years several trees have fallen, masking much of the falls. Due to the fragile area surrounding the waterfall, these trees have not been removed by those who maintain the park. Perhaps natural forces will one day clear these obstructions and bring the splendid beauty of the waterfalls back. Take note that there is no swimming at this particular location. If swimming is what you desire, nearby Livermore Falls will fit the bill.

TRAIL INFORMATION The Ruth Walter Trail begins across the bridge at the nature area sign. Do not be fooled by the small path in front of the parking area. Be sure to walk across the bridge and turn left onto the necessary trail. The trail is well maintained and relatively flat. It tends to be muddy after periods of rain and during high-water runoff.

At the base of the falls there is a loop to the left that crosses a small wooden bridge and circles around to view the falls from above. If you are looking for an extra hike this trail is worth the trip, otherwise the best view of the falls is obtained at the base by the small white sign.

DIRECTIONS From I-93 in Plymouth, take exit 25. Follow signs to US 3 and take a left onto US 3 south (also called Main Street.) Travel on US

3 south for 2.3 miles (passing through a rotary along the way) and take a right onto Cummings Hill Road. Travel on Cummings Hill Road for 0.8 mile to a small parking area on the right.

OTHER WATERFALLS NEARBY Campton Falls, Beede Falls, Sculptured Rocks

130

RIPLEY FALLS

Harts Location, Crawford Notch State Park, Carroll County

Rating: 5.0/5.0
Type: Horsetail and slides
Height: 100-foot total drop
Trail Length: 0.6 mile
Water Source: Avalanche Brook
Altitude Gain/Loss: +400 feet

Difficulty: Easy side of moderate
Hiking Time: 25 minutes
DeLorme Atlas: Page 44, E-4
(marked)
Best Time to Visit: Year-round

THE FALLS (HIGHLY RECOMMENDED) Crawford Notch State Park is rich with noteworthy waterfalls. Toward the north end of the park are Gibbs Falls, Beecher and Pearl Cascades, and the sisters Flume Cascade and Silver Cascade. For the southern half of the state park, you will find popular day-trip destinations of Arethusa Falls and Ripley Falls, the latter being discussed here.

Ripley Falls is a beautiful 100-foot sheet of white water flowing over a smooth rock wall. The rock wall is at about a 60-degree angle, causing the rushing mountain water to maintain contact with the rock during most of its descent. For the best photograph, scramble a few feet downstream and add some scale to your camera's frame, such as a person or rock in the foreground.

There are only short, temporary periods where the water jumps away from the rock wall. Because of this, Ripley Falls, as an entire structure, is one of the most steeply angled slides in all of New England.

TRAIL INFORMATION The trail to the falls is an uphill climb most of the way. At times, it is muddy and moderately steep. From the parking lot, follow the white-blazed Ethan Pond Trail for slightly less than 0.2 mile to a junction with the Arethusa-Ripley Falls Trail. Fork left onto the Arethusa-Ripley Falls Trail, and continue for 0.4 mile farther to the falls.

The trail will be marked with blue blazes from this point forward.

If you feel more adventurous, you can continue along the Arethusa-Ripley Falls Trail to spectacular Arethusa Falls, as part of a long loop. Arethusa Falls can also be visited on its own for a much easier trail. Please refer to the separate Arethusa Falls chapter for information on how to either do the loop or visit each falls on their own.

For those looking for extended overnight trips, Ripley Falls can be complemented with other waterfalls that sprout from short spur trails off the Ethan Pond Trail. Thoreau Falls and Zealand Falls are two waterfalls that can be added to Ripley Falls for either a lengthy day-trip or an overnight backpacking trip. There are several backcountry accommodations one can use for such a trip, including the AMC's Zealand Falls Hut and the Ethan Pond Campsite.

There are also rumored waterfalls upstream of Ripley Falls called Sparkling Cascade and Sylvan Glade Cataract. Reaching these two elusive falls may involve extensive bushwhacking in steep and dangerous terrain, so please take caution.

DIRECTIONS From the junction of US 302 and NH 16 in the section of Bartlett known as Glen, take US 302 west for 16.8 miles. Turn left onto an unmarked road at a sign for RIPLEY FALLS. Drive up this road past the overflow parking area to an upper parking lot. This access road is 2.3 miles west of Arethusa Falls Road and 1.0 mile east of the Willey House Historical Site. *To get to Glen,* take NH 16 north from Conway.

OTHER WATERFALLS NEARBY Arethusa Falls, Kedron Flume, Nancy Cascades, Silver Cascade, Flume Cascade

131

ROCKY GORGE

Albany, White Mountain National Forest, Carroll County

Rating: 3.5/5.0

Type: Cascades

Height: 15-foot total drop

Trail Length: 0.1 mile

Water Source: Swift River

Altitude Gain/Loss: None

Difficulty: Easy

Hiking Time: 5 minutes

DeLorme Atlas: Page 44, J&K-7 (marked as Rocky Gorge Scenic Area)

Best Time to Visit: Year-round

THE FALLS Along with nearby Lower Falls, Champney Falls, and Sabbaday Falls, Rocky Gorge is a popular warm-weather attraction for visitors traveling the Kancamagus Highway. Similar to these other admired waterfalls, Rocky Gorge can be teeming with shutterbugs, swimmers, and other visitors. Despite the crowds, this 15-foot plunge is absolutely worthy of your attention since it is a highly photogenic waterfall set on an open, sunny river.

A bridge has been constructed near the falls to give you one of the better possible perspectives. You do not need the bridge to see the falls, though; the river is easy to navigate around. You will notice signs near the gorge prohibiting swimming. Although swimming in the gorge is prohibited, you may swim both upstream and downstream. The river does have a rather fast current along its entire length, but there are many rock obstacles that create dormant pools that are perfect for a quick dip.

As you walk along the trail to view the falls you will read a story as to why swimming is prohibited at Rocky Gorge. In 1942, Dorothy Sparks went for a swim only to get sucked into the currents and lodged under the rocks beneath the surface. During the three-hour rescue, all thought she was lost, but miraculously she survived. The falls have been off-limits to swimming ever since this event.

There are picnic tables and bathroom facilities here as well, making the area quite visitor friendly.

Rocky Gorge

TRAIL INFORMATION From the parking lot facing the river, take the paved path on your right that travels alongside a log fence. The falls are 0.1 mile away and best viewed by a footbridge that crosses the Swift River. This is a handicap-accessible site, and there are many benches along the short stretch to view the falls. Informational displays along the walk are also worthy of your attention.

DIRECTIONS From the junction of NH 112 and NH 16 in Conway, take NH 112 (the Kancamagus Highway) west for 9.2 miles and the marked parking area will be on your right. If you are traveling from I-93 in Lincoln, take exit 32 and follow NH 112 east for 26.4 miles and the parking area will be on your left. A sign marks the parking area for ROCKY GORGE SCENIC AREA from both sides of the highway. The Rocky Gorge Scenic Area is 2.0 miles west of the parking area for Lower Falls and 1.6 miles east of the parking area for the Champney Falls Trail.

Please be aware that this trailhead is part of the White Mountain National Forest parking fee program. The fee was $3 in 2009 but there is currently a proposal in review to raise this amount to $5.

OTHER WATERFALLS NEARBY Lower Falls, Champney Falls, Sabbaday Falls, Diana's Baths

132

SABBADAY FALLS

Waterville Valley, White Mountain National Forest, Grafton County

Rating: 5.0/5.0
Type: Punchbowl and plunges
Height: 35-foot total drop
Trail Length: 0.3 mile
Water Source: Sabbaday Brook
Altitude Gain/Loss: +100 feet

Difficulty: Easy
Hiking Time: 15 minutes
DeLorme Atlas: Page 44, K-4 (marked)
Best Time to Visit: Year-round

THE FALLS (HIGHLY RECOMMENDED) The main gorge at Sabbaday Falls was allegedly carved over 10,000 years ago by large volumes of water from the last melting glacier. This water carried with it sand, gravel, and boulders, which eventually carved out the gorge. Set inside this gorge are two plunges and a gorgeous punchbowl at the top.

The punchbowl, which is 5 feet in height, falls peacefully into a circular pool about 4 feet wide. Immediately after, Sabbaday Brook plunges about 22 feet. After landing, the waters of the brook turn right and immediately plunge another 8 feet. There are walking bridges and steps so everyone will be able to see all three parts of this fall. Also, be sure to check out the lower pool, which has exceptionally clear water. It is too bad swimming is prohibited here, as this pool would be a perfect place to relax!

Since you are already in the area, you may want to check out nearby Champney Falls, a highly seasonal waterfall with good flow only during the early months of spring.

TRAIL INFORMATION The trail to the falls begins directly in front of the parking lot. It is wide, well marked and well traveled, and mostly flat. Just before the main falls, the trail splits. The left fork takes you close to one of the loveliest pools in the state and provides intimate views of the falls by way of a staircase. If you stay straight, you will stay on the Sabbaday Brook Trail, which is a designated handicap-accessible path (although grades are a bit steep in spots). This will bring you to the top of the falls.

Sabbaday Falls

You will have no problems finding the waterfall on this simple, family-friendly trail. Visitors during the winter season can access the falls via cross-country ski or snowshoe, as the trail is flat and quite easy to navigate.

DIRECTIONS From the junction of NH 112 and NH 16 in Conway, take NH 112 (the Kancamagus Highway) west for 15.5 miles and the marked parking area will be on your left. If you are traveling from I-93 in Lincoln, take exit 32 and follow NH 112 east for 19.9 miles and the parking area will be on your right. A sign marks the parking area for SABBADAY FALLS PICNIC AREA from both directions. Sabbaday Falls Picnic Area is located 1.2 miles west of the Passaconaway Campground and 1.9 miles east of the Sugarhill Overlook.

Please be aware that this trailhead is part of the White Mountain National Forest parking fee program. The fee was $3 in 2009 but there is currently a proposal in review to raise this amount to $5.

OTHER WATERFALLS NEARBY Franconia Falls, Thirteen Falls, Rocky Gorge, Lower Falls, Champney Falls

133

~

SCULPTURED ROCKS
Groton, Sculptured Rocks Natural Area, Grafton County

Rating: 2.5/5.0
Type: Cascades and small plunges
Height: 15-foot total drop
Trail Length: Less than 0.1 mile
Water Source: Cockermouth River

Altitude Gain/Loss: None
Difficulty: Easy
Hiking Time: Negligible
DeLorme Atlas: Page 38, J-7 (marked)
Best Time to Visit: Year-round

THE FALLS If you are passing through the area, this is a nice sight to stop and see. The waterfall itself is nothing spectacular, as there are only the smallest of plunges and cascades here, but the well-carved gorge is quite impressive. This geological wonder is another New Hampshire attraction that is believed to have been formed by a retreated glacier from the great Ice Age, about 10,000 years ago.

Swimming is a locally popular activity at this spot in the summer, but it is only safe in low-water conditions. You might spot people jumping off the gorge walls for a bit of adventure. Others may be enjoying some of the water-filled potholes alongside the river. Swimming can be dangerous here; if the water level looks too high, avoid the temptation, especially within the gorge.

TRAIL INFORMATION From the parking lot, walk back down (heading east) and cross Sculptured Rocks Road. The falls appear shortly after entering the woods on an obvious trail on your left.

DIRECTIONS From I-93 in Plymouth, take exit 26. Follow NH 3a south into Hebron. Continue traveling along NH 3a south for 5.0 miles past the junction of NH 3a and NH 25 in West Plymouth and take a right onto North Shore Road. Follow North Shore Road for 2.4 miles and continue straight onto Groton Road. Follow Groton Road for 1.6 miles and fork left onto Sculptured Rocks Road. Follow this road for 1.2 miles and the large parking area will be on the left. *To get to Plymouth,* take I-93 south from Lincoln or I-93 north from Concord.

OTHER WATERFALLS NEARBY Welton Falls, Profile Falls, Rainbow Falls

Sculptured Rocks

134

SILVER CASCADE

Harts Location, Crawford Notch State Park,
Carroll County

Rating: 5.0/5.0

Type: Plunges and cascades

Height: Approximately 250 feet
of vertical drop is visible from the
road

Trail Length: Roadside

Water Source: Unknown

Altitude Gain/Loss: None to
base of falls

Difficulty: Easy

Hiking Time: Not applicable

DeLorme Atlas: Page 44, D-4
(unmarked)

Best Time to Visit: May to July

THE FALLS (HIGHLY RECOMMENDED) Silver Cascade is a tall mix of
plunges and cascades that hop and skip from left to right down the southwestern side of Mt. Jackson. The falls continue under US 302, eventually
converging with the Saco River below the highway.

Due to the ease of access, this waterfall has dazzled millions of tourists
over the years, making it one of the most popular waterfalls in New England. You will understand why once you see the slender ribbon of water
tumbling over ledges and through chasm walls. The falls are particularly
beautiful during spring runoff and foliage season, and are heavily visited and
photographed as a result.

If you are like most of the visitors to this waterfall, you take a quick look
from the road, snap two pictures, and walk back to your car. We suggest
venturing beyond the roadside views, by climbing up and getting closer to
the falls. If you do, you will find some unexpected privacy. Many of the
great photographs we have seen of this waterfall are taken from such intimate spots.

TRAIL INFORMATION The falls are located across the highway from
the parking areas. Flume Cascade, sister to Silver Cascade and also not to
be missed, is just up the hill on the right.

DIRECTIONS From the junction of US 302 and NH 16 in the section
of Bartlett known as Glen, take US 302 west for 19.7 miles and several
parking areas will be on your left. Silver Cascade is 1.9 miles west of the
Willey House Historic Site and 0.5 mile east of the Crawford Notch State
Park border, marked by signs on both sides of the road. *To get to Glen,* take
NH 16 north from Conway.

OTHER WATERFALLS NEARBY Flume Cascade, Beecher and Pearl Cascades, Gibbs Falls, Kedron Flume, Ripley Falls, Arethusa Falls

135

SWIFTWATER FALLS, BATH
Bath, Grafton County

Rating: 4.0/5.0
Type: Blocks
Height: Tallest block is 8 feet; 12-foot total drop
Trail Length: Less than 0.1 mile
Water Source: Wild Ammonoosuc River

Altitude Gain/Loss: Negligible
Difficulty: Easy
Hiking Time: Negligible
DeLorme Atlas: Page 42, F-5 (unmarked)
Best Time to Visit: Year-round

THE FALLS It would be easy to write off Swiftwater Falls as a waterfall lacking originality, power, or beauty. However, Swiftwater Falls still offers a complete package—a completely worthwhile visit once you consider all the perks. In the background of these falls is a scenic covered bridge, and below the falls lies one of the largest waterfall swimming holes in New England. With its western exposure, the pool soaks up the sun, often heating the water to tolerable temperatures—warm enough to some as early as May.

The Wild Ammonoosuc River drops twice here, with both falls of the block style. The bottom block is the tallest, at 8 feet, and the widest, at about 45 feet. You will notice that on the last cascade, only the bottom half of the cascade is white water, which is highly irregular. The Wild Ammonoosuc River slips for the first half then ripples into white water, which carries on into the pool, creating a natural waterslide perfect for anyone confident of their swimming abilities.

The perfect time to visit this waterfall is during an afternoon on a hot and sunny summer day. Although this is still northern New England, and many will still find the water temperature chilly, it will be considerably warmer than most swimming holes in the region. There is fairly good fishing here too—don't forget your fishing rod!

TRAIL INFORMATION From the parking lot, walk toward the covered bridge and the river to view the falls. A view of the bridge with the

Swiftwater Falls, Bath

falls set in the foreground can be seen by walking down to the rocky beach outlining the swimming hole.

DIRECTIONS From I-93 in Lincoln, take exit 32. Take NH 112 west. Travel on NH 116 as it joins with NH 112, and shortly thereafter, breaks off. Continue traveling on NH 112 west for 6.5 miles past where NH 116 breaks off. At this point, you are about 19.3 miles from I-93. Take a right onto Porter Road. Immediately after, drive through a single-lane covered bridge, and pull into the large parking area on your left.

OTHER WATERFALLS NEARBY Bridal Veil Falls, Beaver Brook Cascades, Paradise Falls, Agassiz Basin

136

∽

THIRTEEN FALLS

Franconia, White Mountain National Forest, Grafton County

Rating: 4.0/5.0

Type: Plunges, horsetails, and cascades

Height: Tallest drop is 18 feet; total drop is 150 feet

Trail Length: 8.0 miles

Water Source: Franconia Brook

Altitude Gain/Loss: +1,000 feet

Difficulty: Moderate, but long

Hiking Time: 4 hours, 30 minutes

DeLorme Atlas: Page 43, E-13 (unmarked)

Best Time to Visit: June to October

THE FALLS For a taste of true backcountry falls, opt to wander deep into the Pemigewasset Wilderness, where you will find Thirteen Falls, a mix of cascades and pools in one of the most remote locations in the White Mountain National Forest. We count five distinct waterfalls here, ranging in height from 5 feet to 25 feet tall. No particular one of the falls is mind-blowing, but as a whole, these wild and secluded gems will surely please all.

The private pools found below several of the falls contain some of the coldest swimming holes around. It would have to be at least 85 degrees on a humid July or August day for us to even consider jumping in. If you are lucky enough to be here on such a day, you will likely forever cherish the moments spent.

The falls are commonly overlooked by peak-baggers passing through who are continuing onto, or returning from, one or several of the many surrounding 4,000-foot mountains that surround the Wilderness area. We believe that the falls deserve more attention than this. At a minimum, plan on an hour or two of tramping your way up and downstream to check out all five of the waterfalls. There is also a real possibility that there are more noteworthy falls here that we missed in our time exploring the area.

Visiting Thirteen Falls is very tiresome on your feet; the total round-trip hike, at 16.0 miles, is the longest hike described in this guide. You should love both hiking and waterfalls to attempt to journey to this natural treasure. Allot about 10 to 14 hours, depending upon your pace and endurance, for this ultimate waterfall expedition. An alternative to a day-hike would be to backpack to one of the nine hardened tent pads nearby at the 13 Falls Campsite (sometimes called Camp 13). These campsites are first-come, first-served and the cost per night in 2009 was $8.00. Check with the Appalachian Mountain Club backcountry rules and regulations before embarking on such an adventure at www.outdoors.org.

TRAIL INFORMATION The trail to the falls begins near the ranger station cabin. Proceed down a wooden staircase, cross a wooden bridge, and follow signs to the trailhead for the LINCOLN WOODS TRAIL. A few hundred feet beyond the visitor center, you will cross a suspension footbridge over the East Branch of the Pemigewasset River.

After crossing the bridge, you will reach a junction with a large sign. Take a right and continue hiking along the wide and nearly completely flat Lincoln Woods Trail. Follow this trail for 2.7 miles and you will reach a stone wall where you will find sign for FRANCONIA FALLS. If you would like to visit two waterfalls today, take this left and hike the final 0.4 mile to this scenic set of cascades and slides (see separate chapter). To continue to Thirteen Falls, continue straight past the stone wall and cross a bridge over Franconia Brook. Hike for about 150 feet beyond the bridge and take a left onto the Franconia Brook Trail.

You will have to follow the Franconia Brook Trail for a total of 5.1 miles as it travels through primarily wilderness terrain. There are several brook crossings that may be difficult during high water; expect some bouts with mud as well. The first waterfall you will approach, an 8-foot plunge easily spotted on the left about 0.1 mile south of the 13 Falls campsite, is the second of the five distinguished falls we have found here.

Enjoying the other four waterfalls here requires short bushwhacks of varying difficulty. Just downstream of the second falls is the lowermost waterfall. This is the most difficult of the five waterfalls to approach; you must travel 100 feet downstream and clamber down a steep 40-foot embankment to reach its base. The reward is a 25-foot-tall slide and horsetail that falls into one the largest and most alluring natural swimming pools in the region. Three more waterfalls are found upstream. The third waterfall is visible off in the distance from the second falls, but requires a 300-foot bushwhack upstream. If you look carefully, you should be able to locate a hard path leading to this 18-foot plunge.

The final two falls are most easily accessed by continuing 300 feet north along the Franconia Brook Trail and taking a left onto the Lincoln Brook Trail at a marked junction. Cross a branch of Franconia Brook and travel on the Lincoln Brook Trail 150 feet beyond this crossing and you should hear the fourth falls. Head off-trail into the woods for 40 feet and you should reach the brook. You will find a 5-foot slide into a 10-foot plunge, along with another gorgeous pool, although more moderately sized com-

Thirteen Falls

pared to the pools downstream. You can also reach this fourth set of falls by traveling directly upstream along the river's edge from the third falls for 100 feet. Be aware that the fourth falls will not be visible to you from the base of the third falls.

The fifth waterfall, a 20-foot mix of small plunges and horsetails with another great swimming hole, perhaps the most private of them all here, is only 100 feet upstream of the fourth falls. This waterfall is just 25 feet off the Lincoln Brook Trail and it is more easily spotted from that trail than is the fourth waterfall. The fifth falls are not visible from the fourth falls, just as the fourth falls are not visible from the third falls.

DIRECTIONS From I-93 in Lincoln, take exit 32. Take NH 112 west for 5.2 miles and take a left into the Lincoln Woods parking area just after crossing a bridge over the East Branch of the Pemigewasset River. The Lincoln Woods parking area is 2.1 miles west of the Big Rock Campground and 0.3 mile east of the Hancock Campground. *To get to Lincoln,* take I-93 north from Concord or I-93 south from Franconia.

Please be aware that this trailhead is part of the White Mountain National Forest parking fee program. The fee was $3 in 2009 but there is currently a proposal in review to raise this amount to $5.

OTHER WATERFALLS NEARBY Franconia Falls, Georgiana Falls, Agassiz Basin, Falls on the Flume–Pool Loop, Sabbaday Falls

137

THOMPSON FALLS

Pinkham's Grant, White Mountain National Forest, Coos County

Rating: 4.5/5.0

Type: Plunges and cascades

Height: Tallest plunge is 20 feet; approximately 150-foot total drop

Trail Length: 0.6 mile

Water Source: Thompson Brook

Altitude Gain/Loss: +150 feet

Difficulty: Easy

Hiking Time: 30 minutes

DeLorme Atlas: Page 45, A&B-8 (unmarked)

Best Time to Visit: May to October

THE FALLS (HIGHLY RECOMMENDED) Three waterfalls are worthy of attention in Pinkham Notch: Glen Ellis Falls and Crystal Cascade, both drops of the Ellis River, and Thompson Falls, a scarcely visited sequence of cascades on Thompson Brook, a mountain stream that flows down the west side of the "A Peak" of Wildcat Mountain.

The lowest cascade of Thompson Falls crashes over an overhanging rock ledge that takes on the shape of a gigantic clam. The clam is roughly 30 feet wide, but water only flows over a portion of that. Below, the waters churn slowly around in an inviting, although very chilly, swimming pool. With some careful footing and a willingness to get wet, it is certainly possible to find a position behind the falling water on the rocks below the overhanging clam-shaped ledge.

Additional cascades can be found upstream, but they lack the bold personality of the lower cascade. There is one waterfall above the main attraction that is worth your while. This 20-foot plunge splashes into a deep and very dark pool below and will certainly make the additional hike all the more gratifying. The gorge surrounding this plunge is stunning but it does prevent the necessary lighting for optimal photographs for most of the day. The upper falls and cascades do offer the advanced possibility of exploring in solitude. However, you are likely to enjoy all of the falls at Thompson Falls entirely to yourself, as waterfall lovers are often caught focusing on the other waterfalls in Pinkham Notch.

To add to the experience be sure to hike the remainder of The Wildcat Way as you stroll back to the parking area. There are some beautiful and rare lady slippers and the smell of cedar along the walk that enhance your experience all the more.

TRAIL INFORMATION From the Wildcat Ski area parking lot, walk behind the lodge and cross over a brook on one of several bridges. Take a left after the bridge, following along the nature trail that runs parallel to the brook. There is a sign for THE WILDCAT WAY marking this trail. Shortly after this sign, you will enter the woods and come to several signs letting you know you are on the THOMPSON FALLS TRAIL, which hikes along a portion of The Wildcat Way loop trail. After walking approximately halfway around the loop, take a left at a sign pointing toward THOMPSON FALLS. Follow this new path and you will soon reach a dirt road. Walk across the road and continue along the trail for another 0.2 mile to the lower falls.

If you continue climbing on the yellow-blazed trail, you will pass a large pool and eventually reach the middle and upper series of falls above. You know you will have reached the final waterfall when you see the carved wooden sign stating END OF TRAIL.

DIRECTIONS From the junction of NH 16 and US 302 in the section of Bartlett known as Glen, take NH 16 north for 12.6 miles and take a right into the Wildcat ski area parking lot. The parking lot is 0.8 mile north of the Pinkham Notch Visitor Center and 2.0 miles south of the Mt. Washington Auto Road entrance. *To get to Glen,* take NH 16 north from Conway.

OTHER WATERFALLS NEARBY Crystal Cascade, Glen Ellis Falls, Winniweta Falls, Jackson Falls

138

THOREAU FALLS

Lincoln, White Mountain National Forest, Grafton County

Rating: 3.5/5.0
Type: Cascades and slides
Height: 80-foot total drop
Trail Length: 4.8 miles
Water Source: North Fork of the East Branch of the Pemigewasset River

Altitude Gain/Loss: +400 feet
Difficulty: Easy side of moderate, but long
Hiking Time: 2 hours, 30 minutes
DeLorme Atlas: Page 44, E-2 (marked)
Best Time to Visit: May to October

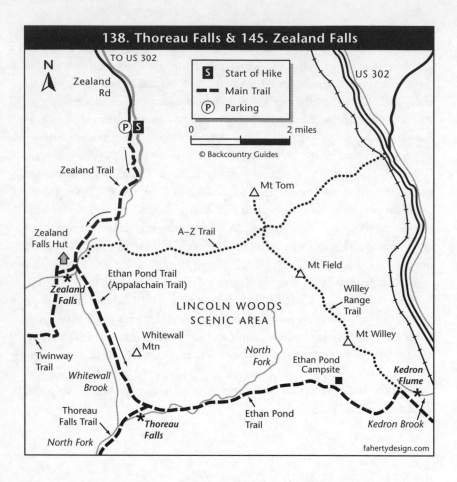

138. Thoreau Falls & 145. Zeeland Falls

N

TO US 302

Zealand Rd

US 302

S   Start of Hike

– –   Main Trail

P   Parking

0   2 miles

© Backcountry Guides

P S

Zealand Trail

Mt Tom

A–Z Trail

Zealand Falls Hut

Ethan Pond Trail (Appalachain Trail)

Mt Field

Zealand Falls

Willey Range Trail

LINCOLN WOODS SCENIC AREA

Mt Willey

Twinway Trail

Whitewall Mtn

North Fork

Ethan Pond Campsite

Kedron Flume

Whitewall Brook

Thoreau Falls Trail

Thoreau Falls

Ethan Pond Trail

Kedron Brook

North Fork

fahertydesign.com

THE FALLS A trip to Thoreau Falls offers many rewards. The waterfall is long, powerful, and set in a wonderfully remote and pleasing setting. The ledges beside the falls are large and flat, creating a fine lunch or rest spot. There is also an impressive scenic view. If you are like most visitors, you will want to relax for at least an hour here.

The waterfall consists mostly of cascades and slides stretching to a total of an 80-foot drop; no single drop is greater than 15 feet in height. Decent wading pools lie upstream and downstream, hidden from most visitors, who are likely to arrive at the top of the falls from the trail. The remoteness of this waterfall makes the wading pools very inviting. If the river water is running low, it is safe to scramble directly alongside the falls to the pools above and below. During high water, some of the river may be spilling onto the ledges; under these conditions, use the developed trail to move up and down the river.

If you are looking to photograph these falls, we recommend the afternoon hours. During the morning hours, the sunlight creates a streaking effect on the water that limits your chance of a good snapshot.

TRAIL INFORMATION From the end of the last parking lot along the Zealand Road, follow the wide trail that immediately enters the woods. This path, the blue-blazed Zealand Trail, covers the first 2.5 miles of this trip. This trail, which is rated as easy side of moderate, is considerably easier once the muddy spring season ends.

At mile 2.5, you will reach a major trail junction between the Zealand Trail, the trail known as the Twinway, and the Ethan Pond Trail. If you take a right onto the Twinway Trail, you can visit Zealand Falls (see separate chapter), and the AMC run Zealand Hut, both less than 0.3 mile away. To reach Thoreau Falls, you will need to continue straight onto the Ethan Pond Trail. This trail, which is also a section of the white-blazed Appalachian Trail, is the next leg of your hiking trip. You will need to follow the Ethan Pond Trail for 2.1 miles to its junction with the Thoreau Falls Trail. When you reach the Thoreau Falls Trail, which is clearly marked, take a right and follow the rough path for 0.2 mile down to the top of the falls. You will want to pay close attention to this trail as you approach the falls as it may be somewhat challenging to locate when you are ready to leave. Primitive paths will also lead you to the base of the falls, but we felt, and believe you will also, that the views from the top of the falls are more than sufficient.

The variety of hiking environments, plus the smooth and gentle stretches spread across the entire trip, craft quite the pleasant family hike, perhaps one of the best hikes suited for the introductory hiker looking to get a feel for long-distance hiking. The most notable section of the trail includes a walk along the unstable cliffs of Whitewall Mountains, where you are exposed to the elements, and afforded with fine views of Zealand Mountain, Mt. Bond, the section of the Zealand Trail that cuts through mountain marshland, and Zealand Pond, where beavers have made their home. A combined trip to Zealand Falls and Thoreau Falls will forever be one of our favorite day-hikes in the White Mountain National Forest.

DIRECTIONS From the junction of US 302 and US 3 in the village of Carroll known as Twin Mountain, take US 302 east. Travel on US 302 east for 2.2 miles and take a right into the marked ZEALAND RECREATION AREA. Follow Zealand Road for 3.4 miles to the end of the road, where large parking lots can be found. There is a main parking lot at the end of the road and an overload parking lot, which is often necessary to use, just before that. *To get to Twin Mountain,* take I-93 north from Lincoln to US 3 north.

Please be aware that this trailhead is part of the White Mountain National Forest parking fee program. The fee was $3 in 2009 but there is currently a proposal in review to raise this amount to $5.

OTHER WATERFALLS NEARBY Zealand Falls, Upper Ammonoosuc Falls, Ammonoosuc Ravine, Gibbs Falls, Beecher and Pearl Cascades, Kedron Flume

139

TRIPLE FALLS

Gorham & Randolph, White Mountain National Forest, Coos County

Rating: 3.0/5.0

Type: Plunges and cascades

Height: Varies (see notes)

Trail Length: 0.2 mile to Evans Falls

Water Source: Town Line Brook

Altitude Gain/Loss: +200 feet to Evans Falls

Difficulty: Easy side of moderate

Hiking Time: 15 minutes to Evans Falls

DeLorme Atlas: Page 48, I-7 (marked)

Best Time to Visit: May to October

THE FALLS In addition the famous waterfalls of Pinkham Notch, more waterfalls lie within a few miles to the north. Specifically, six waterfalls are described in this guide. Three falls—Stairs Fall, Coosauk Falls, and Hitchcock Falls—are described in the section entitled "Falls on the Howker Ridge Trail." The other three falls—Proteus Falls, Erebus Falls, and Evans Falls—are often united together under one fitting name, Triple Falls.

Only minutes from Dolly Copp, one of the largest campgrounds in the White Mountains, Triple Falls can be conveniently accessed via a short drive, long walk, or an easy bike ride.

With 177 campsites nearby, you would expect that any attractions within walking distance would be popular. However, this is not always the case. With only a small sign for the falls revealing its location, Triple Falls still lies nearly as untouched as it ever was. The summit of nearby Pine Mountain, reached via a trailhead that begins just farther down the Pinkham B Road from Triple Falls, attracts a much larger crowd from the campground.

Here is what you can expect to see at Triple Falls: Proteus Falls, the first of the hike, is a 20-foot horsetail that falls into moss-covered chasm walls. Erebus Falls, only feet above Proteus Falls, takes on the form of a segmented 25-foot plunge over a sheath of rock. Just below Erebus is a fast-traveling waterslide. Evans Falls, the final feature of Triple Falls, is a small 12-foot plunge with some cascades and slides varying in size, best viewed by crossing the brook.

The falls are often weak in power—we suspect that Town Line Brook could be dry by July—but you do get three waterfalls for the price of one here. To make a day-trip out of the area, continue driving along the Pinkham B Road. Spend some time climbing to the summit of Pine Mountain, and visiting the other waterfalls nearby. As the years continue, Triple Falls has the potential to become lost in the overgrown woods. Erosion may be sure to tear at the existing trail causing future access to these falls to be limited or nonexistent.

TRAIL INFORMATION From the small parking area, cross the road and start up the fairly well-traveled Town Line Brook Trail to begin your hike. After about 0.1 mile, a spur path will lead toward the brook and, after scrambling around a rock wall, the first waterfall, Proteus Falls, will come into view. Continue climbing up the Town Line Brook for riverside views of Erebus Falls, and then, shortly thereafter, Evans Falls. The trail is thin and can be extremely slippery and muddy, especially as you advance beyond Proteus Falls. Beware of continuing erosion and always check your footing.

DIRECTIONS From the junction of NH 16 and US 302 in the section of Bartlett known as Glen, take NH 16 north. Continue on NH 16 north for 3.4 miles north of the entrance to the Mt. Washington Road and take a left onto Dolly Copp Road. Follow Dolly Copp Road straight for 0.5 mile, passing the entrance to the campground on the left, and you will reach a fork in the road. Take the left fork onto Pinkham B Road. Follow Pinkham B Road for 2.2 miles to a small parking area on the right just after crossing a small bridge over the Town Line Brook. *To get to Glen,* take NH 16 north from Conway.

OTHER WATERFALLS NEARBY Falls on the Howker Ridge Trail, Mossy Glen, Appalachia Waterfalls, Thompson Falls, Crystal Cascade, Dryad Fall, Giant Falls

140

TUCKER BROOK FALLS

Milford, Tucker Brook Town Forest, Hillsborough County

Rating: 2.5/5.0

Type: Horsetail

Height: 10 feet

Trail Length: 0.3 mile

Water Source: Tucker Brook

Altitude Gain/Loss: -50 feet

Difficulty: Easy side of moderate

Hiking Time: 10 minutes

DeLorme Atlas: Page 21, G-11 (unmarked)

Best Time to Visit: April to June

THE FALLS Tucker Brook Town Forest, a 258-acre conservation property, has an extensive network of hiking and mountain biking trails. Strewn across these trails are 10,000-year old glacial erratics—boulders believed to be left over from retreating glaciers of the last Ice Age. The Town Forest also conceals the locally popular 10-foot-tall Tucker Brook Falls. The falls drape over rows of thin ledge, and are accordingly pretty and photograph well. However, they are no match to other grander falls in the area, such as Garwin Falls and Purgatory Falls. With that being said, we would not make a special trip out to Tucker Brook Falls—unless your plan is to visit this trio of waterfalls. Dedicated waterfall hunters will likely object to this statement, as each and every waterfall has its own personality.

TRAIL INFORMATION To find the falls, locate the path that starts at the southern end of the parking lot and follow it parallel to the road for 150 feet. The trail will then swing left and head deeper into the woods. About 50 feet farther, you will reach a billboard with information about the forest. From here, follow the obvious trail for 0.1 mile to a four-way junction of paths. Take the left trail and follow a white-blazed trail for about 300 feet, where you will want to take a right at another junction to continue hiking on the white-blazed trail (a blue-blazed trail continues straight here). Travel for only 50 feet from this junction and you will reach yet another junction. This time, take a left onto a different blue-blazed trail. Follow this blue-blazed trail for 300 feet parallel to the river heading downstream, and you will soon find the falls. The key to the trails near the falls is to always stay close to the river and continue traveling downstream. At no point will it be necessary to cross the brook to find the falls.

Although only a short distance away, the network of trails within this forest can make finding the falls slightly difficult. It can also be slightly challenging to find your way back to the parking area after your visit to the falls is complete. Follow the trail description above very closely and your visit should go as smoothly as planned.

DIRECTIONS From the western junction of NH 101 and NH 101a in Milford, take NH 101 east (take note that the highway actually travels south here) for 0.1 mile and take a right onto Phelan Road. Follow Phelan Road straight through an intersection and for a total of 0.6 mile, where you will want to fork right onto Savage Road. Follow Savage Road for 0.3 mile and take a left into a large dirt parking area for Tucker Brook Town Forest. *To get to Milton,* take NH 101a west from Nashua.

OTHER WATERFALLS NEARBY Purgatory Falls, Garwin Falls

141

UPPER AMMONOOSUC FALLS

Crawfords Purchase, White Mountain National Forest, Coos County

Rating: 3.0/5.0
Type: Plunge and cascades
Height: Tallest drop is 8 feet
Trail Length: Less than 0.1 mile
Water Source: Ammonoosuc River

Altitude Gain/Loss: None
Difficulty: Easy
Hiking Time: Negligible
DeLorme Atlas: Page 44, B-3 (marked)
Best Time to Visit: Year-round

THE FALLS Hundreds of documented fatal tragedies have occurred in New England's swimming holes. After Huntington Gorge of Vermont—the region's deadliest swimming hole—Upper Ammonoosuc Falls is likely to be the second in line. We have nearly seen it first-hand; on one visit, we witnessed a gentleman struggling dearly to find the strength to exit a circular pothole found below the main 8-foot falls. He made it out alive that day, but others have not been so fortunate. Swimming is only possible here in the lowest of currents and it is never safe to swim in the potholes near the main plunge—that is where the accidents have almost always occurred.

The highlight of this place is certainly the pools and the gorge, and not the falls themselves. The tallest drop here, the 8-foot plunge, is roaring in power but a bit lacking in character. It is also tough to photograph well since the sun shines directly on it for most of the day. The best photographs here would likely be taken early in the morning or very late in the afternoon.

Summer brings swarms of thrill seekers, photographers, fishermen, and tourists to these falls daily. Known for years as a place that tolerated the consumption of alcohol along with cliff jumping (an absolutely horrible combination, we should add), the U.S. Forest Service recently decided, after several recent fatal and near-fatal accidents, to place a permanent ban on alcohol consumption at this waterfall. As a result, this place is slowly becoming more family friendly. Children should also be watched carefully here; the best and safest place for them to wade in the river is at least 50 feet downstream of the falls.

As the name of this waterfall might suggest, there exists a Lower Ammonoosuc Falls. It is located a few miles downstream and is accessible via a short and easy 0.2-mile trail that begins at the end of nearby Lower Falls Road. The lower falls were not significant enough to earn a chapter in this guide, but there is another good (and much safer) swimming hole there. If the currents are too strong at Upper Ammonoosuc Falls, you may still have a chance to enjoy the water at Lower Ammonoosuc Falls as the pool there is extremely large.

TRAIL INFORMATION From the parking area, follow the sound of the rushing water for just a few feet into the woods and you will earn an unobstructed view of the falls and gorge. At the top of the gorge is a nice footbridge where you will get a great perspective of the gorge.

DIRECTIONS From the junction of US 302 and US 3 in the village of Carroll known as Twin Mountain, take US 302 east for 4.5 miles and take a left onto Base Road, which is marked by a sign for the Cog Railway. Follow Base Road for 2.2 miles and park on the right side of the road. There is not an official sign for the falls here, but there is a White Mountain National Forest informative display board if you look closely enough. *To get to Twin Mountain,* take US 3 north from Lincoln.

OTHER WATERFALLS NEARBY Ammonoosuc Ravine, Zealand Falls, Thoreau Falls, Gibbs Falls, Beecher and Pearl Cascades, Silver Cascade, Flume Cascade

142

WATERVILLE CASCADES

Waterville Valley, White Mountain National Forest,
Grafton County

Rating: 4.0/5.0

Type: Horsetails, fans, and cascade

Height: Main falls are 18 feet

Trail Length: 1.4 miles to initial cascade; 1.7 miles to end of cascades

Water Source: Cascade Brook

Altitude Gain/Loss: +450 feet, -150 feet to end of cascades

Difficulty: Easy side of moderate

Hiking Time: 45 minutes

DeLorme Atlas: Page 40, A-2 (unmarked)

Best Time to Visit: May to October

THE FALLS If there was some equation matching beauty per foot of height for waterfalls, Waterville Cascades, or The Cascades, as some call them, would certainly surface as a contender for the top title. The main cascades here may be small, at 18 feet of height, but in that short distance, Cascade Brook manages to astonish every visitor with its breathtaking treasure.

This main waterfall begins as a horsetail, quickly descending to a temporary platform of rock at the midway point. From here, the waters converge and fan out in an uprising chute, similar to a ski jump. The waters land in an attractive golden pool below. Close to 4 feet deep, the pool is a fine specimen of cold mountain water. Take a dip if you dare, but be warned that the water temperature is not substantially warmer than freezing for all but a few days of the year. Above the main falls, reachable by continuing up the trail, are various other splendid small falls and cascades.

Nearby, Avalanche Brook has its own small natural feature. The Norway Rapids, a short side trip off Cascade Path, is a long chain of cascades of clear white water. Although the rapids lack the stunning personality of Waterville Cascades, Norway Rapids is still worth the miniscule effort required to reach them.

TRAIL INFORMATION The trail to this waterfall has significantly changed since the first edition, although the trailhead remains the same. The trail to the falls begins at the bottom of Cascade Ridge Road. From here walk uphill on this paved road for about 750 feet, at which point you will enter the woods on your left, marked by a TRAIL sign. Continue walking uphill and you will soon reach a sign pointing right toward CASCADE PATH. Take this right, continuing uphill, where you will cross a paved road. Cross

Waterville Cascades

this road and continue climbing uphill on a ski trail. About 0.1 mile after crossing this road (at this point, you are about 0.4 mile from the parking area), take a left onto Cascade Path, marked by a sign and yellow blazes. From here, continue following the yellow blazes for about 0.2 mile where you will reach a junction. The Cascade Path will continue straight and the Elephant Rock Trail will spur right. Stay straight on the Cascade Path and you will eventually reach a small wooden bridge. This point is about 1.2 miles from the parking lot. Bear right after crossing this 8-foot-long bridge, and in 250 feet, you will reach the Norway Rapids Trail junction. Continue straight (do not cross this bridge) for the Waterville Cascades. The remainder of this walk parallels the brook. The main cascades are only 0.2 mile farther from this point. There are several less significant but still pretty cascades and pools over the next 0.3 mile above the main cascade that are worth exploring as well.

If you wish to visit the Norway Rapids—more cascades than rapids, if you ask us—return to the Cascade Path and Norway Rapids trail junction. Follow the Norway Rapids trail, also yellow-blazed, for 0.4 mile through the woods to Avalanche Brook, where the rapids will be clearly visible.

DIRECTIONS From I-93 in Campton, take exit 28. Turn onto NH 49 east (which actually heads more north than east), heading toward Waterville Valley. Continue traveling along NH 49 east for 5.7 miles past the Waterville Valley town line sign. Take a right onto Boulder Path Road within the ski village area. Travel on Boulder Path Road for 0.4 mile and take a right into a large parking lot for the Snow Mountain ski lift building, which is currently painted red. *To get to Campton,* take I-93 north from Plymouth or I-93 south from Lincoln.

OTHER WATERFALLS NEARBY Campton Falls, Beede Falls

143
~

WELTON FALLS

Alexandria, Welton Falls State Forest, Grafton County

Rating: 4.0/5.0

Type: Plunges

Height: 30-foot total drop

Trail Length: 1.2 miles

Water Source: Fowler River

Altitude Gain/Loss: -300 feet, +100 feet

Difficulty: Moderate

Hiking Time: 40 minutes

DeLorme Atlas: Page 38, K-7 (marked)

Best Time to Visit: May to October

THE FALLS The AMC Cardigan Lodge serves as a trailhead for both the summit of Mt. Cardigan and a delightful package of waterfalls of different shapes and sizes, ranging from a staircase of cascades to a 15-foot-tall plunge surrounded by cliff walls on all sides (the lower half of Welton Falls, to be specific). Above the 15-foot plunge, the upper half of Welton Falls consists of an 8-foot-tall cascade, hidden from most vantage points around the falls by the boulder-strewn river.

The Fowler River offers swimming for nearly the entire section of the Manning Trail that parallels the brook. There are shallow pools scattered just about everywhere, and a few deep pools below the falls. Always take caution when entering any swimming hole. Slippery rocks and strong currents have been merciless before and will likely be again. The best opportunity for swimming would be directly below the main plunge at Welton Falls; unfortunately, we scanned the area and could not determine a feasible route out of the pool. Also, we encourage you to stroll up to the top of the main falls, where you will find an overhanging ledge with safety rails.

There lies another waterfall within a moderate hiking distance of the AMC Cardigan Lodge. Elizabeth Falls, rumored to be 40 feet tall, is allegedly found by bushwhacking a short distance off the Holt Trail toward Bailey Brook. Sources indicate that the falls lie somewhere between 1.0 to 1.5 miles from the lodge. Although we were unable to locate this waterfall on our sole attempt, we are certain of its existence.

TRAIL INFORMATION From the parking area facing the AMC Lodge, take a right and cross a short, grassy field and enter the woods about 150 feet later on. Follow a path about 0.1 mile while passing a few campsites on your left. A more obvious, yellow-blazed trail begins to emerge. This is the Manning Trail, which will lead you to the falls. After hiking on this trail for about 0.8 mile, you will need to cross the river, which may require you to remove your boots and start wading across. Trekking poles are very helpful in such a situation. After crossing the river to the falls, the trail ascends and descends several times, and, at times, the path is somewhat steep. About 0.2 mile beyond where you crossed the river, the trail will descend and turn right. Immediately after, fork left and walk toward a green iron fence for a view of the top of the falls from within a bowl-shaped gap in the gorge. To reach the base of the falls, continue back to the trail and continue downstream about 100 feet. You may even wish to scramble downstream for additional pools and small cascades.

DIRECTIONS From I-93 in New Hampton, take exit 23. Turn onto NH 104 west. Continue traveling on NH 104 west until you reach the

Welton Falls

junction of NH 104 and NH 3a in the center of Bristol. Turn right onto NH 3a north and follow that highway for 2.1 miles. Take a left onto West Shore Road just before a stone church. Follow West Shore Road for 1.5 miles and continue straight onto a new road. Follow this road for 1.1 miles and fork right onto Fowler River Road. Follow Fowler River Road for 3.2 miles and take a left onto Brook Road. Follow Brook Road for 1.1 miles and take a right onto Shem Valley Road. After 0.1 mile on Shem Valley Road, fork right and head toward the Cardigan Lodge. Continue for an additional 1.2 miles and you will reach the AMC Cardigan Lodge. Parking is on the left, opposite the AMC building. *To get to New Hampton,* take I-93 south from Plymouth or I-93 north from Concord.

OTHER WATERFALLS NEARBY Sculptured Rocks, Profile Falls

144

WINNIWETA FALLS

Jackson, White Mountain National Forest, Carroll County

Rating: 4.0/5.0

Type: Cascades, small plunges and a horsetail

Height: Lower falls is 40 feet; upper falls is 20 feet; 60-foot total drop

Trail Length: 0.9 mile

Water Source: Miles Brook

Altitude Gain/Loss: +300 feet

Difficulty: Easy side of moderate (see notes)

Hiking Time: 40 minutes

DeLorme Atlas: Page 44, D&E-7 (marked)

Best Time to Visit: June to October

THE FALLS Winniweta Falls is a seldom-visited little waterfall located off NH 16, just south of the Mt. Washington Auto Road and Pinkham Notch. At this site, there are major cascades, notable plunges, and many slides over rock. Views are usually at least partially limited by plant growth, but it is possible to explore some areas of the falls. Be on the lookout for moose here—we have heard some accounts of sightings, and seen plenty of fresh tracks ourselves. The deep pool below the falls is very inviting and there is definitely the potential to sit in the waterfall with the water crashing over and around you on a hot day.

TRAIL INFORMATION From the parking area, walk west toward the Ellis River on the Winniweta Falls Trail. The trail begins with a hop over many small rocks. At 0.1 mile you must cross the Ellis River. Depending on the season, this may be a difficult task. If you are crossing in early spring, you may get wet up to mid-thigh. If you are crossing in the middle of summer, you may only get your feet wet. After you cross the river, hike for 150 feet and take a right at a fork, currently marked by a small trail sign on a tree. From this point on, the trail is relatively easy as it passes through several trail junctions. Continue straight at each junction and you will reach the falls. After 0.9 mile, a small spur trail turns left and 5 feet beyond is a sign with an arrow pointing to the falls. Feel free to maneuver your way along either of the small paths to view the falls. For the best view be sure to bushwhack down the steep hill to the river, if you feel comfortable doing so, to glimpse this beautiful waterfall at its best.

DIRECTIONS From the junction of NH 16 and US 302 in the section of Bartlett known as Glen, take NH 16 north 5.4 miles and a small parking pull-off will be on the left, marked by an small, rather inconspicuous trail sign for WINNIWETA FALLS. *To get to Glen,* take NH 16 north from Conway.

OTHER WATERFALLS NEARBY Jackson Falls, Glen Ellis Falls, Crystal Cascade, Thompson Falls, Diana's Baths

145

~

ZEALAND FALLS

Bethlehem, White Mountain National Forest, Grafton County

Rating: 2.5/5.0
Type: Plunges
Height: 25-foot total drop
Trail Length: 2.7 miles
Water Source: Whitewall Brook
Altitude Gain/Loss: +575 feet

Difficulty: Easy side of moderate, but long
Hiking Time: 75 minutes
DeLorme Atlas: Page 44, D-2 (marked)
Best Time to Visit: May to June

THE FALLS You get more than just a prized waterfall when you visit Zealand Falls. Along the linking trails, there are scenic marshlands, a mountain body of water known as Zealand Pond, and just above the falls is Zealand Hut, a convenient hiker hut managed by the Appalachian Mountain Club. With drinks (lemonade!), food, and lodging reservation available, the Zealand Hut makes both a great year-round rest stop and an overnight accommodation. Reservations are recommended for those wishing to stay overnight, but be sure to check out the Hut (or any other of the huts within the AMC's system) even if you are just a day visitor. We are sure you will find the structure interesting and the employees inviting, friendly, and full of great outdoor advice.

During the morning hours on a sunny day, light hits the front of the rock faces of Zealand Falls, illuminating the top of the waterfall. The lower part of the fall is tucked a few feet inside a narrow flume, but is visible upon closer inspection. The sound of the water drowns out any other sounds. A smaller 4-foot waterfall is below the main attraction. At the base of this smaller addition there is a circular pool; it is not very deep, but it is fine for sitting or wading.

TRAIL INFORMATION From the end of the last parking lot along Zealand Road, follow the wide trail that immediately enters the woods. This path, the blue-blazed Zealand Trail, covers the first 2.5 miles of this trip. This trail, which is rated as easy side of moderate, is considerably easier once the muddy spring season ends.

At mile 2.5, you will reach a major trail junction between the Zealand Trail, the trail known as the Twinway, and the Ethan Pond Trail. To visit Zealand Falls, take a right onto the Twinway. The falls are a short 0.2-mile climb up this trail, and the AMC Zealand Hut, only 250 feet farther.

Unless you happen to embark on this trail during the spring muddy season, traveling is extremely easy, with generous sections of flat, smooth hiking. To add a few hours to your trip, add nearby Thoreau Falls to your itinerary. With Thoreau Falls, the trip grows to be a total of about 10 easy-going miles. This hike was one of the most pleasant half-day hikes we encountered while producing this guide. See the chapter on Thoreau Falls for more trail details.

DIRECTIONS From the junction of US 302 and US 3 in the village of Carroll known as Twin Mountain, take US 302 east. Travel on US 302 east for 2.2 miles and take a right into the marked ZEALAND RECREATION AREA. Follow Zealand Road for 3.4 miles to the end of the road, where large parking lots can be found. There is a main parking lot at the end of the road and an overload parking lot, which is often necessary to use, just before that. *To get to Twin Mountain,* take I-93 north from Lincoln to US 3 north.

Please be aware that this trailhead is part of the White Mountain National Forest parking fee program. The fee was $3 in 2009 but there is currently a proposal in review to raise this amount to $5.

OTHER WATERFALLS NEARBY Thoreau Falls, Beecher and Pearl Cascades, Gibbs Falls, Upper Ammonoosuc Falls, Ammonoosuc Ravine

V. Rhode Island

146

∽

STEPSTONE FALLS

West Greenwich, Arcadia Management Area, Kent County

Rating: 2.0/5.0

Type: Small plunges and cascades

Height: 10-foot total drop

Trail Length: Less than 0.1 mile

Water Source: Wood River

Altitude Gain/Loss: None

Difficulty: Easy

Hiking Time: Negligible

DeLorme Atlas: Page 70, C-3 (marked)

Best Time to Visit: April to November

THE FALLS The state of Rhode Island does not contain mountainous terrain anywhere near the level found in the five other New England states. The highest point of the state is Jerimoth Hill, which is only 812 feet above sea level. Only 4 of the 50 states have a lower highest point: Mississippi, Louisiana, Delaware, and Florida.

With such a smooth, gentle landscape covering the majority of the state, it is no surprise that we could only find one notable natural waterfall. You could surely find other chains of cascades in the state, but not ones that have water flow year-round like Stepstone Falls of West Greenwich does.

Dropping 10 feet over about 100 feet of distance, the falls are by no means massive or spectacular. Instead, they are peaceful little cascades falling over overhanging ledges. The tallest drop, at only 3 feet, is surprisingly photogenic and charming. The water flows over a broad, flat ledge, creating a long curtain.

For those seeking additional outdoor activities, the Arcadia Management Area offers extensive hiking and horseback-riding trails. A number of animals reside in the park, including cottontail rabbits, white-tailed deer, fox, and mink. Fishing is another common activity—trout can be caught in the Wood River and its tributaries, and several ponds contain bass and pickerel.

TRAIL INFORMATION The falls are located only a few feet downstream of the parking area. There are other petite cascades upstream and downstream from the main waterfall, which is approximately 100 feet from the parking area. Each side of the river offers different perspectives on the falls and cascades

DIRECTIONS From Providence, take I-95 south to exit 5a. Turn onto RI 102 south and follow signs to RI 3 south. Take a right onto RI 3 south.

Travel for 1.2 miles on RI 3 south and take a right onto RI 165 west. Follow RI 165 west for 5.1 miles and take a right onto Escoheag Hill Road. After 2.4 miles on Escoheag Hill Road, take a right onto Falls River Road, a somewhat rough dirt road that should be passable by the average car from April to November. Travel down Falls River Road for 0.6 mile and the pull-off will be on the right just before crossing the bridge over the Wood River.

OTHER WATERFALLS NEARBY None

Abbey Pond Cascades, VT

VI. Vermont

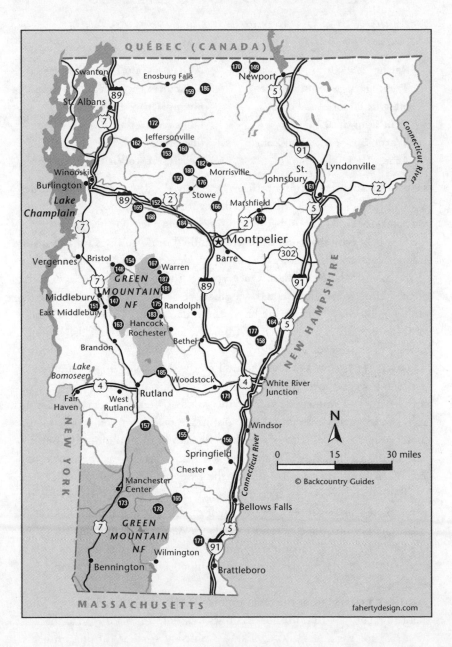

QUÉBEC (CANADA)

Swanton

Enosburg Falls

Newport

170 149

89

159 186

5

St. Albans

7

172

Jeffersonville

91

162

160

St.
Johnsbury

Lyndonville

153

182

Winooski

180

Morrisville

2

Burlington

150 176

161

5

89 152 2

Stowe

166 Marshfield

5

*Lake
Champlain*

169

Montpelier

302

7

168

184

2 174

2

Barre

Vergennes

Bristol

154 167

Warren

89

*GREEN
MOUNTAIN
NF*

148

187

91

Middlebury

147 181

East Middlebury

151 175 Randolph

NEW HAMPSHIRE

163 183

Hancock
Rochester

164

177

Brandon

Bethel

158

5

*Lake
Bomoseen*

185 Woodstock

4

White River
Junction

4

Rutland

179

Fair
Haven

West
Rutland

Windsor

N

NEW YORK

157

155 156

Springfield

0   15   30 miles

Chester

Connecticut River

© Backcountry Guides

Manchester
Center

165

173

Bellows Falls

178

7 *GREEN
MOUNTAIN
NF*

171

91 5

Wilmington

Bennington

Brattleboro

MASSACHUSETTS

fahertydesign.com

147

ABBEY POND CASCADES

Middlebury, Green Mountain National Forest, Addison County

Rating: 3.5/5.0

Type: Horsetails and cascades

Height: 80-foot total drop

Trail Length: 0.2 mile

Water Source: Stream from Abbey Pond

Altitude Gain/Loss: +100 feet

Difficulty: Easy side of moderate

Hiking Time: 10 minutes

DeLorme Atlas: Page 39, K-10 (unmarked)

Best Time to Visit: May to June

THE FALLS Powered from upstream by Abbey Pond, Abbey Pond Cascades is a sequence of cascades and horsetails that drop a combined 80 feet. From the footbridge that the Abbey Pond Trail travels over, you will notice that the area is heavily shaded and there are limited opportunities for capturing a good photograph. To solve this problem, deviate from the trail and hike to the base of the entire falls. Once you get there, you will notice a completely different perspective and will likely be able to obtain a much better photograph. Gravel pits in the background detract from the delightfulness of this waterfall a bit, especially from the bottom of the falls, but not enough to thwart you from visiting.

TRAIL INFORMATION The trail you will be following to the falls is the blue-blazed Abbey Pond Trail. Begin traveling up this trail via a wide gravel path and immediately enter the woods. After a moderate 0.2-mile uphill walk, you will reach a short footbridge placed approximately in the center of the cascades. The best view to be had, in our opinion, is from the base of the entire cascade chain with the bridge serving as the center object. There are several paths to reach the base of the falls, all of which can be slippery and muddy, so take caution. It is also possible to scramble up and explore the area around the top half of the falls, with care.

If time permits, hike beyond the falls to Abbey Pond, a remote mountain pond frequently inhabited by great blue herons. From the falls, it is a moderate hike of 1.7 miles farther to the pond (with 1,100 additional feet of elevation gain).

DIRECTIONS From the junction of VT 116 and VT 125 in East Middlebury, take VT 116 north for 4.2 miles to a right onto a dirt road marked by a sign for the ABBEY POND TRAIL. Immediately after turning onto the dirt road, take a left at a fork and follow the road for 0.3 mile to a large parking area at the end. *To get to East Middlebury,* take US 7 south from Middlebury to VT 125 east.

OTHER WATERFALLS NEARBY Texas Falls, Falls of Lana, Bittersweet Falls, Bartlett Falls, Bristol Memorial Park Falls

148

BARTLETT FALLS
Bristol, Addison County

Rating: 4.5/5.0
Type: Block
Height: 15 feet
Trail Length: Less than 0.1 mile
Water Source: New Haven River
Altitude Gain/Loss: None
Difficulty: Easy to initial viewpoint; easy side of moderate down to the base of the falls

Hiking Time: Negligible
DeLorme Atlas: Page 39, H-10 (unmarked)
Best Time to Visit: Year-round

Bartlett Falls

THE FALLS (HIGHLY RECOMMENDED) There are several extraordinary features of Bartlett Falls; a 40-foot-wide, 120-foot-long sparkling pool below the falls is one of them. With its inviting yellow green waters, and depths ranging from ankle deep to well over your head, this pool has been known to attract five hundred people in a single day! The second is the falls themselves. A block-style falls, about 15 feet in height, drops over a broad overhanging ledge, creating a large alcove behind the falling water. The flat slabs of rock to the side of the falls allow you access to this alcove. From within this alcove, a new perspective on waterfalls is formed. All sounds are drowned out and all you can see are the walls of the alcove and the power of the river falling in front of you. There are few waterfalls in New England where this is possible, none as appealing and easy to get into as Bartlett Falls. If the current is weak enough, you can jump or swim through the waterfall and be carried slowly downstream through a gorge.

Bartlett Falls is also commonly known as Bristol Falls or New Haven River Gorge. We strongly suggest when visiting this waterfall that you bring a bathing suit and lunch, and plan to spend a few hours basking in the sun. If the popularity of the falls is too much to handle, more pools, and a quieter atmosphere, can be found both upstream and downstream. Regardless of how popular this place is, if you visit on a hot day, you are sure to cherish this place and will want to return to it many more times throughout your life.

TRAIL INFORMATION There are a number of trails stemming from the road. Some will lead you to the top of the gorge for a bird's-eye view of the falls. Others will climb down to the level of the river, where you will find one of the largest swimming holes in the state. This swimming hole probably provides the best perspective and photographic opportunity of the falls, so try to time your visit for summer or early fall, where water levels are typically lower. If the water level is indeed low enough, it is challenging but possible to swim up to the falls and explore a cave behind the plunging water. There is enough room here for several people. If you decide to attempt this, please take extreme caution as the ledges behind the falls are exceptionally slippery. Do not attempt in moderate or high water. Bartlett Falls is one of only two waterfalls in New England that we are aware of that you can easily get behind.

There are other interesting natural features over the course of the next 0.25 mile upstream of the main falls. There are many slides, cascades, and pools to be enjoyed, including the natural waterslide known as Circle Current. These areas can be considerably more private than Bartlett Falls, but there are almost always a few people around on a hot summer weekend.

DIRECTIONS From the western junction of VT 17 and VT 116 in Bristol, take the combined highway VT 116 north and VT 17 east for 2.8 miles to a right onto Lincoln Road. After 0.2 mile, park on either side of Lincoln Road. *To get to Bristol,* take US 7 north from Middlebury to VT 17 east.

OTHER WATERFALLS NEARBY Bristol Memorial Park Falls, Abbey Pond Cascades, Bittersweet Falls, Hartshorn Falls, Warren Falls, Stetson Hollow Falls

149

BIG FALLS

Troy, Big Falls of the Missisquoi Natural Area, Orleans County

Rating: 4.0/5.0

Type: Cascades

Height: 40-foot total drop

Trail Length: Less than 0.1 mile

Water Source: Missisquoi River

Altitude Gain/Loss: None

Difficulty: Easy

Hiking Time: Negligible

DeLorme Atlas: Page 53, A&B-11 (marked)

Best Time to Visit: Year-round

THE FALLS Though very simple, the name of this waterfall fits it perfectly. The water rushing through the gorge creates a big, roaring waterfall, and the gorge itself is noteworthy, with very high walls. The currents here are powerful and strong, and the water color is usually a mixture of ivory, white, and yellow. Considering the volume of the water rushing through the gorge, it is surprising that this waterfall has never been developed as a hydroelectric project, as have most of the waterfalls with similar strength in Vermont. The falls are now officially managed by the Vermont Department of Forests, Parks, and Recreation, so they are likely to remain natural forever.

The best observation point we found was from the highest cliff, which rises 80 feet above the river below. Several segments of cascades make up the total waterfall. Before rushing down this formation, the water condenses into a bubbling and impressive rapid. This is where the powerful, almost certainly deadly, currents can best be viewed.

TRAIL INFORMATION From the parking lot, enter the open woods behind the boulders outlining the parking area. Walk past some small cascades on your distant left, and a vantage point for the falls will be straight ahead, on top of the soaring gorge wall. From this cliff you will be able to admire the deadly power of the Missisquoi River at Big Falls, and the giant gorge walls that continue downstream.

DIRECTIONS From Newport, take VT 105 west. Continue traveling on VT 105 west to the junction of VT 105 and VT 100. Take a right to continue on VT 105 west, travel for 7.0 miles, and take a left onto River

Big Falls

Road, a dirt road. This road is about 1.0 mile east of the center of North Troy. Follow River Road south for 1.4 miles to a small marked parking area on the right. *To get to Newport,* take I-91 north from St. Johnsbury to exit 27. Take VT 191 west to US 5 south.

OTHER WATERFALLS NEARBY Jay Branch Gorge, Trout River Falls, Crystal Falls

150

∽

BINGHAM FALLS
Stowe, Mt. Mansfield State Forest, Lamoille County

Rating: 5.0/5.0
Type: Plunges and cascades
Height: Tallest plunge is 25 feet
Trail Length: 0.3 mile to lowermost plunge
Water Source: West Branch of the Waterbury River
Altitude Gain/Loss: -150 feet

Difficulty: Easy to first falls; moderate thereafter
Hiking Time: 20 minutes
DeLorme Atlas: Page 46, F-3 (marked)
Best Time to Visit: May to October

THE FALLS (HIGHLY RECOMMENDED) This waterfall is a secluded, geologically interesting natural wonder. The long, tight gorge walls along the river cause the water to create a deep, rumbling, thunderous sound as it is forced downstream and eventually over the main 25-foot falls. This gorge is one of the prettiest in the state. The water is a beautiful teal color for its entire distance—even as it plunges over the falls. This is unlike most waterfalls in the Northeast, as they tend to have a more white-water appearance as they fall and settle in pools beneath the base of the falls.

Various cascades and plunges adorn the river as you hike toward the main attraction. At the main falls, water projects away from the rocks at an angle and falls into an ultra-enticing pool—one of the greatest we have ever seen. It is deep, clean, and absolutely stunning; if you did not bring your swimming trunks, you will wish you did. If you do swim here, stay to the left side to avoid the stronger currents on the right.

There is a history of tragedy here, so always use your personal judgment before swimming here. Children should always be supervised and adults need to be equally careful due to the often very strong currents.

TRAIL INFORMATION Access to this waterfall has been greatly improved since the original edition of this guide. From the unmarked dirt pull-offs, continue down the only trail on the east side of the state highway. After an easy 0.2-mile walk, you will reach the first falls. When you first reach the falls, follow the trail right (downstream) to discover more natural wonders

Bingham Falls

and the primary falls below. The trail becomes moderately steep and often slippery as it descends a newly constructed rock staircase to the base of spectacular Bingham Falls.

DIRECTIONS From the junction of VT 108 and VT 100 in Stowe, take VT 108 north for 6.3 miles to the unmarked dirt parking areas that are on both sides of the road. This parking area is 0.1 mile south of the entrance to the Smugglers Notch State Park campground. *To get to Stowe,* take I-89 north from Montpelier or I-89 east from Burlington to exit 10 in Waterbury. Follow VT 100 north.

OTHER WATERFALLS NEARBY Brewster River Gorge, Moss Glen Falls–Stowe, Sterling Brook Gorge, Terrill Gorge

151

BITTERSWEET FALLS
Weybridge, Addison County

Rating: 2.5/5.0
Type: Plunges
Height: 20 feet
Trail Length: Less than 0.1 mile
Water Source: Beaver Brook
Altitude Gain/Loss: None

Difficulty: Easy
Hiking Time: Negligible
DeLorme Atlas: Page 32, A-6
(unmarked)
Best Time to Visit: April to June

THE FALLS Vermont has dozens of roadside waterfalls, and Bittersweet Falls is a fine example of these easily viewed falls. Although highly seasonal, Beaver Brook takes the stage during the spring with a tumbling two-sided plunge, each side dropping 18 to 20 feet. In low-water conditions, a thin ribbon of water is seen falling along a wall of moss on only one side.

The name of this waterfall is a mystery to us. The term *bittersweet* could be referring to the low volume of water often seen here, or it could be indicative of the smell of fertilizer that is carried to the falls from nearby agricultural zones.

TRAIL INFORMATION To reach the falls, walk across the short field on your left and you will be at the base of the falls after only about 175 feet. You can often hear and see the falls from the parking area if there is enough of a water flow.

DIRECTIONS From the junction of VT 125 and US 7 in the center of Middlebury, take VT 125 west to a right onto VT 23 north. Follow VT 23 north for 2.8 miles and take a left onto James Road. Follow James Road for 0.1 mile and take a right onto Bittersweet Falls Road. Go 0.6 mile on this road and park on the small pull-off on the left just before crossing a bridge.

OTHER WATERFALLS NEARBY Falls of Lana, Abbey Pond Cascades, Bartlett Falls, Bristol Memorial Park Falls

152

BOLTON POTHOLES
Bolton, Chittenden County

Rating: 4.5/5.0
Type: Plunges and cascades
Height: 45-foot total drop
Trail Length: Less than 0.1 mile
Water Source: Joiner Brook
Altitude Gain/Loss: Negligible

Difficulty: Easy
Hiking Time: Negligible
DeLorme Atlas: Page 45, K-14 (unmarked)
Best Time to Visit: Year-round

THE FALLS (HIGHLY RECOMMENDED) This is the waterfall that fits everyone well: It is perfect for children, teens, and adults alike. There are plenty of flat rock surfaces for picnickers and sunbathers, swimming pools and potholes for waders and swimmers, and a stunning set of waterfalls sure to please anyone.

Bolton Potholes, which is frequently called The Potholes or Devil's Potholes, consists of three sets of falls. The first plunge drops into a small, round pothole about 5 feet wide by 7 feet long. The second plunge, only feet downstream, drops into an almost perfectly circular pothole about 25 feet in diameter and 10 feet at its deepest point. The lips of the surrounding cliff walls overhang slightly over the pool, allowing daring souls an opportunity to cliff jump. If you partake in this activity, take extreme caution as the edge of the cliff is very slippery. We have seen several people slip off this overhang and land in the pool below in unintended positions.

Each of the two potholes is filled with the deep, emerald green water that is so common to Vermont swimming holes, yet still breathtaking every time we see it. The third waterfall, a cascade about 5 feet tall, slips into a narrow river channel. Below these falls, the water calms as it enters a very large, round pool that is perfect for younger children. Small sand and pebble beaches line the riverbank, creating ideal conditions for a picnic.

Although it is probably one of the coldest of Vermont's swimming holes, you are likely to see a swimmer or two anytime from June to September. On a recent 80-degree August afternoon, we shared a swim with over 100 people! The Potholes, regardless of how crowded it can become, retains high scenic character and are highly recommended.

TRAIL INFORMATION From any of the parking areas, walk east toward the brook. There are a half-dozen or so short paths leading to the upper, middle, and bottom viewpoints of the falls from the road.

DIRECTIONS From Burlington, take I-89 east to exit 11. Follow US 2 east through Richmond and into Bolton. Continue traveling on US 2 for 0.4 mile past the green BOLTON town sign and take a left onto Bolton Valley Access Road. This is the road that leads to the Bolton Valley Ski Area. Follow Bolton Valley Access Road for 0.2 mile and park on the shoulder on either side of the road. If you are traveling from the east, Bolton Valley Access Road is located on US 2 about 6.6 miles west of the junction of VT 100 and US 2 in Waterbury (which is accessible from exit 10 off I-89).

OTHER WATERFALLS NEARBY Huntington Gorge, Honey Hollow Falls, Thatcher Brook Falls

Bolton Potholes

153

BREWSTER RIVER GORGE
Cambridge, Lamoille County

Rating: 3.0/5.0

Type: Horsetails

Height: 75-foot total drop

Trail Length: 0.3 mile to lower falls; 0.5 mile to upper falls

Water Source: Brewster River

Altitude Gain/Loss: +30 feet, -20 feet to lower falls; +100 feet, -20 feet to upper falls

Difficulty: Easy side of moderate

Hiking Time: 10 minutes to lower falls; 15 minutes to upper falls

DeLorme Atlas: Page 46, B-1 (unmarked)

Best Time to Visit: May to October

THE FALLS Thanks to recent conservation efforts, your experience at Brewster River Gorge, commonly called Jefferson Falls by some, is now a simpler and perhaps more enjoyable experience. Years ago, it could take upwards of a half hour to reach the waterfall, due mostly in part to a then-required river crossing, which typically meant taking off your shoes and rock-hopping across the river. New trails on the opposite side of the river now guide you easily to the lower and upper segments of the gorge.

From the base of the lower falls, the water picks its way through and around boulders that appear to have fallen on top of one another throughout the years. There are small greenish pools at the base of several of these boulders. The river below the falls is quite wide with an extended riverbank—containing a mix of tough sand, soft grass, and small pebbles. There are lots of boulders to scramble over and play on here if you choose.

The upper viewpoint provides you with a look down into the wild and powerful gorge. There is no swimming here for obvious reasons. For those wishing to spend more time at this destination, a rough trail continues on a lovely river walk above the falls, offering many opportunities for children to wade or splash in small pools.

If swimming is what you desire, there is a small set of cascades, Jeff Falls, nearby that offers much better opportunities than Brewster River Gorge. It is located on a short 250-foot trail that is only 0.5 mile south of town on VT 108. It is currently private property, but access is allowed on the condition that all visitors respect the natural surroundings and clean up after themselves.

TRAIL INFORMATION The trail to both the lower and upper viewpoints starts across the street from the parking area and is marked by a sign for the ALDEN BRYAN BREWSTER RIVER TRAIL. To begin this hike, start into the woods on this charming and straightforward white-blazed trail. After about 0.3 mile on this trail, you will reach a junction. *To reach the base of the falls,* take a right and you will reach the base of the falls in about 400 feet. *To reach the top of the falls,* where the best views of the gorge are found, continue left and keep hiking uphill for 0.2 mile on moderate terrain.

DIRECTIONS From the junction of VT 108 and VT 15 that is just to the northeast of the center of Jeffersonville, take VT 108 south through town for 0.8 mile and take a left onto Canyon Road. Travel down Canyon Road for less than 0.1 mile, go through a covered bridge, and immediately park on your left. *To get to Jeffersonville,* take VT 15 east from Burlington or VT 108 north from Stowe.

OTHER WATERFALLS NEARBY Bingham Falls, Fairfax Falls, Dog's Head Falls, Terrill Gorge

154

BRISTOL MEMORIAL PARK FALLS

Bristol, Memorial Forest Park, Addison County

Rating: 3.0/5.0
Type: Plunges and horsetails
Height: 10 feet and 15 feet
Trail Length: 0.1 mile
Water Source: Baldwin Creek
Altitude Gain/Loss: -50 feet

Difficulty: Easy
Hiking Time: 5 minutes
DeLorme Atlas: Page 39, G-11 (unmarked)
Best Time to Visit: Year-round

THE FALLS The best view of this waterfall is from the narrow bridge that is perched above the head of the gorge below the falls. From this bridge, you will see both a side view of the impressive upper plunge and the lower horsetail, which falls into an oyster-shaped rock surface. Framing the two falls into a single photograph can produce great results.

Beginning directly under the bridge and continuing downstream is the very narrow 50-foot-long gorge. The creek is condensed drastically here, often resulting in roaring sounds of water.

Bristol Memorial Park Falls may not be the most highly recommended waterfall in the area, but its proximity to nearby Bartlett Falls means it should not be neglected.

TRAIL INFORMATION From the parking lot, follow an easy boardwalk trail a few minutes until you reach the falls and gorge. For those wary of ladders, be aware that there is a 15-foot section you must descend to obtain an unobstructed view of the falls.

DIRECTIONS From Bristol, follow the combined highway VT 116 north and VT 17 east. Take a right onto VT 17 east and travel on that highway for 1.6 miles after it breaks away from VT 116. Pull into the parking lot marked with a sign for the MEMORIAL FOREST PARK on the right. *To get to Bristol,* take US 7 north from Middlebury to VT-17 east.

OTHER WATERFALLS NEARBY Bartlett Falls, Abbey Pond Cascades, Hartshorn Falls, Stetson Hollow Falls, Warren Falls

Bristol Memorial Park Falls

155

BUTTERMILK FALLS

Ludlow, Windsor County

Rating: 4.0/5.0

Type: Horsetails and cascades

Height: Lower falls is 8 feet; middle falls is 20 feet; upper falls is 15 feet

Trail Length: 0.2 mile to visit all three falls

Water Source: Branch Brook

Altitude Gain/Loss: +25 feet to visit all three falls

Difficulty: Easy side of moderate to visit all three falls

Hiking Time: 10 minutes to visit all three falls

DeLorme Atlas: Page 30, J-4 (marked)

Best Time to Visit: Year-round

THE FALLS This waterfall is one of several classic swimming holes in southern Vermont. There is a large pool below both the middle and upper falls, each being deep enough for complete submersion. The middle falls flows into a deep 25-foot-wide pool of clear, olive green water. Later in the season, a twist of water, which wraps itself around a slightly wetted boulder, adds character to what is usually a typical plunge over the ledge during times of high water.

The upper waterfall is a segmented horsetail, with the right side being the predominant one. The left horsetail is only strong during the spring or after heavy rains. This horsetail is steeper and slightly taller, at 15 feet, whereas the right horsetail is about 12 feet in height. Both streams of water flow into another large swimming pool with clear water and a pebble-covered bottom. These waterfalls should be visited both in spring and later on in the summer, as you will experience two different personalities of the falls.

The lower waterfall, a set of cascades 8 feet tall, lacks a pool of any real significance, but is considerably less crowded than the two falls above.

TRAIL INFORMATION There are many trails that lead to each of the three sets of falls from the road. Follow any of the paths a few feet and you will reach the brook. You can scramble your way upstream or downstream to each of the three falls without returning to the road. The best trail to the upper falls is 30 feet downstream of the end of the road.

DIRECTIONS From Ludlow, take the combined highway VT 100 and VT 103 north. Continue traveling on VT 103 north for 0.2 mile after VT 100 breaks off. Take a right onto Buttermilk Falls Road. Follow this road

Buttermilk Falls

for 1.3 miles and park on any of the dirt pull-offs on the right. *To get to Ludlow,* take I-91 south from White River Junction to exit 8. Follow VT 131 west to VT 103 north.

OTHER WATERFALLS NEARBY Clarendon Gorge, Lower Falls, Cascade Falls

156

CASCADE FALLS

Weathersfield, Mount Ascutney State Park, Windsor County

Rating: 3.0/5.0

Type: Horsetail

Height: 84 feet

Trail Length: 0.4 mile to Little Cascade Falls; 1.1 miles to Cascade Falls

Water Source: Ascutney Brook

Altitude Gain/Loss: +700 feet to Cascade Falls

Difficulty: Moderate

Hiking Time: 45 minutes to Cascade Falls

DeLorme Atlas: Page 31, J-9 (unmarked)

Best Time to Visit: May to June

THE FALLS Two waterfalls can be found off the Weathersfield Trail on Mt. Ascutney, the tallest mountain in southeastern Vermont. Cascade Falls, and its sister, Little Cascade Falls, are two highly seasonal waterfalls that are quite attractive when water is actually flowing over them. Due to their high elevation on the slopes of Mt. Ascutney, both waterfalls are often reduced to just a trickle by June or July of every year, except after heavy rains.

Little Cascade Falls is exceptionally seasonal. During a period of drought, there may be such a lack of water that you would be hard-pressed to find any evidence that a waterfall exists here. A visit during a high-water period will unveil a pretty horsetail falling approximately 45 feet over several drops.

Cascade Falls, which is often called Crystal Cascade Falls, drains more water off the mountain, and so is a bit less seasonal. The trail to these falls brings you to where the brook drops over a broad ledge. This ledge is 30 feet wide, but the falls are not more than a few feet wide. A perfectly placed boulder near the ledge makes for a great seat from which to admire the scenic panorama. Better views can be obtained from the base of the falls, but this requires a difficult bushwhack down a very steep slope.

TRAIL INFORMATION The trail to the falls is a nearly continuous climb of 1.1 miles, but there are a few re-energizing flat stretches. From the parking area, begin ascending Mt. Ascutney via the white-blazed Weathersfield Trail. The distance from the parking area to Little Cascade Falls is only 0.4 mile, and is only 250 feet in elevation gain.

When you reach Little Cascade Falls, continue climbing along the Weathersfield Trail and you will soon reach a trail ladder. Climb the sturdy ladder and the first scenic vista of the trail is to the left. There is a nice rock outcropping here for a quick rest. After admiring the view, continue climbing the moderately steep trail to Cascade Falls. A little over 1 mile from the parking lot, you will reach a sign directing you left to the falls and right toward the rest of the 1.8 miles of the Weathersfield Trail needed to reach the summit of Mt. Ascutney. Take a left at this sign and begin walking toward the clearing.

As you walk down the large, flat rock toward the ledge over which the brook tumbles, you will be rewarded with another scenic vista. This one has views of approximately 80 miles or more, especially on very clear days. There is a perfectly placed boulder that overlooks the waterfall and the panorama near the ledge of the fall.

As far as we could tell, there is no safe means by which to scramble down to the base of Cascade Falls. Perhaps a trail will one day be constructed by state park personnel to offer viewers a new perspective on this lovely waterfall.

SPECIAL NOTE If you are willing, keep hiking on the Weathersfield Trail beyond Cascades Falls all the way to the summit of Mt. Ascutney. From Cascade Falls, it is an additional 1.8 miles with 1,400 feet more elevation gain on moderate terrain to the summit. A fire tower survives on the summit, offering some of the very best views that Vermont has to offer. This round trip hike of 5.8 miles is highly recommended for those in good physical condition.

DIRECTIONS From White River Junction, take I-91 south to exit 8. Take VT 131 west for 3.1 miles and take a right onto Cascade Falls Road. Follow Cascade Falls Road for 400 feet and take a left onto High Meadow Road. Follow this road for 0.4 mile to the end of the road to reach the parking lot.

OTHER WATERFALLS NEARBY Buttermilk Falls, Quechee Gorge

157

CLARENDON GORGE, LOWER FALLS

Clarendon, Rutland County

Rating: 2.5/5.0

Type: Plunge and cascades

Height: 15-foot total drop

Trail Length: 0.1 mile

Water Source: Mill River

Altitude Gain/Loss: -50 feet

Difficulty: Moderate

Hiking Time: 5 minutes

DeLorme Atlas: Page 29, G-12 (unmarked)

Best Time to Visit: May to October

THE FALLS Mill River offers at least three separate sections of falls and cascades worthy of mention. The upper falls, which were described in full detail in our original guide, are seen below a suspension bridge along a combined section of the Long and Appalachian Trails. These cascades are tiny and somewhat run-of-the-mill, but the suspension bridge adds great appeal.

The lower waterfall of Clarendon Gorge is a more recent discovery of ours. At this site, the river violently thrashes through a tan-colored gorge. Swimming is not feasible anywhere near the gorge, but tiny pools may be available upstream if the current is calm enough. These falls are locally known as Devil's Gorge and are also often called Lower Clarendon Gorge.

Another unnamed set of cascades is downstream of the lower falls. It is not advisable to hike along the gorge to find them. Instead, follow the directions below to an alternative trailhead, where an easy stroll will bring you downhill to the cascades.

TRAIL INFORMATION From the parking pull-off located 0.5 mile up Gorge Road, walk 300 feet south on the only obvious path and then take a left to descend a steep and moderately difficult 100-foot section of trail to the river's edge. Once you reach the river, bear right, and walk a very short distance to obtain a good view of the falls from the top of the gorge. Be very careful around the end of the gorge as the ledges here can be extremely slippery.

DIRECTIONS From the junction of VT 7B and VT 103 in Clarendon, take VT 7B south for 1.9 miles and take a left onto Gorge Road. Follow Gorge Road for 0.5 mile and there will be a parking pull-off on the right with room for two or three cars. This is the trailhead for the lower falls, also known as Devil's Gorge. There is another set of 8-foot-tall cascades really close by, as well, accessed by a different trailhead that is located only 0.2 mile up Gorge Road from VT 7B. *To get to Clarendon,* take US 7 south from Rutland or US 7 north from Manchester.

OTHER WATERFALLS NEARBY Buttermilk Falls

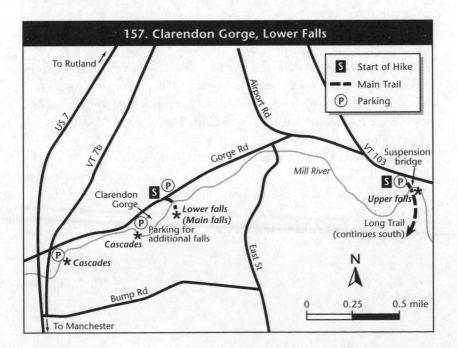

157. Clarendon Gorge, Lower Falls

158

COVERED BRIDGE FALLS
Thetford, Orange County

Rating: 2.5/5.0
Type: Cascades
Height: 25-foot total drop
Trail Length: Less than 0.1 mile
Water Source: Ompompanoosuc River
Altitude Gain/Loss: -25 feet

Difficulty: Moderate side of difficult
Hiking Time: 5 minutes
DeLorme Atlas: Page 35, G-14 (unmarked)
Best Time to Visit: Year-round

THE FALLS Covered Bridge Falls, is, as the name suggests, a waterfall that neighbors a covered bridge. The bridge, which is approximately 50 feet in length, sits just above this 25-foot chain of cascades in the town of Thetford. This waterfall is also known as Thetford Center Falls.

Although the bridge is only several yards above the falls, accessing any good view of these cascades, other than from the road or bridge, is surprisingly difficult. However, do not leave the area without a closer look. If its location were more publicly disclosed, it would certainly receive more attention from painters and photographers, as the waterfall and covered bridge create quite an artistic frame.

TRAIL INFORMATION The falls begin only 50 feet downstream from the covered bridge, accessible by a barely used trail on your left just before the river. In the past, we have seen this trail become a little overgrown. The cascades are quite worth the effort of making it successfully down the trail, in our opinion.

DIRECTIONS Take I-91 north from White River Junction to exit 14 in Thetford. Take VT 113 west for 2.3 miles and take a left onto Tucker Hill Road. Follow this road for 0.25 mile and park before the covered bridge on the left.

OTHER WATERFALLS NEARBY Old City Falls, Glen Falls, Quechee Gorge

159

CRYSTAL FALLS

Montgomery, Franklin County

Rating: 2.5/5.0

Type: Cascades and slides

Height: 15-foot total drop

Trail Length: Less than 0.1 mile

Water Source: West Hill Brook

Altitude Gain/Loss: -15 feet

Difficulty: Easy

Hiking Time: Negligible

DeLorme Atlas: Page 52, E-5 (unmarked)

Best Time to Visit: May to October

THE FALLS The Creamery Bridge, or West Hill Bridge, as it is often called, is a covered bridge of the lattice design, spanning West Hill Brook in the town of Montgomery. It is one of seven covered bridges located in this town, considered by many to be the covered bridge capital of Vermont. Officially closed to automobile use in September of 1999, the bridge is now only accessible by foot, but this may change with a restoration project currently underway.

While there are over one hundred covered bridges in the state, only a small handful have waterfalls below them. Crystal Falls, which we incorrectly labeled as West Hill Brook Falls in the first edition of this guide, is a 15-foot drop that begins its descent starting just below the bridge. Beginning as a stretch of slides and cascades falling at an angle of about 45 degrees, the waterfall first takes on the appearance of a thick blanket, before dropping the final few feet as a steep cascade.

Many guidebooks are currently available for sale on the covered bridges of Vermont and the rest of New England. A few new passions for us emerged as we visited more and more waterfalls; a love for covered bridges was one of them. If you found that you enjoyed the waterfall-covered bridge combination, check out Covered Bridge Falls of Vermont, and Swiftwater Falls of Bath, New Hampshire. These are two other similar and special places.

TRAIL INFORMATION The falls are only a few feet downstream from the covered bridge. There is a faint path to the left of the bridge that leads you to the base of the falls, where a temping pool can be found. Downstream of the falls is West Hill Brook Falls, although we are not certain of the absolute location or whether or not it is located on private property. If you do go searching for this second set of falls, please respect any private property you encounter.

DIRECTIONS From the junction of VT 118, VT 58, and VT 242 in Montgomery Center, take VT 118 north for 2.9 miles to a left onto West Hill Road. Another road nearby, Hill West Road, should not be confused with West Hill Road. Follow West Hill Road for 2.7 miles to a left onto Creamery Bridge Road, which is currently an unmarked road. Take this road for 0.7 mile and the parking area will be on your right just before a covered bridge. *To get to Montgomery Center,* take VT 105 west from Newport to VT 100 south to VT 58 west. As a note of caution, be aware that VT 58 is a seasonal road and is typically closed from late fall to early spring.

Be aware that during our visit in 2009, construction was in progress to restore the bridge. It is uncertain whether this construction will have any effect on your visit. Future editions of this guide will reflect any changes.

OTHER WATERFALLS NEARBY Trout River Falls, Big Falls, Jay Branch Gorge, Kings Hill Brook Falls

160

DOG'S HEAD FALLS
Johnson, Lamoille County

Rating: 2.0/5.0

Type: Cascades

Height: 6 feet

Trail Length: 0.1 mile

Water Source: Lamoille River

Altitude Gain/Loss: Negligible

Difficulty: Easy

Hiking Time: 5 minutes

DeLorme Atlas: Page 46, B-5 (unmarked)

Best Time to Visit: Year-round

THE FALLS The best view of this waterfall used to be from the road, River Road East, before you reached the path to the falls. Strong plant growth over the years has made hiking necessary to obtain a good view. From the trail, a massive profile of a canine quickly indicates the origin of this waterfalls' name. A topic of controversy is what breed of dog; in our opinion, it can only be a Saint Bernard!

This waterfall is actually known as Upper Dog's Head Falls to some. Directly upstream of the dog's head profile is 6 feet of incredibly powerful cascades. The water has a yellowish tint, and the very strong currents in the entire river prevent swimming in the deep pools below.

Lower Dog's Head Falls, sometimes called Sloping Falls, consist of two sections of 5-foot cascades and rapids, and are found just back down the road. It is said that during low water, the entire volume of the Lamoille River travels hidden underneath a wide natural bridge that spans the entire river, although we have yet to see such a natural wonder.

TRAIL INFORMATION Depending on the season, the waterfall and the dog's head profile from which this waterfall derives its name are both visible off in the distance after traveling 0.7 mile on River Road East.

For a closer view, a rough path begins 0.1 mile farther up the road at the pull-off described in the directions below. From the pull-off, walk through a small field and then bear left into a short stretch of wooded area. The falls will be just ahead, accessed by a relatively easy walk across rock ledge. Take caution if the ledge is wet, as it can be very slippery.

DIRECTIONS From the junction of VT 15 and VT 108 in Jeffersonville, take VT 15 east. Continue traveling on VT 15 east for 0.7 mile past the WELCOME TO JOHNSON sign. Please note that this is not actually the town's border. Take a right onto Railroad Street just before reaching the center of Johnson and follow it for 0.3 mile. Take a left onto River Road East immediately after going through an old iron bridge. Follow River Road East for 0.8 mile to a small pull-off on the left side of the road. To get to Jeffersonville, take VT 15 east from Burlington or VT 108 north from Stowe.

OTHER WATERFALLS NEARBY Brewster River Gorge, Fairfax Falls, Terrill Gorge, Sterling Brook Gorge, Bingham Falls, Moss Glen Falls–Stowe

161

EMERSON FALLS
St. Johnsbury, Caledonia County

Rating: 2.5/5.0
Type: Cascades
Height: 25-foot total drop
Trail Length: Less than 0.1 mile
Water Source: Sleepers River
Altitude Gain/Loss: Negligible

Difficulty: Easy side of moderate
Hiking Time: Negligible
DeLorme Atlas: Page 48, I-5 (unmarked)
Best Time to Visit: April to June

THE FALLS Controlled upstream by a hydroelectric project, Emerson Falls is a low-angle cascade that should always have some water flow. As the water jumps down over jagged bedrock, some small pools are created, and these little potholes of water attract the majority of visitors to this waterfall.

The site is unfortunately quite urban; there are businesses and other buildings directly behind the waterfall. This distracts from the natural beauty of Emerson Falls. Luckily, if you hike down to the base of the waterfall, you quickly forget that you are surrounded by society. The waterfall, with its rugged, irregular nature, still manages to drown out the sounds and human-made structures just downstream.

TRAIL INFORMATION The trail to the falls is located adjacent to the Emerson Falls Business Center. It is a very short path, but it has been getting progressively narrower over the years. It is possible that the trail will become so eroded that it will become unsafe to travel on. If you find the trail to be in poor condition, please limit your viewing of these falls from the business center and the road.

DIRECTIONS From I-91 in St. Johnsbury, take exit 21. Take US 2 west for 0.7 mile to a right onto North Danville Road. Take an immediate right onto Emerson Falls Road. Follow this road for 0.25 mile and the falls will be on your left. There is no official parking area, so you may have to park farther or back up the road.

OTHER WATERFALLS NEARBY Marshfield Falls

162

~

FAIRFAX FALLS
Fairfax, Franklin County

Rating: 2.0/5.0
Type: Cascades
Height: Approximately 80-foot total drop
Trail Length: Roadside
Water Source: Lamoille River

Altitude Gain/Loss: None
Difficulty: Easy
Hiking Time: Not applicable
DeLorme Atlas: Page 45, A-12 (marked)
Best Time to Visit: Year-round

THE FALLS Once an untouched, massive, and high-volume waterfall, since 1918 Fairfax Falls has been used as a hydroelectric dam to supply the ever-growing demand for electricity. Although the power station next to the waterfall detracts significantly from the natural setting, the waterfall still retains much of its original beauty.

Spring runoff guarantees a powerful show at Fairfax Falls. Yet even in times of low water, this waterfall is still of interest; small rivulets of water pick their way down over the 80-foot rock wall.

TRAIL INFORMATION Fairfax Falls is clearly visible from VT 104, but the views are much better from the designated picnic area that is off River Road.

DIRECTIONS From I-89 in Burlington, take exit 15. Follow VT 15 east to a left turn onto VT 128 north in the village of Essex Center. Take VT 128 north and take a right onto VT 104 south in Fairfax. Follow VT 104 south for 1.0 mile and the falls will be visible on your left. Continue 0.1 mile beyond your first glimpse of the falls and take a left to cross a bridge at the top of the dam. Immediately after crossing the bridge, take a left onto River Road. Follow River Road for 0.2 mile and take a left into the marked Fairfax Falls Picnic Area. This road is only about 300 feet long, but it may be in rough condition and not suitable for low-clearance vehicles.

OTHER WATERFALLS NEARBY Brewster River Gorge, Dog's Head Falls

163

FALLS OF LANA
Salisbury, Addison County

Rating: 5.0/5.0
Type: Horsetails and cascades
Height: 100-foot total drop
Trail Length: 0.4 mile to either lower falls or upper falls viewpoint; 0.7 mile to base of upper falls
Water Source: Sucker Brook
Altitude Gain/Loss: +100 feet, -25 feet to lower falls viewpoint; +200 feet to upper falls viewpoint; +250 feet, -100 feet to base of upper falls

Difficulty: Easy side of moderate to lower falls viewpoint; moderate to upper falls viewpoint; moderate side of difficult to base of upper falls.
Hiking Time: 15 minutes to either lower falls or upper falls viewpoints; 25 minutes to base of upper falls
DeLorme Atlas: Page 33, E-10 (marked)
Best Time to Visit: May to October

THE FALLS (HIGHLY RECOMMENDED) Have you ever seen one of those waterfalls in romance movies where the leading characters fall in love?

The upper section of the Falls of Lana certainly qualifies as one of those waterfalls, and, if Hollywood film location scouts were aware of this waterfall, Falls of Lana could become a star.

The top horsetail at the Falls of Lana snakes down through a gorge into a stunning and deep swimming pool. This pool has little to no current at all, and with minimal tree coverage overhead, is highly exposed to the sun's rays. Yet even with the sun beating onto the surface of the pool, the water tends to be cooler than most swimming holes, mostly due to its high elevation.

The lower sections of this waterfall are equally beautiful, but it is much more difficult to get a good view of them. This section of falls consists of horsetails and cascades winding down through a gorge into another tempting pool. Plan to spend some time exploring here and you will find nooks and crannies that many have likely missed during their visits.

TRAIL INFORMATION Access to this waterfall has significantly changed since the first edition of this book. We are now describing the trail to the falls as traveled from the paved parking area that is 0.2 mile south of the old dirt parking area.

From the large paved parking area, take the narrow trail uphill (sometimes called the Silver Lake Trail) for 100 feet, where you will reach a junction with a dirt road. Take a right and follow this dirt road. After about 0.3 mile, the road will cross under a large black pipe (called a penstock). This is time for you to make a decision. *To reach the lower falls viewpoint,* scramble downhill alongside the penstock for 200 feet and there will be a fence with a good view of the falls on your right.

To reach the upper falls viewpoint and the base of the upper falls, continue straight ahead on the dirt road. In only 400 feet, take one of the rough paths on your left for just 50 feet and you will reach any one of the several viewpoints of the upper falls. During our visit, there was a NO CAMPING sign here to mark the spot where you should leave the dirt road. To continue to the base of the upper falls, you will have to hike straight and travel farther along the dirt road. Continue another 0.2 mile farther and you should reach a trail sign for RATTLESNAKE CLIFFS. Take a left and cross a bridge over Sucker Brook (see warning, below), and take a left to head downstream on a sometimes steep and rough blue-blazed trail. You will reach the base of the upper falls, with one of Vermont's most gorgeous pools to refresh yourself in, after about 0.2 mile on this trail.

Warning! During a massive flood in 2008, a bridge over Sucker Brook, critical to visiting the base of the upper falls, was destroyed. Although there are rumors of plans to replace the bridge in 2010, there is a chance that this bridge may take longer to be replaced, or even not be replaced at all.

Without the bridge intact, it may be difficult or impossible to cross the brook in all but the lowest of water levels. You may be able to find other areas downstream of the bridge site to cross safely, though.

DIRECTIONS There are two parking areas along VT 53 in the town of Salisbury that access this waterfall. The following directions are based on the parking area that we felt provided the easiest and safest access.

From Middlebury, take US 7 south into the town of Salisbury and take a left onto VT 53 south. Follow VT 53 south for 4.0 miles and you will reach a large paved parking area on the left. This parking area is 0.4 mile south of the Branbury State Park entrance on the eastern shore of Lake Dunmore.

OTHER WATERFALLS NEARBY Abbey Pond Cascades, Texas Falls, Bittersweet Falls

164

GLEN FALLS
Fairlee, Orange County

Rating: 4.0/5.0
Type: Plunge and cascades
Height: 80-foot total drop
Trail Length: To main plunge, 0.2 mile; to upper cascades, 0.3 mile
Water Source: Glen Falls Brook
Altitude Gain/Loss: +50 feet to main plunge

Difficulty: Easy to main plunge; moderate side of difficult thereafter
Hiking Time: 10 minutes to main plunge
DeLorme Atlas: Page 36, D-2 (unmarked)
Best Time to Visit: Year-round

THE FALLS What makes this waterfall so exceptional is how narrow the main 25-foot plunge is. It pours through a small opening cut between the gorge walls. For such a normally small and weak stream, the plunge takes on a commanding appearance. It is set back from the road, completely hidden and heavily shaded, but just enough sunlight forces its way through the woods to allow for a nice picture. The plunge drops into an almost perfect circular pool—a bit shallow, but that has not seemed to matter to the many children we have seen playing here.

Downstream from this plunge are small cascades and medium-sized plunges. Above the main falls are additional cascades and plunges. Most visitors stop at the main falls, so you if you venture farther you may be able to earn yourself some solitude.

TRAIL INFORMATION From the parking area, walk back down Lake Morey Road until you see a tennis court on your left. Across from the tennis court is a well-used path that will lead you on a gently uphill sloping trail past several unnamed cascades and plunges to the main star of the show, Glen Falls. After hiking about 0.1 mile, you will reach a noteworthy but unnamed 12-foot segmented plunge with a clear, moss-surrounded pool. Continue hiking upstream with the brook on your left a short distance farther to Glen Falls. When you reach the main falls, you can choose to hike the moderately difficult trail to less attractive cascades above.

The parking area for the falls also serves as the trailhead for the newly constructed Cross Rivendell Trail. From the parking area, it is a 3.3-mile moderate hike to the 360-degree viewpoint called Bald Top. More information about this increasingly popular 36-mile long trail can be found at www.crossrivendelltrail.org.

DIRECTIONS Take I-91 north from White River Junction to exit 15 in Fairlee. Follow signs to LAKE MOREY ROAD and you will soon reach an intersection with Lake Morey Road. Continue straight through the intersection and drive for 1.3 miles as the road travels along the west shoreline of Lake Morey. You will find a parking area on the left, across from a Vermont Department of Fish and Wildlife boat launch site.

OTHER WATERFALLS NEARBY Covered Bridge Falls, Old City Falls

165
❧

HAMILTON FALLS
Jamaica, Hamilton Falls Natural Area,
Windham County

Rating: 4.5/5.0

Type: Horsetails and slides

Height: Approximately 125-foot total drop

Trail Length: 0.2 mile to base of falls

Water Source: Cobb Brook

Altitude Gain/Loss: -150 feet to base of falls

Difficulty: Easy side of moderate

Hiking Time: 10 minutes

DeLorme Atlas: Page 26, I-3 (marked)

Best Time to Visit: May to October

THE FALLS (HIGHLY RECOMMENDED) A short distance northeast of Jamaica State Park is the final mile of Cobb Brook, a water source renowned for one of Vermont's tallest waterfalls, 125-foot Hamilton Falls. The waters of the brook literally slice their way sideways through deeply cut gorge walls before landing in popular wading pools below the entire formation. At the top of the falls is a deep pool and rock ledges that people often illegally jump from. For your own safety, swimming is prohibited here, and for good reason. A sign at the falls states that 10 people have died here. *The currents in this pool are deadly and should be avoided.*

Hamilton Falls

Hamilton Falls is an amazing place to bring children and have a picnic. There are sunny areas for tanning, but still enough shade along the side to keep cool. You will find that this waterfall is very popular and there will be other people there relaxing, as well. Most of these visitors tend to be out-of-staters, which is rather surprising, because most refreshing waterfalls in Vermont are only locally known.

Nearby Jamaica State Park also offers hiking, camping, hunting, fishing, and white-water kayaking (one weekend in spring and fall, the Ball Mountain Dam releases high levels of water and kayakers and canoeists have made events out of these dates). The area inside Jamaica State Park also has some history of particular interest. In 1748, the last year of King George's War, the debate over the borders of New France and the British Colonies was still in full disagreement. On the night of May 31, 1748, two Frenchmen and nine Native Americans crept up the West River in what is now the town of Londonderry and attacked British troops, killing five and wounding another. This massacre occurred at Salmon Hole, a popular fishing spot during that time period on the West River (it is now known more as a popular swimming hole).

TRAIL INFORMATION Two separate trails lead to observation points at the base and top of the falls. To reach the base of the falls, where the best views are to be had in our opinion, follow Switch Road for 0.1 mile as it gradually walks down through the woods to a sign for the falls. Take a right at the sign and continue climbing down to the base of the falls. A shorter trail, accessed by walking a few feet farther down Windham Road from the parking area, leads left to the top of Hamilton Falls.

You may notice some other visitors using the steep and very rough trail to the right of the falls to travel between the lower and upper viewpoints of the falls. This looked moderately risky and is therefore not recommended.

DIRECTIONS From the junction of VT 30 and VT 35 in Townshend, take VT 30 north for 4.5 miles into the village of West Townshend. Take a right onto Windham Hill Road and follow that for 4.3 miles to a left onto Burbee Pond Road. Follow this road for 0.8 mile to a left onto West Windham Road. Follow West Windham Road for 2.8 miles and the parking lot will be on your left, marked by a sign for the SWITCH ROAD. *To get to Townsend,* take exit 2 off I-91 in Brattleboro. Follow VT 9 east to VT 30 north.

OTHER WATERFALLS NEARBY Pikes Falls, Lye Brook Falls, Jelly Mill Falls

166

HANCOCK BROOK FALLS
Worcester, Washington County

Rating: 3.0/5.0
Type: Plunges and slides
Height: Tallest is 8 feet
Trail Length: Less than 0.1 mile
to each falls
Water Source: Hancock Brook
Altitude Gain/Loss: -20 feet to
each falls

Difficulty: Easy side of moderate
Hiking Time: Negligible
DeLorme Atlas: Page 46, J-7
(unmarked)
Best Time to Visit: May to
October

THE FALLS Hancock Brook Falls is one of the more recent success stories of the Vermont River Conservancy, an organization whose resumé for conserving sections of important and scenic rivers across the state is becoming legendary. Acquired in 2007, this property includes several small waterfalls and a classic swimming hole known as the Upper Pot.

We found three waterfalls along a short section of the brook. A lower set of falls is a 6-foot slide that slips into a shallow pool. The middle falls fea-

Hancock Brook Falls

ture a 5-foot-tall plunge into a deeper pool perfectly sized for two. The third and final falls are our favorite; you will find a trio of adjacent plunges, each dropping 6 to 8 feet into the Upper Pot, perhaps the finest of the swimming holes in the vicinity.

TRAIL INFORMATION The lower, middle, and upper falls can be seen from the road if you look carefully enough. In order to visit each of them, you will have to scramble down rough and somewhat steep paths. The middle falls are only 50 feet upstream of the lower falls. The upper and final waterfall is 300 feet upstream of the middle falls. The best way to visit each of them is to park at the lower falls and walk along the road.

DIRECTIONS From I-89 in Montpelier, take exit 8. Follow VT 2 east and signs to VT 12 north. Follow VT 12 north through Middlesex and into Worcester. Continue traveling along VT 12 north for 2.1 miles beyond its junction with Calais Road and take a left onto Hancock Brook Road. Follow Hancock Brook Road for 0.3 mile and there will be a pull-off with room for one car on the right. The lower falls are directly across the street, reached by a 20-foot moderate scramble down to the base of the falls. The middle falls and the premier swimming hole in the area are 50 feet farther up the road from the lower falls. The upper falls are about 300 feet farther up the road from the middle falls. There really is not any suitable or safe place to park beyond the lower falls, so you might just want to park there and walk up the road to view the middle and upper falls.

OTHER WATERFALLS NEARBY Marshfield Falls, Terrill Gorge

167

HARTSHORN FALLS
Warren, Washington County

Rating: 3.0/5.0

Type: Plunges and cascades

Height: Tallest is 12 feet

Trail Length: 0.1 mile to upper falls

Water Source: Lincoln Brook

Altitude Gain/Loss: +50 feet to upper falls

Difficulty: Easy

Hiking Time: 5 minutes to upper falls

DeLorme Atlas: Page 39, I-14 (unmarked)

Best Time to Visit: May to October

THE FALLS Hartshorn Falls is located in the Mad River Valley, a region that can boast about the fact that it has an assortment of celebrated watering holes. Hartshorn Falls, which is commonly called Lincoln Brook Falls and Bobbin Mill, is one of the more pristine of them.

The waters of Lincoln Brook plunge into a narrow recess between huge gorge walls at the lowest set of falls on this parcel of property. These falls are the tallest, at 12 feet. Wading across the brook to the other side will reward you with an obstructed view of these falls.

A short distance upstream you will find the middle falls, a 6-foot horsetail. This waterfall is visible off in the distance from the trail, beyond a rocky beach and an elongated pool. The upper falls are just as easily accessed, and they feature a two-tiered 6-foot cascade that winds its way along the side of a broad ledge. In low-water conditions, a very fun thing to do is to lie down between the two tiers of cascades and let the water pour on top of you. We have seen other visitors doing exactly this on several occasions.

This is a great place to spend hours splashing in the numerous small pools along the brook. Children will especially enjoy themselves here, and parents should feel comfortable knowing that this is one of the safer, more family-friendly swimming holes in the area.

TRAIL INFORMATION From the parking lot, head slightly uphill into the woods. After only 75 feet, bear left to reach the first and tallest set of falls, a 12-foot plunge. In order to visit more falls, continue only 100 feet farther up the main trail and you will see the middle falls off in the distance. The third and final significant waterfall here is only 150 feet upstream of this point.

DIRECTIONS From the junction of VT 100 and VT 125 in Hancock, take VT 100 north through Granville and into Warren. Continue traveling on VT 100 north for 2.1 miles past Stetson Hollow Road and take a left onto Bobbin Mill Road. Bobbin Mill Road is 200 feet south of Lincoln Gap Road, which heads west to Lincoln and Bristol. Follow Bobbin Mill Road for 0.2 mile and park at the end of the road next to an old building. Look for the FRIENDS OF THE MAD RIVER sign that marks the parking area. This parking area is on private property, but the owners have allowed public access for many years. We all need to do our part to respect this special place to prevent it from becoming posted in the future. *To get to Hancock,* take exit 3 off I-89 and follow VT 107 east to VT 100 north.

OTHER WATERFALLS NEARBY Warren Falls, Stetson Hollow Falls, Moss Glen Falls–Granville, Bartlett Falls, Bristol Memorial Park Falls

168

HONEY HOLLOW FALLS

Bolton, Chittenden County

Rating: 4.0/5.0
Type: Plunges, horsetails and cascades
Height: 55-foot total drop
Trail Length: Less than 0.1 mile
Water Source: Preston Brook
Altitude Gain/Loss: -50 feet to base of falls

Difficulty: Moderate
Hiking Time: 5 minutes
DeLorme Atlas: Page 45, K-13 (unmarked)
Best Time to Visit: Year-round

THE FALLS The towns of Waterbury and Stowe never cease to astonish us as we seem to continue discovering new waterfalls in this general area practically every year. Honey Hollow Falls is our latest find. Located within minutes of other fantastic falls in the area, "absolutely gorgeous" and "extraordinarily photogenic" were our first reactions to this wonderful waterfall and hollow. The brook tumbles a total of 55 feet over a 150-foot-long section of near-continuous plunges, horsetails, and cascades. The falls and hollow, bordered by pretty ferns and thick moss, are a photographers' dream. Some of our all-time favorite shots have been taken here.

Honey Hollow Falls

TRAIL INFORMATION From the parking area, rough paths lead toward the top of the upper falls. Once you reach the upper falls, far rougher trails lead down steep, slippery, and often muddy terrain to the lower falls. It is possible but difficult to descend into nice but shallow pools below several of the falls.

DIRECTIONS Take I-89 east from Burlington or I-89 west from Waterbury to exit 11. Follow US 2 east for 5.3 miles through Richmond and into Bolton. Take a right onto Cochran Road. Go 0.1 mile on Cochran Road and take a left onto Duxbury Road. Follow Duxbury Road along the Winooski River for 1.7 miles and take a right onto Honey Hollow Road. Follow Honey Hollow Road for 0.3 mile and a parking area fit for two cars will be on your left. This parking area is marked by several large boulders.

OTHER WATERFALLS NEARBY Thatcher Brook Falls, Bolton Potholes, Huntington Gorge

169

HUNTINGTON GORGE
Richmond, Chittenden County

Rating: 4.0/5.0

Type: Horsetails and cascades

Height: Main horsetail is 15 feet; 30-foot total drop

Trail Length: Less than 0.1 mile

Water Source: Huntington River

Altitude Gain/Loss: None

Difficulty: Easy

Hiking Time: Negligible

DeLorme Atlas: Page 45, K-12 (unmarked)

Best Time to Visit: Year-round

THE FALLS Huntington Gorge is as famous for its swimming holes as it is for its frightening death toll racked up in the last half-century. A sign at the falls indicates the tragic fates of almost two dozen visitors over the last 60 years. With some common sense, and some careful scouting, visitors can bypass the obvious dangers here, enjoy the popular swimming holes, and marvel at the gorge and falls.

This gorge certainly attracts the foolhardy. We have seen many young adults leaping off sloping gorge walls, and others diving into swimming pools nowhere near deep enough to dive into safely.

For falls, the gorge has many small treasures, approximately half of which can be seen at each vantage point. There is also one main horsetail falling into the pool at the end of the gorge. The currents between the falls continue through the popular swimming pools within the gorge. We urge you to bypass these dangerous spots and restrict swimming to the large channel below the bottom falls.

There also happens to be a little history regarding this waterfall. By 1802, a gristmill opened at the site and operated continuously for over a century. The Richmond Light and Power Company converted the mill in 1903 to generate electricity for the nearby villages. Nowadays, the gorge lies in its natural state, with evidence of past use nearly nonexistent. Make sure to plan on spending hours at Huntington Gorge and many more if you visit the other must-see waterfalls of the area, The Potholes and Honey Hollow Falls.

TRAIL INFORMATION Several very short trails begin about 200 feet farther up the road (downstream) of the parking area and lead to views of the falls and gorge. Once you reach the gorge, it is fairly easy to explore the entire area, including the large pool at the base of the lowermost falls. Swimming here is almost never completely safe due to the normal high flow of the river, so do so at your own risk.

DIRECTIONS Take I-89 east from Burlington or I-89 west from Waterbury to exit 11. Take US 2 east for 1.7 miles into Richmond and take a right onto Bridge Street. Follow Bridge Street for 0.5 mile to a right onto Huntington Road. Follow Huntington Road while following signs to HUNTINGTON for 3.5 miles and take a left onto Dugway Road, currently an unmarked dirt road. Follow this road for 1.4 miles and park at the designated parking area on the right. There is room for eight or so cars here.

OTHER WATERFALLS NEARBY Bolton Potholes, Honey Hollow Falls, Thatcher Brook Falls

170

JAY BRANCH GORGE
Troy, Orleans County

Rating: 3.0/5.0

Type: Plunges

Height: 12 feet

Trail Length: Less than 0.1 mile

Water Source: Jay Branch

Altitude Gain/Loss: -30 feet

Difficulty: Easy

Hiking Time: 5 minutes

DeLorme Atlas: Page 53, B-11 (unmarked)

Best Time to Visit: Year-round

THE FALLS We arrived at Jay Branch Gorge, or Four Corners, an alternative name commonly used, expecting to find a lackluster waterfall. What we found was a pretty plunge and one of Vermont's premier swimming holes. The falls are short of amazing, but the site is welcoming and encourages photography. From the cliffs beside the falls, a gigantic pool full of olive green water appears bottomless. Those in search of swimming holes could do much worse than here.

Despite our persistent research, we could not determine the owner of this property, although public access is clearly well tolerated. If you encounter private property signs on your visit, please respect the wishes of the landowner and skip this one. There are more falls and swimming holes within a short drive of here. As long as we do our part to keep places like this natural and clean, public access is likely to continue. Losing the ability to visit such special places would surely be a shame.

TRAIL INFORMATION From the parking area, head east and straight into the woods. A trail will bring you down to the river. Continue downstream for 100 feet and you will reach the top of the falls. If you wish to enjoy the swimming hole below the falls, walk farther downstream and negotiate a moderate scramble down to the water. From here, you can wade back upstream to the swimming hole as long as the water levels are not too high.

DIRECTIONS From the junction of VT 101 and VT 242 in Troy, take VT 101 north for 1.1 miles and pull into the large dirt parking area on the

Jay Branch Gorge

right. This parking area is 50 feet beyond the (currently named) Four Corners Mini Mart, and is also 0.1 mile south of the junction of VT 101 and VT 105. *To get to Troy,* take VT 105 west from Newport to VT 100 south. Follow VT 100 south to a right turn onto VT 101 north.

OTHER WATERFALLS NEARBY Big Falls, Trout River Falls, Crystal Falls

|7|

JELLY MILL FALLS

Dummerston, Windham County

Rating: 2.5/5.0
Type: Small plunges and cascades
Height: Tallest drop is 8 feet; 30-foot total drop
Trail Length: Roadside
Water Source: Stickney Brook

Altitude Gain/Loss: None
Difficulty: Easy
Hiking Time: Not applicable
DeLorme Atlas: Page 22, F-6 (unmarked)
Best Time to Visit: Year-round

THE FALLS A favorite wading and swimming spot for local residents for years, Jelly Mill Falls is a petite little formation on a mountain stream in

Jelly Mill Falls

Dummerston. The waterfall consists of a series of step falls and miniature cascades carrying the water downstream a few feet south to the mouth of the brook.

The total drop may be 30 feet, but no individual fall is greater than 8 feet. As such, the falls are not exceptional. However, we felt the urge to include this falls in our guide solely because it manages to draw a significant number of visitors to its shallow pools and its broad, flat slabs of rock that provide ideal tables for picnics. With others loving to spend their days at this waterfall, we know this will be an experience that you will enjoy as well.

TRAIL INFORMATION The falls are to the right of the road and are clearly visible. There are several paths leading to the various cascades and small plunges. The flat rocks around the falls can be quite slippery, so take caution when stepping in the heavy moss growth surrounding the falls.

DIRECTIONS From I-91 in Brattleboro, take exit 2. Take VT 9 east for 1.4 miles to VT 30 north, which spins off to the left after passing through town. Follow VT 30 north for 5.0 miles and take a left onto Stickney Brook Road (which is often confused with Pleasant Valley Road). Take this road for 300 feet and several pull-offs will be on the right.

OTHER WATERFALLS NEARBY Hamilton Falls, Pikes Falls, Beaver Brook Falls, Keene (NH)

172

KINGS HILL BROOK FALLS
Bakersfield, Franklin County

Rating: 3.0/5.0
Type: Fan
Height: 25 feet
Trail Length: Less than 0.1 mile
Water Source: Kings Hill Brook
Altitude Gain/Loss: -10 feet to initial viewpoint; -30 feet to base of falls

Difficulty: Moderate side of difficult
Hiking Time: Negligible
DeLorme Atlas: Page 52, I-1 (unmarked)
Best Time to Visit: April to July

THE FALLS Waterfalls set directly below man-made bridges are rarely this memorable. Despite the bridge, the falls have a wild and secluded aura.

Kings Hill Brook Falls

The water of Kings Hill Brook veils softly over metamorphic rock into an intimate pool, which beckons you from the trail high above. As these falls are fairly seasonal, the optimal time to visit this waterfall is after heavy rain.

TRAIL INFORMATION There is only one path that enters the woods from where you have parked. You might need to spend a second or two trying to find it since it is a rough and infrequently used trail. Once you do find it, head down this steep and slippery trail and you will reach a view of the falls after descending only 10 feet in elevation. Beyond this viewpoint, the trail becomes more hazardous as it climbs down to the base of the falls, where you will find a nice shallow pool, perfect for a quick swim, during periods of low water.

DIRECTIONS From the junction of VT 108 and VT 36 in Bakersfield, take VT 108 south for 2.4 miles and take a right onto the northern end of Lost Nation Road. Follow Lost Nation Road for 0.1 mile and take a right onto an unmarked road. There is a parking spot with room for one car on the left side of the road, after only 20 feet. *To get to Bakersfield,* take VT 36 east from St. Albans or VT 108 north from Jeffersonville.

OTHER WATERFALLS NEARBY Crystal Falls, Trout River Falls

173

⟋

LYE BROOK FALLS

Manchester, Green Mountain National Forest,
Bennington County

Rating: 4.5/5.0

Type: Horsetail

Height: Approximately 125-foot
total drop

Trail Length: 2.3 miles

Water Source: Lye Brook

Altitude Gain/Loss: +750 feet,
-150 feet

Difficulty: Moderate

Hiking Time: 90 minutes

DeLorme Atlas: Page 25, I-10
(unmarked)

Best Time to Visit: May to June

THE FALLS (HIGHLY RECOMMENDED) Lye Brook Falls is a steep, seasonal waterfall that you will need to visit by the end of June each year. When we arrived at the falls one July, only dribbles of water were cascading down the rocks. It was still intriguing as the water dropped in sheets of thin veils, and we assume it will have a much different and more powerful look during parts of the season with high-water volume. Some hiking friends of ours have suggested the elegance of the low-water flow is more picturesque at Lye Brook Falls. We recommend that you try visiting during multiple seasons and form your own opinion.

Near the top of the waterfall, portions of the falls are somewhat hidden by rocks and trees. Sunlight penetrates this waterfall because of its western exposure. At the top, there are larger step cascades that start out narrow and spread as the water finds its way down over the rock surfaces. About halfway down, most of the water condenses into a strong angular horsetail, while other trickles of water hop down the smaller steps alongside the horsetail.

The hike to the falls is an enjoyable one, as long as you are comfortable with a bit of a climb. We consider this one of the great introductory family hikes you can take in the state. It is also the longest waterfall hike for Vermont in this guide. It is certainly worth every footstep required in order to reach it.

TRAIL INFORMATION To reach Lye Brook Falls, follow the only trail that begins at the parking area. After only 75 feet into the woods, you will reach a billboard with information on the surrounding area, including the Lye Brook Wilderness Area. From here, you must follow the Lye Brook Trail for 1.8 miles until you come to a fork. The Lye Brook Trail will fork left and will lead you deep into the Lye Brook Wilderness to Bourn Pond and Stratton Pond. Instead, you will want to fork right and continue on a gently downsloping spur trail for 0.5 mile to the falls.

From the parking area, your hike to the falls will begin as a gradual and manageable uphill walk. As you hike farther along the trail, it will become progressively steeper. Those unfamiliar with hiking uphill for great distances may find the middle section of this trail to be an uphill battle. The final 0.5-mile spur trail down to the falls is very easy and enjoyable.

This hike, although challenging, is very popular and easy to follow. The 125-foot spectacle of falling water at the trail's end should justify the effort involved. This waterfall is best visited in the late months of spring, or after heavy rains.

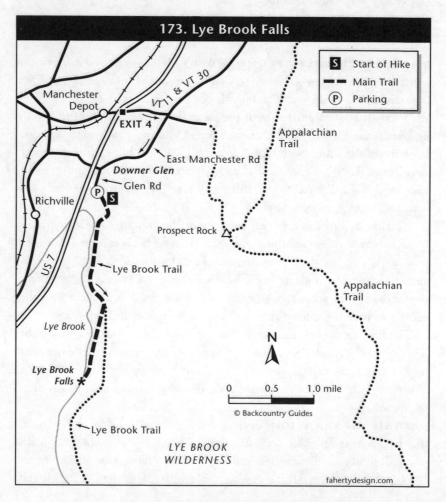

173. Lye Brook Falls

DIRECTIONS From US 7 in Manchester, take exit 4. Take the combined highway VT 11 and VT 30 east for 0.4 mile and take a right onto East Manchester Road. Follow this road for 1.1 miles to a left onto Glen Road. A few hundred feet down this road, fork right and follow this new road to its end where you will find the parking area.

OTHER WATERFALLS NEARBY Pikes Falls, Hamilton Falls

174

MARSHFIELD FALLS
Marshfield, Washington County

Rating: 3.0/5.0
Type: Cascades
Height: 100-foot total drop
Trail Length: Roadside
Water Source: Marshfield Brook
Altitude Gain/Loss: None

Difficulty: Easy
Hiking Time: Not applicable
DeLorme Atlas: Page 41, A-12 (unmarked)
Best Time to Visit: Year-round

THE FALLS Years ago, this waterfall stood alone in the quiet woods. Today, Marshfield Falls is split into upper and lower falls by a paved road. The lower waterfall is a fan that travels down and divides into a plunge on the left side and a staircase of cascades on the right. The total drop of the lower falls reaches about 40 feet.

The upper section of Marshfield Falls is taller, but there is no parking pull-off in which to stop and admire it. This section of falls is narrow with a less apparent staircase of cascades. The water flow here is more intense as it gradually spreads out on its way down to the lower falls. It is more shaded, too, making photography very difficult. Only the absolute top of the upper falls segment is exposed to the sun.

TRAIL INFORMATION There is no formal trail network or even rough paths around the falls. This waterfall is best suited for quick glimpses from the road. If you only have a short amount of time available, skip the top viewpoint and enjoy the bottom one.

DIRECTIONS From the junction of US 2 and VT 215 in Marshfield, take US 2 west for 0.2 mile and take a left onto School Street. Follow School Street straight for 0.2 mile and you will come to a fork. The right fork, Lower Depot Road, will lead to the bottom of the cascades after 0.1 mile

Marshfield Falls

and they will be on your left. The left fork, Upper Depot Road, will lead
to the remaining portion of the cascades. *To get to Marshfield,* take US 2
west from St. Johnsbury (exit 21 off I-91) or take US 2 east from Montpelier (exit 8 of I-89). If you are traveling from Montpelier on US 2 east,
School Street will be on your right 0.3 mile after passing the green MARSH-
FIELD town sign (this is not the actual town border).

OTHER WATERFALLS NEARBY Hancock Brook Falls, Emerson Falls

175

MOSS GLEN FALLS, GRANVILLE

*Granville, White Mountain National Forest,
Addison County*

Rating: 5.0/5.0

Type: Horsetail

Height: 35 feet

Trail Length: Less than 0.1 mile

Water Source: Deer Hollow
Brook

Altitude Gain/Loss: None

Difficulty: Easy

Hiking Time: Negligible

DeLorme Atlas: Page 34, A-1
(marked)

Best Time to Visit: Year-round

THE FALLS (HIGHLY RECOMMENDED) Two of the most charming waterfalls in Vermont have the same name. There is Moss Glen Falls of Stowe, and there is Moss Glen Falls of Granville, a roadside attraction featured in nearly every photographic portrait of Vermont ever published. The second is the focus of this chapter. This waterfall is a gorgeous horsetail with thin streams of water that choose their path down a slightly angled rock face. The falls start out by bubbling down over some short steps before spreading out to dance down into a light teal pool about 20 feet wide.

There are good views all around these falls, from the river to the end of the boardwalk to the road itself. If you are as lucky as we have been during two visits, dozens of pretty black-and-white butterflies soaring around the falls will help create a mystical atmosphere here.

Moss Glen Falls is a quick stop for many highway travelers, but if you take the time to admire it fully you will see how indescribably beautiful this place is. There is even an added waterfall bonus if the season is right. In the spring, a thin horsetail about 50 feet tall, often referred to as Little Moss Glen Falls, is found close to the star of the show. If you are not looking carefully along the boardwalk, you might miss it.

TRAIL INFORMATION The waterfall is located at the end of the boardwalk trail that starts at the designated parking area. As you approach the main falls, you may notice Little Moss Glen Falls to your right, especially if enough water is flowing down. We suspect that many visitors walk right past this additional set of falls without even noticing them, as they are

Moss Glen Falls, Granville

set a little ways back in the woods and are a minor attraction in comparison to the main falls here.

DIRECTIONS From Middlebury, take US 7 south to VT 125 east. Take VT 125 east through Ripton and into Hancock. Take a left onto VT 100 north and follow this highway for 6.8 miles. You will see the falls on your left and a small parking area immediately after on the left. This parking area is 4.2 miles north of the green LOWER GRANVILLE town sign.

OTHER WATERFALLS NEARBY Stetson Hollow Falls, Warren Falls, Hartshorn Falls, Texas Falls

176

MOSS GLEN FALLS, STOWE

Stowe, C. C. Putnam State Forest, Lamoille County

Rating: 5.0/5.0
Type: Plunge, horsetail, and a fan
Height: 125-foot total drop
Trail Length: 0.2 mile to middle viewpoint
Water Source: Moss Glen Brook
Altitude Gain/Loss: +50 feet to middle viewpoint

Difficulty: Easy to middle viewpoint; easy side of moderate to enter gorge
Hiking Time: 10 minutes
DeLorme Atlas: Page 46, G-6 (marked)
Best Time to Visit: May to October

THE FALLS (HIGHLY RECOMMENDED) Every year, a local class of artists convenes at this waterfall to paint a portrait of Moss Glen Falls, in an attempt to capture the beauty which can only be found here. This waterfall is worthy of their attention because it consists of a spectacular 125-foot-tall combination of several drops falling one after another.

There are a few dramatically different viewpoints of the falls available for you to enjoy, each magnificent in its own way. The upper viewpoints, from high above the brook at the top of precipitous gorge walls, give the best view of the upper half of the falls, which features a 20-foot plunge followed by a curving horsetail. From the lower viewpoint, accessed by wading your way upstream into the gorge, you get an improved perspective of the lower half of the falls, although you can see the formation in its entirety as well. This half of the falls features a beautiful wide fan followed by two short cascades.

Moss Glen Falls, Stowe

Add Moss Glen Falls to other waterfalls nearby—specifically Bingham Falls, Terrill Gorge, and Sterling Brook Gorge—for an amazing waterfall day-trip.

TRAIL INFORMATION Follow the skinny path in front of the parking lot as it winds its way through several fields before entering the woods. Seconds after you enter the woods, you will begin climbing a steep 50-foot-tall ridge. As you climb, you will hear the falls on the other side. At the top of the ridge, the incredible 100-foot drop is unveiled.

After serious consideration, we have decided to let you in on Moss Glen Falls' biggest secret. Not many are aware of this, but you can backtrack on the trail and wade your way upstream along the riverbed into the gorge. Inside, you will be surrounded by tall gorge walls and a totally secluded view of the falls awaits you. While the rest of Moss Glen Falls can be nearly overrun with visitors, you may find solitude standing inside the gorge. The gorge drowns all outside noises, making this spot feel wildly remote.

DIRECTIONS From the junction of VT 100 and VT 108 in Stowe, take VT 100 north for 3.0 miles to a right onto Randolph Road. After 0.3 mile on Randolph Road, take a right turn onto Moss Glen Falls Road. Follow Moss Glen Falls Road for 0.5 mile and the parking area will be on your left, marked by a sign for the C. C. PUTNAM STATE FOREST. *To get to Stowe,* take I-89 north from Montpelier or I-89 south from Burlington to exit 10 in Waterbury. Follow VT 100 north.

OTHER WATERFALLS NEARBY Bingham Falls, Sterling Brook Gorge, Terrill Gorge, Dog's Head Falls, Thatcher Brook Falls

177

OLD CITY FALLS
Strafford, Orange County

Rating: 4.5/5.0
Type: Plunge and cascades
Height: 45-foot total drop
Trail Length: 0.3 mile
Water Source: Old City Brook
Altitude Gain/Loss: -125 feet

Difficulty: Moderate side of difficult
Hiking Time: 15 minutes
DeLorme Atlas: Page 35, E-12 (unmarked)
Best Time to Visit: May to October

THE FALLS (HIGHLY RECOMMENDED) When we informed two local residents that we had come from another state to see Old City Falls, they were shocked; for as long as they had enjoyed this waterfall it had remained a local hidden secret, far from a tourist attraction that drew visitors from all over the region.

The best view of these falls is seen by hiking past the trail and climbing up to the base of the highest fall. Both the upper plunge and the lower cascade flow into refreshing pools. Each of the pools is waist deep—enough to cool you off on a hot day. At the upper pool, in the correct conditions, you can lean against the rock and enjoy the splashing waters cascading over you.

A good picnic area surrounds the parking lot for the falls, and it is complete with picnic tables, trash barrels, and a shelter from the rain. Old City Falls offers hours of enjoyment, so be sure to bring the bathing suit, towels, and a picnic. Visitors will surely love eating their peanut butter and jelly sandwiches at this locally famous place.

TRAIL INFORMATION The trail to the falls begins at the end of the parking area and soon enters the forest. Although the trail to the base of the falls is not all that difficult, with only a few short stretches of steep terrain to climb down, exploring the area around the falls is much more of a

Old City Falls

challenge. The official trail ends at the brook. From here to the falls, you must rock hop, carefully making sure not to fall into the brook's chilly waters.

There is plenty of exploring to do around the falls, most of which is considered challenging and sometimes, highly dangerous. Technically, you could stand underneath the upper plunge or swim in the mid-level pool. Accessing the mid-level pool is done by making use of your upper body strength and climbing up the roots to the left of the waterfall. This trail is quite difficult but it may be manageable, depending on current conditions and with due care. The trail to the upper plunge is extremely dangerous and is not recommended.

DIRECTIONS From White River Junction, take I-89 north to exit 2 in Sharon. Take VT 132 east through Sharon and into the village of South Strafford. In South Strafford, take a left onto the Justin Morrill Memorial Highway. Follow this road for 2.2 miles to the center of Strafford where you will reach a fork. Fork right and continue on the Justin Morrill Memorial Highway for 0.7 mile farther to a right onto Old City Falls Road. Follow Old City Falls Road for 0.8 mile and turn left into a dirt road just after crossing a bridge over Old City Brook. This road will lead you a short distance to the parking area.

OTHER WATERFALLS NEARBY Covered Bridge Falls, Glen Falls

178

PIKES FALLS

Jamaica, Pikes Falls Natural Area, Windham County

Rating: 3.0/5.0

Type: Cascades and slides

Height: 20-foot total drop

Trail Length: Less than 0.1 mile

Water Source: North Branch Brook

Altitude Gain/Loss: -40 feet

Difficulty: Easy

Hiking Time: Negligible

DeLorme Atlas: Page 26, J-1 (unmarked)

Best Time to Visit: May to October

THE FALLS Children probably enjoy Pikes Falls more than any other age group. During hot, summer days, children can be seen sliding down a 10-foot-long rock slide into a pool at Pikes Falls. The looks of pure pleasure on their faces confirm their love for this place.

Is it the slide they love, or the fact that below this waterfall is one of the largest swimming holes in the state? About 40 feet wide, 25 feet long, and up to 10 feet deep, this pool, with its clear, olive green water, is complemented by a large, rocky beach running along its edges. With such a large pool and a suitable beach for relaxing or eating a snack, one could imagine that Pikes Falls would be crowded. However, that is not usually the case; it has a few friendly swimmers on a hot day, but not nearly like other swimming holes in the state, such as nearby Hamilton Falls.

TRAIL INFORMATION The trail begins at the parking pull-off. Enter the woods and in approximately 20 feet, fork left to descend a set of stairs to the base of the falls and the swimming pools. Fork right if you wish to visit the top of the falls. Either approach is short and easy.

DIRECTIONS From the junction of VT 30 and VT 35 in Townsend, take VT 30 north into Jamaica to its junction with VT 100 in the village of East Jamaica. From here, continue straight onto the combined VT 100 north and VT 30 north, drive 3.2 miles, and take a left onto South Hill Road. Drive for 200 feet on South Hill Road and fork right onto Pikes Falls Road. Follow this road for 2.3 miles. After 2.3 miles, Pikes Falls Road will continue right and cross a bridge. Drive for an additional 2.4 miles on this road and you will find a wide shoulder on the left to park. *To get to Townsend,* take exit 2 off I-91 in Brattleboro. Follow VT 9 east to VT 30 north.

OTHER WATERFALLS NEARBY Hamilton Falls, Lye Brook Falls, Jelly Mill Falls

Pikes Falls

179

QUECHEE GORGE

Hartford, Quechee Gorge State Park, Windsor County

Rating: 2.0/5.0

Type: Mill Pond Falls is a horsetail; cascades are inside Quechee Gorge

Height: Mill Pond Falls is 30 feet

Trail Length: 0.3 mile to Mill Pond Falls or 0.4 mile to bottom of the gorge; 1.4 miles for entire tour of gorge

Water Source: Ottauquechee River

Altitude Gain/Loss: +25 feet, -25 feet to Mill Pond Falls; -200 feet, +200 feet for entire tour of gorge

Difficulty: Easy

Hiking Time: 10 minutes to Mill Pond Falls; 60 minutes for entire tour of gorge

DeLorme Atlas: Page 31, C-11 (marked)

Best Time to Visit: Year-round

THE FALLS Vermont's Little Grand Canyon is the phrase thrown around to describe the mile-long Quechee Gorge. While you really cannot compare the gorge here to the mile-deep, 277-mile-long Grand Canyon in Arizona, it is impressive compared to all others in New England.

Quechee Gorge (top of gorge)

You can overlook the entire gorge from the VT 4 highway bridge. From the bridge, it is a jawdropping 165 feet to the river below. This provides quite a scenic and wild view of the shallow valley that the Ottauquechee River has cut. As for a waterfall or a set of cascades, you cannot really see either from the bridge without a pair of binoculars.

By following the network of trails that parallels the river downstream, you can get a closer inspection of the small cascades within the gorge. If you are looking for major waterfalls, you will not find any within the gorge—for that you have to hike to the head of the gorge. There you will find Mill Pond Falls—occasionally referred to as Dewey's Mill—flowing below a dam. This falls is a horsetail that very few visitors to the gorge bother to find. It is neither powerful nor scenic, but it helps conclude a fine trip to Quechee Gorge, Vermont's longest and most famous gorge.

TRAIL INFORMATION The trails that lead to both the gorge and Mill Pond Falls begin behind the gift shop. From the parking area, walk behind the gift shop and down a short staircase where you will reach a trail-head sign. Continue beyond the sign by climbing a short staircase straight ahead of you. At this point, you will have a decision to make. You can either take a left and continue 0.4 mile downstream to the base of the gorge, or you can take a right and head 0.3 mile upstream to Mill Pond Falls. Both trails are well maintained and provide easy access to the gorge and falls. A trip to both the upper and lower ends of the gorge is 1.4 miles.

Also be sure to see Quechee Gorge from the elevated position of the highway bridge. The distance from the bridge to the river below is an astonishing 165 feet and the views are impressive.

DIRECTIONS From White River Junction, take I-89 north to exit 1. Take US 4 west for 2.6 miles and park on the right in a gift shop parking lot just before crossing a bridge over the gorge. Several signs for QUECHEE GORGE along this road will help guide you.

OTHER WATERFALLS NEARBY Cascade Falls, Covered Bridge Falls, Old City Falls, Thundering Brook Gorge

180

~

STERLING BROOK GORGE

Stowe, Lamoille County

Rating: 3.5/5.0
Type: Plunges, horsetails and cascades
Height: 105-foot total drop
Trail Length: 0.2 mile to end of gorge
Water Source: Sterling Brook

Altitude Gain/Loss: -125 feet
Difficulty: Easy side of moderate
Hiking Time: 15 minutes
DeLorme Atlas: Page 46, E-4 (unmarked)
Best Time to Visit: Year-round

THE FALLS This waterfall is the perfect place to take a class for a field trip. Reached by following a self-guided interpretative trail, you will notice many small tablets describing the history, geology, and lore about Sterling Brook Gorge. You learn at one of the stops that there are three falls, six cascade sets, and eight pools within the gorge.

No falls or cascades are greater than a few yards tall, and unfortunately, the pools are out of reach. In addition, only about half the drops or cascades are fully visible during the summer, when the leaves on the trees hinder your view. Currently there are also some roped-off sections of the trail. The good news is that this place is significantly less crowded than other waterfalls in Stowe. Another plus is that many of the falls and cascades are indeed still visible from the trail. There is also a quiet picnic spot at the end of the gorge, great for a snack or a light lunch.

TRAIL INFORMATION From the parking lot, cross the bridge marked with a RESIDENT VEHICLES ONLY sign. The trailhead is just after the bridge on the left, marked with a billboard describing the park rules and the gorge's geology. The trail you are about to embark on is an interpretative one with several stops along the trail outlying key geological features and facts from the beginning to the end of the gorge. The falls begin shortly after the trail begins. Continue along the trail downstream for more plunges, cascades, pools, and the gorge. If you continue traveling down the trail past where the interpretative signs end, about 0.3 mile from the road, you will eventually descend a wooden staircase and arrive at the brook well beyond the end of the gorge. To our surprise, we found the most unexpected picnic table we've ever seen. It turns out to be a truly wonderful and secluded place for a picnic.

DIRECTIONS From the junction of VT 100 and VT 108 in Stowe, take VT 100 north for 1.7 miles to a left onto Stage Coach Road. Follow this road for 1.7 miles to a left onto Sterling Valley Road. After 1.6 miles on Sterling Valley Road, you will come to a four-way intersection. Take the right hand fork that does *not* pass through a covered bridge (there are two right turns here). Continue for 2.8 miles farther (staying straight at mile 1.1) and take a left onto Sterling Gorge Road at a sign for STERLING GORGE PARKING. Continue down Sterling Gorge Road for 0.1 mile and park in the parking area at the end of the road on the right. *To get to Stowe,* take I-89 north from Montpelier or I-89 south from Burlington to exit 10 in Waterbury. Follow VT 100 north.

OTHER WATERFALLS NEARBY Terrill Gorge; Moss Glen Falls, Stowe; Bingham Falls; Dog's Head Falls; Brewster River Gorge

|8|

STETSON HOLLOW FALLS
Warren, Washington County

Rating: 2.5/5.0
Type: Horsetail
Height: 40 feet
Trail Length: 1.2 mile (see notes)
Water Source: Unknown
Altitude Gain/Loss: +150 feet

Difficulty: Easy
Hiking Time: 40 minutes
DeLorme Atlas: Page 39, J-14
(unmarked)
Best Time to Visit: May to October

THE FALLS Stetson Hollow Falls was not originally on our radar screen. We stumbled upon it by accident while on a hike into the Breadloaf Wilderness. To our surprise, we spotted a 40-foot-tall horsetail tumbling down from out of the sky, landing in Stetson Brook just in front of our feet.

These falls are not well known; in fact, the name Stetson Hollow Falls is not an official name. Rather than refer to them as *Unnamed Falls,* we chose to name them after Stetson Hollow, which the trail (forest road) passes through. These falls are very seasonal, so early in the season is the best time to catch the falls at their fullest.

TRAIL INFORMATION Unless you have a high-clearance vehicle (see directions, below), the hike to this waterfall will be an easy 1.2-mile walk west along Stetson Hollow Road. The falls will be visible on your right, seen falling from the mountainside down into the stream that parallels the road.

DIRECTIONS From the junction of VT 100 and VT 125 in Hancock, take VT 100 north for 12.3 miles through Granville and into Warren. At 12.3 miles, take a left onto Stetson Hollow Road. If you are traveling south on VT 100 from Waterbury, Stetson Hollow Road will be on your right 2.1 miles south of Lincoln Gap Road, which heads west to Lincoln and Bristol.

It is a total of 1.3 miles from VT 100 to the falls along Stetson Hollow Road, but how much of this road you will be able to drive on depends upon your vehicle. Most will want to park at a small parking area on the left after 0.1 mile and walk along the road an easy 1.2 miles farther. In an SUV with good ground clearance, you may be able to make it about 0.8 mile down the road. *To get to Hancock,* take exit 3 off I-89 and follow VT 107 east to VT 100 north.

OTHER WATERFALLS NEARBY Warren Falls; Hartshorn Falls; Moss Glen Falls, Granville; Bartlett Falls; Bristol Memorial Park Falls

182

&

TERRILL GORGE

Morristown, Lamoille County

Rating: 2.5/5.0
Type: Block
Height: 5 feet
Trail Length: 0.5 mile
Water Source: Kenfield Brook
Altitude Gain/Loss: -80 feet, +20 feet

Difficulty: Moderate to initial viewpoint; moderate side of difficult to base of falls and pool
Hiking Time: 20 minutes
DeLorme Atlas: Page 46, D-6 (marked)
Best Time to Visit: May to October

THE FALLS There are a few falls of significance on Kenfield Brook. Unfortunately, only the lower falls are easily accessible. The falls upstream supposedly require miles of bushwhacking—not exactly leisurely family hiking. From pictures, the upper falls look nice, but they are basically typical cascades. For purposes of this guide, we are only describing the lower falls, leaving the upper falls to be uncovered by avid hikers.

A half-mile walk from the parking area leads to the popular, but not overly crowded, swimming hole at the lower falls. The waterfall itself is rather small and if it were not for the beautiful pool, we might have lowered our overall rating. The falls are only 5 feet tall, but the 10-foot width does add character and makes the waterfall slightly more impressive. Water flows over a flat angled rock that could possibly be the remnants of an old dam, although we are not sure. The pool is perhaps 15 feet deep and full of cold, yellow green water. Its shape is nearly a perfect oval, being about 35 feet wide by 25 feet long. You may see careless people leaping off the rock wall to the left of the falls and be tempted to do the same. We are against this idea, because reaching the ledge they jump off is extraordinarily difficult. There is also a high risk of slipping off the edge accidently.

TRAIL INFORMATION From the small pull-off, immediately enter the woods and head down the trail toward the brook. After 0.25 mile on the trail, you will reach the river, which must be crossed. After crossing the river, which usually requires the removal of your shoes and socks, climb up the riverbank and take a left as soon as you reach a field. Follow the path along the field for a few hundred feet back into the woods. Continue along the trail 0.1 mile farther into the woods. Just as you begin climbing a steep hill, the falls and pool will be visible on your left. One steep and slippery trail leads down to the pool. Most visitors are better off enjoying the falls without taking this extra step down. Many more cascades are rumored to lie upstream, but this allegedly requires almost 1.5 miles of tough bushwhacking along the brook.

Terrill Gorge

DIRECTIONS From the junction of VT 100 and VT 108 in Stowe, take VT 100 north for 1.7 miles to a left onto Stage Coach Road. Follow this road for 6.5 miles to a three-car-sized dirt pullout on the left just before a large field. This lot is 0.9 mile north of the four-way intersection of Stage Coach Road and Walton Road. *To get to Stowe,* take I-89 north from Montpelier or I-89 south from Burlington to exit 10. Follow VT 100 north.

OTHER WATERFALLS NEARBY Sterling Brook Gorge; Moss Glen Falls, Stowe; Dog's Head Falls; Bingham Falls; Brewster River Gorge; Hancock Brook Falls

183

~

TEXAS FALLS

Hancock, Green Mountain National Forest, Addison County

Rating: 4.0/5.0
Type: Punchbowls
Height: 35-foot total drop
Trail Length: Less than 0.1 mile
Water Source: Texas Brook
Altitude Gain/Loss: None

Difficulty: Easy
Hiking Time: Negligible
DeLorme Atlas: Page 33, D-14 (marked)
Best Time to Visit: May to October

THE FALLS Texas Falls has long been a favorite Green Mountain National Forest attraction, visited by many and seen in books and photographs by thousands more. If the falls look familiar, they should. Hundreds of postcards, hiking guides, and portraits of Vermont have included Texas Falls. So although you may not have had the chance to visit this classic waterfall, its structure may seem familiar to you.

Managed by the U.S. Forest Service, Texas Falls, once a favorite swimming hole, is now off-limits to swimmers after several injuries occurred here. Wooden fencing surrounds the flume and falls, and the only views are from a boardwalk trail, from which you are asked not to stray. The best view is from the bridge that crosses over the stream. From there, you will see two small plunges with a deep, greenish blue pool in between them. Both plunges are of equal beauty, as they flow through a narrow ravine. Because of the beauty and the compactness of the gorge walls both sets of plunges look more like a flume rushing downstream.

If you drive up the road a small distance, you will find picnic tables where you can sit and have a nice lunch. You should not miss this classic, well-known waterfall.

TRAIL INFORMATION The trail begins across the street from the parking lot. The path to the falls is enclosed entirely by rail fencing and you are asked not to deviate from the path. The waterfall is only several yards from the road, making viewing rather easy. Another trail continues at the falls. This is the Texas Falls Nature trail, a 1.2-mile loop, which begins at the falls and travels around the surrounding woods only to return back to the waterfall.

SPECIAL NOTE Due to a strong flood in August of 2008, the old bridge over Texas Brook at the falls was destroyed. A new bridge is currently scheduled to be constructed to replace the old one. It is expected to be finished by the summer of 2010. Until then, be aware that your enjoyment of this place may be limited, as many of the best viewpoints are inaccessible until this occurs.

DIRECTIONS From Middlebury, take US 7 south to VT 125 east. Travel on VT 125 east past Middlebury Gap and take a left onto the road marked by a GREEN MOUNTAIN RECREATION AREA sign. This sign is visible from both sides of the road. The parking area is 0.4 mile down the road on the left. This access road is 3.0 miles west of the VT 100 and VT 125 junction in Hancock.

OTHER WATERFALLS NEARBY Moss Glen Falls, Granville; Warren Falls; Falls of Lana; Abbey Pond Cascades

184

THATCHER BROOK FALLS
Waterbury, Washington County

Rating: 3.0/5.0
Type: Horsetails and cascades
Height: 40-foot total drop
Trail Length: Less than 0.1 mile
Water Source: Thatcher Brook
Altitude Gain/Loss: None

Difficulty: Easy
Hiking Time: Negligible
DeLorme Atlas: Page 40, A-3 (unmarked)
Best Time to Visit: Year-round

THE FALLS Thatcher Brook Falls provides you with the rare opportunity to pair fine dining with a heads-on, full view of a cascading brook. As a matter of fact, unless you are one of the lucky landowners who also share the view, the restaurant will have the best perspective by which the public can witness these falls. The 40-foot drop of the falls mostly consists of robust cascades, with some steeper sections of horsetails. Exploration of the brook along the falls is limited due to the lack of any safe access to water level.

Historically, three dams within the town provided power along this brook, and some of the remnants of one of them still exist today at the falls. The restaurant, which is currently only open for dinner from Tuesday through Saturday, is an interesting 19th-century mill building. Reviews of the restaurant have been overwhelmingly positive, but we have not dined there.

Thatcher Brook Falls

TRAIL INFORMATION The falls are located behind the restaurant. There is a path beside the restaurant that leads to an observation platform. The restaurant has limited outdoor seating with an exceptional view of the falls. Be sure to arrive early for dinner to request one of these special tables.

DIRECTIONS From the junction of I-89 and VT 100 in Waterbury, take VT 100 north for 0.2 mile and take your first right onto Stowe St. just before a Shaw's supermarket. Follow Stowe St. for 750 feet and take a right into the Hen of the Wood restaurant, which is on the site of an old mill. If parking here is not available (or appropriate—use your own judgment), there is a small town-maintained parking area about 300 feet down the road below the I-89 bridges. *To get to Waterbury,* take I-89 north from Montpelier or I-89 south from Burlington to exit 10. Follow VT 100 north.

OTHER WATERFALLS NEARBY Honey Hollow Falls; Bolton Potholes; Moss Glen Falls, Stowe; Huntington Gorge

185

THUNDERING BROOK FALLS
Killington, Rutland County

Rating: 3.5/5.0
Type: Horsetails
Height: Approximately 125-foot total drop
Trail Length: 0.1 mile to upper falls; 0.2 mile on separate trail to lower falls
Water Source: Thundering Brook
Altitude Gain/Loss: −50 feet to upper falls; −150 feet to lower falls

Difficulty: Moderate side of difficult to upper falls; easy side of moderate to lower falls
Hiking Time: 10 minutes to either upper falls or lower falls
DeLorme Atlas: Page 30, B-2 (unmarked)
Best Time to Visit: May to June

THE FALLS The Appalachian Trail is marked by white-blazed trees and rocks all the way from Springer Mountain, Georgia to the mountain known as Katahdin in Maine. Along this famed route are hundreds upon hundreds of spur trails, often leading to marvelous natural features that cannot be seen from the main trail. Thundering Brook Falls is one such diversion.

With a total drop of about 125 feet, these falls are undeniably fantastic. The principal waterfall here is the 80-foot lower falls, which horsetail above and past an observation deck elevated two stories above the brook. Do not overlook the 22-foot upper falls—also a horsetail—which is camera-friendly in any water conditions.

Thundering Brook Falls

TRAIL INFORMATION There is a separate trail to reach the upper and lower falls. *To get to the upper falls,* take that path that begins at the parking area. It closely follows the stream and heads very steeply 0.1 mile down to the falls. This is an extremely rough trail that demands good boot traction. It is not recommended for children. *To get to the lower falls,* continue walking up Thundering Brook Road for 300 feet from the parking area and take a left onto the white-blazed Appalachian Trail. It is a relatively easy walk of 0.2 mile downhill to a junction with a blue-blazed spur trail on the left. Take this left and the falls are only 150 feet away. An observation deck with good views of the falls marks the end of the trail.

It is possible to scramble alongside the brook to connect the upper and lower falls. However, this is rather dangerous due to the inherent hazards of the steep terrain here.

DIRECTIONS From the junction of US 4 and VT 100 in Killington, take the combined highway US 4 east and VT 100 south for 0.5 mile and take a left onto Thundering Brook Road. Follow Thundering Brook Road for 1.3 miles and there will be a parking pull-off on the left with room for a few cars. *To get to Killington,* take US 4 east from Rutland or US 4 west from Woodstock.

OTHER WATERFALLS NEARBY Quechee Gorge

186

TROUT RIVER FALLS
Montgomery, Franklin County

Rating: 2.5/5.0
Type: Small plunges and cascades
Height: 10 feet
Trail Length: 0.2 mile
Water Source: Trout River and Hunnah Clark Brook
Altitude Gain/Loss: +10 feet

Difficulty: Difficult
Hiking Time: 15 minutes
DeLorme Atlas: Page 52, E-6 (unmarked)
Best Time to Visit: July and August

THE FALLS Two brooks converge into a popular swimming hole at Trout River Falls, or Three Holes, as the locals tend to call it. Both falls are 10 feet in height and they fall into the same alluring lime green pool. The swirling currents of this pool are famous for containing trout. On one visit, we saw a family of three catch over half a dozen trout.

The left waterfall consists of many low-angle cascades that twist and turn in and around boulders. The waterfall on the right side is a set of punch-bowls. While both falls are attractive, the real attraction here is the swimming hole. Visit during the summer for a pleasantly refreshing swim.

TRAIL INFORMATION Access to this waterfall has significantly changed since the first edition of this guide. The trail now begins off VT 58 and is now considerably more difficult. Your trip here is likely to be more of a private experience than it was in the past, due to these changes.

From the parking pull-off on VT 58, follow the steep trail that leads down to the edge of the river. From here, you will have to travel upstream in and along the edge of the river for 0.2 mile to the falls. How you get there is up to you, but there is really no simple or easy way to do it. We suggest bringing water shoes to greatly assist you and provide a higher degree of safety. Depending on the season and recent rainfall, you may find yourself in knee-deep (or higher) water. In high water, these falls are simply too dangerous to visit. To increase your chance of being able to safely reach the falls and swimming hole, save this place for a hot summer afternoon following several precipitation-free days.

DIRECTIONS From the junction of VT 58, VT 118, and VT 242 in Montgomery Center, take VT 58 east (Hazens Notch Road) for 0.1 mile and there will be a small gravel pull-off on the left side of the road, with room for only a car or two. *To get to Montgomery Center,* take VT 105 west from Newport to VT 100 south to VT 58 west. As a note of caution, be aware that VT 58 is a seasonal road and is typically closed from late fall to early spring.

OTHER WATERFALLS NEARBY Crystal Falls, Big Falls, Jay Branch Gorge, Kings Hill Brook Falls

187

WARREN FALLS

Warren, Green Mountain National Forest,
Washington County

Rating: 3.5/5.0
Type: Plunges
Height: 20-foot total drop
Trail Length: 0.1 mile
Water Source: Mad River
Altitude Gain/Loss: -20 feet

Difficulty: Easy to initial viewpoints;
easy side of moderate to base of falls
Hiking Time: 5 minutes
DeLorme Atlas: Page 39, J-14
(unmarked)
Best Time to Visit: Year-round

THE FALLS The Mad River harbors a collection of first-class swimming holes, including our absolute favorite in Vermont, Warren Falls. We have had the pleasure of swimming in dozens of waterfalls in the state, and this one is simply unmatched, in our opinion. The pools below the falls are spacious and full of clear, green-tinted water. Cliff jumping is a true pastime here, and you would be hard-pressed to find a safer spot to partake in this activity. Of course, this sport always carries a high degree of risk, so use caution if you decide to join the conga line of jumpers.

The falls themselves, a series of several small plunges, are not particularly exciting and, as a result, are mostly overshadowed by the allure of the pools. Our original guidebook made no mention of Warren Falls or its pools because it only recently surfaced in our research. Although it is certainly not a private or secluded place, the falls would likely be exponentially more popular if there was actually sign on the highway indicating its location. We wonder if the U.S. Forest Service intentionally leaves the parking pull-off unmarked to keep the falls in their natural state and the area clean. Despite the crowds that are still likely to be here on weekends, there is always enough room for all to savor this jewel of an attraction.

TRAIL INFORMATION From the parking area, head into the woods on an obvious trail and bear right at an informational billboard containing information about the falls. After about 250 feet, you will reach a fork. If you take the left fork, you will reach the top of the uppermost falls. If you take the right fork, the trail will guide you to additional viewpoints along the river and ultimately down to the base of the falls. The trail down to the base of the falls (and the gorgeous swimming hole!) is a bit steep, so take caution here.

Warren Falls

DIRECTIONS From the junction of VT 100 and VT 125 in Hancock, take VT 100 north through Granville and into Warren. Continue traveling on VT 100 north for 1.1 miles north of Stetson Hollow Road and you will find a medium-sized dirt parking pull-off on the left. If you look 20 feet into the woods, you should be able to spot an informative billboard here. If you are traveling south on VT 100, the parking area will be on your right 6.5 miles south of the junction of VT 100 and VT 17 in the village of Irasville. *To get to Hancock,* take exit 3 off I-89 and follow VT 107 east to VT 100 north.

OTHER WATERFALLS NEARBY Stetson Hollow Falls; Hartshorn Falls; Moss Glen Falls, Granville; Texas Falls

Appendixes

Appendix A

TOP 40 WATERFALLS
IN NEW ENGLAND

Although we would love to say that all waterfalls are equally beautiful, and that no waterfall deserves any more attention than another, the fact is we have some personal favorites. Here are our picks of the top 40 waterfalls in New England. Each one has earned an overall rating of either 4.5 or 5.0.

Angel Falls (ME)

Arethusa Falls (NH)

Bash Bish Falls (MA)

Beaver Brook Cascades (NH)

Beaver Brook Falls, Colebrook (NH)

Bingham Falls (VT)

Bridal Veil Falls (NH)

Campbell Falls (MA)

Chapman Falls (CT)

Crystal Cascade (NH)

Diana's Baths (NH)

Dunn Falls (ME)

Eagle Cascade (NH)

Enders Falls (CT)

Falls of Lana (VT)

Falls on the Basin-Cascades Trail (NH)

Falls on the Falling Waters Trail (NH)

Falls on the Flume–Pool Loop (NH)

Garfield Falls (NH)

Giant Falls (NH)

Glen Ellis Falls (NH)

Gulf Hagas (ME)

Hamilton Falls (VT)

Houston Brook Falls (ME)

Kent Falls (CT)

Lye Brook Falls (VT)

Mosher Hill Falls (ME)

Moss Glen Falls, Granville (VT)

Moss Glen Falls, Stowe (VT)

Moxie Falls (ME)

Nancy Cascades (NH)

Old City Falls (VT)

Race Brook Falls (MA)

Ripley Falls (NH)

Sabbaday Falls (NH)

Screw Auger Falls, Grafton (ME)

Silver Cascade (NH)

Smalls Falls (ME)

Step Falls (ME)

Tannery Falls (MA)

Appendix B

TOP 30 WATERFALL SWIMMING HOLES

These are our selections for the premier 30 swimming holes in New England that also feature a waterfall. There are other excellent swimming holes throughout this region that are not included here because they either do not contain a significant waterfall or do not have one at all.

Bartlett Falls (VT)

Bellevue Falls (MA)

Bingham Falls (VT)

Bolton Potholes (VT)

Buttermilk Falls (VT)

Diana's Baths (NH)

Emerald Pool (NH) *

Enders Falls (CT)

Frenchmen's Hole (ME)

Falls of Lana (VT)

Franconia Falls (NH)

Gulf Hagas (ME)

Huston Brook Falls (ME) *

Jackson Falls (NH)

Jay Branch Gorge (VT)

Ledge Falls-T4, R10 (ME) *

Lower Ammonoosuc Falls (NH) *

Lower Falls (NH)

Pikes Falls (VT)

Pitcher Falls (MA)

Pollards Mills (NH)

Rattlesnake Flume and Pool (ME)

Smalls Falls (ME)

Step Falls (ME)

Swiftwater Falls (Bath, NH)

Terrill Gorge (VT)

Thirteen Falls (NH)

Twenty Foot Hole (VT) *

Upper Ammonoosuc Falls (NH)

Warren Falls (VT)

* See Appendix F for information on this waterfall as it does not have its own chapter in this guide.

Appendix C

THE BEST WATERFALL
DAY TRIPS

In our opinion, nothing reenergizes the soul like the splendor of spending a full day with nature. Make the most of your day-trip by connecting nearby waterfalls together. Here are our suggestions for multiple-waterfall day-trips, organized by state.

❧

Great Falls, Dean's Ravine Falls, Pine Swamp Brook Falls,
Kent Falls (CT)

❧

Westfield Falls, Little Wadsworth Falls, Big Wadsworth Falls,
The Cascade (CT)

❧

Bash Bish Falls, Race Brook Falls, Campbell Falls (MA)

❧

March Cataract Falls, Money Brook Falls, The Cascade,
Tannery Falls (MA)

❧

Trap Falls, Doane's Falls, Spirit Falls, Royalston Falls (MA)

❧

Gibbs Falls, Flume Cascade, Silver Cascade,
Ripley Falls, Arethusa Falls (NH)

❧

Diana's Baths, Winniweta Falls, Thompson Falls,
Glen Ellis Falls, Crystal Cascade (NH)

❧

Pond Brook Falls, Beaver Brook Falls, Colebrook, Dixville Flume,
Huntington Cascades (NH)

❧

Falls on the Flume–Pool Loop, Falls on the Basin-Cascades Trail,
Georgiana Falls (NH)

❧

Eagle Cascade, Brickett Falls, Rattlesnake Flume and Pool,
Bickford Slides (NH & ME)

～

Screw Auger Falls, Grafton, Step Falls, Dunn Falls, Ellis Falls,
Coos Canyon, Angel Falls (ME)

～

Brewster River Gorge, Bingham Falls, Moss Glen Falls, Stowe,
Sterling Brook Gorge, Terrill Gorge (VT)

～

Falls of Lana, Abbey Pond Cascades, Bittersweet Falls, Bartlett Falls,
Bristol Memorial Park Falls (VT)

～

Texas Falls, Moss Glen Falls, Granville, Stetson Hollow Falls,
Warren Falls, Hancock Brook Falls (VT)

Appendix D

THE BEST LONG-DISTANCE WATERFALL DAY HIKES

(In no particular order)

Falls on the Falling Waters Trail and Mt. Lafayette, NH
(page 181)

Total Hiking Distance: **8.9 miles**

Altitude Gain: **3,900 feet**

Difficulty: **Extremely difficult**

∽

Katahdin Stream Falls and Baxter Peak, ME *(page 326)*

Total Hiking Distance: **10.4 miles**

Altitude Gain: **4,200 feet**

Difficulty: **Extremely difficult**

∽

Zealand Falls and Thoreau Falls, NH *(pages 246 and 233)*

Total Hiking Distance: **10.0 miles**

Altitude Gain: **500 feet**

Difficulty: **Moderate**

∽

Crystal Cascade and Mt. Washington, NH *(page 166)*

Total Hiking Distance: **8.2 miles**

Altitude Gain: **4,200 feet**

Difficulty: **Extremely difficult**

∽

Gulf Hagas, ME *(page 58)*

Total Hiking Distance: **8.6 miles**

Altitude Gain: **600 feet**

Difficulty: **Moderate side of difficult**

Race Brook Falls, Mt. Race, and Mt. Everett, MA
(page 123)

Total Hiking Distance: **7.0 miles**
Altitude Gain: **2,300 feet**
Difficulty: **Moderate side of difficult**

~

Beaver Brook Cascades and Mt. Moosilauke, NH
(page 151)

Total Hiking Distance: **7.6 miles**
Altitude Gain: **3,100 feet**
Difficulty: **Difficult**

~

Falls on the Basin-Cascades Trail and Lonesome Lake, NH
(page 177)

Total Hiking Distance: **5.4 miles**
Altitude Gain: **1,200 feet**
Difficulty: **Moderate**

~

Franconia Falls and Thirteen Falls, NH *(pages 189 and 229)*

Total Hiking Distance: **17.0 miles**
Altitude Gain: **1,000 feet**
Difficulty: **Moderate, but long**

Appendix E

SCENIC WATERFALLS OF BAXTER STATE PARK IN MAINE

Many of the waterfalls of Baxter State Park are extremely appealing. It will take a fair amount of planning on your part to visit most of them, however. The rules and regulations of the park, which are designed to preserve the natural setting for eternity, include restrictions on the number of visitors that can enter the park and the backcountry. For more information, visit the official Web site of Baxter State Park, www.baxterstateparkauthority.com.

Katahdin Stream Falls

Trail Length:	**1.2 miles**
Water Source:	**Katahdin Stream**
DeLorme Atlas:	**Page 50, D-5 (marked)**

NOTES: Katahdin Stream Falls is the culmination of three drops totaling 60 feet in height. The waterfall maintains a strong year-round flow. Perhaps the best known of Baxter's waterfalls, this natural feature can be seen from the Hunt Trail, which is one of the more popular routes to the summit of Mt. Katahdin. Be aware that Baxter Peak, Katahdin's tallest point, requires a strenuous round-trip hike totaling 10.4 miles and an elevation gain of 4,200 feet. The trailhead for the falls and the Hunt Trail is at the Katahdin Stream Campground. The optional round-trip to the summit of Katahdin is one of the best alpine hikes New England has to offer.

∽

Grand Falls

Trail Length:	**From Roaring Brook Campground to falls,**
	10.0 miles; from Russell Pond to falls, 2.8 miles
Water Source:	**Wassataquoik Stream**
DeLorme Atlas:	**Page 51, B-1 (marked)**

NOTES: The Grand Falls Trail leaves from Russell Pond, a backcountry campsite reached only by hiking one of several long access trails. Although we have yet to visit Grand Falls, we have heard that it is quite magnificent and makes for a pleasant half-day trip from the pond.

Green Falls

Trail Length: **From Roaring Brook Campground to falls, 10.4 miles; from Russell Pond to falls, 3.2 miles**

Water Source: **unnamed water source**

DeLorme Atlas: **Page 50, B-5 (marked)**

NOTES: Green Falls is a remote waterfall just south of Wassataquoik Lake. Just like nearby Grand Falls, Green Falls is accessed via a wilderness trail (the Wassataquoik Lake Trail) that starts at Russell Pond. There is a sketch of Green Falls in DeLorme's "Map and Guide to Baxter State Park"—an essential map if you are visiting the area—that will give you a good idea of how beautiful the falls is. The falls are named for the emerald green moss that borders the flow of water.

Little Abol Falls

Trail Length: **0.8 miles**

Water Source: **Tributary of Abol Stream**

DeLorme Atlas: **Page 50, D-5 (marked)**

NOTES: The Little Abol Falls Trail begins at the Abol Campground and leads to a mountain stream with 15 feet of cascades over pink brown Katahdin granite. Little Abol Falls provides a nice place for a picnic, and is an easy stroll from the campground.

South Branch Falls

Trail Length: **0.5 mile**

Water Source: **South Branch Ponds Brook**

DeLorme Atlas: **Page 51, A-1 (unmarked)**

NOTES: This small set of cascades is accessed by the South Branch Falls Trail. The trail leaves the west side of the road that leads to the South Branch Pond Campground. The trail descends at a moderate rate, without any particular hiking dangers or challenges. Several small pools for swimming can be found here.

Niagara Falls

Trail Length: **1.25 miles**
Water Source: **Nesowadnehunk Stream**
DeLorme Atlas: **Page 50, D-4 (marked)**

NOTES: Two falls, Little Niagara Falls and Big Niagara Falls, are located just south of the Daicey Pond Campground on Nesowadnehunk Stream. To access these waterfalls, connect with the Appalachian Trail at the campground and head south. Little Niagara Falls is reached after hiking for about 1.0 mile, with Big Niagara Falls 0.25 mile beyond that.

Howe Brook Falls

Trail Length: **3.0 miles**
Water Source: **Howe Brook**
DeLorme Atlas: **Page 51, A-1 (marked)**

NOTES: Take the Pogy Notch Trail for 1.0 mile south of the South Branch Pond Campground to a left onto the Howe Brook Trail. Follow the Howe Brook Trail 2.0 miles to a large waterfall. Many other small falls and cascades are seen before reaching the main attraction.

Appendix F

STATE-BY-STATE AND ADDITIONAL WATERFALLS LIST

This list includes each waterfall mentioned throughout the guide, whether they had their own chapter or were included as part of another. Additional waterfalls not otherwise mentioned are also listed here for dedicated waterfall hunters.

CONNECTICUT

Ayers Gap (see Bailey's Ravine)

Bailey's Ravine, 2

Bear Hill Falls
LOCATION: Unnamed source, Middletown
HEIGHT: 30-foot total drop
HIKING DISTANCE: 0.6 mile
COMMENTS: Highly seasonal and unattractive waterfall on the Mattabasset Trail; access off north side of Airport Road.

Blackledge Falls, 3

Burlington Falls
LOCATION: Bunnell Brook, Burlington
HEIGHT: Unknown
HIKING DISTANCE: Unknown
COMMENTS: Appears promising based on pictures we have seen; public access unknown.

Burr Falls
LOCATION: Outlet from Burr Pond, Torrington
HEIGHT: 45-foot total drop
HIKING DISTANCE: Roadside
COMMENTS: Somewhat appealing cascades clearly visible along Burr Mountain Road.

Buttermilk Falls, Norfolk
LOCATION: Blackberry Creek, Norfolk
HEIGHT: 20-foot total drop
HIKING DISTANCE: Roadside
COMMENTS: Recent residential development has limited public access to this pretty horsetail-fan.

Buttermilk Falls, Plymouth, 5

Carpenter's Falls, 7

Cascades, The, 9

Chapman Falls, 10

Codfish Falls, 12

Dean's Ravine Falls, 13

Enders Falls, 15

Falls Brook Falls
LOCATION: Falls Brook, Hartland
HEIGHT: Unknown
HIKING DISTANCE: Unknown
COMMENTS: Promising waterfall on a lovely hike in Tunxis State Forest; off CT 20.

Gorge Cascade Falls
LOCATION: Unknown source, Hamden
HEIGHT: Unknown
HIKING DISTANCE: Unknown
COMMENTS: Highly seasonal horsetails within Sleeping Giant State Park; unofficial name.

Great Falls, 17

Indian Well Falls, 18

Kent Falls, 19

Kettletown Brook Falls
LOCATION: Kettletown Brook, Southbury
HEIGHT: 5 feet
HIKING DISTANCE: 0.2 mile
COMMENTS: Small but attractive falls in Kettletown State Park; falls alone is not really worth the expensive entrance fee.

Mill Pond Falls, 21

Big Falls, Lower Cupsuptic
LOCATION: Cupsuptic River, Lower
Cupsuptic
HEIGHT: Unknown
HIKING DISTANCE: Unknown
COMMENTS: Access may be possible off
Big Falls Road; most likely a set of small
cascades or rapids.

Big Falls, Washington
LOCATION: Grand Lake Stream,
Washington
HEIGHT: Unknown
HIKING DISTANCE: Unknown
COMMENTS: Likely to be small cascades
or rapids; downstream of Milford Road;
may only be accessible by canoe.

Big Niagara Falls (see Waterfalls of Baxter State Park, appendix E)

Big Wilson Falls
LOCATION: Big Wilson Stream, Elliottsville
HEIGHT: 20-foot total drop
HIKING DISTANCE: Less than 0.1 mile
COMMENTS: Access via short trail
downstream from Elliottsville Road;
good swimming hole.

Billings Falls (see Gulf Hagas)

Bottle Brook Falls
LOCATION: Bottle Brook, Kingsbury
HEIGHT: 20 feet
HIKING DISTANCE: 0.3 mile
COMMENTS: No trails; requires short
bushwhack; best access via ME 16.

Buttermilk Falls (see Gulf Hagas)

Cascade Brook Falls
LOCATION: Cascade Brook, Grafton
HEIGHT: Unknown
HIKING DISTANCE: 0.2 mile
COMMENTS: Pretty falls, but requires
bushwhack; north of Mother Walker
Falls on ME 26.

Cascade Falls
LOCATION: Cascade Brook, Saco
HEIGHT: 20 feet
HIKING DISTANCE: Estimated at 0.1–0.3
mile
COMMENTS: Downstream of ME 98
bridge over Cascade Brook; may require

short bushwhack.

Cascades, The
LOCATION: Cascade Stream, Sandy River
HEIGHT: Estimated at 75-foot total drop
HIKING DISTANCE: 0.25 mile
COMMENTS: Access off Town Hall Road,
which loops off ME 4; also called
Cascade Stream Gorge.

Cataracts, The, 46

Cliffs, The
LOCATION: Big Wilson Stream, Greenville
HEIGHT: Unknown
HIKING DISTANCE: Estimated at 0.5–1.0
mile;
COMMENTS: Several drops near dam;
swimming generally considered
dangerous; could be private property.

Cold Stream Falls
LOCATION: Cold Stream, Johnson
Mountain
HEIGHT: Unknown
HIKING DISTANCE: Unknown
COMMENTS: Access via dirt road off US-
201; high probability this one is
off-limits (private property); marked on
DeLorme atlas.

Cooper Brook Falls
LOCATION: Cooper Brook, TA R11
HEIGHT: Estimated at 30-foot total drop
HIKING DISTANCE: 3.7 miles (south from
Jo-Mary Road)
COMMENTS: Low-angle cascades with
good swimming hole below; located on
the Appalachian Trail; lean-to shelter just
below falls.

Coos Canyon, 48

Duck Brook Falls
LOCATION: Duck Brook, Bar Harbor
HEIGHT: Unknown
HIKING DISTANCE: Roadside
COMMENTS: Seasonal falls viewable from
Duck Brook Road.

Dunn Falls, 49

Earley Landing Falls
LOCATION: Big Wilson Stream, Willimantic
HEIGHT: 6-foot total drop

HIKING DISTANCE: Roadside
COMMENTS: Private property with no public access allowed; skip this one.

Ellis Falls, 53

Falls at Frenchmen's Hole
(see Frenchmen's Hole)

Falls, The, 54

Fish River Falls
LOCATION: Fish River, T14 R8
HEIGHT: 60-foot total drop
HIKING DISTANCE: Unknown
COMMENTS: Likely to be roadside or very short hike; near start of Fish River canoe trip.

Frenchmen's Hole, 55

Gauntlet Falls
LOCATION: East Branch of the Pleasant River, TB R10
HEIGHT: Unknown
HIKING DISTANCE: 0.1 or 0.6 mile, depending on status of Gauntlet Falls Road
COMMENTS: Several campsites in vicinity; within KI-Jo-Mary Multiple Use Forest (access fee charged).

Goodell Brook Falls
LOCATION: Goodell Brook, Monson
HEIGHT: 22-foot total drop
HIKING DISTANCE: 0.3 mile
COMMENTS: Steep horsetails and cascades; take Appalachian Trail north 0.2 mile from ME 15 and bushwhack downstream for 0.1 mile before crossing brook.

Grand Falls—T3 R4
LOCATION: Dead River, T3 R4
HEIGHT: 30 feet
HIKING DISTANCE: Unknown, but likely to be short
COMMENTS: Very impressive block-style falls; proposed site of the third hut within the Maine Huts and Trails hut system; access may be possible off Lower Enchanted Road; short hike may be required.

Grand Falls—T4 R9 (see Waterfalls of Baxter State Park, appendix E)

Grand Pitch
LOCATION: West Branch of the Penobscot River, T5 R8
HEIGHT: 21 feet
HIKING DISTANCE: Unknown
COMMENTS: Wide and powerful cascades; canoe portage site; popular with white-water kayakers; campsites nearby; may have access trail but likely to be accessible by canoe only.

Green Falls (see Waterfalls of Baxter State Park, appendix E)

Greenwood Falls
LOCATION: Green Brook, Bowdoin College Grant East
HEIGHT: 20 feet
HIKING DISTANCE: 0.4 mile
COMMENTS: Light bushwhack off logging road; great swimming hole; not well known; fee charged to enter multiple-use forest.

Grindstone Falls
LOCATION: Penobscot River, Grindstone
HEIGHT: 2 feet
HIKING DISTANCE: Roadside
COMMENTS: Pretty site and picnic area; wide row of very tiny cascades on scenic river.

Gulf Hagas, 58

Gully Brook Falls
LOCATION: Gully Brook, Blanchard
HEIGHT: Unknown
HIKING DISTANCE: 0.25 mile
COMMENTS: Series of cascades; requires short bushwhack downstream off Blanchard-Shirley Road.

Hadlock Falls
LOCATION: Hadlock Brook, Mt. Desert
HEIGHT: 40 feet
HIKING DISTANCE: 1.0 mile
COMMENTS: Clearly visible from carriage road between marked posts #12 and #19; hiking access easiest from parking area on ME 3; several other waterfalls can be found along interconnected carriage roads.

Hay Brook Falls, 61

Heald Stream Falls, 63

High Bridge
LOCATION: White Brook, Bowdoin College Grant East
HEIGHT: 5 feet
HIKING DISTANCE: Roadside
COMMENTS: Can be seen along drive to Hay Brook Falls; visible from bridge over White Brook; campsite adjacent to falls.

Holeb Falls
LOCATION: Moose River, Somerset
HEIGHT: 24 feet
HIKING DISTANCE: Unknown
COMMENTS: Powerful cascades on scenic river; research suggests this is only accessible by canoe/kayak; good chance that unmapped logging roads contain a trailhead.

Horseshoe Canyon
LOCATION: West Branch of the Piscataquis River, Blanchard
HEIGHT: Unknown
HIKING DISTANCE: Estimated at 3.5–4.5 miles
COMMENTS: Series of cascades along the Appalachian Trail; best access via Blanchard-Shirley Road; lean-to shelter is above the falls.

Houston Brook Falls, 64

Howe Brook Falls (see Waterfalls of Baxter State Park, appendix E)

Huston Brook Falls
LOCATION: Huston Brook, Carrabassett Valley
HEIGHT: 18-foot total drop
HIKING DISTANCE: 0.1 mile
COMMENTS: Excellent swimming hole with two miniature sets of falls; also called Bunchberry Falls.

Indian Stream Falls
LOCATION: Indian Stream, Elliottsville
HEIGHT: 80 feet
HIKING DISTANCE: Estimated at 1.5–2.0 miles one way
COMMENTS: Impressive and remote falls; several means of access; bring good map.

Jail Falls

LOCATION: Bear River, Grafton
HEIGHT: 25 feet
HIKING DISTANCE: 0.1 mile
COMMENTS: Pretty two-tier horsetail; short bushwhack from parking pull-off 0.3 mile north of Screw Auger Falls, Grafton.

Jewell Falls
LOCATION: Fore River, Portland
HEIGHT: Estimated at 20-foot total drop
HIKING DISTANCE: Unknown
COMMENTS: Located within the Fore River Sanctuary; best access likely off Congress Street.

Katahdin Falls
LOCATION: Katahdin Stream, T3 R10
HEIGHT: Unknown
HIKING DISTANCE: Unknown
COMMENTS: Located in Baxter State Park; no trail so access is most likely prohibited; tallest waterfall chain in Maine

Katahdin Stream Falls (see Waterfalls of Baxter State Park, appendix E)

Kees Falls, 66

Kezar Falls, 67

Ledge Falls—T4 R9
LOCATION: Wassataquoik Stream, T4 R10
HEIGHT: Unknown
HIKING DISTANCE: Approximately 6.5 miles from Roaring Brook Campground in eastern side of Baxter SP
COMMENTS: Small cascades and rapids en route to more impressive Grand Falls.

Ledge Falls—T4 R10
LOCATION: Nesowadnehunk Stream, T4 R10
HEIGHT: Tallest drop is 4 feet; 12-foot total drop
HIKING DISTANCE: Visible from road, but parking area is a few hundred feet downstream
COMMENTS: Thoroughly enjoyable waterslides and pools; bring a tube with you, but be careful of currents; within Baxter State Park (access fee for non-residents).

Little Abol Falls (see Waterfalls of Baxter State Park, appendix E)

Little Canada Falls
LOCATION: South Branch of the Penobscot River, Prentiss
HEIGHT: Unknown
HIKING DISTANCE: Unknown
COMMENTS: A lost waterfall; most likely a short bushwhack off Old Kelly Dam Road.

Little Falls
LOCATION: Cupsuptic River, Lower Cupsuptic Township
HEIGHT: Unknown
HIKING DISTANCE: Estimated at 0.5–1.0 mile
COMMENTS: Marked on DeLorme Atlas; access likely off Fanjoy Road, but may be private property.

Little Niagara Falls (see Waterfalls of Baxter State Park, appendix E)

Little Wilson Falls, 68

Logan Brook
LOCATION: Logan Brook, TB R11
HEIGHT: Unknown
HIKING DISTANCE: Estimated at 1.6 miles one-way
COMMENTS: Near the Logan Brook lean-to on the Appalachian Trail; hike south from Logan Brook Road.

Lower Falls
LOCATION: East Hastings Brook, Moro
HEIGHT: Unknown
HIKING DISTANCE: Estimated at 1.0–2.0 miles one way
COMMENTS: Marked on DeLorme map, along with nearby Upper Falls in Merrill; access unknown.

Lower Gauntlet Falls
LOCATION: East Branch of the Pleasant River, TB R10
HEIGHT: 20 feet
HIKING DISTANCE: 0.3 or 0.8 miles, depending on status of Gauntlet Falls Road
COMMENTS: Only 0.2 mile downstream of Gauntlet Falls; rough access along river;

no official trails.

Mad River Falls, 69

Man of War Brook Falls
LOCATION: Man of War Brook, Mt. Desert
HEIGHT: Unknown
HIKING DISTANCE: Estimated at 1.3 miles
COMMENTS: Seasonal falls that dumps directly into Somes Sound; access from parking area off ME 102; connect Man O' War Brook Fire Road with Acadia NP hiking trails.

Megunticook Falls
LOCATION: Megunticook River, Camden
HEIGHT: 25 feet
HIKING DISTANCE: Less than 0.1 mile
COMMENTS: Set of cascades located in downtown Camden; allegedly behind stores on Main Street; public viewing may not be possible.

Millinocket Falls
LOCATION: Millinocket Stream, T8 R8
HEIGHT: Unknown
HIKING DISTANCE: Unknown
COMMENTS: Marked on DeLorme Atlas; trail access unlikely.

Mosher Hill Falls, 70

Mother Walker Falls
LOCATION: Bear River, Grafton
HEIGHT: 98 feet
HIKING DISTANCE: Less than 0.2 mile
COMMENTS: Cascades are heavily obstructed by boulders; skip this one.

Moxie Falls, 72

Mud Gauntlet Falls
LOCATION: East Branch of the Pleasant River, TB R10
HEIGHT: Estimated 20-foot total drop
HIKING DISTANCE: Estimated at 0.5 or 1.0 mile, depending on status of Gauntlet Falls Road
COMMENTS: Downstream of Lower Gauntlet Falls; requires short but difficult bushwhack along streambed.

Mud Pond Stream
LOCATION: Outlet from Mud Pond, Greenville

HEIGHT: 60 feet
HIKING DISTANCE: Less than 0.1 mile
COMMENTS: Seldom-visited seasonal horsetail; located off confusing network of logging roads.

Nesowadnehunk Falls, 73

Niagara Falls (see Waterfalls of Baxter State Park, appendix E)

Norway Falls
LOCATION: Wassataquoik Stream, T4 R9
HEIGHT: Unknown
HIKING DISTANCE: Unknown
COMMENTS: Located in Baxter State Park; would require bushwhack, but public access is likely not permitted; may be small cascades or rapids anyway.

Parlin Falls, 74

Phillips Falls, 76

Poplar Stream Falls, 77

Rattlesnake Flume & Pool, 80

Red River Falls
LOCATION: Red River, T14 R8
HEIGHT: Unknown
HIKING DISTANCE: Unknown
COMMENTS: Short plunge and horsetail combination; most likely off Hewes Brook Road.

Redington Pond Falls
LOCATION: Unknown source, Redington
HEIGHT: 321 feet
HIKING DISTANCE: Unknown
COMMENTS: One of Maine's tallest waterfalls, but located on restricted U.S. Navy property.

Rocky Brook Falls
LOCATION: Rocky Brook, T15 R8
HEIGHT: 27 feet
HIKING DISTANCE: Unknown
COMMENTS: Very scenic drop in northern Maine; requires hike of unknown distance and difficulty.

Rumford Falls, 83

Sarampus Falls
LOCATION: North Branch of the Dead River, Alder Stream
HEIGHT: 5 feet

HIKING DISTANCE: Roadside
COMMENTS: Short and wide drop with huge pool below; marked pull-off on ME 27.

Sawtelle Falls, 84

Screw Auger Falls, Bowdoin College Grant East (see Gulf Hagas)

Screw Auger Falls, Grafton, 85

Shin Falls, 87

Shirley Gorge
LOCATION: East Branch of the Piscataquis River, Shirley
HEIGHT: Unknown
HIKING DISTANCE: Unknown
COMMENTS: Various falls and cascades below dam on Shirley Pond; requires bushwhack of unknown difficulty.

Silver Ripple Cascade
LOCATION: Black Brook, Andover
HEIGHT: 30-foot total drop
HIKING DISTANCE: Less than 0.1 mile
COMMENTS: Access off Devil's Den Road; interesting gorge and swimming hole; runnable by experienced white-water kayakers in high water.

Slugundy Falls
LOCATION: Long Pond Stream, Elliottsville
HEIGHT: Two drops, each estimated at 12 feet
HIKING DISTANCE: 0.8 mile (unverified)
COMMENTS: Small falls visible from the Appalachian Trail near Barren Mountain; lean-to shelter nearby.

Smalls Falls, 89

Snow Falls, 90

South Branch Falls (see Waterfalls of Baxter State Park, appendix E)

Stair Falls (see Gulf Hagas chapter)

Steep Falls
LOCATION: Saco River, Limington & Baldwin
HEIGHT: 6 feet
HIKING DISTANCE: Roadside
COMMENTS: Falls are visible from ME 11 bridge; area next to falls is now private property.

Step Falls, 92

Swift River Falls
  LOCATION: Swift River Falls, Roxbury
  HEIGHT: 6 feet
  HIKING DISTANCE: Roadside
  COMMENTS: Recent residential
  development has extremely limited
  access; public no longer welcome.

Thirtyfoot Falls
  LOCATION: Second Currier Brook,
  T9 R11
  HEIGHT: 30 feet
  HIKING DISTANCE: Unknown
  COMMENTS: Remote waterfall deep
  in northern Maine woods. Access may
  be possible via trail from Pelletier Road.

Thompson Brook Falls
  LOCATION: Thompson Brook, Elliottsville
  HEIGHT: 70-foot total drop
  HIKING DISTANCE: Estimated at 3–4 miles
  one way
  COMMENTS: Several scenic drops; long
  and challenging hike

Tobey Falls, 93

Tumbledown Dick Falls
  LOCATION: Tumbledown Dick Stream, T1
  R11
  HEIGHT: Unknown
  HIKING DISTANCE: Unknown
  COMMENTS: Rumored waterfall on a spur
  trail off the Appalachian Trail east of
  Nahmakanta Stream Road.

Valley Brook Falls
  LOCATION: Tucker Valley Brook, Dixfield
  HEIGHT: 30 feet
  HIKING DISTANCE: Roadside or close to it
  COMMENTS: Research indicates easy
  access off Tucker Valley Brook Road;
  possible this is private property.

Vaughan Stream Falls
  LOCATION: Vaughan Stream, Elliottsville
  HEIGHT: 20 feet
  HIKING DISTANCE: Unknown
  COMMENTS: Impressive set of cascades;
  trailhead is difficult to find; falls are off the
  Appalachian Trail.

Warren Falls
  LOCATION: West Branch Mattawamkeag
  River, Hersey
  HEIGHT: Unknown
  HIKING DISTANCE: Unknown
  COMMENTS: Small cascades on wide
  stream; popular fly-fishing spot.

Webhannet Falls
  LOCATION: Webhannet River, Wells
  HEIGHT: 12 feet
  HIKING DISTANCE: Roadside or close to it
  COMMENTS: Small cascades upstream of
  US-1 bridge north of Ogunquit; unsure if
  visible from road.

West Chairback Pond Falls
  LOCATION: West Chairback Pond Stream,
  T7 R9
  HEIGHT: 54 feet
  HIKING DISTANCE: Estimated at 2.5–3.0
  miles one-way from Katahdin Iron
  Works Road
  COMMENTS: Along the Appalachian Trail
  between Cloud Pond and Chairback Gap
  lean-tos; best access probably from
  Katahdin Iron Works Road.

MASSACHUSETTS

Bash Bish Falls, 96

Bear Rock Falls
  LOCATION: Bear Rock Stream,
  Mt. Washington
  HEIGHT: Approximately 100-foot total
  drop
  HIKING DISTANCE: 3.0 miles
  COMMENTS: Rest stop along the
  Appalachian Trail; viewing limited to top
  of falls; backcountry camping at nearby
  Laurel Ridge campsite.

Bear's Den Falls, 97

Beaver Brook
  LOCATION: Unknown source, Waltham
  HEIGHT: 8 feet
  HIKING DISTANCE: Roadside
  COMMENTS: Small falls located within the
  Beaver Brook Reservation.

Bellevue Falls, 99

Bradley Falls
  LOCATION: Little River, Worthington

HEIGHT: 30 feet
HIKING DISTANCE: Roadside
COMMENTS: High probability of private property, so may only be viewable from roadside.

Briggs Brook Falls
LOCATION: Briggs Brook, Erving
HEIGHT: 60-foot total drop
HIKING DISTANCE: 0.3 mile
COMMENTS: Seasonal set of cascades on Metacomet-Monadnock Trail; new parking area on Briggs Street.

Buffam Falls, 100

Campbell Falls, 102

Cascade on South Brook
LOCATION: South Brook, Cheshire
HEIGHT: 8 feet
HIKING DISTANCE: Less than 0.1 mile
COMMENTS: Small set of cascades located in interesting but short gorge.

Cascade, The, Melrose
LOCATION: Unnamed source, Melrose
HEIGHT: 20 feet
HIKING DISTANCE: 0.1 mile
COMMENTS: Extremely seasonal horsetail in Middlesex Fells Reservation; very close to Boston; off Goodyear Avenue.

Cascade, The, North Adams, 103

Cascade, The
LOCATION: Unnamed source, Worcester
HEIGHT: 40-foot total drop
HIKING DISTANCE: Roadside
COMMENTS: Seasonal but pretty falls in high water; viewable from Cataract Street in southeastern end of Cascade Park.

Chapel Falls, 105

Danforth Falls
LOCATION: Danforth Brook, Hudson
HEIGHT: 6 feet
HIKING DISTANCE: 0.3 mile
COMMENTS: Small and very seasonal; only slightly appealing site.

Daniels Brook Chasm
LOCATION: Daniels Brook, Lanesborough
HEIGHT: 25-foot total drop
HIKING DISTANCE: 0.5 mile

COMMENTS: Small but interesting chasm; access via popular shared ATV and hiking trails.

Deer Hill Falls (see March Cataract Falls)

Doane's Falls, 107

Falls on the Overbrook Trail
LOCATION: Unknown source, Lenox
HEIGHT: Tallest cascade is 20 feet
HIKING DISTANCE: 0.9 mile to uppermost falls
COMMENTS: Located within the Audubon Society's Pleasant Valley Wildlife Sanctuary; very seasonal falls, but lovely hike; admission fee.

Falls on the Bellows Pipe/ Thunderbolt Ski Trails
LOCATION: Unnamed source, Adams
HEIGHT: Unknown
HIKING DISTANCE: Unknown
COMMENTS: Series of impressive seasonal cascades on the east side of Mt. Greylock.

Falls on Camp Brook
LOCATION: Camp Brook, Tyringham
HEIGHT: 20-foot total drop
HIKING DISTANCE: 2.3 mile loop
COMMENTS: Within the McLennan Reservation, a Trustees of Reservations property; small falls but enjoyable loop hike.

Falls on Peck's Brook
LOCATION: Peck's Brook, Adams
HEIGHT: Unknown
HIKING DISTANCE: 1.0 mile
COMMENTS: Backcountry camping in near vicinity at Peck's Brook shelter; seasonal falls; accessible from town of Adams or Mt. Greylock Reservation roads.

Galloway Brook Falls
LOCATION: Galloway Brook, Barre
HEIGHT: 50-foot total drop
HIKING DISTANCE: 0.5 mile
COMMENTS: Interesting cascades and gorge below rock dam; within the borders of Cook's Canyon Wildlife Sanctuary.

Glacial Potholes (also called Shelburne
Falls, see p. 339)

Glen Brook Falls
LOCATION: Glen Brook, Sheffield
HEIGHT: Upper falls is 40-foot total drop;
lower falls is 30-foot total drop
HIKING DISTANCE: 0.6 mile to lower falls;
0.9 mile to upper falls
COMMENTS: Located on Berkshire School
property; very seasonal, but quiet,
peaceful area.

Glendale Falls, 108

Goldmine Brook Falls, 110

Gunn Brook Falls
LOCATION: Gunn Brook, Sunderland
HEIGHT: 35 feet
HIKING DISTANCE: Less than 0.1 mile
COMMENTS: Public is no longer welcome
at these falls; skip this one.

Haley Brook Falls
LOCATION: Haley Brook, Williamstown
HEIGHT: 15-foot total drop
HIKING DISTANCE: 0.2 mile
COMMENTS: Observation deck for
viewing nice falls; small but delightful
pool below; off Berlin Road.

Hawthorne Falls
LOCATION: Unnamed source, Great
Barrington
HEIGHT: 30 feet
HIKING DISTANCE: 0.5 mile
COMMENTS: Exceptionally seasonal, but
worthwhile destination in high water;
combine with hike up Monument
Mountain.

Holland Glen
LOCATION: Hop Brook, Belchertown
HEIGHT: Tallest drop is 15 feet
HIKING DISTANCE: 0.5 mile
COMMENTS: Picturesque setting, but
recommended in high water only; access
via Metacomet-Monadnock Trail.

Hop Brook (also called Holland Glen,
see p. 338)

Hubbard River Gorge & Falls
LOCATION: Hubbard River, Granville
HEIGHT: Tallest is 8 feet
HIKING DISTANCE: 1.2 miles to lowermost
falls
COMMENTS: Scenic mix of five notable
sets of cascades and slides; within
Granville State Forest; access recently
closed due to bridge repair; current
status unknown.

Hudson Brook Chasm, 111

Konkapot Falls
LOCATION: Konkapot River, Monterey
HEIGHT: 12-foot total drop
HIKING DISTANCE: Less than 0.1 mile
COMMENTS: Somewhat impressive
sequence of low-angle cascades; easy
access off River Road.

Lulu Cascade, 113

Lynne's Falls
LOCATION: Lyon's Brook, Wendell
HEIGHT: 25-foot total drop
HIKING DISTANCE: 0.5 mile
COMMENTS: Very seasonal set of several
falls; access via Metacomet-Monadnock
Trail.

March Cataract Falls, 115

Marguerite Falls
LOCATION: Unnamed source, Sandisfield
HEIGHT: 40 feet
HIKING DISTANCE: Roadside
COMMENTS: Somewhat seasonal, but one
of Massachusetts' best roadside falls;
viewable from MA 8.

Mohawk Brook Falls
LOCATION: Mohawk Brook, Leverett
HEIGHT: 50-foot total drop
HIKING DISTANCE: 1.0 mile
COMMENTS: Extremely seasonal
and only worthwhile after extreme rain;
access via Robert Frost Trail and spur
path.

Money Brook Falls, 117

Monument Mountain Falls (also called
Hawthorne Falls, see p. 338)

Notch Brook Cascade
(see The Cascade, North Adams)

Otis Falls

LOCATION: Fall River, Otis
HEIGHT: 50-foot total drop
HIKING DISTANCE: Less than 0.1 mile
COMMENTS: Scenic value reliant upon dam releases; outstanding in high water; within Tolland State Forest.

Parker Brook Falls (see Tannery Falls)

Pauchaug Brook Falls
LOCATION: Pauchaug Brook, Northfield
HEIGHT: 15-foot total drop
HIKING DISTANCE: Roadside
COMMENTS: Shrub growth has limited views of this falls; at the junction of MA 63 and MA 10; best viewed in early spring.

Pecks Falls, 118

Pitcher Falls, 120

Race Brook Falls, 123

Roaring Falls, 126

Royalston Falls, 128

Sages Ravine (Lower)
LOCATION: Sages Ravine Brook, Mt. Washington
HEIGHT: Unknown
HIKING DISTANCE: Estimated at 1.0 mile
COMMENTS: More impressive than upper falls; bushwhack of unknown difficulty required; access via MA 41.

Sages Ravine (Upper)
LOCATION: Sages Ravine Brook, Mt. Washington
HEIGHT: Unknown
HIKING DISTANCE: Estimated at 1.8 miles
COMMENTS: Less impressive than lower falls; easiest approach is via East Street; visible from Appalachian Trail; camp at nearby Sages Ravine backcountry campsite.

Salmon Falls (also called Shelburne Falls, see p. 339)

Sanderson Brook Falls, 131

Schermerhorn Gorge
LOCATION: Unknown source, Lee
HEIGHT: Unknown
HIKING DISTANCE: Unknown

COMMENTS: Rumored waterfall in October Mountain State Forest; access via Gorge Trail.

Shelburne Falls
LOCATION: Deerfield River
HEIGHT: 35-foot total drop
HIKING DISTANCE: Less than 0.1 mile
COMMENTS: Cascades below a dam; viewing now limited to new observation deck.

Slatestone Brook Falls, 132

Slip Dog Falls
LOCATION: Gunn Brook, Sunderland
HEIGHT: 10 feet
HIKING DISTANCE: 1.0 mile
COMMENTS: Highly seasonal; trailhead off Reservation Road.

Sluice Brook Falls
LOCATION: Sluice Brook, Shelburne
HEIGHT: Lower falls is 30 feet, upper falls is 12 feet
HIKING DISTANCE: Lower falls is 1.0 mile paddle; upper falls are 1.8 miles
COMMENTS: Access for lower falls is canoe only; easy side of moderate hike to upper falls.

South Worthington Falls (also called Bradley Falls, see p. 336)

Spirit Falls, 133

Stafford Brook Cascade
LOCATION: Stafford Brook, Colrain
HEIGHT: 12 feet
HIKING DISTANCE: Less than 0.1 mile
COMMENTS: Seasonal but pretty and photogenic falls just downstream of Green River Road; possible this is private property.

Stevens Glen
LOCATION: Lenox Mountain Brook, Richmond
HEIGHT: 40 feet
HIKING DISTANCE: 0.7 mile
COMMENTS: Chain of thin and steep cascades; marked parking area off Lenox Branch Road; historically significant.

Tannery Falls, 134

the Great Gulf Trail; access may be possible from Great Glen ski trail network.

Lower Ammonoosuc Falls
LOCATION: Ammonoosuc River, Carroll
HEIGHT: 8-foot total drop
HIKING DISTANCE: 0.25 mile
COMMENTS: Classic swimming hole but unimpressive falls; easy access off Lower Falls Road.

Marian Fall (see Appalachia Waterfalls)

Moriah Brook Gorge & Cascades
LOCATION: Moriah Brook, Beans Purchase
HEIGHT: Tallest is 10 feet
HIKING DISTANCE: 1.4 miles to Moriah Gorge; 3.4 miles to uppermost cascades
COMMENTS: Lovely gorge and several small falls along long stretch of brook; several swimming holes.

Mossy Fall (see Appalachia Waterfalls)

Muscanigra Fall (see Falls on the Howker Ridge Trail)

No. 13 Falls (see Thirteen Falls)

Noble Falls (see Bridal Veil Falls)

Norway Rapids
LOCATION: Avalanche Brook, Waterville Valley
HEIGHT: 20-foot total drop
HIKING DISTANCE: 1.6 miles
COMMENTS: Just tiny rapids; worthwhile only if visiting nearby Waterville Cascades.

Pearl Cascade (see Beecher and Pearl Cascades)

Peboamauk Fall
LOCATION: Moose Brook, Randolph
HEIGHT: Unknown
HIKING DISTANCE: 2.3 miles
COMMENTS: On the Peboamauk Loop, which connects to the Ice Gulch Path.

Pitcher Falls (see Champney Falls)

Pleiades Cascades
LOCATION: Baker River, Woodstock
HEIGHT: Unknown
HIKING DISTANCE: Unknown
COMMENTS: Access probably involves difficult bushwhack off Asquam Ridge Trail on Mt. Moosilauke.

Pool, The (see Falls on the Flume–Pool Loop)

Proteus Falls (see Triple Falls)

Pulpit Falls
LOCATION: Pauchaug Brook, Winchester
HEIGHT: Unknown
HIKING DISTANCE: 0.25 mile
COMMENTS: Seasonal falls close to Massachusetts border on NH 10; may require short bushwhack.

Raymond Cataract
LOCATION: Branch of the Cutler River, Sargents Purchase
HEIGHT: At least 300 feet
HIKING DISTANCE: Unknown
COMMENTS: Located between Huntington and Tuckerman Ravines; extremely difficult and potentially dangerous bushwhack; occasionally skied in winter by experts under optimal conditions.

Roaring Falls (see Fall of Song)

Rocky Glen Falls (see Falls on the Basin-Cascades Trail)

Salmacis Fall (see Appalachia Waterfalls)

Salroc Falls (see Appalachia Waterfalls)

Sawhegenet Falls
LOCATION: Pemigewasset River, Bridgewater

HEIGHT: 2 feet
HIKING DISTANCE: 0.1 mile
COMMENTS: Just a set of rapids; skip this one.

Sculptured Rocks, 224

Senter Falls
LOCATION: Cold Brook, Lyndeborough
HEIGHT: At least 100 feet
HIKING DISTANCE: Unknown
COMMENTS: Falls are located on newly designated conservation land; off the Two Brooks Trail.

Shell Cascade
LOCATION: Hardy Brook, Waterville Valley
HEIGHT: Unknown
HIKING DISTANCE: 0.5 mile
COMMENTS: Bushwhack of unknown difficulty; may be private property.

Silver Cascade, 226

Soup Bowl Glide
LOCATION: Atwell Brook, Groton
HEIGHT: Unknown
HIKING DISTANCE: Less than 0.25 mile
COMMENTS: Likely to be more of a natural waterslide than a waterfall; appears to be a short hike or quick bushwhack off Orange Road.

Sparkling Cascade (see Ripley Falls)

Sphinx Cascades
LOCATION: Sphinx Brook, Thompson and Meserves Purchase
HEIGHT: Unknown
HIKING DISTANCE: 6.1 miles
COMMENTS: Best combined with trip to Weetamoo Falls; several sets of cascades and falls here.

Spur Brook Fall (see Appalachia Waterfalls)

Stairs Fall (see Falls on the Howker Ridge Trail)

Stairs Falls (see Falls on the Falling Waters Trail)

Stark Falls
LOCATION: Stark Falls Brook, Woodstock
HEIGHT: Unknown
HIKING DISTANCE: Unknown

COMMENTS: Short bushwhack off NH 112.

Stepped Falls
LOCATION: Brown Brook, Ellsworth
HEIGHT: 30-foot total drop
HIKING DISTANCE: Lower falls are roadside; 0.2 mile to upper cascades
COMMENTS: Seasonal but photogenic falls in less-visited section of the White Mountain National Forest; lower falls visible from Ellsworth Hill Road.

Swiftwater Falls, Bath, 227

Swiftwater Falls, Franconia (see Falls on the Falling Waters Trail)

Sylvan Cascade
LOCATION: Parapet Brook, Thompson, and Meserves Purchase
HEIGHT: Unknown
HIKING DISTANCE: 4.1 miles
COMMENTS: Off the Madison Gulf Trail between the Great Gulf Trail and Mt. Madison; pictures we have seen look promising.

Sylvan Glade Cataract (see Ripley Falls)

Tama Fall (see Appalachia Waterfalls)

Thirteen Falls, 229

Thompson Falls, Hales Location
LOCATION: Unknown source, Hales Location
HEIGHT: Unknown
HIKING DISTANCE: Unknown
COMMENTS: Access via abandoned trail that is now probably heavily overgrown; could be private property.

Thompson Falls, Pinkham's Grant, 232

Thoreau Falls, 233

Thorndike Fall (see Appalachia Waterfalls)

Triple Falls, 236

Tucker Brook Falls, 238

Twin Falls (see Fall of Song)

Upper Ammonoosuc Falls, 239

Walker Cascade
LOCATION: Walker Brook, Lincoln
HEIGHT: Estimated at 100-foot total drop

RHODE ISLAND

VERMONT

dam; off Carvers Falls Lane on the border of Vermont and New York.

Carwash Falls
LOCATION: Unnamed source, Cambridge
HEIGHT: Unknown
HIKING DISTANCE: Roadside
COMMENTS: Tall but very seasonal waterfall visible on VT 108; near Smuggler's Notch.

Cascade Falls, 268

Cavendish Gorge
LOCATION: Black River, Cavendish
HEIGHT: Tallest plunge is 10 feet; 80-foot total drop
HIKING DISTANCE: 0.3 mile to viewpoint at middle of gorge
COMMENTS: Rugged and remote gorge, but falls lack character; access off Elton Brown Road.

Cheever Falls
LOCATION: Unknown source, Walden
HEIGHT: Unknown
HIKING DISTANCE: Unknown
COMMENTS: Pretty set of falls and cascades based on pictures we have seen; access unknown.

Circle Current (see Bartlett Falls)

Clarendon Gorge, Lower, 270

Clarendon Gorge, Upper
LOCATION: Mill River, Clarendon
HEIGHT: 8-foot total drop
HIKING DISTANCE: 0.1 mile
COMMENTS: Small cascades below shaky suspension bridge; access via Long Trail parking area on VT 103.

Covered Bridge Falls, 272

Cox Brook Cascades (also called Northfield Falls, see p. 347)

Crystal Cascade Falls (see Cascade Falls)

Crystal Falls, 273

Danby Waterslide
LOCATION: Mill Brook, Danby
HEIGHT: 20-foot total drop
HIKING DISTANCE: Less than 0.1 mile
COMMENTS: Beautiful swimming hole but average falls; possible this is located on

private property.

Dead Creek Falls
LOCATION: Dead Creek, Swanton
HEIGHT: 30 feet
HIKING DISTANCE: 0.2 mile
COMMENTS: Powerful falls near boundary of Fairfield Swamp Wildlife Management Area; high probability this is private property.

Devil's Gorge (see Clarendon Gorge, Lower)

Devil's Potholes (see Bolton Potholes)

Deweys Mill (see Quechee Gorge)

Dog Team Falls
LOCATION: New Haven River, New Haven
HEIGHT: 6 feet
HIKING DISTANCE: Less than 0.1 mile
COMMENTS: Popular swimming hole; block-style falls; public access appears to be allowed, but may be private property.

Dog's Head Falls, 274

Downer Glen
LOCATION: Bourne Brook, Manchester
HEIGHT: Unknown
HIKING DISTANCE: Unknown
COMMENTS: Public access doubtful; bushwhack likely required if access is allowed.

Duck Brook Cascades
LOCATION: Duck Brook, Bolton
HEIGHT: Over 100-foot total drop
HIKING DISTANCE: Unknown
COMMENTS: Series of small falls and cascades; visible from the Long Trail north of Jonesville.

Emerson Falls, 275

Fairfax Falls, 276

Falls of Lana, 277

Four Corners (see Jay Branch Gorge)

Gerrys Falls
LOCATION: Mountain Brook, Windsor
HEIGHT: Unknown
HIKING DISTANCE: 1.9 miles
COMMENTS: Located on a short spur trail off the Windsor Trail on Mt.

LOCATION: Pekin Brook, Calais
HEIGHT: Unknown
HIKING DISTANCE: Roadside
COMMENTS: Falls are located between two private residences; skip this one.

Pike River Falls
LOCATION: Pike River, Berkshire
HEIGHT: 10 feet
HIKING DISTANCE: Unknown
COMMENTS: Also called Ferland Falls; extremely likely to be private property.

Pikes Falls, 302

Pool of Jalna
LOCATION: Unknown source, Salisbury
HEIGHT: Unknown, but small
HIKING DISTANCE: Unknown
COMMENTS: Private small horsetails and swimming hole for guests of the Kingsley Mill Manor.

Potholes, The (see Bolton Potholes)

Power Plant Falls
LOCATION: Winooski River, Marshfield
HEIGHT: Unknown
HIKING DISTANCE: Unknown
COMMENTS: Small horsetail; access off Power Plant Road.

Proctor Falls
LOCATION: Otter Creek, Proctor
HEIGHT: 50 feet
HIKING DISTANCE: Less than 0.1 mile
COMMENTS: Dazzling in high water, but dependent upon dam releases; access via Patch Street.

Quechee Gorge, 304

Reeds Falls
LOCATION: Catamount Brook, Worcester
HEIGHT: Unknown
HIKING DISTANCE: Unknown
COMMENTS: Difficult bushwhack of unknown distance required.

Ridley Brook Cascades
LOCATION: Ridley Brook, Duxbury
HEIGHT: 6 feet
HIKING DISTANCE: Roadside
COMMENTS: Small cascades off Camel's Hump Road; best cascades along brook

are off-limits (private property).

Riverton Falls
LOCATION: Dog River, Berlin
HEIGHT: 5 feet
HIKING DISTANCE: 0.6 mile
COMMENTS: Small but powerful; follow train tracks south from VT 12 south in the village of West Berlin.

Roxbury Falls
LOCATION: Dog River, Roxbury
HEIGHT: 15 feet
HIKING DISTANCE: Roadside
COMMENTS: Photogenic falls somewhat visible from Warren Mountain Road; recent residential development has reduced extent of exploration.

Sacketts Brook Falls
LOCATION: Sacketts Brook, Putney
HEIGHT: 8-foot total drop
HIKING DISTANCE: Less than 0.1 mile
COMMENTS: Small falls on conservation site; may be additional cascades upstream, but this is private property.

Seven Falls
LOCATION: Huntington River, Huntington
HEIGHT: 20-foot total drop
HIKING DISTANCE: Less than 0.1 mile
COMMENTS: Seven small cascades, some with alluring swimming holes; parking on Gore Road 0.1 south of Weaver Road.

Sheep's Hole
LOCATION: Foot Brook, Johnson
HEIGHT: 4-foot total drop
HIKING DISTANCE: Roadside
COMMENTS: Short cascades, but tempting small swimming hole; limited privacy; off Foot Brook Road.

Shelburne Falls
LOCATION: La Platte River, Shelburne
HEIGHT: Main falls is 5 feet; 15-foot total drop
HIKING DISTANCE: Less than 0.1 mile
COMMENTS: High probability of private property, so access is discouraged.

Sloping Falls (see Dog's Head Falls)

Smugglers Falls
LOCATION: Unknown source, Stowe

HEIGHT: Estimated at 800-foot total drop
HIKING DISTANCE: Unknown
COMMENTS: One of the tallest chains of waterfalls in the Northeast; requires extremely difficult bushwhack.

South Branch Falls
LOCATION: South Branch of the Trout River, Montgomery
HEIGHT: 25-foot total drop
HIKING DISTANCE: Less than 0.1 mile
COMMENTS: Lower falls has small pool for swimming; upper falls viewable from roadside only; off Gibou Road.

Spaulding Falls
LOCATION: Jail Branch, Barre
HEIGHT: Unknown
HIKING DISTANCE: Unknown
COMMENTS: Set of falls in residential area; most likely private property.

State Prison Hollow Falls
LOCATION: Lewis Creek, Starksboro
HEIGHT: 15 feet
HIKING DISTANCE: Less than 0.1 mile
COMMENTS: Rough and steep access trail to scenic horsetail; may be other waterfalls along creek.

Sterling Brook Gorge, 306

Stetson Hollow Waterfall, 307

Sutherland Falls (also called Proctor Falls, see p. 348)

Terrill Gorge, 308

Texas Falls, 310

Thatcher Brook Falls, 311

Thetford Center Falls (see Covered Bridge Falls)

Three Holes (see Trout River Falls)

Thundering Brook Falls, 313

Tinker Brook Cascades
LOCATION: Tinker Brook, Plymouth
HEIGHT: Unknown
HIKING DISTANCE: Unknown
COMMENTS: Set of cascades within the Tinker Brook Natural Area; hike of unknown difficulty off Shrewsbury Road.

Tollgate Falls

LOCATION: Winhall River, Londonderry Falls
HEIGHT: 10 feet
HIKING DISTANCE: Roadside
COMMENTS: Small and unremarkable cascades; easy access off Cohen Road.

Trout River Falls, 315

Twenty Foot Hole
LOCATION: North Branch of the Black River, Reading
HEIGHT: Tallest is 5 feet
HIKING DISTANCE: Less than 0.1 mile to upper falls; 0.2 mile to lowermost falls
COMMENTS: Three outstanding swimming holes, but falls lack character; recently protected by Vermont River Conservancy; unmarked parking area off Tyson Road.

Twin Falls
LOCATION: Saxtons River, Westminster
HEIGHT: 20-foot total drop
HIKING DISTANCE: Roadside
COMMENTS: Impressive falls, but now marked private property with no public access.

Upper Crossett Brook Falls
LOCATION: Crossett Brook, Duxbury
HEIGHT: 13 feet
HIKING DISTANCE: Roadside
COMMENTS: Small but nice falls visible from Crossett Hill Road; lower falls are on private property.

Warren Falls, 317

Waterman Brook Falls
LOCATION: Waterman Brook, Johnson
HEIGHT: Unknown
HIKING DISTANCE: Unknown
COMMENTS: Set of cascades on gently flowing stream; high probability of private property, though.

Waterslide, The (also called Danby Waterslide, see p. 345)

West Hill Brook Falls (See Crystal Falls)

Willoughby Falls
LOCATION: Willoughby River, Barton
HEIGHT: 15-foot total drop

HIKING DISTANCE: Less than 0.1 mile
COMMENTS: Long chain of low-angle cascades; park in VT Fish and Game parking area off East Street.

Woodbury Falls
LOCATION: Stream from Mud Pond, Woodbury
HEIGHT: 35 feet

HIKING DISTANCE: Visible from roadside, parking area 0.1 mile
COMMENTS: Only impressive in very high water; upper falls are private property and therefore off-limits.